SPECIAL DELIVERY

WOMEN IN CULTURE AND SOCIETY

A series edited by Catharine R. Stimpson

LINDA S. KAUFFMAN

SPECIAL DELIVERY

Epistolary Modes in Modern Fiction

FOREWORD BY CATHARINE R. STIMPSON

THE UNIVERSITY OF CHICAGO PRESS
Chicago and London

Linda S. Kauffman is professor of English at the University of Maryland, College Park.

The University of Chicago Press, Chicago 60637
The University of Chicago Press, Ltd., London
© 1992 by The University of Chicago
All rights reserved. Published 1992
Printed in the United States of America
01 00 99 98 97 96 95 94 93 92   54321

ISBN (cloth): 0-226-42680-7 (cloth)
ISBN (paper): 0-226-42681-5 (paper)

Library of Congress Cataloging-in-Publication Data
Kauffman, Linda S., 1949–
    Special delivery : epistolary modes in modern fiction / Linda S. Kauffman.
        p.   cm. — (Women in culture and society)
    Includes index.
    1. Epistolary fiction—History and criticism.   2. Fiction—20th century—History and criticism.   3. Women in literature.   4. Letters in literature.   I. Title.   II. Series.
    PN3448.E6K38   1992
    809.3'04—dc20   91-23819
                                                                           CIP

Postage-stamp illustrations by Kathryn Jacobi.

Chapter 2 is a revised and expanded version of Linda S. Kauffman's "Framing Lolita," in *Refiguring the Father: New Feminist Readings of Patriarchy*, edited by Patricia Yaeger and Beth Kowaleski-Wallace (Carbondale: Southern Illinois University Press, 1989); reprinted with permission. Chapter 4, revised and expanded, is reprinted with permission from *Theorizing Feminist Writing Practices*, edited by Elizabeth A. Meese and Alice Parker (Amsterdam: John Benjamins, in press). An earlier version of Chapter 6 appeared in *Writing the Female Voice: Essays on Epistolary Literature*, edited by Elizabeth C. Goldsmith (Boston: Northeastern University Press, 1989); reprinted with permission.

⊚ The paper used in this publication meets the minimum requirements of the American National Standard for Information Sciences—Permanence of Paper for Printed Library Materials, ANSI Z39.48-1984.

FOR KAY AUSTEN

CONTENTS

FOREWORD

"This is my letter to the World/That never wrote to Me—." So Emily Dickinson begins one of her most famous poems. Born in 1847, Alexander Graham Bell was an adolescent when she wrote it. In 1876, the year in which he started to patent the inventions that were the basis for the telephone, she was forty-six. She was to die a decade later. However, let us imagine that history had a different sequence, that Dickinson had been born after Bell; that her Amherst study had contained a telephone, fax machine, tape recorder, cassettes. Let us imagine, moreover, that Dickinson had found letters from the contemporary world in her mailbox: junk mail, fund-raising appeals, L. L. Bean catalogs, Visa and American Express bills, and, occasionally, a personal letter, printed out on pinfed paper by a daisy wheel. What then might the first words of her poem have been?

Special Delivery has provoked this fanciful question. For Linda S. Kauffman is writing about nothing less than the letter in literature in the twentieth-century. I first discovered Kauffman's ideas in 1986 when I heard her read a paper about Vladimir Nabokov and *Lolita*. Her voice was distinctive, at once incisive and subtle, sophisticated and shrewd, eloquent and witty. In the same year, she published her first book, *Discourses of Desire*, an analysis of the genre of the love letter from Ovid to *The Three Marias: New Portuguese Letters* (1972). A critic who refuses to be boxed in, she synthesized a number of critical approaches: a structuralist interest in genre and the relations of texts to each other; a poststructuralist interest in the "politics of representation," in questions of who gets to say what and to whom; a psychoanalytic interest in desire, the wish for that which we do not have; a Bakhtinian interest in dialogue and polyvocality, in the clash and convergence of several languages; and, finally, an interest in gender. As a feminist critic, Kauffman insisted that women's subjectivity is not only the product of language, not only the product of material reality, not only the product of individual will and grit, but of all three.

Special Delivery now deepens Kauffman's methods and extends her reach. She is taking up seven books written between 1923 and 1986, all of which use letters. Four of these epistolary adventures are by men (Viktor Shklovsky, Vladimir Nabokov, Roland Barthes, Jacques Derrida) who produce, among other things, a picture of women. Three of these adventures are by women (Doris Lessing, Alice Walker, Margaret Atwood). They generate their own narratives about gender and its meaning. Kauffman, however, asks us to revel in the complexity these books share, their invitation to readers to enter into a restless, unstable, dramatic world. For each of these texts makes "different discourses interrupt each other dialogically in order to initiate a crisis." With a fine lucidity, Kauffman also shows us what this crisis is, the postmodern necessity of questioning older and reassuring myths about the self-willed potencies of the individual; about romantic love; about language as the mirror of nature; about the reliability of distinctions between theory and practice, between fact and fiction.

Although Kauffman demonstrates how much language talks about itself and how much language tells us who we are, she refuses to abandon the realities of history and twentieth-century society from the Russian Revolution to the dismantling of the Soviet empire. *Lolita*, for example, is a novel "about" father-daughter incest and a dazzling display of the novel as a fiction, as a mansion of mirrors. Beyond *Lolita*, incest happens, painfully, destructively. The task of the critic, Kauffman persuasively argues, is to measure the encounters between language and the history that language inexorably, cunningly interprets. In part, these encounters are epistemological; in part, they are literary. For Kauffman, they are also moral and political. They either increase or constrict human freedoms. *Special Delivery* seeks to expand our sense of how free a text can be, and in so doing, to remind us of how free we, too, might be. Surely, this is a message worth sending and receiving.

CATHARINE R. STIMPSON
Rutgers University

ACKNOWLEDGMENTS

*S*ince *Special Delivery* focuses on writing as a contested dialogue and struggle, I must thank those quarrelsome critics who constantly questioned my perceptions and prose: I'm indebted to Melissa Lentricchia for *The Handmaid's Tale* and segments on feminist criticism, and to Jane Tompkins and Patricia Yaeger for *Lolita*. Louise Yelin honed *The Golden Notebook* chapter, as did Lee Greene and Michael Awkward with *The Color Purple*. Martha Nell Smith livened up many passages, and Lorrie Sprecher was an energetic assistant. Kathy Jacobi's illustrations teach us how to see all over again; she has my deepest thanks for myriad illuminations—verbal as well as visual.

I am grateful for a National Endowment for the Humanities Fellowship in 1987–88, for leave from the University of Maryland in 1990, and for five indefatigable friends who racked their brains recommending me for grants: Myra Jehlen, Toril Moi, Garrett Stewart, Frank Lentricchia, and Deirdre David. Many discussions with them, as well as with James Thompson, Marilee Lindemann, Susan Leonardi, Rebecca Pope, and Deborah Rosenfelt, are reflected in these pages.

Feminists owe an incalculable debt to Catharine Stimpson, whose activism (not to mention her savoir faire and joie de vivre) are inspiration to us all. My thanks to her and to Karen Wilson for their editorial acumen, and to Lila Weinberg for meticulous copyediting. Judith Kegan Gardiner, as a reader for the University of Chicago Press, made many suggestions that immeasurably improved the manuscript.

I also wish to thank the conference organizers who invited me to lecture: I spoke on *Lolita* at Emory University, Florida State University, Goethe University in Frankfurt, West Germany, and in 1986 at the Modern Language Association convention. *The Color Purple* chapter first took shape at a symposium for the University of North Carolina's Program in the Humanities in Chapel Hill in 1986. I spoke on Margaret Atwood at the MLA Convention in 1987, on Doris Lessing at the International Conference on Feminist Critical Practice and Theory in Dubrovnik, Yugoslavia, in 1988, and on Barthes and Derrida at Brigham Young University in 1990. Various segments on feminist theory were presented at Brooklyn College; the University of North Carolina, Chapel Hill; the University of Tulsa; the University of California, Riverside; and the University of Maryland. Greater coherence and rigor resulted from the audience's challenges on these occasions.

I thank the Women's Caucus of the Modern Language Association for awarding me first prize in the Florence Howe Essay Contest in 1988 for "Twenty-first Century Epistolarity in *The Handmaid's Tale*," which is reprinted with an "Afterword" in *"Courage and Tools:" The Florence Howe Award Essays*, edited by Joanne Glasgow and Angela Ingram (New York: Modern Language Association, 1990).

Special Delivery is dedicated to my sister, Kay, who helped raise me, and from whom I continue to discover the meaning of perception, perseverance, and courage.

PROLOGUE

Since *Special Delivery*'s subject is antinarrative as well as narrative, it is, appropriately, both sequel and antisequel to *Discourses of Desire: Gender, Genre, and Epistolary Fictions* (1986). The earlier study traces the love letter as a genre from Ovid's *Heroides* to *The Three Marias: New Portuguese Letters* (1972), with chapters on Héloise's letters to Abelard, *The Letters of a Portuguese Nun* (1669), and *Clarissa*. Many of the characteristics that make the love letter an identifiable genre in those texts also can be found in the present study: writing in the absence of the beloved, mourning the inadequacies of language, transgressing generic boundaries, subverting gender roles, staging revolt through the act of writing. My aim in the earlier study was to delineate a tradition, to demonstrate how "amorous epistolary discourse" remains identifiable even when it becomes assimilated into such first-person narratives as *Jane Eyre, The Turn of the Screw,* and *Absalom, Absalom!* I also illustrated how, in the process of reaccentuating its predecessors, each text engages in intertextual dialogue; thus Ovid invokes Sappho, Héloise invokes Ovid, *The Letters of a Portugese Nun* invokes Héloise, *Jane Eyre* is a subtext in *The Turn of the Screw,* and *The Three Marias* turns back to *The Letters of a Portuguese Nun.*

Special *Delivery* is a sequel in the sense that this tradition is never far from mind; the landmark texts in *Discourses of Desire* reappear from time to time. Given the ambitiousness of a temporal time frame that begins with Ovid, *Discourses of Desire* is of necessity drawn with broad brush strokes. *Special Delivery* frames a much smaller canvas. With the exception of two "novelized" theoretical texts, Roland Barthes's *A Lover's Discourse* and Jacques Derrida's *The Post Card,* the study is limited to novels from 1923 to 1986. It is nonetheless an antisequel, for where *Discourses of Desire* emphasized the value of sentimentality, *Special Delivery* satirizes it. Where the former study emphasized generic continuity, the present one emphasizes discontinuity, which is why I have shifted my focus from genre to mode. Alastair Fowler explains the difference by noting that mode, unlike genre, seldom implies a complete external form; to define Sidney's *Arcadia* as pastoral, for instance, conveys no information about its external form. The epistolary mode, however, has a broader function than many other modes.[1] It is able to combine with other kinds; the very looseness of its conventions has made it resilient, adaptable, and relevant in diverse historical epochs. *Special Delivery* examines the ruptures in both literature and history that make it impossible to forget that the epistolary mode is neither timeless nor transcendent. Indeed, in the 1990s it may seem quixotic to study "epistolarity" (defined as the theory and practice of writing letter fiction), when letter writing has practically become a lost art, supplanted by telephones, fax machines, computers, camrecorders, and tape cassettes (video as well as audio). In fact, in Margaret Atwood's *The Handmaid's Tale*, writing has all but disappeared: the "epistolary" heroine records her memories on audio tapes, which are salvaged some hundred and fifty years in the future. Yet Atwood memorializes and mines all the classic conventions of epistolarity. Each of the seven texts in my study has the same Janus-like ability to look backward and forward, as remembrance and prophecy.

The first part of this study, "Producing Woman," concentrates on four texts that are love letters or about love and letters: Viktor Shklovsky's *Zoo, or Letters Not about Love* (1923), Vladimir Nabokov's *Lolita* (1955), Roland Barthes's *A Lover's Discourse: Fragments* (1978), and Jacques Derrida's *The Post Card: From Socrates to Freud and Beyond* (1980). *Zoo* is a novel-in-progress, ostensibly written to a woman who has forbidden Shklovsky to speak of love (hence the subtitle). So he muses on Russian history and literature, avant-garde art, cinema, literary criticism, and theory. He disassembles the classic tenets of mimesis in order to defamiliarize the artificiality of language. Writing in the wake of Héloise and Rousseau's *La nouvelle Héloise* (*Zoo's* second subtitle: *The Third Héloise*), Shklovsky accentuates his generic legacy of belatedness by parodic distortion and dimunition. Shklovsky wrote the novel in exile in Berlin, surrounded by the Russian diaspora that fled in the wake of revolution and world war. His addressees range from the beloved, to Mother Russia, to the censors and party officials who have banished him. He combines the lyrical lament for unrequited love with a skeptical assessment of a new world order, transforming *Zoo* into an allegory of exile.

1. Alastair Fowler, *Kinds of Literature: An Introduction to the Theory of Genres and Modes* (Cambridge, Mass.: Harvard Univ. Press, 1982), pp. 106–11, see also pp. 167–69; hereinafter cited parenthetically.

Lolita also deals with unrequited love and exile. It, too, portrays the problematics of address: Humbert variously addresses the reader, the editor, the typesetter, the gentlemen and gentlewomen of the jury, Charlotte Haze, and Lolita herself. Perhaps what Humbert's narrative most resembles is a love letter to Lolita, composed in jail, a series of death sentences. Like *Zoo*, *Lolita* is a patchwork of modes and genres, combining literary criticism, newspaper reports, fragments of diaries, journals, and memoirs. By framing Humbert's narrative between John Ray's spurious forward and his own afterword, Nabokov underscores its artificiality. Nevertheless, few have noticed how consistently Humbert elides Lolita. He "produces Woman" by reinscribing misogynistic stereotypes of femininity; critics of the novel follow suit.

In Roland Barthes's *A Lover's Discourse* and Jacques Derrida's *The Post Card: From Socrates to Freud and Beyond*, the notion of "beyond" is crucial: they each attempt to go beyond the narratable, beyond logic, beyond totalizing theories, beyond the boundaries of gender and genre. Each stresses the performative aspects of language, using amorous discourse to stage his speculations about love, literature, identity, difference. They deconstruct the dichotomies dividing love from scholarship, margin from center, fiction from theory. Both experiment with "writing unprotectedly"; they present themselves as fictional characters, consciously "novelized" and "feminized." Sometimes they nostalgically reinscribe the feminine stereotypes they mean to mock, but at other points they show what can be gained by destabilizing the assumed relationships between gender and identity.

In Part Two, "Women's Productions," my perspective shifts to three novels by women: Doris Lessing's *The Golden Notebook* (1962), Alice Walker's *The Color Purple* (1982), and *The Handmaid's Tale* (1986). Whereas the men are all continental (only Nabokov writes in English), the women are native English speakers; two are North American. Such particularities inevitably alter the study of mode and generic history. Just as the texts themselves highlight their constructedness, I wish to highlight my study's constructedness; a different selection of texts would have produced a different structural configuration. Since I emphasize the material conditions of production, I can hardly ignore the differences that language, location, nationality, individual and world history make for each of these writers. Even given Shklovsky's and Nabokov's Russian and Barthes's and Derrida's

French backgrounds, in temperament, training, and worldview, far more divides than unites them. Although Shklovsky and Nabokov found themselves in Berlin at approximately the same time, their views on politics and art diverge dramatically. Derrida is a robust Algerian Jew; Barthes's health was delicate, his background (though he was born in Cherbourg) is Protestant and Parisian. Each material circumstance inevitably alters the meaning of exile and address for the women writers too: Persian-born, Doris Lessing grew up in Rhodesia (now Zimbabwe); her outsider status shapes her view of England, where she emigrated at the age of thirty in 1949. Margaret Atwood's Canadian citizenship sharpens her satiric perspective of imperialism and hypocrisy in the United States. For an African-American woman, the meaning of exile and address is transformed yet again when one turns to Alice Walker.

The binary division of the two parts of my study is not meant to reinforce but to defamiliarize the assumed polarities between male/female, theory/fiction, male theory/feminist criticism. For example, some readers might expect the women writers to promote the authority of individual experience—to insist that identity, gender, and the female voice are inviolable—but that is not always the case. Similarly, literary history and epistolary tradition lead one to expect the women's novels to focus solely on love, as in the classic *Letters of a Portuguese Nun*, in which a solitary nun in her convent cell pours out her feelings in letters to the chevalier who has abandoned her. Instead, these three novels repudiate the claustrophobia of private emotions; they are preoccupied with pressing social issues: racial injustice, political persecution, the decimation of nature and culture.

The Golden Notebook's vision of postmodern fragmentation is reflected in the form (a combination of letters, diaries, notebooks, novellas, journals, and news reports) and in the characterization of Anna Wulf. To Lessing, the nostalgia for a coherent, unified identity is a disabling fiction, closely aligned to the limitations of the conventional realist novel as a genre. Language encourages us to dichotomize and to label those in foreign lands as alien, threatening "others." By undergoing the process of "schizoanalysis," Anna achieves an imaginative awareness of her correspondences with others around the globe.

Alice Walker portrays the ideology of otherness as the rationale for racial persecution in *The Color Purple*. She fuses epistolarity with slave narrative, creating a dialogic hybrid that is "womanist" in focus. She depicts the mechanisms of colonization at home and abroad, shifting the frame of reference back and forth to reveal parallel structures of oppression in Africa and America, giving voice to those whose collective histories have been eradicated.

The Handmaid's Tale also depicts the erasure of history, the silencing of women, and the persecution of marginalized groups defined as "other." It is a symptomatic narrative of the historical transformation of the social relations of production and reproduction, a fact that underscores my point that (as with Lessing and Walker) the female novelists draw upon theoretical paradigms, just as the male theorists draw upon fictional ones. As in Lessing, Atwood denaturalizes and decenters the concept of the self, showing how its construction is shaped by technology, surveillance, and ideology.

While all share an interest in epistolary production, I have purposely selected seven texts that are more notable for their differences than their similarities, another departure from *Discourses of Desire*. Rather than artificially imposing a foolish generic consistency, I emphasize each text's innovative contribution to modal transformation, focusing on the distinctive treatment of seven major motifs:

1. *Representation.* Each writer interrogates the proposition that the function of art is to hold the mirror up to nature. Among critical theorists, that proposition has become known as "the representational or mimetic fallacy." Each writer in my study attempts to expose the underlying ideological assumptions of mimesis, demonstrating that what appears "natural" (history, economics, gender, class, racial classifications) is instead socially constructed. In markedly different ways, each writer self-consciously dramatizes the processes of textual production and reception to undermine the tenets of representation.

2. *Individualism.* At least since 1740, the rise of the novel has been linked to the rise of the middle class. The burgeoning prosperity of the bourgeoisie led to increased literacy, which created a mass market for the novel as a genre. The emerging middle class avidly desired to read about itself—its problems, its triumphs, its desires. Realism became a dominant aesthetic criterion, propelled by the bourgeoisie's self-regard (in both senses of the word). When I allude to "bourgeois individualism" or "bourgeois realism," then, I have in mind the middle class's insistence that (*a*) fiction reflect (what

they recognize as) "reality," (b) character and plot revolve around privatized emotions and problems, (c) the (bourgeois, Western European) individual's experience is universal.[2] In this regard, each text in my study is an anatomy of ideology.

3. *The ideology of romantic love.* Special Delivery is also an anatomy of this ideology. Love letters have a lot to answer for. Through the ages, they have been instrumental in disguising relationships of power, politics, and economics by glorifying fulfillment as something only love can bring. The writers in my study sometimes confess their nostalgia, but they also expose the snares and delusions of this myth—and literature's complicity in perpetuating it. Satire displaces sentimentality, which leaves its traces nonetheless.

4. *The Oedipus myth as universal trope.* The Oedipus myth constrains us to view the family as the type for society, encouraging an endless search (in church, school, and nation) for imaginary surrogates. The writers in *Special Delivery* posit alternative paradigms of desire, paradigms that (implicitly or explicitly) criticize the relentless familialism and rigid normalization of Western thought. In various contexts, "oedipalization" connotes the triangle of the nuclear family, repressive socialization, or an aggressive will to power.

5. *Generic disruption and defamiliarization.* Each text in my study is written against the grain in multiple senses. At least since *The Letters of a Portuguese Nun,* the letter has been identified as "the voice of true feeling"; traditionally, the solitary heroine's letters are testaments to sincerity, authenticity, and spontaneity. (The criteria were suspect even at their inception, since there is ample speculation and considerable evidence that the "feminine" disorder of the *Portuguese Letters* probably came from a masculine pen.)[3] The texts in *Special Delivery* use a variety of strategies to

2. Among the many studies that relate the rise of the novel to the rise of the bourgeoisie, see Ian Watt's *The Rise of the Novel* (Berkeley: Univ. of California Press, 1957); Terry Eagleton, *The Rape of Clarissa: Writing, Sexuality, and Class Struggle in Samuel Richardson* (Minneapolis: Univ. of Minnesota Press, 1982); Nancy Armstrong, *Desire and Domestic Fiction: A Political History of the Novel* (Oxford: Oxford Univ. Press, 1987); Lennard J. Davis, *Resisting Novels: Ideology and Fiction* (New York: Methuen, 1987).

3. The literary history and debate over authorship of *The Letters of a Portuguese Nun* is rehearsed by Linda S. Kauffman, *Discourses of Desire: Gender, Genre, and Epistolary Fictions* (Ithaca: Cornell Univ. Press, 1986), chap. 3; its continuing relevance is discussed below in chap. 1 (p. 49), chap. 3 (pp. 103–5), and chap. 6 (pp. 226, 231).

question those traditional criteria of value. One strategy is exaggeration, as when Shklovsky turns himself into a fictional character in *Zoo*. He is the man without qualities, the Dostoyevskian antihero who cannot express any emotion without a sideward satiric glance in his antinarrative. Moreover, he includes actual letters from Elsa Triolet, the woman who spurns him. Not only does she make him the butt of satire, but her authentic letters make his look more hysterical. By undermining sincerity and authenticity, *Zoo* effects a perceptible displacement on the genre; after 1923, it will never again be quite the same.

6. *Dialogism.* My views of genre are informed by Mikhail Bakhtin's theories; while each new contribution to a genre bears a "family resemblance" to its predecessors, it engages in "dialogic" contestation with them: it draws on multiple languages and sources, it posits an alternative logic, it eschews resolution and closure, it depicts ideologues in conflict, it creates an open-ended dialogue that encourages further innovation. The dialogue within the letter novel between letter writer and addressee is doubled by the dialogue between writer and reader. Dialogism is also crucial in representing the writer *as* reader: Shklovsky writes to Rousseau, Nabokov to Poe, Barthes to Werther, Derrida to Joyce, Lessing to Laing, Walker to Hurston, Atwood to Hawthorne. Many other influences—ranging from Sterne to Orwell—also enlarge the dialogic frame of reference. As my allusion to slave narratives suggests, borrowings from multiple genres and non-literary sources consistently revitalize epistolary production. Dialogism also signifies the speaking voice, a crucial aspect of the letter, which is written solely because the writer cannot speak to the addressee. The traditional *je crois te parler* motif informs all epistolary production: writing nurtures the illusion of speaking with one whose absence is intolerable.

7. *Decentering the subject.* In "The Death of the Author," Roland Barthes maintains that neither the author's origins, life, or intentions explain the art; that biography and identity are irrelevant in analyzing the writing. This hypothesis is part of a larger poststructuralist project of showing the relativity of relations between writer, reader, and critic. The legacy of Saussurean linguistics is that symbols become "denaturalized." Meaning is no longer viewed as immanent or transcendent; rather it results from internally generated differential relations. Not only does this paradigm shift undermine referentiality, but some feminist critics worry that it simultaneously undermines the female voice.

In my study, the issue is a fraught one. Epistolarity is a fertile field of investigation in this debate precisely because the authors must repudiate authorial omniscience when they create fictional correspondents. Because epistolarity highlights writing as sheer process, each writer can record numerous speculations that seem to go against the grain of the expectations usually associated with him or her. For example, Shklovsky is customarily known as the father of Russian Formalism, the leading proponent of the objective theory of literature (literature as autonomous object). By the time he wrote *Zoo*, however, Shklovsky had considerably modified his views. *Zoo* records the extraliterary aspects that go into the production of the text and the historical upheavals of his age. He reproduces stereotypes of femininity, but he simultaneously inscribes the female voice by transcribing Elsa Triolet's authentic letters. Her counterdiscourse undermines his stereotypes. By situating these ideologues dialogically in his novel-in-progress, *Zoo* has far more in common with the theories of Mikhail Bakhtin (who is commonly credited with "ruining" Russian Formalism)[4] than one would suspect.

The same surprising reversals of expectation occur in all the texts in my study. Like Shklovsky, Barthes and Derrida assume fictional postures, place their proper names in inverted commas, and put the meaning of signature, the "proper," and naming under constant scrutiny. They dismantle the dichotomy between theory/fiction and theory/practice by using their amorous discourses to record their reservations about poststructuralism as well as their practice of it. Invoking a writing strategy of infidelity to all axiomatics, they frequently interrogate even poststructuralism. Barthes's discourse grows out of his seminar on *The Sorrows of Young Werther*: on the one hand he identifies with Werther (thus defying one of poststructuralism's tenets), while insisting on the impossibility of writing like Goethe in the twentieth century. Derrida proclaims that he aims to write against the grain of deconstructive practice—to write the "opposite." In a similarly paradoxical gesture, he exhaustively compiles all the major characteristics of the love letter as a genre, while declaring its end. Lessing's novel, similarly, is usu-

---

4. See Julia Kristeva, "The Ruin of a Poetics," trans. Vivienne Mylne, in *Russian Formalism*, ed. Stephen Bann and John E. Bowlt (Edinburgh: Scottish Academic Press, 1973), pp. 102–19. Kristeva does not take Shklovsky's prose works, his theories of prose, or the evolution of his ideas into consideration.

ally heralded as one of the first manifestos of the modern women's movement, but the novel itself is a sustained critique of the limitations of feminism as well as of Marxism and psychoanalysis. When Shklovsky wrests
signification away from the mystique of the author, Barthes and Derrida
predictably follow suit. Unpredictably, so does Doris Lessing, for she satirizes how fetishizing the author results in making art a commodity and perpetuating bourgeois ideology. She purposely decenters plot, characterization, and identity and dramatizes the relativity of writer, reader, and critic
throughout the novel.

If the four texts above convince us to repudiate the claims of authority
and identity associated with signature, *Lolita*, *The Color Purple*, and *The
Handmaid's Tale* force us to reconsider. Each text has different reasons and
strategies for doing so. Humbert's prose style is so dazzling that it has
blinded critics to his brutality toward Lolita. One must read against the grain
of Humbert's aesthetic manifesto to discover what he consistently erases:
the material suffering of a raped, drugged, and kidnapped girl. *The Color
Purple* suggests that perhaps one must first have the opportunity to be constituted *as* a subject before one can endorse the "death" of the author or the
subject's decentering. Nevertheless, the deconstructive strategy of decentering need not result in renewed silencing of those who never got to speak
in the first place. Instead, it can serve to expose the strategies of silencing,
the tensions in power relations, and the mechanics of constructing those oppressed as "other." In *The Handmaid's Tale*, for instance, the question of
signature is crucial. Offred's voice, her pain, her horror, and the material
aspects of her oppression remain vivid, despite the interventions of time,
technology, and masculine authority. What she "signs" (what she tape-
records) is not a paean to individualism; it testifies instead to the urgency of
collective action of apocalyptic proportions.

Thus, rather than simply urging feminist literary critics either to endorse or to repudiate the decentered subject, one must first find out who is
speaking, and by what authority. We now see that identity, like meaning,
is not intrinsic but situational and relational. As Offred remarks, "Context is
all." What we define as individual experience is shaped externally as well as
internally. Subjectivity seems to arise solely from personal experience, but
what one perceives as subjective are in fact material, economic, and historical
interrelations.

Similarly, gender and genre are often represented as being diametrically opposed: gender is a social construction, while genre is a formal one. The texts in my study interrogate those dichotomies. Deciphering signifying systems does not eradicate social responsibility; it augments it: only by decoding the culture's mythologies can one learn how to defuse them. One can examine the decentering of the human subject without repudiating the notion of agency. Indeed, while decentering their own authorial privilege, Lessing, Walker, and Atwood depict heroines who are haunted by their roles as moral agents, by their failure to act in specific historical circumstances, by their complicity and collusion with oppressive forces.

Far from seeing desire as static, timeless, or universal then, each writer in my study historicizes it. Each seeks to show how desire is shaped by politics, economics, and commodity culture in a specific historical moment. By sustaining the illusion of writing-to-the-moment, each text highlights the partiality (in both senses of the word) of all constructions: politics, history, and aesthetic principles alike. In these texts, the dichotomies between "high" and "low" culture, between private and public break down. Crucial questions are ceaselessly reiterated: to whom, for whom, why does one write? What is the letter's destination and destiny, and how is that determined? What criteria of value shape the writing and reception of these texts? How does the letter simultaneously reinforce and subvert the culture's dominant ideologies?

Since every letter writer is also a reader, epistolarity exposes the internal processes of the reading subject. What we call unique, transcendent passion is a compendium of the already read, the already said—that is what makes the letter such a fascinating challenge for these twentieth-century innovators, who use language to lament language's inadequacy. Each epistolary narrator is engaged in the interpretation of a trauma and the trauma of interpretation. Each text is a *traumscrapt*, a transcript, trauma, script (predestined, already written), a scrap, combining the scraps of dreams, sounds, visual images, conscious and unconscious desires.

I have purposely selected texts that suggest ways to push beyond the confines of representation, beyond the ideology of bourgeois individualism, beyond the romanticism of the expressive theory of art. The word "post" resonates throughout *Special Delivery*. In addition to the obvious connection to mail, "post" implies something we have gone beyond, as in "postfeminist" or "postmodern." Derrida's subtitle simultaneously suggests the infallibility and fallibility of authorial function: the subtitle may mean that the authority vested in authors extends from Socrates to Freud and even beyond, or it may mean that something different has emerged—or will eventually emerge—after Freud. The ambiguity suggests that the subtitle is not so much an example of "wish-fulfillment" as "wish-formulation." Similarly, as a supplement to feminism and modernism, "post" reveals as much anxiety about what comes next as certainty about what has been. The anxiety about beginnings and endings, origins and supplements extends even to chronology: The historical movement that binds *Special Delivery* is postmodernism, adumbrated in 1923 by Shklovsky and reaccentuated in all the subsequent texts I select. Chronologically, *Zoo* is modernist, but Shklovsky anticipates many stylistic techniques we tend to associate with postmodernism. Moreover, like so many other Russian texts from the 1920s through the 1960s, the novel enters the Western discourse of postmodernism in the 1960s (translated into French in 1963, German in 1965, Italian in 1966, and English in 1971). Postmodernism, as a guiding principle of selection, also helps to account for the presence of both *Lolita* and *The Golden Notebook*; although neither is an epistolary novel per se, they both combine epistolary modes with postmodern experimentation.

Far from perpetuating the clichéd dichotomies polarizing (female) feminist criticism versus (male) critical theory, *Special Delivery* demonstrates a mutual indebtedness. For example, reading Derrida's theories of enframing in conjunction with feminist and clinical studies of incest enabled me to see how Humbert "frames" Lolita. Deleuze and Guattari's exploration of capitalism and schizophrenia helped me see how radical Doris Lessing's experiment is in *The Golden Notebook*. I do not endorse the hyperbolically sexualized rhetoric which describes feminists as being "seduced" by "male" theory, for this rhetoric falsely refigures the feminist as Clarissa, virtuous victim who must vigilantly ward off the masculine seductions of loveless, disembodied "Theory." Those who perpetuate this rhetoric may (like Clarissa) end up starving to death. Conversely, instead of scolding those (males) who have "appropriated" (female) feminist theory, I acknowledge how profoundly feminism has transformed the theoretical (poststructuralist, materialist, semiotic, reader response, new historicist) foundations of literary studies.[5] My own analysis draws (in varying degrees) on the theories of Bakhtin, Foucault, and Lacan. I am not only aware of the disagreements among these theorists but I am also aware that each has a very different relationship to feminism. Rather than serving as their apologist, I instead investigate what can be gained by a feminist intervention in these theoretical dialogues; my thesis is that such interventions will raise different questions, through which the original question will be dislocated, radically transformed. For instance, despite my indebtedness to Bakhtin's insights, he is myopic where gender *and* epistolarity are concerned. Not only does he ignore their interrelatedness but he argues that the novel of pathos expired with eighteenth-century sentimentalism; "openly pathetic discourse . . . was never again the stylistic base for any of the important novel-types."[6] In both *Discourses of Desire* and *Special Delivery*, I attempt to show how resilient the novel of pathos is, specifically in its epistolary forms, whether one thinks of Henry James's *The Turn of the Screw*, William Faulkner's *Absalom, Absalom!*, or of *Lolita* and *The Color Purple*.

Far from being an "application" of a particular theory, my study is a feminist intervention, a contested dialogue. To take another example, Derrida's view that sexual categories can be freely appropriated and deconstructed seems to contradict Foucault's insistence that sexual identity is historically determined. In *The Post Card*, however, Derrida speculates about all the ways in which we are historically determined; the multiple meanings of "determination" reverberate throughout his text. Shklovsky, Barthes, Lessing, Walker, and Atwood all search for ways to convey a dy-

---

5. Elaine Showalter invokes the rhetoric of seduction and scolds male feminists in "Critical Cross-Dressing: Male Feminists and the Woman of the Year," *Raritan Review* 3 (Fall 1983): 130–49. Jane Tompkins describes theory as "one of the patriarchal gestures women and men ought to avoid . . . the female subject par excellence, which is her self and her experiences, has once more been elided by literary criticism," in "Me and My Shadow," in *Gender and Theory: Dialogues on Feminist Criticism,* ed. Linda Kauffman (Oxford: Basil Blackwell, 1989), pp. 121–39. Nancy Miller confesses that "Barthes has seduced me . . . [I do not ignore] the appeal of a headier (sexier . . .) destabilization from deconstructive, psychoanalytic, and neo-Marxist perspectives. . . . The chapters of this book all testify to my awareness of their seductions," in *Subject to Change: Reading Feminist Writing* (New York: Columbia Univ. Press, 1988).

6. See Mikhail M. Bakhtin, *The Dialogic Imagination: Four Esssays,* ed. Michael Holquist, trans. Holquist and Caryl Emerson (Austin: Univ. of Texas Press, 1981), p. 398.

namic sense of how society comes to dwell within individuals and how individuality comes to be socially constituted.[7]

My method makes different discourses interrupt each other dialogically in order to initiate a crisis—which is a good description of what happens *within* each text in my study. It also describes what happens *among* them: on the issue of signature, for instance, *Lolita, The Color Purple*, and *The Handmaid's Tale* undermine the view of signature put forward in *Zoo, A Lover's Discourse, The Post Card*, and *The Golden Notebook*. Regarding each of the seven major issues cited above, one will find a different alignment among the seven texts.

I make no attempt to provide a chronological overview of all the remarkable epistolary texts written in the twentieth century, including Madeleine L'Engle's *Love Letters*, John Barth's *Letters*, Peter Handke's novella, *Short Letter, Long Farewell*, Elizabeth Hailey's *A Woman of Independent Means*, Bob Randall's *The Fan*, Manuel Puig's *Heartbreak Tango*, Lee Smith's *Fair and Tender Ladies*, John Updike's *S.*, or novels in which letters figure prominently, like Saul Bellow's *Herzog*, D. M. Thomas's *The White Hotel*, J. M. Coetzee's *Foe* and *Age of Iron*. Nor do I discuss the contribution of epistolarity in such stage dramas as Jean Cocteau's classic "The Human Voice," A. R. Gurney's "Love Letters," Helene Hanff's "84 Charing Cross Road," Jerome Kilty's "Dear Liar," or "Ivy Rowe," the "monodrama" based on Lee Smith's epistolary novel. New fiction indebted to epistolarity continues to appear at a prodigious pace: Kathy Acker's *Great Expectations*, Carol Muske-Duke's *Dear Digby*, Michael Frayn's *The Trick of It*, Julian Barnes's *A History of the World in 10½ Chapters*, Robert Steiner's *Matinee: A Novel*, A. S. Byatt's *Possession*, and Michael Dorris and Louise Erdrich's *The Crown of Columbus* are notable examples.[8]

Alastair Fowler suggests substituting *type* for the notion of *class* in dis-

---

7. I am indebted to Deborah Rosenfelt for drawing my attention to Steven Epstein's formulation of these paradoxes in "Gay Politics, Ethnic Identity: The Limits of Social Constructionism," *Socialist Review* 93–94 (May–August 1987): 9–54.

8. My thanks to Charles Caramello for bringing Steiner's novel to my attention. Recent scholarship continues to uncover notable precursors to twentieth-century epistolarity, such as *Love Letters between a Certain Late Nobleman and the Famous Mr. Wilson*. Originally published in 1723, the letters offer an astonishing glimpse into the sexual underworld and homosexual practices in eighteenth-century England; edited by Michael S. Kimmel, they were reprinted in New York by Harrington Park Press in 1990.

cussing genres, because a single example can represent a type, whereas a class consists of an array of examples (38–39). (It is this sense of "type" that led Shklovsky to proclaim *Tristram Shandy* the most "typical" novel in the world.) Far from being a systematic survey, *Special Delivery* seizes on certain symptomatic narratives to mark a discontinuous history (literary and social) of radical ruptures. That is precisely how Shklovsky conceives of both generic evolution and social change. He predicted that a new fictional form would emerge by combining parody, nonliterary modes, and documentary. Very early, he perceived that language and technology would be indissolubly connected in twentieth-century literature, art, and architecture. The inevitable result would be the interpenetration of "high" and "low" culture—a laudatory result, in the minds of the Formalists and Futurists engaged in a class rebellion against the previous generation's aestheticism.[9] The profound impact of "low" culture—newspapers, comics, songs, cheap novels, and popular movies—extends from *Zoo* to *The Handmaid's Tale;* the myriad ways in which popular culture continues to revitalize the novel are abundantly manifested here.

Shklovsky's awareness of the impact of technology and popular culture permeates his view of aesthetics, cinema, politics, and literary systems, and explains why the construct is so central in *Zoo;* making, reading, writing, and meaning are all portrayed in process. He also realized that Saussure's denaturalization of symbol systems would irretrievably alter our perception of signification, which would henceforth rely on internally generated relational differences rather than on external representational ones. Despite this emphasis on formalist signification, Shklovsky is nevertheless equally obsessed with history in *Zoo.*

Those twin obsessions—language and history—are shared by all the other writers in my study. *Special Delivery* looks backward at the history of criticism over the past seventy-five years and forward toward apocalypse. History is a pervasive presence in these pages, ranging from the Russian

9. Marjorie Perloff points out that "almost all the poets and painters in the Russian avant-garde came from lower middle class or lower-class provincial families, unlike their predecessors, the Symbolists, who tended to belong to the aristocracy or upper middle class of Moscow and Petersburg" (*The Futurist Moment: Avant-Garde, Avant Guerre, and the Language of Rupture* [Chicago: Univ. of Chicago Press, 1986], pp. 38, 126; hereinafter cited parenthetically as *FM*).

Revolution to the Gileadeans' genius in synthesizing historical strategies of urban siege, genocide, torture, and terrorism. In different ways, many of these texts confront a politically exhausted culture, whether one thinks of the Olinka in *The Color Purple* or the Gildeadeans in *The Handmaid's Tale*. Yet another aspect of postmodernism in these texts concerns their ability to combine self-reflexivity and history in what might be described as "histo-riographic metafiction": "a popular form today which is . . . paradoxically and self-reflexively parodic and yet laying claim to actual historical charac-ters or events."[10] Paradoxically, the plethora of historical figures contribute to the "decreation of history" by problematizing the relationships of text, identity, and the authorial self.[11] In each text in my study, history is being rewritten before the narrator's eyes. In each, the narrator scrutinizes the power of the image (and the Imaginary) to shape desire. In his search for "decisive novelty" in *Zoo*, Shklovsky links material history to aesthetic dis-ruption and innovation. By combining theory and fiction, scholarship and love, high and low culture in a letter novel-in-progress, he maps new territory—territory Nabokov, Barthes, Derrida, Lessing, Walker, and Atwood all expand by different routes, while putting their own distinctive stamp on epistolarity.

Linda S. Kauffman
Washington, D.C.
27 April 1991

10. Linda Hutcheon, "The Post-Modern Ex-Centric: The Center That Will Not Hold," in *Feminism and Institutions: Dialogues on Feminist Theory*, ed. Linda Kauffman (Oxford: Basil Blackwell, 1989), p. 158n.l.

11. Richard Martin uses the term "decreation of history" in "Clio Bemused: The Uses of History in Contemporary American Fiction," *Sub-Stance* 27 (1980): 14; see also Naomi Jacobs's discussion of the technique in "Kathy Acker and the Plagiarized Self," *Review of Contemporary Fiction* 9, no. 3 (Fall 1989): 50–55.

ABBREVIATIONS

AA   Hal Foster, ed. *The Anti-Aesthetic: Essays on Postmodern Culture* (Port Townsend, Wash.: Bay Press, 1983).

ALD   Roland Barthes, *A Lover's Discourse: Fragments*, trans. Richard Howard (New York: Hill and Wang, 1978).

CS   Deborah E. McDowell, "'The Changing Same': Generational Connections and Black Women Novelists," *New Literary History* 12, no. 2 (Winter 1987): 281–302.

D&G   Gilles Deleuze and Félix Guattari, *Anti-Oedipus: Capitalism and Schizophrenia*, trans. Robert Hurley, Mark Seem, and Helen R. Lane (Minneapolis: Univ. of Minnesota Press, 1983).

DI   Mikhail M. Bakhtin, *The Dialogic Imagination: Four Essays*, ed. Michael Holquist, trans. Holquist and Caryl Emerson (Austin: Univ. of Texas Press, 1981).

DP   Michel Foucault, *Discipline and Punish: The Birth of the Prison*, trans. Alan Sheridan (New York: Vintage, 1979).

DS   Garrett Stewart, *Death Sentences: Styles of Dying in British Fiction* (Cambridge, Mass.: Harvard Univ. Press, 1984).

FM   Marjorie Perloff, *The Futurist Moment: Avant-Garde, Avant Guerre, and the Language of Rupture* (Chicago: Univ. of Chicago Press, 1986).

FS   Jacques Lacan, *Feminine Sexuality: Jacques Lacan and the école freudienne*, ed. Juliet Mitchell and Jacqueline Rose (New York: W. W. Norton, 1982).

GEB   Douglas R. Hofstadter, *Gödel, Escher, Bach: An Eternal Golden Braid* (New York: Vintage, 1989).

GN   Doris Lessing, *The Golden Notebook* (New York: Simon and Schuster, 1962; reprinted, Bantam Books, 1981).

GV   Roland Barthes, *The Grain of the Voice: Interviews, 1962–1980*, trans. Linda Coverdale (New York: Hill and Wang, 1985).

ISMG   Alice Walker, *In Search of Our Mothers' Gardens* (San Diego: Harcourt Brace Jovanovich, 1983).

LE   John Barth, "The Literature of Exhaustion," *The Atlantic* (August 1967): 29–34.

LG   Jacques Derrida, "La loi du genre/The Law of Genre," trans. Avital Ronell, *Glyph 7* (Spring 1980): 177–232.

LMRB   Jacques Derrida, "Les morts de Roland Barthes," *Poetique 47* (1981): 269–92.

MA   Abdul JanMohamed, *Manichean Aesthetics: The Politics of Literature in Colonial Africa* (Amherst: Univ. of Massachusetts, 1983).

PC   Jacques Derrida, *The Post Card: From Socrates to Freud and Beyond*, trans. Alan Bass (Chicago: Univ. of Chicago Press, 1980).

PE   R. D. Laing, *The Politics of Experience* (New York: Ballantine Books, 1968).

PF   Juliet Mitchell, *Psychoanalysis and Feminism: Freud, Reich, Laing and Women* (New York: Random House, 1975).

PHL   Fredric Jameson, *The Prison-House of Language: A Critical Account of Structuralism and Russian Formalism* (Princeton: Princeton Univ. Press, 1972).

PME   Linda Hutcheon, "The Post-Modern Ex-Centric: The Center That Will Not Hold," in *Feminism and Institutions: Dialogues on Feminist Theory*, ed. Linda Kauffman (Oxford: Basil Blackwell, 1989).

RF   Victor Erlich, *Russian Formalism: History-Doctrine* (The Hague: Mouton, 1969).

RFM   Deborah E. McDowell, "Reading Family Matters," in *Changing Our Own Words: Essays on Criticism, Theory, and Writing by Black Women*, ed. Cheryl A. Wall (New Brunswick, N.J.: Rutgers Univ. Press, 1989).

SJ   Viktor Shklovsky, *A Sentimental Journey: Memoirs, 1917–1922*, trans. Richard Sheldon (Ithaca: Cornell Univ. Press, 1970).

SM   Henry Louis Gates, Jr., *The Signifying Monkey: A Theory of African-American Literary Criticism* (New York: Oxford Univ. Press, 1988).

SSD   Orlando Patterson, *Slavery and Social Death* (Cambridge, Mass.: Harvard Univ. Press, 1982).

TM   Maria Isabel Barreño, Maria Teresa Horta, and Maria Velho da Costa, *The Three Marias: New Portuguese Letters*, trans. Helen R. Lane (New York: Bantam, 1976).

TP   Viktor Shklovsky, *Theory of Prose*, trans. Benjamin Sher (Elmwood Park, Ill.: Dalkey Archive Press, 1990).

TTFS   William L. Andrews, *To Tell a Free Story: The First Century of Afro-American Autobiography, 1760–1865* (Urbana: Univ. of Illinois, 1986).

Producing Woman

From Russia with Love:
Zoo, or Letters Not about Love

HISTORICAL AND THEORETICAL BACKGROUND

Zoo (1923) is one of the oddest epistolary novels ever written. Viktor Shklovsky mixes fictional love letters with real ones; sketches of friends and enemies; essays on literary theory, cinema, and art. He simultaneously defends Russian Formalism and modifies it. One of three million Russians who fled Russia following World War I, the Revolution, and civil war, Shklovsky wrote *Zoo* between the summers of 1922 and 1923 in Berlin. The Russian diaspora there included Aleksei Remizov, Andrei Bely, Ivan Puni, Marc Chagall, Ilya Ehrenburg, Boris Pasternak, Maxim Gorky, Sergei Esenin, Isadora Duncan, Vladimir Mayakovsky, Aleksei Tolstoy, Roman Jakobson, and Vladimir Nabokov.[1]

1. Richard Sheldon, trans. and ed., "Introduction," in *Zoo, or Letters Not about Love*, by Viktor Shklovsky (Ithaca: Cornell Univ. Press, 1971), pp. xiii, xvii; hereinafter cited parenthetically in the text by page number.

CHAPTER ONE

He compares his compatriots to a zoo menagerie: their antics amaze and delight, but they are caged in Berlin, exiled from their native habitats, facing the danger that they may "lose their marvelous potentialities" (8). The novel is an allegory of exile.

Shklovsky's sense of artistic impotence magnifies his emotional state. Not only is his love unrequited, but Alya has forbidden him to speak of it (hence his first subtitle). Alya is the fictional counterpart of Elsa Triolet, who came from a prominent Russian family, married a Frenchman, and, after divorcing him, was courted by Shklovsky. Elsa actually wrote seven of the letters in Zoo, which launched her own literary career. Eventually she married Louis Aragon, the Communist surrealist writer, and became a celebrated writer in her own right. She and Aragon were instrumental in getting Zoo published in French. [2]

Zoo appears at a number of critical crossroads. The first is temporal: its energy, wit, and impudence evoke the earlier heady years of avant-garde Formalist manifestos and Futurist experiments. It looks forward as well as back, diverging from Formalist theory, modifying earlier views of history, aesthetics, poetics. The second crossroads is ideological: Zoo appears at a crucial moment of struggle between competing groups fighting to establish a definitive Marxist-Leninist aesthetic. Lenin's New Economic Policy in the early twenties gave way to a period of intense ideological struggle as Stalin sought to consolidate his position. Shklovsky's retrospective contemplation of this history is illuminated in the prefaces and letters added to later editions of Zoo between 1924 and 1964; he is increasingly chastened and subdued by what is past, passing, and to come in a tortuous century.

Zoo appears at a critical crossroads where the theory of dialogism is concerned, too. Mikhail Bakhtin's theories may seem diametrically opposed to Shklovsky's, but Zoo uncannily captures the heteroglossia of multiple voices, depicts ideologues in conflict, and records extraliterary concerns—traits we tend to associate with Bakhtin rather than Shklovsky. Conversely, it is important to remember that Bakhtin did not merely repudiate Formal-

2. Ibid., pp. xix–xxi. Vladimir Mayakovsky subsequently fell in love with Lilya, Elsa's sister. Lilya was the wife of Osip Brik, another of the architects of Russian Formalism. Mayakovsky composed a remarkable poem "Pro eto" ("About This") about his unrequited love for Lilya. Sheldon compares the stylistic and thematic affinities between Zoo and Mayakovsky's poem, p. xx. See also Sheldon, "Viktor Borisovic Shklovsky: Literary Theory and Practice, 1914–1930" (Ph.D. diss., Univ. of Michigan, 1966), 188; hereinafter cited parenthetically in the text as "Sheldon diss."

ism. Instead, he wanted to reconcile the best in Formalism (namely, a far more sophisticated poetics than anything yet put forward by the Marxists) with the best in Marxism (attention to history and the social sphere). Expressed another way, Bakhtin tried to prevent Formalism from taking precisely the kind of classical structuralist position eventually adopted in France. Moreover, although the solutions he proposed were different, he shared Shklovsky's dread of the growing rigidity of Marxist-Leninist dogma—the dread that led Shklovsky to reject content in favor of form in the first place. These struggles and contradictions presage those to come between structuralists and poststructuralists, as Wlad Godzich explains. The Formalists are to structuralism as Bakhtin is to poststructuralism: Bakhtin tried to foreclose some of the Formalist theoretical options that are very close to structuralism by using procedures that bear "quite a great deal of resemblance to some of today's deconstructive practices."[3] Lamentably, the differences between their interventionist strategies were moot; neither Shklovsky's approach nor Bakhtin's managed to prevent Stalin's repressive enforcement of Marxist-Leninist dogma. Zoo is poised, Janus-faced, between past and future, between Formalist poetics and Bakhtinian dialogism, between remembrance and prophecy.

Zoo also stands at the crossroads between modernity and postmodernity: chronologically it is modernist, but Shklovsky anticipates many of the stylistic experiments commonly associated with postmodernity: discontinuous narrative, illogical associations, self-referentiality, cinematic montage, codeterminous images, the destruction of plot, character, story. Postmodernism has been described as consisting of "three waves of developments occurring at multiple sites within the culture, including literature and science." Beginning with Saussurrean linguistics, symbol systems were "denaturalized." Signification was no longer created by mimesis but by internally generated differential relations.[4] Zoo belongs to this first wave. Be-

3. "Foreword," by Wlad Godzich, in *The Formal Method in Literary Scholarship*, by M. M. Bakhtin and P. M. Medvedev, trans. Albert J. Wehrle (Cambridge, Mass.: Harvard Univ. Press, 1985), pp. vii–xiv.

4. Katherine N. Hayles, "Denaturalizing Experience: Postmodern Literature and Science," *Literature and Science as Modes of Expression* (unpublished abstract from a conference, 8–11 October 1987), Society for Literature and Science, Worcester Polytechnic, cited in Donna Haraway, "The Biopolitics of Postmodern Bodies: Determinations of Self in Immune System Discourse," *Differences* 1, no. 1 (Winter 1989): 3–43.

tween 1919 and 1922, Shklovsky was already assimilating the radical transformations Einstein's theories had begun to make on our consciousness of space and time. Rather than perceiving time as an inevitable linear progression, he saw that henceforth it would be perceived as a relative construct that could be variously conceptualized. Artists and writers would attempt to represent fragmentation and simultaneity, experimenting verbally with the kinds of altered perceptual schemas that had already begun to mark Cubism and Futurism visually.[5]

The theory of relativity transforms plot, characterization, and identity as well. By appearing as a character in Zoo, Shklovsky undermines the traditional authorial privileges of omnipotence and omniscience. His technique of blurring the boundaries between fiction and reality resembles the metafictional strategies we usually associate with such contemporary writers as John Barth, who observes: "When the characters in a work of fiction become readers or authors of the fiction they're in, we're reminded of the fictitious aspect of our own existence."[6] Although Shklovsky took elaborate pains in Zoo to highlight the novel's artificiality and distance from "real life," critics have had the maddening tendency of interpreting it wholly in autobiographical terms. Not only does this tendency minimize the novel's formal qualities, it also diminishes its theoretical force. The love letter's signification changes drastically after Shklovsky; far from epitomizing the "spontaneous overflow of powerful feelings," the criteria of value changes from authenticity to artifice; the more saccharine the device, the better the letter. Alya, the addressee in Zoo, is "the realization of a metaphor"—of

5. Linda Dalrymple Henderson, in "Appendix A: The Question of Cubism and Relativity," in *The Fourth Dimension and Non-Euclidean Geometry in Modern Art* (Princeton: Princeton Univ. Press, 1983), pp. 353–65, points out:

> The mistake of art historians dealing with Cubism [or Futurism] and Relativity has been to read back into Cubist literature of 1911 and 1912 the development in physics of a non-Euclidean space-time continuum that was not completed until 1915 or 1916. . . . Einstein emerged as a celebrity only in November 1919, when the findings of an English astronomical expedition to photograph the May 1919 eclipse were announced by the Royal Society in London. Such displacement photographed at the rim of the sun had confirmed that light rays from stars were indeed bent by the gravitational mass of the sun. With this observational validation, the General Theory of Relativity suddenly gained a new legitimacy that scientists and laymen alike could no longer ignore. (358)

6. John Barth, "The Literature of Exhaustion," *The Atlantic* (August 1967): 29–34; hereinafter cited parenthetically as LE.

love, bourgeois culture, and exile. Alya provides what Shklovsky calls the "motivation" for the devices he puts into play. Since he satirizes the conventions (and conventionality) of genre, genre is the focus of the first part of my chapter. The second part focuses on gender, for while self-consciously dramatizing its own production *Zoo* simultaneously reproduces numerous stereotypes of femininity.

Since there have been numerous misconceptions about Russian Formalism, particularly in America, how exactly can one summarize it? Victor Erlich describes Shklovsky as a chief architect of this remarkable movement, the "product of intellectual teamwork rarely paralleled in the history of literary scholarship."[7] Because of its emphasis on form, it is sometimes compared to Anglo-American New Criticism, but where the New Critics divorced art from politics, the Formalists' avant-garde experiments were politically contemporaneous—if not always "politically correct" in the eyes of the bureaucrats (*RF*, 79). In contrast to the reactionary parochialism of New Criticism, Russian Formalism resembles such movements as German Romanticism and Surrealism in its scope and range. The *Opojaz* (Society for the Investigation of Poetic Language), the group founded by Shklovsky, Boris Eikhenbaum, and Yury Tynyanov, consisted of literary historians who drew upon Saussurean linguistics to make the study of poetic language more rigorous and scientific (*RF*, 94). Their collaborative projects involved poetry, prose, art, cinema, linguistics, literary history, and aesthetic theory. The emphasis on interdisciplinary collaboration is crucial; Shklovsky is to Formalism what Ezra Pound is to modernism. As Fredric Jameson points out:

> Like other literary schools . . . the Opajaz seems to have developed a doctrine of *Geselligkeit* to justify its own collective unity. Shklovsky himself has much in common with the directors of other literary movements in analogous moments of fusion and formation, with Pound, with Friedrich Schlegel, with Breton: a union of seminal ideas, intellectual impudence, and a fragmentary artistic performance which results in the canonization of the fragment as a genre, whether explicitly in Schlegel and in the Surrealists' discontinuous view of lived experience; or implicitly in the ideogrammatic practice of the

---

7. Victor Erlich, *Russian Formalism: History-Doctrine* (The Hague: Mouton, 1969), p. 70; hereinafter cited parenthetically in the text as *RF*.

Cantos, and in Shklovsky's single-sentence paragraphs and deliberate inter-
polation of heterogeneous anecdotes and materials.[8]
Shklovsky's collaborators included theorists, poets, novelists, artists, architects, and cinematographers, ranging from the poet Mayakovsky and the
filmmaker Eisenstein to the "Serapion Brothers," a group of novelists who
(under the influence of Shklovsky and Gorky) regenerated Russian literature after the Revolution. Their aim was to restore the native raciness of the
language and to free it from Europeanization, an effort that partially explains Shklovsky's unremitting critique of "pan-Europeanism" in *Zoo*
(Sheldon, 148–49n.1). One of the abiding paradoxes of the international climate after the First World War was that it combined cosmopolitanism with
an intensely nationalistic fervor and rivalry.[9]

One cannot understand the Formalists unless one perceives what they
were reacting against. One point is not readily apparent in the manifestos:
most of the poets and painters in the Russian avant-garde were either from
the lower middle class or from lowly provincial families; in contrast, the
Symbolists whom they were reacting against were upper middle class or
aristocrats (*FM*, 126). The Formalists' aim was to invent a discourse appropriate to the new century's transformed class relations, receptive to science
and technology, responsive to and representative of mass society. These
aims help to explain why they insist on the interpenetration of "low" culture and "high." They reacted against the dominant academic approach to
literature at the beginning of the twentieth century, which focused on biography, genetic criticism, influence and source studies. The Formalists
attacked their predecessors' sloppy eclecticism, religious-philosophical criticism, and emphasis on symbolism. They shifted the analytic emphasis from
literary meaning to literary production. Where their predecessors argued
that symbols and images were part of a work's organic wholeness, the Formalists' objective was to distinguish intrinsic characteristics that define its
"literariness." They analyzed how textual devices are assembled and how
they function.

By stressing devices instead of themes, Shklovsky also undermined the

8. Fredric Jameson, *The Prison-House of Language: A Critical Account of Structuralism and Russian Formalism* (Princeton: Princeton Univ. Press, 1972), pp. 47–48; hereinafter cited parenthetically in the text as *PHL*.

9. See Marjorie Perloff, *The Futurist Moment,* chap. 1; hereinafter cited parenthetically as *FM*.

sacrosanct notion of an inviolate literary canon. Literary works, he argued, are collections of devices that interact in a textual field; the result may or may not produce aesthetic effects.[10] Just as Shklovsky and other Formalists debunked the notion of "high" versus "low" literature by analyzing the verbal devices in popular songs, folktales, myths, or riddles, the Futurists in the visual arts were making collages from newspaper fragments, advertising posters, popular songs. As Marjorie Perloff points out,

> It is this straining of the artwork to assimilate and respond to that which is not art that characterizes the Futurist moment. It represents the brief phase when the avant-garde defined itself by its relation to the mass audience. As such, its extraordinary interest . . . is as the climactic moment of rupture, the moment when the integrity of the medium, of genre, of categories such as "prose" and "verse," and, most important, of "art" and "life" were questioned. It is the moment when collage, the *mise en question* of painting as the representation of "reality," first makes its appearance, when the political manifesto is perceived aesthetically even as the aesthetic object—painting, poem, drama—is politicized. (*FM*, 38)

In contrast to the high priests of New Criticism who were obsessed with canon formation, Shklovsky's interest was artisanal; canonicity bored him. As he explains in his memoirs, "The formal method is fundamentally very simple—a return to craftsmanship. Its most remarkable feature is that it doesn't deny the idea content of art, but treats the so-called content as one of the manifestations of form."[11]

Shklovsky's *Resurrection of the Word* (1914) is often considered the first historical document of Formalist theory. His "Art as Technique" (1917) further defines the agenda of the emerging Formalist movement. He attacks Symbolism and Imagism for assuming the "givenness" of images and ignoring their fabrication: "Art is a way of experiencing the artfulness of an object; the object is not important."[12] Rather than "thinking in images," like the Symbolists and Imagists, Shklovsky recommends using metaphor and

10. Robert Con Davis, ed., "Viktor Shklovsky," in *Contemporary Literary Criticism: Modernism through Structuralism* (New York: Longman, 1986), p. 51.

11. Viktor Shklovsky, *A Sentimental Journey: Memoirs, 1917–1922*, trans. Richard Sheldon (Ithaca: Cornell Univ. Press, 1970), p. 232; hereinafter cited parenthetically as *SJ*.

12. Viktor Shklovsky, "Art as Technique," in *Contemporary Literary Criticism*, ed. Robert Con Davis (New York: Longman, 1986), p. 55, and Viktor Shklovsky, *Resurrection of the Word* (St. Petersburg, 1914).

metonymy (linguistically based devices) to create works that are more complex, less coherent. [13] Poetry, he argues, is not a specialized part of everyday language but a linguistic system in its own right (*PHL*, 49). Poetry's function isn't to recognize familiarity in unfamiliarity; instead, the poetic use of the image results in a "peculiar semantic shift,"which transfers the object depicted to a different plane of reality (*RF*, 76). Art's purpose is not to convey transcendent philosophical messages but to destroy the habitual associations and automatic responses that have dulled our perception of the world. "Habitualization," Shklovsky wrote, "devours works, clothes, furniture, one's wife, and the fear of war. . . . Art exists that one may recover the sensation of life; it exists to make one feel things, to make the stone *stony*. The purpose of art is to impart the sensation of things as they are perceived and not as they are known."[14] The same hatred of habitualization dominates *Zoo*: "Human routine is awful, meaningless, sluggish, inflexible. . . . Routine we transform into anecdotes. Between the world and ourselves, we build our own little menagerie worlds" (24). Anecdotes and fragments—Shklovsky's trademarks in *Zoo*—transform perception through distortion.

This goal of transforming perception by highlighting production is one of the aims the Formalists shared with such Russian Futurist painters as Kazimir Malevich, who declared in 1915–16, "We must see everything in nature, not as real objects and forms, but as *material*, as masses from which forms must be made that have nothing in common with nature."[15] The Formalists maintained that rather than holding the mirror up to nature, literature is always mirroring its own making. This explains why Boris Eikhenbaum wrote "How [Gogol's] 'The Overcoat' Was Made" (1919) and why Shklovsky wrote "How *Don Quixote* Was Made" (1921). Rather than analyzing Cervantes's psychology, Shklovsky demonstrated that the hero's fate, characterization, setting, and themes all exist solely to serve as a "motivation of the artifice" (*RF*, 196). Similar logic informs Shklovsky's famous declaration that *Tristram Shandy* is "the most typical novel in world literature" because it heightens our perception of its constructedness, its self-

13. Robert Con Davis, "Viktor Shklovsky," pp. 50–51.

14. Shklovsky, "Art as Technique," p. 55.

15. Kazimir Malevich, "From Cubism and Futurism to Suprematism," cited in Perloff, p. 119.

reflexivity: "It is the consciousness of form through its violation that constitutes the content of the novel." The devices are organized to achieve *ostranenie*, which is variously translated as "defamiliarization," "making it strange," or "estrangement." In the recent English translation of *Theory of Prose*, Benjamin Sher coins the word *enstrangement*, noting that previous English translations of *ostraniene* are misleading, for Shklovsky's neologism simultaneously signifies "a process or act that endows an object or image with 'strangeness' by 'removing' it from the network of conventional, formulaic, stereotypical perceptions and linguistic expressions." "Defamiliarization" suggests a transition from the familiar to the unknown, whereas Shklovsky wants to suggest the opposite movement: "from the cognitively known (the language of science), the rules and formulas that arise from a search for an economy of mental effort, to the familiarly known, that is, to real knowledge that expands and 'complicates' our perceptual process in the rich use of metaphors, similes and a host of other figures of speech."[16] Perhaps we had to wait for Derrida to understand Shklovsky better, for Derrida shares Shklovsky's motives for inventing neologisms. Instead of creating a fictional illusion of time progressing, all Shklovsky's sentences lead us back to their writing (*PHL*, 75). That particular form of temporal manipulation not only operates throughout *Zoo* but is one of the trademarks of epistolarity. Retarding and impeding devices, artificial obstacles, narrative disruption all work to break the chain of habitual association and automatic responses. The aim of art is thus not reflection but distortion of nature by means of sets of devices (*RF*, 76).

The impulse to strip the veil and evil of familiarity from the world extends from Aristotle to the Romantics, but the Formalists substitute a linguistic metaphor of artistic creation for the organic one, and approach the text as a field of activity in which linguistically based devices create a more complex analysis than a study of mere images can encompass.[17] The primacy of the linguistic model, as Jameson points out, is the point of departure

---

16. Viktor Shklovsky, *Theory of Prose*, trans. Benjamin Sher (Elmwood Park, Ill.: Dalkey Archive Press, 1990), p. 149, and "Translator's Introduction," pp. viii–ix, hereinafter cited parenthetically as *TP*. Originally published in 1925, *Theory of Prose* was expanded in 1929; Ardis Press chose the 1929 ed. for its facsimile reprint in 1971; Sher's translation also relies on the 1929 ed.

17. Robert Con Davis, "Viktor Shklovsky," p. 51.

first for the Formalists and later for the structuralists: "Language as a model! To rethink everything through once again in terms of linguistics!" (*PHL*, vii). At stake is not freedom from meaning but emancipation from the referent (*RF*, 185). By divorcing the sign from the referent, the Formalists laid the groundwork for structuralism and, by extension, for poststructuralism. The result of this divorce is not an absence of meaning but a multiplicity of signifiers colliding on a textual field, a result Roland Barthes and Jacques Derrida will later take pains to exploit.

Formalism, which preceded the Revolution, was attacked during and after it as "an asylum for the advocates of 'pure,' 'apolitical' art," but it nonetheless reflected the Zeitgeist of the age, as Erlich points out: "The Formalist School is apt to appear for better or worse as a legitimate, if somewhat eccentric, child of the revolutionary period, as part and parcel of its peculiar intellectual atmosphere" (*RF*, 78n.51, and 80). Its insistence on scientific rigor, its materialist base, and particularly its emphasis on the laws of literary production paralleled the industrial enthusiasms of the post-October period (*RF*, 81). The specific art forms scrutinized by the Formalists reflected the material conditions of literary production in these tumultuous years: research was difficult, books were hastily published. One reason for proclaiming poetry rather than prose the chief literary genre was the scarcity of paper. Shklovsky valorizes the aphorism and the fragment, nonstories and unfinished anecdotes for practical as well as theoretical reasons: the chaotic times and scarcity of materials prohibited extensive bibliographic scholarship and leisurely exegesis; necessity was the mother of inventive brevity. In several senses, then, the materialist base is the foundation upon which Shklovsky's theories are built.

Shklovsky's extreme proclamations and insistence on the primacy of form must thus be contextualized, for the years 1916–20 were, in Boris Eikhenbaum's words, "years of struggle and polemics"; they were among the "most turbulent periods of Russian letters" (*RF*, 78–79). Since each competing literary school was struggling to devise a program of proletarian art and a definitive Marxist-Leninist aesthetic, their polemical rhetoric was seldom measured or moderate; it was the rhetoric of manifestos, slogans, and propaganda. One ridiculed one's opponents as "obsolete, reactionary, bourgeois, decadent, or mechanistic" (*RF*, 70–86).[18] It was only in the

18. See also Sheldon diss., p. 84.

preceding decade, commencing with Marinetti's *Foundation et manifeste du futurisme* (1909), that the manifesto itself began to emerge as a new literary genre, one designed to reach a mass audience while simultaneously promoting the avant-garde, the antibourgeois. Marinetti's prescription for excelling in the art of writing manifestos: combine violence and precision; "l'accusation précise, l'insulte bien définie" (*FM*, 81–82).

Shklovsky became one of the most violent and precise practitioners of the genre in the years between 1914 and 1920. He subsequently championed artistic freedom and protested against the doctrinaire insistence of early Marxist-Leninist practice, which in his view wholly sacrificed form and craft to ideological content. But by the time he wrote *Zoo*, the verve, wit, and impudence of his manifesto style was becoming subdued. He modified his theories, conceding that the "insistence on the primacy of form was as mechanistic as the utilitarian's call for the hegemony of content."[19] He also modified his theories of genre and literary evolution. Initially, he had insisted that "a work of literature is the sum-total of all stylistic devices employed in it,"[20] but he later decided that such a definition could not account for the dynamism of literature as a system. He initially felt that each literary genre completely overturns the old genres. He saw perpetual change and permanent artistic revolt as inherent in artistic form itself (*PHL*, 52–53). Eventually, he realized that this theory did not permit him to explain how genres are transformed; how, for instance, comic devices in one historical period could become tragic in the next. (The grotesque is a case in point.) Nor did his initial theory enable him to reconcile the literary work of ideology with the nonliterary, a failing Bakhtin and Medvedev were quick to point out.[21]

Shklovsky's subsequent work with Tynyanov and Eikhenbaum convinced him that literature is more than the sum of its devices. Literature is not a closed, symmetrical whole, says Tynyanov in 1924, but a dynamic process (*RF*, 90–91). Shklovsky embraced this view, acknowledged Tynyanov's constructive modifications, and substituted a dynamic concept of literary process for his initial static view of literary form; he proceeds to show how

19. Sklovskij, *Literatura i kinematograf* (Berlin, 1923), p. 3, cited in Erlich, *Russian Formalism*, p. 197.

20. Sklovskij, *Rozanov* (Petersburg, 1921), p. 15, cited in Erlich, *Russian Formalism*, p. 90.

21. Bakhtin and Medvedev, *The Formal Method in Literary Scholarship*, pp. 92, 103–4, 110, 140–41, 158–65.

the same literary device performs different functions in different historical contexts (*RF*, 137). Tynyanov recast the problem of the relation of the literary system to nonliterary systems by arguing for overlapping and cross-fertilization of literature and life. This development bears directly on *Zoo*, for nonliterary modes, such as letter writing, provide the verbal raw material, which under certain circumstances is absorbed into the literary system in the form of the letter novel (*PHL*, 94). In *Zoo*, Shklovsky takes the "raw material" of Elsa Triolet's letters and absorbs them into the fabric of the novel. Conversely, a document recounting an authentic event may qualify as literature (*RF*, 121–22). That, too, is the case in *Zoo*: Russian emigration to Berlin becomes the occasion for an extended allegory of internal and external exile. Shklovsky exploits Tynyanov's ideas in *Zoo* by combining allusions to epistolary conventions with memoirs, diaries, conversations, and literary criticism; he weaves the nonliterary and the literary together dialogically.

In his later writings, Shklovsky continued to define art as a process of defamiliarization, but he expanded the definition to include analysis of the extraliterary. By 1926, he coined the word "factography" to describe the mode that combines literary with such nonliterary genres as newpaper reportage, cinema, or semijournalistic feuilletons. Since the debate over the relationship of form to content had been so vehement in the early 1920s, "factography" was hailed as the perfect example of the integration of form and content. Shklovsky expected a new literary form based on facts recorded in fragmentary notebooks to emerge from this fusion (Sheldon diss., 283–84)—a prophecy Doris Lessing fulfills in *The Golden Notebook*, which similarly incorporates newpaper articles, anecdotes, undeveloped story lines, historical events and people, literary criticism, and cinematic techniques in attempting to go beyond the conventional novel form. Erlich comments that "one may wonder how Sklovskij managed to reconcile his enthusiasm for reportage with a literary theory which saw the chief aim of art in the creative deformation of reality" (*RF*, 120–21). But if postmodern readers and poststructuralist theorists have learned anything, it is to see the extent to which so-called objective reporting is itself a deformation of "reality" and that "reality" is subject to numerous competing constructions. By seizing on language to launch a new perception of history as *text* and of writing as *production*, rather than representation, Shklovsky paves the way in *Zoo* for the production of plural histories and plural writing practices in a specific historical milieu. Historical characters like Roman Jakobson, Elsa Triolet, and Shklovsky himself become "novelized," which heightens our awareness of the fictiveness of reality. (Barthes and Derrida follow suit in their amorous discourses.) Contemporary readers of John Barth, Truman Capote (*In Cold Blood*), Norman Mailer (*The Executioner's Song*), Joan Didion (*Salvador, Democracy*), and Don DeLillo (*Libra*) would not see Shklovsky's twin enthusiasms for fact and fiction as mutually irreconcilable in the least.

Confronted with dramatic evidence of how literary forms adapt to and reflect social change during the turbulent years of 1917–26, the Formalists modified their views of a pure Formalism and developed more complex analyses of the relationship between literature and history in their literary as well as their theoretical writings. In addition to penetrating reevaluations of the Golden Age of Russian Literature in such works as Tynyanov's *Dostoevskij and Gogol* (1921), Tomashevsky's *Pushkin* (1925), Eikhenbaum's *The Young Tolstoi* (1922) and *Lermontov* (1924), the Formalists studied contemporary writers like Anna Axmatova and Vasily Rozanov (*RF*, 91–92). Rozanov's radically disruptive compositions profoundly influenced Shklovsky. He was influenced also by Eikhenbaum, who shifted the question from how to write to how to be a writer, a question of increasing urgency given the growing political regimentation of literature.

By the time Shklovsky wrote *Zoo*, he was thus already formulating a socio-formalist approach which analyzed the impact of social environment on the literary process. *Zoo*, indeed, demonstrates just how forceful that impact can be: the writers are stifled because exiled, and (to paraphrase Flaubert) they long to make music to melt the stars while tapping crude rhythms for caged bears to dance to. One reason that *Zoo* seems so anomalous is that Shklovsky's views are purposely contradictory. On one page, he declares his faith in love; on the next, his cynicism. On one page, he defends Formalist theory; on the next he criticizes it. The whole purpose of staging a discourse that places "ideologues" in conflict, according to Bakhtin, is to resist synthesis, harmony, and closure, to prevent orthodoxy from rigidifying.[22] Ironically, the value of such a procedure was forcibly brought home to

22. Mikhail Bakhtin, *The Dialogic Imagination*, pp. 259–422; hereinafter cited parenthetically in the text as *DI*.

Shklovsky, for to gain readmittance to Russia he had to respond to an increasingly doctrinaire political climate at home, a climate that made political allegory and coded writing necessary. Jakobson speculates that Eikhenbaum's analysis of Lermontov's work and the oppressions of the 1830s is a thinly veiled account of Eikhenbaum's own recent ordeal (RF, 143). Michael Holquist argues convincingly that Bakhtin's theories of dialogism, of utterance as a contest and a struggle, are veiled in parable and allegory for similar reasons:

> Bakhtin has appropriated the code of one ideology to make public the message of quite another. . . . For Russians, utterance has ever been a contest, a struggle. The need to speak indirectly has resulted in a Russian discourse that is always fabular precisely when it is fueled by the most intense desire to mean. Such indirection has resulted in an allegorical mode known as "Aesopic" language. [23]

Similar motives inform Shklovsky's use of "Aesopic language" throughout Zoo. From Velimir Khlebnikov's poem about the demoralization of zoo animals, which Shklovsky takes as his opening epigraph, to his description of the anthropoid ape in Letter 6, to his discussion of the "Order of Monkeys" with their monkey language and monkey economy in Letter Five, Shklovsky exploits Aesopic language to ridicule and subvert Soviet censorship practices. The multilayered text, embedding as many competing voices as possible in dialogic contest, was thus a cunning response to the political realities of repression. Despite such efforts, by the end of the 1920s literature, art, and criticism which do not serve the official party line is suppressed (RF, 135).

GENERIC REACCENTUATION AND INNOVATION IN ZOO

Zoo exemplifies both the originality of Shklovsky's initial theories and their subsequent modification. It reflects the Formalist quest for unorthodox and difficult modes of expression and the quest for "decisive novelty" (RF, 149). In one preface, Shklovsky describes his problems in constructing the novel: how "to motivate the appearance of the unrelated pieces"; he explains the justification for including devices that are not integrated into the whole. His

---

23. Michael Holquist, "The Politics of Representation," in *Allegory and Representation*, ed. Stephen J. Greenblatt (Baltimore: Johns Hopkins Univ. Press, 1981), pp. 176, 181.

solution: "I introduced the theme of a prohibition against writing about love, and this prohibition let into the book autobiographical passages and the love theme" (xxvii). *Zoo* is an experiment in writing a new kind of documentary novel—one that extends the borders of literature and breaks new ground (xxix). One of the most innovative techniques was the combination of scholarly letters and letters of love, as Tynyanov points out:

> [A] single emotional core provides the basis for a novel, and a feuilleton, and a scholarly paper. We are not accustomed to reading a novel which is at the same time a scholarly paper. We are not accustomed to scholarship in "letters about love," or, for that matter, in "letters not about love." Our culture is built on a rigid differentiation between scholarship and art. Only in certain instances— very few at that—have these areas overlapped. Heine, for example, in his "Reisebilder," his "Parisian Letters," and, in particular, in his *History of Philosophy and Literature in Germany*, combined newspaper correspondence, portraits of a very personal nature, and the coarse salt of scholarly thought.[24]

Richard Sheldon argues that "Shklovsky's letters represent the revival and transformation of a genre canonized during the first quarter of the nineteenth century" (xxxi–xxxii). Like Aleksei Remizov and Vasily Rozanov, Shklovsky sought ways to strip the Russian language of foreign derivations and to restore its robust vernacular in *Zoo*. Letters play a seminal role in this process, for they are characteristically colloquial, intimate, devoted to the dailiness of life. Not only were Rozanov's letters turned into a book by Remizov (a fact discussed by Shklovsky in Letter 5 in *Zoo*), but Shklovsky's critical study of Rozanov was published shortly before he wrote *Zoo*. Shklovsky was particularly influenced by Rozanov's rebellion against coherence and cohesiveness in literature. He also disrupted logical composition and adopted Rozanov's nonchalant, conversational tone (Sheldon diss., 335). This helps to explain why *Zoo* seems unfinished, tentative, and improvised: these were the effects Shklovsky was striving for. The aim is to make the text seem "as if it were written and read in the twinkling of an eye! (singing, splash, dance, throwing down of clumsy structures, forgetting, unlearning)" (*FM*, 122). This description appears in Kruchenyk's *The Word as Such* and is practiced by Khlebnikov as well as Shklovsky. Shklovsky eulo-

---

24. Yury Tynyanov, "Literaturnoe segodnia" [The Literary Today], *Russkii sovremennik* [The Russian Contemporary], no. 1 (1924), pp. 305–6; cited in Sheldon's intro. to *Zoo*, p. xxxi.

gizes Khlebnikov in Letter 4; and throughout *Zoo* he assimilates the notions of "transrational" language that Kruchenyk and Khlebnikov put forth in their manifestos: "language that undermines or ignores the conventional meanings of a given word, thus allowing its sound to generate its own range of significations, or, in its more extreme form, the invention of new words based purely on sound" (*FM*, 121). The willing suspension of rationality, the allusions to private meanings, and the valorization of non-sense help to explain some of Shklovsky's more puzzling sentences. To take one example, after lyrically lamenting, "Life tailors us for a certain person and laughs when we are drawn to someone unable to love us," Shklovsky comments enigmatically, "All this is simple—like postage stamps" (*Zoo*, 19). He thus draws attention to a neglected aspect of material production that goes into communicating by love letter, and obliquely comments on its futility, since the letter's *destinataire* is someone who doesn't love the sender. Despite his disclaimer, there is nothing "simple" either about unrequited love or about writing and mailing love letters, or, for that matter, about the postal system—as Derrida will demonstrate.

Shklovsky reveals his attitude toward literary predecessors and generic reaccentuation in *Zoo*'s second subtitle, *The Third Héloise*, an ironic allusion both to Héloise's letters to Abelard and to Rousseau's *La nouvelle Héloise*. (The subtitle also alludes to Laurence Sterne's *Journal to Eliza*, a name that puns on both Elsa Triolet [Elza in Russian] and Héloise) (Sheldon, xxv–xxvi). Shklovsky identifies with Héloise, who was similarly forbidden by Abelard to speak of love; she can only lure him into a correspondence by disguising her letters as a search for spiritual guidance and a philosophical inquiry. Nevertheless, far from merely imitating Héloise's correspondence and Rousseau's novel, Shklovsky purposely highlights the incongruity of the comparisons through ironic deflation: Alya lacks Héloise's unswerving devotion and Julie's sentimentality. As a lover, Shklovsky is no match for the tragic Abelard or the charismatic St. Preux (Sheldon diss., 198–99). Instead, he is a malicious, spiteful, vindictive antihero. Like Dostoyevsky's narrator in *Notes from Underground*, *Zoo*'s narrator is a paradoxicalist. Roland Barthes reminds us of the etymological meaning of *paradox*:

> The Text is that which goes to the limit of the rules of enunciation (rationality, readability, and so on). The Text tries to situate itself exactly *behind* the limit of *doxa* (is not public opinion—constitutive of our democratic societies and

powerfully aided by mass communication—defined by its limits, its energy of exclusion, its *censorship*?). One could literally say that the Text is always *paradoxical*.[25]

Shklovsky's dilemma is that, despite his obsession, Alya forbids him to mention love. Her injunction has the effect of making him desire to write of love all the more, just as political censorship instills a desire to defy its limits. The novel becomes a patchwork of strategies of paralepsis, evasion, and subversion. Despite the twin censors, Alya and Russia, the narrator writes compulsively. What can he talk about? Himself. Russia. The state of modern letters. Politics. The Russian diaspora in Berlin. Homesickness. Disillusionment. Time. Memory. Literary production. His theories of prose. Desire. The novel's *donnée* thus seizes on one of the fundamental characteristics of epistolarity: the narrative invariably springs from an injunction, a prohibition against writing: Abelard's decree of silence compels Héloise's defiant address; Clarissa's parents have commanded her silence before she ever puts pen to paper. "At the origin of narrative, Desire," Barthes observes:[26] narrating is compulsive, insatiable, and unsatisfying. The union we seek in the imaginary or with the beloved can never be fulfilled.

Although Shklovsky's initial theory of estrangement focused primarily on poetry, *Zoo* demonstrates its relevance to prose. The relationship of title to subtitles is estranging, for the zoo is Berlin, and its captive animals are the Russian emigrés. The primary focus of the text seems to be political: what social, historical, and economic factors led to this exile and captivity? But the subtitle reaccentuates one of the oldest and most cunning epistolary strategies: *praeteritio*. From the subtitle forward then, Shklovsky demonstrates that his epistolary novel is already embedded in a complex textual system of signification. The referent is systematically displaced: Shklovsky's aim in *Zoo* resembles Barthes's in *A Lover's Discourse* and Derrida's in *The Post Card*: he wants to create a text that cannot be naturalized, one freed from a fixed signified and which draws attention to its self-referentiality.

Shklovsky also defamiliarizes the text by encoding multiple prohibitions. Letter 19, written by Alya, is "the best one in the whole book," but he

25. Roland Barthes, "From Work to Text," in *Textual Strategies: Perspectives in Post-Structuralist Criticism*, ed. Josué V. Harari (Ithaca: Cornell Univ. Press, 1979), p. 75.

26. Roland Barthes, *S/Z*, trans. Richard Miller (New York: Hill and Wang, 1974), p. 88.

commands the reader not to read it now. "Skip it and read it after you've finished the book. . . . Even I didn't read it when it first arrived, I did kiss it and I skimmed certain passages, but it was written in pencil so I didn't read it. . . . I read Alya's letter only recently, on March 10, after I had already finished writing the book" (70). This cunning passage imitates *Tristram Shandy* by placing in the foreground the literal reading time of the letter and writing time of the novel; by alluding to the date of its completion he reminds us that writing is a process. He then highlights the process of consumption, describing when and how he read Alya's letter. Next, he evokes the ancient epistolary *je crois te parler* motif: in writing, I imagine I am speaking to the beloved; since I could not kiss her, I kissed her letter. The letter is a metonym for the beloved's body, which he cannot hold in his hands. Not only is he probably lying, but he must know that we suspect him of lying: it is too implausible that the impatient lover could defer the pleasure of reading a letter from the beloved until after he finished writing the book! But Shklovsky realizes how much the reading experience depends on delay and deferral (what Derrida will later call *différance*), and he commands the reader to repeat his own reading experience—(or the experience he *claims* he had). Shklovsky thus mocks the convention of authorial intrusion and the illusion of authorial control and authority, for he knows that, once the text leaves his table, he has no control over its destination or dissemination (one of Derrida's obsessions in *The Post Card*). Nevertheless, to enforce the injunction against reading, he crosses out the letter with red *XX*s (see fig. 1). The result is to make the reader want to read the letter all the more—just as the effect of Alya's command not to write of love is to make the narrator's desire all the stronger. By crossing out her letter, Shklovsky highlights the materiality of the text, combines the verbal and the visual, and turns the tables by taking revenge on Alya for the injunction she imposed on him. Since his political exile and Alya's injunction mean that his writing must be devious, written "under erasure," as Derrida will later put it, he reproduces visibly the violence of being doubly crossed out.

Shklovsky consistently lays bare the devices of literary production to estrange reality and to reveal the materialist base of creation. He wants to dismantle its mystique and expose its labor. This strategy is one of the underlying tenets of Russian Formalism, as Fredric Jameson explains:

> There is a certain sense in which . . . all literary works, at the same time that they speak the language of reference, also emit a kind of lateral message about

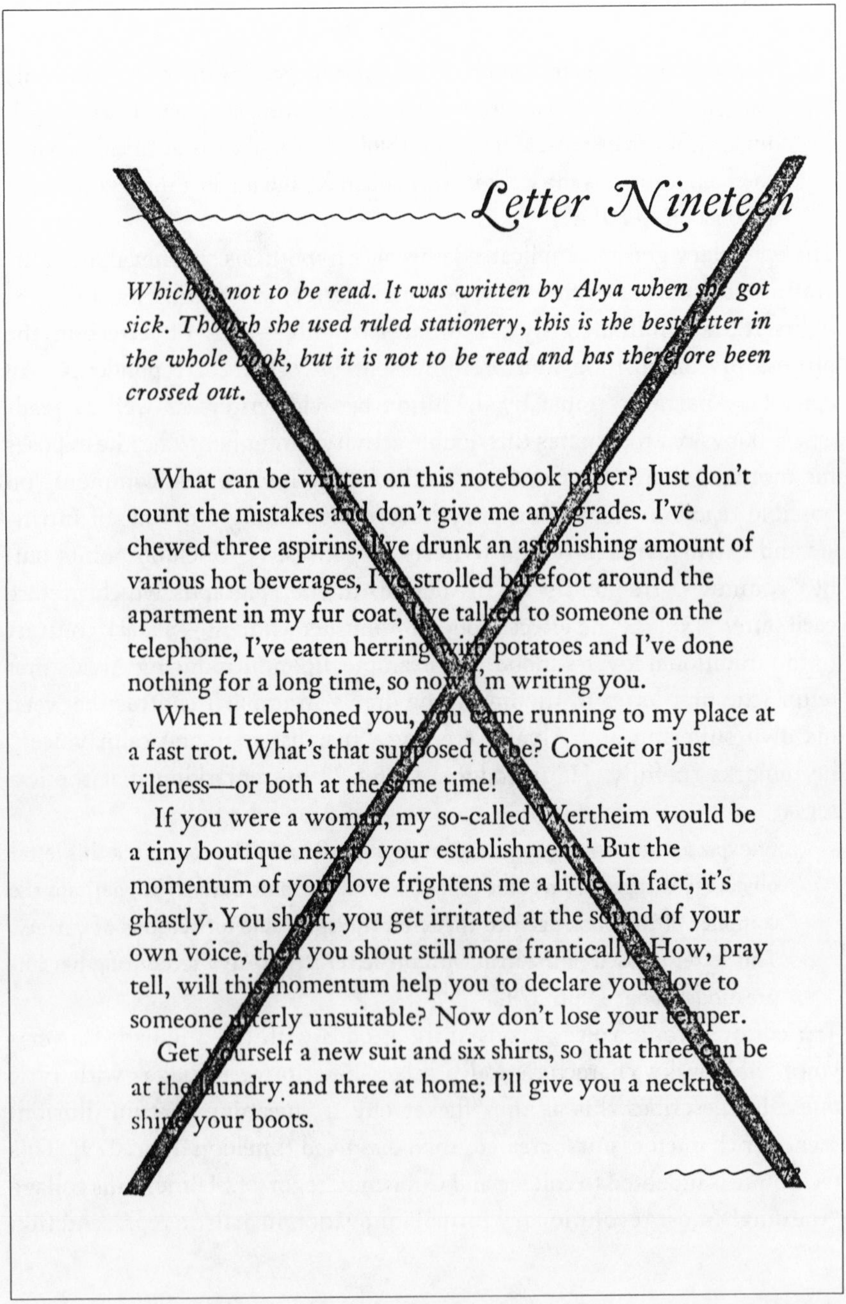

Letter Nineteen

Which is not to be read. It was written by Alya when she got sick. Though she used ruled stationery, this is the best letter in the whole book, but it is not to be read and has therefore been crossed out.

What can be written on this notebook paper? Just don't count the mistakes and don't give me any grades. I've chewed three aspirins, I've drunk an astonishing amount of various hot beverages, I've strolled barefoot around the apartment in my fur coat, I've talked to someone on the telephone, I've eaten herring with potatoes and I've done nothing for a long time, so now I'm writing you.

When I telephoned you, you came running to my place at a fast trot. What's that supposed to be? Conceit or just vileness—or both at the same time!

If you were a woman, my so-called Wertheim would be a tiny boutique next to your establishment.[1] But the momentum of your love frightens me a little. In fact, it's ghastly. You shout, you get irritated at the sound of your own voice, then you shout still more frantically. How, pray tell, will this momentum help you to declare your love to someone utterly unsuitable? Now don't lose your temper.

Get yourself a new suit and six shirts, so that three can be at the laundry and three at home; I'll give you a necktie; shine your boots.

Fig. 1 Reprinted from Victor Shklovsky, _Zoo, or Letters Not about Love_. Edited and translated from the Russian by Richard Sheldon. English edition copyright © 1971 by Cornell University. Used by permission of the publisher, Cornell University Press.

their own process of formation. The event of the reading, in other words, only partially obliterates that earlier event of the writing upon which, as in a palimpsest, it is superposed. Such is, I think, the social basis of Formalism as a method, insofar as the work is work solidified, the product the end-result of production. (*PHL*, 89)

The epistolary genre complicates Jameson's hypothesis. Rather than obliterating "the earlier event of the writing," letter fiction consciously highlights it. It simultaneously accentuates *reading*—both of letters in the process of composition and of those sent by other correspondents. All epistolary narrators must by definition be avid writers as well as readers. Shklovsky accentuates this double activity throughout *Zoo*: he exposes his motives, shares his responses to the letters he receives, comments on possible reactions his readers may have, thus making a mosaic of intrinsic and extrinsic readerly and writerly responses. As Sheldon points out, he "comments frequently on his devices in the epigraphs which preface each letter" (xxix). The effect is one of ironic detachment—a stark contrast to the traditional lover's mood. For example, upon introducing Alya's first letter (the first letter in the novel), he draws an implicit contrast between his own suffering and Alya's serenity: "Just listen to the calm voice!" he remarks ruefully. He introduces Letter 22 by remarking that the letter is

> unexpected and, in my opinion, utterly superfluous. The content of this letter obviously escaped from some other book by the same author, but perhaps the compiler of the book deemed the letter indispensable for reasons of variety. This letter crossed in the mail with the letter [from Alya recounting her impressions] about Tahiti. (79)

The editor's ironic voice is constantly at odds with the anguished lover's voice. Shklovsky characteristically mixes descriptive passages with lyric ones. He describes this as the "flicker effect," meaning that an illusion, scene, or character is first created, then dissolved (Sheldon diss., 279). This technique is indebted to collage and Cubism. Gregory L. Ulmer calls collage "the single most revolutionary formal innovation in artistic representation

27. Gregory L. Ulmer, "The Object of Post-Criticism," in *The Anti-Aesthetic: Essays on Postmodern Culture*, ed. Hal Foster (Port Townsend, Wash.: Bay Press, 1983), p. 84; hereinafter cited as *AA*.

to occur in our century."[27] This revolution, the origin of which is usually attributed to Picasso's *Still Life with Chair Caning* and Braque's *Fruit Dish*, both made in 1912, quickly spread from visual to verbal representation. In both,

> Each cited element breaks the continuity or the linearity of the discourse and leads necessarily to a double reading: that of the fragment perceived in relation to its text of origin; that of the same fragment as incorporated into a new whole, a different totality. The trick of collage consists also of never entirely suppressing the alterity of these elements reunited in a temporary composition.[28]

That is a good description of Shklovsky's methodical madness throughout *Zoo*: he destroys the ground (foundation, origin) that would enable us merely to classify the novel generically; he exploits every possibility of double reading at his disposal; he leaves the alterity of the disparate elements, as well as the traces of a generic legacy, visible. Louis Aragon observes "The principle of collage is the introduction of an object, a substance, taken from the real world and by means of which the painting, that is to say the world that is imitated, finds its whole self once again open to question."[29] "Flicker effect" resonates across several media: Malevich's 1913 Cubist painting "Knife Grinder/Principle of Flickering," epitomizes the simultaneity of the action represented, while simultaneously revealing its mechanistic beauty. The debt to cinematography in general and to Eisenstein in particular is also clear. As Barthes observes, Eisenstein's genius lay in creating oscillating visual images in a succinct manner, images that oscillate between manifest and latent levels of signification; his emphases are so elliptical that it is difficult to guarantee their intentionality.[30] Shklovsky often uses codeterminious images to organize the text, estranging it by distorting our perception of the material and seizing, as Eisenstein does, on a metonymic detail. This tech-

28. Group *MU*, eds., *Collages: Revue d'esthétique*, nos. 3–4 (Paris: Union Générale d'Editions, 1978), pp. 34–35, trans. Ulmer, cited in Perloff, p. 47.

29. Louis Aragon, "Collage dans le roman et dans le film" (1965), in *Les collages* (Paris: Hermann, 1980), p. 119, cited in Perloff, pp. 47–48.

30. Roland Barthes, "Le troisième sens: notes de recherche sur quelques photogrammes de S. M. Eisenstein," *Cahiers du Cinéma* 222 (July 1970); reprinted in *Roland Barthes: Le texte et l'image*, catalogue for an exhibition at the Pavillon des Arts, 1986, pp. 48–51; my translation.

nique reduces all aspects of the work to integration in a few key phrases or words.[31] As Shklovsky notes in *A Sentimental Journey*:

> [E]verything—the fate of heroes, the epoch in which the action takes place— everything is the motivation of forms. . . . The motivation . . . is a story, a manuscript, reminiscence, a mistake by the bookbinder (Immermann), the forgetfulness of the author (Sterne, Pushkin) or a cat's coming along and mixing up the pages (Hoffmann). (*SJ*, 233)

The purpose of the device is to retard the reading process, another strategy commonly associated with postmodernism, exploited in such parodies of production as John Ray's preface in *Lolita*, Barthes's *S/Z*, John Barth's *Letters* and *Lost in the Funhouse*, and Italo Calvino's *If on a Winter's Night a Traveller*, which contains numerous discontinuous narratives mixed up in production.

The role of chance, fortune-telling, gambits, and gambling recurs frequently in modern epistolary narratives, ranging from Humbert Humbert's obsession with "McFate" in *Lolita* to Derrida's obsession with astrology and numerology in *The Post Card*. In Shklovsky's view, "The artist needs to know the laws of chance in art. . . . Art lives by changing its raw material. By chance."[32] This is another legacy from the Futurists and Cubists; they were charmed by the improvised, the accidental, the chance happening, the uncanny. Chronological displacement and digression serve a similar function of disrupting logic, causality, and temporality. Traditionally, the date, location, and signature on a love letter orients the reader and maps the letter writer's emotional state. In Ovid's *Heroides*, for example, each heroine locates herself—spatially, temporally, emotionally—vis-à-vis her beloved.[33] Shklovsky purposely withholds all such psychological signposts and thwarts the reader's attempt to approach the characters as "real people" instead of devices. He suppresses the connective tissue in his text, violates the laws of unity and harmony, and substitutes one-sentence paragraphs, incongruous images, illogical ideas, hyperbolic aphorisms.

In Shklovsky's view, artists have such a limited number of techniques

31. Sheldon diss., pp. 191–93, 201, 256; see also Albert J. Guerard, *The Triumph of the Novel: Dickens, Dostoyevsky, Faulkner* (New York: Oxford Univ. Press, 1976).

32. Shklovsky, *The Third Factory*, cited in Sheldon diss., p. 266.

33. See Kauffman, *Discourses of Desire*, p. 35.

available to them that they must constantly strive to use the limited repertoire in new ways (Sheldon diss., 79). His favorite analogy is chess: the artist
has only a set number of pieces and must play according to a set of rules; to
Shklovsky, plot corresponds to gambits. His view of language as a game thus
anticipates the poststructuralist emphasis on *jeu* (play, game, activity) in
Barthes's "The Structuralist Activity" and Derrida's "Structure, Sign, and
Play." *Jeu's* connotations also suggest gambit (the role of chance again) and
tension, as in the "play" of a door on its hinges. Shklovsky believed that
literary genres are continually exhausted, which is why worn-out modes
and genres have dulled our perception of words and images. He shrewdly
anticipates the "postmodern" preoccupation with imitation and the fic-
titiousness of reality, perceiving that parody of a form usually marks the
beginning of a new form, which is why he stresses marginal modes like
newspapers, sketches, and letters: they hold the best hope of producing a
genre that consciously parodies its predecessors. Texts that were once highly
favored and original, like Héloise's letters or *Lettres portugaises*, cease to be
perceived by succeeding generations in the same way. The love letter, in
Shklovsky's hands, is a case in point, for after *Zoo* one cannot respond to the
love letter's pathos and sentimentality without a sideward satiric glance.

SHKLOVSKY'S ADDRESSEES: DIALOGIC CONTESTATION

Shklovsky variously assumes the roles of author, editor, besotted writer of
love letters, and reader; all these roles are thrown into a contested polyphonic dialogue, which serves multiple functions. For example, the epigraphs often include editorial comments which directly contradict the
contents of the letters they are supposed to introduce. This technique parallels Rousseau's use of ironic footnotes as a counterdiscourse in *La nouvelle
Héloise* (Sheldon, xxvi). In one epigraph, Shklovsky says that in what follows "the author attempts to be lighthearted and cheerful, but I know for
sure that in the next letter he won't be able to carry it off" (37). We are a long
way from Balzac's omniscient creation of a "realist" cosmos in miniature,
for Shklovsky-as-editor has information of which Shklovsky-as-besotted
love letter writer is ignorant. *Zoo* anticipates the postmodern delight John
Barth describes in "The Literature of Exhaustion" of imitating "the form of
the Novel, by an author who imitates the role of Author" (LE, 33). It is not

just the perspective that is fragmented, but the "I" itself. The letters are produced by a split—or more accurately, a multiply fractured—writing subject. Epistolary narratives have always exploited the ambiguities that result when letter writers are also letter readers; opportunities for self-reflexivity are built into the genre, but Shklovsky simultaneously exploits and estranges these devices. He alludes to the travails of literary production, the necessity of selling the manuscript, and his frustrations with proofreaders, copyeditors, etc. Another major characteristic of epistolarity involves the story of the making of the book, the process of epistolary transmission by which letters are exchanged, copied, collected, and turned over to the editor(s). The letter writer is frequently at the mercy of an editor or a compiler, whether one thinks of William's censorious comments about Werther's letters, or John Ray's sociological interpretation of Humbert's narrative in *Lolita*, or the archivist's pious moralizings in *The Handmaid's Tale*'s "Historical Notes."

Since dialogism consists of contesting discourses among antagonists, these voices are "ideologues" (as opposed to characters) representing mutually irreconcilable positions. In Dostoyevsky's *Notes from Underground*, for example, the narrator addresses an imaginary audience of "gentlemen" whose illusions of Enlightenment progress and benevolent self-interest he systematically shatters. In *Zoo* as in *Notes from Underground*, the narrator often detests his readers, whose values and intelligence the narrator finds dubious. Shklovsky thwarts the reader's attempt to read for the plot by drawing attention to method: "What," he demands in his preface to Letter 19, "is the structural function of this letter?" The question is presented by one impatient voice and is answered by a different, belligerent voice: "Why the devil do you want structure?" Having invented his adversary and posed the question, Shklovsky the theorist proceeds to answer it:

> You insist? Then allow me! To make a work ironic, you need a double interpretation of the action, which is usually achieved by the technique of reduction. . . . In my book, though, I'm using the technique of enhancement to give a second interpretation of the woman I've been writing to; in addition, I'm providing a second interpretation of myself. . . .
>
> If you believe my explanation of the structure, then you will also have to believe that the letter ascribed to Alya was written by me.
>
> That would not be wise. (71)

Every seemingly explanatory sentence is undermined by contradiction. Shklovsky's *mise en question* method is the verbal equivalent of collage's insistence on forcing a double reading of the canvas, one in which the alterity of disparate elements remains unassimilated, unresolved. What I describe as the novel's "dialogic" structure, Barthes will define as "contrapuntal," and Derrida will call "postcarded," but all three writers share the same motive of dismantling authorial omniscience and undermining representational systems.

In the passage quoted above, Shklovsky exploits the ambiguity between fiction and reality: Is Alya real? Did she write the letter, or did Shklovsky invent it (and her)? The reader is confronted with an either/or dichotomy: one must either believe his structural explanation or believe that someone else wrote Alya's letter. In fact, the truth is both/and: Alya is fictional, *and* Shklovsky did not write this letter. Instead, Elsa Triolet wrote it. While grappling with these ambiguities, the reader is further thwarted by Shklovsky's abrupt conclusion: "the crucial sections were pruned by the proofreader" (71). Once again, he highlights the materiality of the text in the process of production, and mockingly thwarts the reader's desire for answers.

In keeping with the precision and violence of his manifesto writing, Shklovsky viewed art as being "fundamentally ironic and destructive. . . . Its function is to create inequalities, which it does by means of contrasts" (*SJ*, 252). Shklovsky constantly searched for strategies to surprise readers out of their habitual reading patterns, like embedding the work of other writers in his own: "It's impossible to write a book in the old way. . . . We have introduced into our work the intimate, identified by first and last name, because of this same necessity for new material in art" (23). Epistolary novels are uniquely suited for such experiments, since they usually consist of letters by a variety of hands. The use of real names, places, and events as well as of intimate letters from other correspondents enhances the illusion of authenticity, but Shklovsky succeeds precisely because one is never permitted to forget that what is being created is merely the *illusion* of intimacy. As in his reference to the proofreader, Shklovsky reminds us repeatedly that the surface is an imaginary representation—one in which readers nonetheless desire to lose themselves (*PHL*, 78–80). As in such Cubist paintings as Malevich's "Knife Grinder/Principle of Flickering," *Zoo* links event, memory, and prophecy in a shimmering verbal surface; perception shifts, merges, evaporates, and returns.

Readers' desire to lose themselves in the representation is nonetheless compelling. No matter how hard one tries to discourage them, readers perversely continue to respond to characters and authors through empathetic identification. In his literary criticism Shklovsky confesses his own desire to lose himself through identification: "Sterne, whom I revived, confuses me. Not only do I make writers, but I myself became him."[34] Such identification seems to be especially tempting when the mode is epistolary, the tone amorous. Barthes goes further, speculating that such identification is a structural characteristic of amorous discourse:

> The subject painfully identifies himself with some person (or character) who occupies the same position as himself in the amorous structure. . . .
>
> Werther identifies himself with every lost lover: he is the madman who loved Charlotte and goes out picking flowers in midwinter; he is the young footman in love with a widow, who has just killed his rival. . . . Identification is not a psychological process; it is a pure structural operation: I am the one who has the same place I have. . . .
>
> Since Heinrich and I occupy the same place, it is no longer merely with Heinrich's place that I identify myself, but with his image as well. A hallucination seizes me: *I am Heinrich!*[35]

One of the reasons that Shklovsky's literary criticism seems so weird is that he frequently takes on the style and adopts the devices of the author he is discussing. He self-consciously criticizes his own essay on *Don Quixote*, for instance, by confessing that "I am beginning to feel that the influence of the novel being analyzed is affecting me: I put episode after episode, forgetting about the central movement of the article" (Sheldon diss., 134). One would think that such identification would cease in light of theoretical postulates about "the death of the author"; instead, one continues to desire what one knows is theoretically unorthodox and untenable. (Derrida, as well as Barthes, repeats this gesture.) Shklovsky foregrounds the gap between desire and the inevitable frustration of that desire throughout *Zoo*.

34. Shklovsky, *The Third Factory*, p. 94, cited in Sheldon diss., p. 267.

35. Roland Barthes, *A Lover's Discourse: Fragments*, trans. Richard Howard (New York: Hill and Wang, 1978), pp. 129–30; hereinafter cited parenthetically in the text as *ALD*.

In analyzing Sterne, Shklovsky explains how Sterne's parody of the traditional adventure novel in *Tristram Shandy* reduces the genre to shambles: "the consciousness of form through its violation . . . constitutes the content of the novel" (*TP*, 149).

Transferential relations may also lead the reader to interpret autobiographically. In *Zoo*, such confusion is understandable since Shklovsky purposefully blurs the boundaries, but sometimes critics fall into the trap he sets. Richard Sheldon, for example, reminds us that Shklovsky

> was on the verge of a nervous breakdown when he wrote *Zoo*. The entire book is not so much a product scrupulously constructed as it is an exercise in sublimation. . . . Out of the torments of an unrequited love, Shklovsky has fashioned a book, and he suggests that a similar motivation has provided man with most of his cultural achievements. (*Zoo*, "Introduction," xxx)

Zoo is scrupulously constructed *precisely to give the impression* of a lover undergoing a breakdown. Shklovsky exploits the reader's naiveté, for he is well aware that readers have mistaken the sincerity and authenticity of epistolary lovers at least since Goethe's *The Sorrows of Young Werther*. Although the impulse to read autobiographically is almost irresistible, Shklovsky repeatedly exposes its duplicity and doubleness: not only is writing conventional, but so are the codes of love. In many respects, we have had to wait for Roland Barthes's *A Lover's Discourse* and Derrida's *The Post Card* to learn better how to read *Zoo*, for the lover is simultaneously a structural figure and a rhetorician of amorous discourse.

Not only does Shklovsky place historical figures in his fiction, but he repeatedly dramatizes the fictiveness and duplicity of his endeavor. He offers a "double interpretation of myself" and exposes the doubleness of his enterprise: he is a spurned lover who simultaneously laments his fate and self-ironically mocks his role, underscoring its literariness. He sees his similarity to previous epistolary lovers who rail against fate and bewail their destiny—Ovid's heroines in the *Heroides*, Rousseau's characters, Héloise, Werther. When he reflects, "Life tailors us for a certain person and laughs when we are drawn to someone unable to love us" (19), he seems to echo the Portuguese nun when she asks, "What blind and malicious fate is it that drives us irresistibly to those who have feelings only for others?" Yet, elsewhere, she confesses that "[m]y despair exists only in my letters"; she

writes to keep her passion and her despair alive.[36] Shklovsky seizes the itera-
tive and imitative potential of the language of love:

> I see myself at a remove; I fear my destiny.
>
> I fear its literary quality. I am becoming part of a book. (121)

Writing thus becomes the means of manufacturing the requisite passion, and even the emotions of the spurned lover are revealed to be a reproduction, categorized and quantified in terms of the number of pages he has
written:

> My hallucination is only a literary phenomenon.
>
> Sorrow comes to see me. I talk to him while inwardly counting up pages.
>
> There are only a hundred pages or so.
>
> Such a brief sorrow! (129)

Thus throughout *Zoo* what the reader would like to think is sentiment is
wholly style; *Zoo* is a novel held together by style alone. *Zoo* returns *auto-
bio-graphy* to its etymological roots, radically subverting the search for
sincerity and—long before Barthes—demonstrating the extent to which
epistolary lovers are "paper authors": "the *I* that writes the text is never,
itself, anything more than a paper *I*."[37]

Zoo exemplifies one of the major tenets of Russian Formalism: the subject of art is its own coming into being. Works only seem to have referents
and determinant content; they are always discussing their own construction
(*PHL*, 86). At one point the narrator reflects,

> I am completely bewildered, Alya! This is the problem: I'm writing letters to
> you, and, at the same time, I'm writing a book. And what's in the book and
> what's in life have gotten hopelessly jumbled. You recall that I wrote you
> about Andrei Bely and about method. Love has its own methods, its own
> logic—set moves established without consulting either me or us. I pro-
> nounced the word "love" and set the whole thing in motion. The game began.
> And I no longer know where love ends and the book begins. The game is un-
> derway. After a hundred pages or so, I will be checkmated. The beginning is
> already played out. No one can change the denouement.

---

36. Frédéric Deloffre and J. Rougeot, eds., *Lettres portugaises, Valentins, et autres oeuvres
de Guilleragues* (Paris: Garnier, 1962), pp. 358, 351; my translation; see also Kauffman, *Discourses of Desire*, chap. 3.

37. Barthes, "From Work to Text," p. 79.

> Tragic endings—at the very least, a broken heart—are inevitable in an
> epistolary novel. (64)

That can be read in two ways: either as an observation about emotion or
about language. The first is the old-fashioned interpretation: passion has its
own logic and leads inevitably to tragedy for the doomed lover. The second is
a commentary on language: "love" is a word which prescribes certain linguistic responses, sets certain plots, sentences and devices in motion. Amorous discourse has its own inexorable logic, which determines the tone
(pathos) of the speaking subject and circumscribes the set moves within a
certain field of activity. That is why Shklovsky is so fond of the chessboard
analogy.

If Shklovsky sounds the death knell of the realistic novel by insisting
that a character is not a person but a device, he hammers the nails in the
coffin by insisting that emotion is method, not content. Shklovsky's view of
sentimentality marks a significant departure from the traditional association
of the love letter with sincerity, for sentimentality cannot be considered the
content of art, if only because in art there is no separate content. The depiction of things from a sentimental viewpoint is a special method of depiction,
just as depiction from the point of view of a horse (in a story by Tolstoy) is
(Sheldon diss., 79). Shklovsky similarly subverts verisimilitude by highlighting the temporality of novelistic construction. Like all previous epistolary heroes, the narrator in *Zoo* is obsessed with time and duration: he
records minutely the number of hours between visits with the beloved, the
length of his love, and the length of the time he has been writing:

> I have your permission to telephone at 10:30.
>
> Four and a half hours, then another twenty empty hours, and between
> them your voice. . . .
>
> I can divide the waiting into hours and minutes; I can count them. I wait
> and wait. (47, 49)

Writing passes the time, but if the beloved were present he would not need to
write. Since one can no longer write in the old way, and since the beloved
refuses to let the lover "throw scenes," he stages his own dramas to pass the
time, turning himself into a dramatic character—a strategy repeated by
Barthes:

> There is a scenography of waiting: I organize it, manipulate it, cut out a por-
> tion of time in which I shall mime the loss of the loved object and provoke all

the effects of a minor mourning. This is then acted out as a play. . . . The lover's fatal identity is precisely: *I am the one who waits*. (*ALD*, 37, 40)

All aspects of temporality—waiting, duration, frequency, repetition, iteration—are consciously exploited by the lover in order to keep the circuit of both his desire and his writing open. Shklovsky is well aware that these strategies are as old as Ovid. In a passage from his theoretical work, which reveals much about his technique in *Zoo*, Shklovsky asks:

> Why is it that, in fashioning an *Art of Love* out of love, Ovid counsels us not to rush into the arms of pleasure?
>
> A crooked road, a road in which the foot feels acutely the stones beneath it, a road that turns back on itself—this is the road of art.
>
> One word fits another. One word feels another word, as one cheek feels another cheek. Words are taken apart and, instead of one complex word handed over like a chocolate bar at a candy store, we see before us a word-sound, a word-movement. Dance is movement that can be felt. Or more accurately, it is movement formed in order to be felt. (*TP*, 15)

Like Ovid, Shklovsky transforms love into art, emotion into artifice. The emphasis on movement is crucial, for the lover is meant to be perceived as mobile, as if to defamiliarize the etymological significance of *discourse:* "*dis-cursus*—originally the action of running here and there" (*ALD*, 3). In the absence of the beloved's body, the abandoned lover has only words to play with, evoking the sensuousness of language and exploiting its seductive nuances. Barthes emphasizes that sensuousness in words that are almost identical to Shklovsky's:

> Language is a skin: I rub my language against the other. It is as if I had words instead of fingers, or fingers at the tip of my words. My language trembles with desire. The emotion derives from a double contact: on the one hand, a whole activity of discourse discretely, indirectly focuses upon a single signified, which is "I desire you," and releases, nourishes, ramifies it to the point of explosion (language experiences orgasm upon touching itself); on the other hand, I enwrap the other in my words, I caress, brush against, talk up this contact, I extend myself to make the commentary to which I submit the relation endure. (*ALD*, 73)

Zoo keeps desire circulating—the many epigraphs, prefaces, and additional letters appended to subsequent editions attest to the infinite extension of the commentary.

In *Zoo*, Shklovsky seems to fulfill the Flaubertian desire to write a novel about nothing, held together by style alone: "How I want simply to describe objects as if literature had never existed; that way one could write literarily" (*Zoo*, 84). If Shklovsky looks backward to Flaubert he also looks forward to Barthes, anticipating the Barthesian distinction between work and text: readerly works, epitomized by Balzac, remind one that literature has always existed; they are closed, seemingly impervious to rewriting, reassembling. They perpetuate old lies, old codes, old conventions. Writerly texts, in contrast, expose those conventions; in them, the reader is free to dissemble and reassemble.[38] Shklovsky multiplies the ways in which discourse is segmented and invents new ways to break it up. Not only does he celebrate the smashing of outworn conventions, he electrifies us with the shock of the new:

> Our business is the creation of new things. At the moment, Remizov wants to create a book with no plot, with no "man's fate" lodged at the base of the composition. He's writing one book made from bits and pieces—that's *Russia in Writ*, a book made from scraps of books; he's writing another one built on Rozanov's letters. (23–24)

He ironically embeds praise for the innovative novel built on epistolary techniques in his own attempt at the same kind of novel—one as dependent on "scraps, bits, and pieces" as the Cubists were for their collages. Through such strategies, he continually draws attention to the theory and method underlying his narrative construction. At one point he refers directly to the experiment in which he is engaged:

> A more interesting case is the book which I am currently writing. It is called *Zoo, Letters Not about Love* or *The Third Héloise*. There the individual components are connected; in fact, everything is tied together by the history of a man's love for a woman. This book is an attempt to go outside the framework of the ordinary novel. (82)

Zoo repeatedly forces us to reflect on the raw materials that go into novelistic creation: journal entries, newspaper clippings, letters, notes on scraps of paper, interpolated stories—all contribute to the collage that makes up the

---

38. Barthes makes the distinction between the readerly and the writerly text in "From Work to Text," pp. 79–81; in *S/Z*, he dismantles Balzac's *Sarrasine* in order to demonstrate that even the most readerly text is not impervious to intervention.

novel, which is purposely plotless: "I could have embedded a plot in the novel. . . . [But] I have the same attitude toward a plot of the usual type as a dentist to teeth" (4). The novel purposely repudiates the kind of "truth" associated with realism by remaining on the horizontal level, unfolding minute by minute without recourse either to unifying strategies or transcendent symbolism. Epistolary novels have always been celebrated for the ways in which they mime the technique of writing-to-the-moment; one of Shklovsky's innovations is to present bundles of sentences which are not integrated on a higher level; he refuses to construct a realistic novel with a beginning, middle, and end, which he sees as a worn-out device.

Zoo also epitomizes Shklovsky's interest in what has variously been called "negative form," or "zero degree writing" (PHL, 63–64). Like the Futurists, he valued improvisation, nonstories, and unfinished anecdotes full of tentative potential. He praises Sterne, Maupassant, and Flaubert for novels that conclude with an uncompleted action: "Sterne left his Tristram Shandy unfinished. His Sentimental Journey ends in the middle of an erotic scene" (SJ, 233). Barthes follows suit with Writing Degree Zero and with an "absolutely arbitrary" order in A Lover's Discourse: the alphabet. Thus when Shklovsky proclaims, "My fate was completely predetermined. But everything might have been different" (130), he means that a different bundle of linguistic relations would have produced an entirely different discourse. Although he makes this statement in the final letter of the second edition, the letter hardly qualifies as a conclusion or a resolution. Instead, like epistolary narratives from Clarissa to The Three Marias, Zoo uses a dizzying array of devices to forestall closure. He offers several alternative "endings." Embroidering tales borrowed from Hans Christian Andersen about a prince and a princess, he defamiliarizes the fairy tales to demonstrate that what one perceives depends on how the devices are assembled. In one version: "The princess eats and sleeps in [the prince's] house. But she sleeps with others. It turns out that between a given point and a straight line, one can draw several perpendiculars" (132). These bawdy puns simultaneously attack Alya's lack of fidelity and comment on the construction of narratives. They demonstrate that "for Shklovsky, the completed narrative, the story that works and has a point, is analogous to word play. For the tying up or unravelling of the knot is like the coincidence of two verbal series in the pun"

(*PHL*, 63). Only by embracing alogic and the kind of non-sense one finds in riddles or puns does the text "make sense":

> All this makes sense . . . if one reaches the point where a pun amuses him about as much as an ulcer.
>
> It's all a matter of "how much."
>
> All my letters are about "how much" I love you. (132)

"How much" can never be quantified—either in language or in love. No matter "how much" he loves, it is not enough to make Alya love him in return. No matter how much he speaks, he cannot sum up. No ending can resolve the dilemmas he confronts. Although the first edition of *Zoo* ends with letter 29, Shklovsky added more prefaces to the second and third editions (1924, 1929), two prefaces to the fourth edition (1964), and more letters (nos. 30–34), in addition to a postscript. What constantly eludes him is a sense of proportion, some balance between excess and austerity. Barthes confronts the same dilemma:

> To try to write love is to confront the *muck* of language: that region of hysteria where language is both *too much* and *too little*, excessive (by the limitless expansion of the *ego*, by emotive submersion) and impoverished (by the codes on which love diminishes and levels it). (*ALD*, 99)

That is why *Zoo* relies on reduction as well as irony: the codes of love themselves diminish and impoverish the lover's sentiments, robbing them of originality and authenticity. This strategy of devaluing content within the content itself (*PHL*, 78) is one that we shall see repeated by Nabokov, Barthes, Derrida, Lessing, and Atwood. Although Shklovsky often comments on the inadequacy of the letter form, at some points his frustration is intensely focused on the telephone, which seems almost to become a character in the novel. As in Cocteau's *The Human Voice* (1930), the telephone influences the direction of the action, determines how the narrator allots his time, and acts as chorus, sometimes seeming to mock and sometimes to pity the narrator. He is well aware of the irony that the technological advances that have brought the entire world into closer communication bring him no nearer to Alya. (Derrida's laments in *The Post Card* are equally rueful.)

History is as palpable as love in Shklovsky's pages. In many letters, Shklovsky is simultaneously overwhelmed by the weight of Alya's rejection, and by the weight of history, as when he contrasts his youth to his maturity: in his youth he

> did not yet know loneliness . . . and did not tremble at the sound of a telephone—when life had not yet slammed the door to Russia shut on my fingers, when I thought that I could break history on my knee. . . . Now . . . I too am thirty, . . . I wait for the telephone to ring—though I've been told not to expect a call . . . life has slammed the door on my fingers and history is too busy even to write letters. (27–28)

Far from being too busy, Shklovsky has nothing to do but write letters. His is a conscious attempt to expose language's limitations, its inability ever adequately to reproduce the raw materials of experience. Shklovsky thus repeatedly repudiates the very thing he has just finished constructing, as when he makes puns and then compares them to ulcers. The arbitrary jump cuts from one topic to another, the uncompleted actions, the refusal to satisfy the reader's desire for narrative coherence, logic, and unity all throw what we normally think of as novelistic content into disarray. His description of Andrei Bely's construction of *Notes of an Eccentric* (1922) is equally applicable to the juxtaposition of the lyric, satiric, and descriptive planes in *Zoo*. Bely

> creates several planes. One is strong, almost real; the others move beneath it and seem like its shadows, thrown by many light sources, but it is these many planes that seem real, while the other one seems quite incidental. There is no reality of soul in the one or in the others: there is only method, a technique of deploying things in rows. (36)

Such insights are interesting because they rely on the kinds of metaphors one finds in Cubist painting, and because they help to explain the serial construction that leads from *Zoo* to *A Lover's Discourse*. In one letter (no. 26), he discusses automobile design as an extended metaphor for narrative design, commenting, "All this I find more interesting than the life and times of the Russian emigration" (97). In some epigraphs, he describes the content of the letter to come as "an experiment in the pathetic style" (83) or as "didactic" (55), thus undermining its emotional impact in advance. Perhaps his most damning indictment of content comes in Letter 22, which is also perhaps the clearest exposition of his literary method. After first describing a variety show, he notes that "what struck me most about this show was the total discontinuity of its program" (80). He proceeds to contrast artists who are "translators"—those who view art as a window on the world—with those who see art as "only a sketched window." "The most vital genres in contemporary art are the collection of articles and the variety show" (81). In a passage that seems to anticipate such postmodern narratives as Robert Coover's "The Hat Act," Shklovsky describes narratives like his own, in which

> the master of ceremonies emerges as the hero whose fate connects the individual parts of the work. In a Czech theater . . . I had occasion to see one other device, which has apparently been used for a long time in circuses. At the end of the show, a clown runs through all the acts, parodying and exposing them. For example, he does magic tricks standing with his back to the audience, which sees where the missing card disappeared. (82)

As in "The Hat Act," Shklovsky sees the artist as a trickster and a con man. Forced to come up with new tricks for an increasingly restive and hostile audience, the artist turns to parody, laying bare the devices he has used to create his illusions. If love letters traditionally stage the private theater of the emotions, Shklovsky's resemble the Futurist Variety Theater, notable for its amazing novelty, its evocation of a carnivalesque body madness, and its attempt to combine eroticism with nihilism. This theater, as described in Marinetti's 1913 manifesto, celebrated the new man created by technology, glorified the automobile as symbol of technology's promise, and predicted that the machine would redraw the cultural and aesthetic map of Europe.

The impact of Futurism can been seen throughout Zoo, sometimes in discussions of specific works and sometimes illuminating Shklovsky's own method. Following Einstein's discovery, one of the Futurist aims was to portray the interaction of time and space—a dilemma Shklovsky alludes to when he uses Einstein as a gloss on the experience of exile from the beloved and from Russia. He introduces one letter by noting "how hard it is, even after Einstein's discovery, to live without taking up either time or space" (53). Elsewhere he notes that art renews perception by wresting an object from a flat surface and lifting it into relief, by changing a square into a cube, for instance (Sheldon diss., 239–40). The Futurists drew on Cubism and photography to depict simultaneous action, dislocation, and dismemberment. The aim was to make the painting or the text into a node of associations, fragmentary but evocative—a motive clearly delineated in Zoo when he describes the action in terms of a Cubist painting: "He opened the door and (let's try some cubism) the wind hurled into the rectangle prisms of rain and the spherical sectors of an umbrella" (131). Like the Futurist painters, Shklovsky uses the technique of montage to portray the simultaneity of experience and to render the sum total of visual sensations. Like Shklovsky's torn, illegible, defaced, crumpled letters, consigned to the wastebasket, the Futurists frequently alluded to the act of production by experimenting with collages consisting of stained, peeling, rusty, bent, torn, crumpled fragments. The Futurist aim was to dismantle the transcendental mysticism of Logos and to express the modern sensibility in the language of the mechanical age (*RF*, 43–44); but we must wait for poststructuralism to fully expand the attack on Logos, translating the sensibility of the postmodern age into the medium of telecommunications, for one of the things the Formalists underestimated was the opacity of the sign and of representation.[39]

The Futurist enchantment with machines and technological advances— airplane, automobile, cinema, telephone, and telegraph—are all evoked by Shklovsky, who frequently uses the machine as a metaphor for the forward movement of history. It is difficult for contemporary readers to share the Futurist visionary enthusiasm, but as Marjorie Perloff points out:

> We take for granted today that World War I was the most futile war of all. . . .
> The fact is, however, that until late in 1915, the war was celebrated by most of the poets and painters who enlisted as the culmination of a thrilling new adventure with technology; as the revolution that would remove the shackles of monarchy, papacy, and class structure. (*FM*, xxi)

Shklovsky's confidence in progress and technology in his early Futurist proclamations has wholly disappeared by the time he writes *Zoo*; his tone is subdued by the awareness of the destruction the machine has wrought in the aftermath of the Revolution, civil war, and World War I. In one letter, he contrasts automobiles and luxury ocean liners to comment on the propulsion of history:

> All your sensations are different in an automobile: you feel PROPULSION and peace of mind, PROPULSION and anxiety. But everything you feel is conditioned by the sensation of movement pressing against you. . . .
> A new world is being born, new sensations; not everyone is aware of them yet. Our country is being pulled somewhere by a tugboat. . . .

39. Kristeva, "The Ruin of a Poetics," p. 105.

Russian Berlin is going nowhere. It has no destiny.

No propulsion. . . .

The revolution has lost its propulsion. (61–63)

On the one hand, Shklovsky contrasts the propulsion of events in Russia with the stagnation of Berlin; the emigrés are frozen in time while history marches on. On the other hand, however, he astutely realizes that one of the most pressing problems of exile is that one imagines the country in an arrested moment, and one forgets that Russia in 1923 is not the same as the Russia he left a year before. He not only exposes the illusions he uses to create his narrative but he exposes his political illusions as well.

Zoo records the momentous changes history and technology have wrought in art and in society. The willful exposure of the illusion as illusion leads inevitably to the devaluation of content—a devaluation endemic in modern literature from Bely to Breton, Beckett, and Barthes. In both personal and political terms, the exiled lover is barraged by signifying systems, messages that he can decipher but not interpret definitively. Barthes argues that such failure is one of the distinguishing characteristics of amorous discourse: the lover "doesn't know where or how to make signs stop. He deciphers perfectly, but he's unable to arrive at a definite interpretation, and he's swept away by a perpetual circus, where he'll never find peace."[40] Zoo and circus animals are apt emblems in such discourses: they are forced into unnatural poses and postures, put through their paces in alien environments. In one sense, the spurned lover has already had to confront the illusory nature of his writing simply to put pen to paper, for he writes to sustain the illusion of dialogue, of *correspondence* with the beloved. In contrast to the beloved's physical presence, the act of writing cannot but seem reductive, diminished, a meager mirroring. What is one to do, confronted with the fictive quality of one's desire and one's predicament? "Give everything a cosmic dimension, take your heart in your teeth, write a book" (20). (Elsewhere, Shklovsky substitutes the word "comic" for "cosmic.")

Shklovsky's most innovative contribution to the traditional love letter is comedy. Gone are the days when the whole world wept for the Portuguese nun, or when distraught lovers blew their brains out, à la Werther. Does the

40. Roland Barthes, *The Grain of the Voice: Interviews, 1962–1980*, trans. Linda Coverdale (New York: Hill and Wang, 1985), p. 303.

devaluation of sentimentality follow inevitably from the devaluation of content? Perhaps. Mayakovsky boasts, "We have invaded the love whispers of the cozy porches with the thousand-foot step of the ages. These are our rhythms—the cacophony of wars and revolutions."[41] Sentimentality gives way to irony, pathos to comedy, and no one is more aware of the irrelevance of the lover in the twentieth century than Shklovsky. His model is not Werther but Charlie Chaplin:

> Chaplin said that the most comical effects are obtained when a man in an unlikely situation pretends that nothing has happened.
>
> It is comical, for instance, when a man hanging upside down attempts to straighten his tie. . . . But my tie . . . still chafes my neck.
>
> And I, having gotten myself into a literary predicament, don't know what to do. (122)

Like vaudeville, variety shows, circuses, zoos, films, and comedies (all forms of "low" culture), *Zoo* is intensely and intentionally artificial. Every element in the text has a signification which can be interpreted according to some literary code. Rather than examining love as emotion, Shklovsky presents it as a *type of discursivity.* It "motivates" the devices; its subject matter is consciously "deformed." Shklovsky insists that the individual components are connected by the history of a man's love for a woman (80–82), but this connection is fragmented and tenuous. He has purposely constructed a piecemeal novel, one influenced by his theory of the fragment, the aphorism, the one-page essay. No one element is directly linked with any other; the relation is established according to a hierarchy of planes (strata) and levels (ranks) along the axis of substitutions and the axis of connections.[42] As Shklovsky explains, "[T]he events mentioned in the text serve only as material for the metaphors. This is a common device in erotic things, where real norms are repudiated and metaphoric norms affirmed" (4). Similarly, he praises artists who consistently draw attention to the artificiality of their sentiment, like Ksana Boguslavskaya, whom Shklovsky describes as "[n]ot a bad painter, either, though somewhat saccharine. In fact, probably a good painter, because the saccharine quality is intentional—a device. It has nothing to do with tears" (57).

---

41. Mayakovsky, *Sobranie socinenij* (Moscow, 1928–33), 3:18, cited in Erlich, p. 43.
42. Tzevtan Todorov, *The Poetics of Prose,* trans. Richard Howard (Ithaca: Cornell Univ. Press, 1977), p. 251.

THE PRODUCTION OF WOMAN

Shklovsky is meticulous in describing the strategies he employs to expose the artificiality of the text he is in the process of producing. But he is simultaneously producing a stereotype of femininity, which he less meticulously "lays bare." While he defamiliarizes the codes related to the lover (obsessional, thwarted, furious, comical, romantic, pathetic), he sometimes presents the codes of femininity (duplicitous, cold, vain, heartless) at face value. Alya is alien: "the woman . . . acquired a certain configuration, that of a person from an alien culture, because there's no point in writing descriptive letters to a person of your own culture" (3–4). Alya's European tastes and sensibilities alienate Shklovsky; her heart doesn't ache for Petersburg. Her otherness sometimes signifies the chasm between men and women and, at other times, the chasm between Russia and Europe. Shklovsky links Alya's conspicuous consumption to her femininity when he says, "I'm writing about an alien culture and an alien woman. The woman is perhaps not totally alien. I'm not complaining about you, Alya. But you are an utter woman" (40). What exactly is an "utter woman"? One who "flirts with the things in the store: she likes everything. That's the European mentality" (40). Shklovsky thus accuses her of lacking discrimination, of being promiscuous in her tastes in material goods and, by implication, promiscuous with men. Yet the irony cannot be lost on Shklovsky that, if she were truly promiscuous, she would be willing to extend her favors to *him*. The love letter thus becomes the vehicle of revenge and exorcism—two motives that have traditionally characterized it at least since Richardson. Lovelace confesses: "[I have] written . . . upon . . . REVENGE, which I love; upon LOVE, which I hate, heartily hate, because 'tis my master: And upon the devil knows what besides."[43]

Shklovsky's portrayal of Alya reaccentuates other major motifs in epistolary tradition. He refers repeatedly to the power she has over his life, frequently comparing himself metonymically to the letter that she either holds in her hands, or tears up and throws away:

I, torn and shredded like a letter, keep climbing out of the wastebasket for your

---

43. Samuel Richardson, *Clarissa: or, The History of a Young Lady*, Shakespeare Head Edition (Oxford: Basil Blackwell, 1930), vol. 1, letter 31, pp. 221–22; hereinafter cited parenthetically in the text by volume, letter number, and page.

broken toys. I will survive dozens more of your passing fancies; every day you tear me up and every night I revive, like the letters. . . .

You have turned my life the way a worm screw turns a rack. (48)

Men are passing fancies that she devours and destroys before moving on. Elsewhere, Alya is a metonym for the letter, as when he laments her absence and finds substitutes for her face and body in the placing of black marks on white paper. The activity is a conscious exercise in supplementation: "How hard it is—even in letters, even through the black paper mask I make you wear, even in dreams—how hard it is for me to see your face" (55). Shklovsky evokes the *je crois te parler* motif, but rather than being able to sustain that illusion when he writes, he aggravates his condition by forcibly reminding himself that it *is* an illusion—merely black marks on white paper.

Shklovsky is equally aware that sublimation is illusory: "All we have are the yellow walls of houses, lit by the sun; we have our books and we have man's entire civilization, built by us on the way to love" (20). We are always *en route* to love; it is a destination forever elusive. The letter's transit is a metaphor for the transitory, circuitous *routing* of love. (*Routing* should be understood in both senses of the word, as the route love takes to its destination, and as the rejection it encounters when (and if) it arrives there.) Indeed, in numerous epistolary novels after *Zoo*, the lovers' obsession with the relays, detours, and dissemination of their letters and desire becomes an *idée fixe*. This explains why Shklovsky often depicts himself as a sentinel at his post; he is waiting either for a telephone call or for the mail. "Alya," he insists, "you know yourself that one's letters have to be sent somewhere" (32), even if they end up in the wastebasket.

The knowledge that desire by definition cannot be fulfilled is what keeps letters circulating; it is a space, a gap that we seek to fill with one simulacrum after another.[44] That is why shadows are frequently associated with Alya: "She, my Alya, loves the dance because it's the shadow of love" (39). To Shklovsky, Alya prefers the dance of courtship, wooing, and adoration to a lasting commitment; she does not love love but its shadow. Alya's narcissism is stereotypically feminine too. Yet Shklovsky nonetheless pursues his

44. See Jacques Lacan, "The Mirror Stage," in *Ecrits*, trans. Alan Sheridan (New York: W. W. Norton, 1977), pp. 1–7.

quest for love, communication, correspondence, obsessively writing letters, tearing them up, then mending, copying, and mailing them.

Shklovsky "produces" Woman by recording her capriciousness, perversity, and inconstancy. One letter is a fable of a hermit and a woman who keeps changing the object of her love from one element to a mightier element: the sun, the cloud, the wind, the mountain (99). Another fable contrasts woman's superficiality with man's devotion (127). In Letter 25, Shklovsky implicitly compares *Candide*'s Cunégonde and Alya:

> while people look for Cunégonde, she is sleeping with everybody and aging. . . . This plot—more accurately, this critical orientation on the idea that "time passes" and betrayals take place—was already being processed by Boccaccio. There the betrothed woman passes from hand to hand and finally winds up with her husband, assuring him of her virginity. The discoveries she made during her travels were not limited to hands. (92)

From Boccaccio to Voltaire, Woman's treachery and infidelity are legendary. Not only does Alya change lovers frequently, but she is capable of changing her mind, and indeed her entire personality, as often as she changes clothes. She is a remorseless liar. Her attention span is also deficient:

> No matter what you say to a woman, demand an answer immediately; otherwise, she'll take a hot bath, change her dress and you'll have to say the whole thing all over again. Changing clothes makes a woman forget even gestures. I strongly advise you to demand a rapid answer from women. Otherwise, you will find yourself constantly bewildered by some new and unexpected statement. A woman's life is almost devoid of syntax. (114)

Woman, Shklovsky implies, speaks a language man cannot translate; her heart, sexuality, and reasoning processes are utterly inscrutable. Paradoxically, while Shklovsky's declared purpose is to estrange the reading process, he exposes his own estrangement (in both senses of the word, as *ostranenie* and emotional alienation) in his portrait of Alya. Sometimes his parody is more bitter than comic. Although Alya is supposed to be from an alien culture, Shklovsky draws extensive parallels between her treatment of him and Russia's. The woman and the country have both conspired to constrain his desires and confine his creativity. Just as Alya forbids him to write of love, Russia orders him to "[g]o on living, but don't take up either my time or my space" (53). Shklovsky feels as if he has been "disappeared"; he exists in limbo, in a twilight zone that is both personal and political.

Since one of Shklovsky's motives for writing is to try to persuade Alya to relent, he tries valiantly to provide testimony of his sincerity. Such testimony, ranging from tearstains on the paper to bloodstains, is traditional in love letters: tangible signs of suffering document the sincerity of the sentiment and the materiality of the letter—hence its authenticity. Typically, the lover glorifies his heart over his intellect and laments the beloved's indifference: "Of all these contradictions, the most painful to me is that while the lips in question [Alya's] are busy renewing themselves, [my] heart is being worn to a frazzle; and with it go the forgotten things, undetected" (93). Shklovsky exploits yet another feminine stereotype: Alya is not only cold but vain and superficial. She restores herself artificially, by painting her face, while he remains depleted and demoralized. Such contrasts reaccentuate the epistolary code of pathos. Like epistolary lovers from Werther to Humbert, Shklovsky fears that the beloved has forgotten what they shared, so tears authenticate his feelings: "I float, salty and heavy with tears, barely keeping my head above water. I seem to be sinking. . . . In Russia I was strong; here I have begun to weep" (11–12).

In another letter his tears flood Alya's apartment and drag away "a briefcase full of page proofs" (39). Shklovsky strives for sincerity, but such exaggerated hyperbole inevitably undermines it. By this means, he defamiliarizes the lover's discourse as a genre; the very extremity of his descriptions indicates that he is aware that he is playing a role, assuming a pose, but at the same time he exalts his suffering, luxuriates in self-pity, and indicts Alya for his unhappiness.

ELSA TRIOLET'S LETTERS IN *ZOO*

Ironically, while Shklovsky strives for authenticity and sincerity, the letters attributed to Alya, which were written by Elsa Triolet, consistently undermine Shklovsky's poses. Shklovsky purposely blurs the boundaries between fiction and reality and raises numerous questions about the status of the text. Did Elsa mail these letters to Shklovsky without knowing the use to which he would put them? Or did she consciously collaborate with him in the creation of a fiction, as the three Marias would later do in *New Por-*

tuguese Letters (1972)?[45] Internal evidence from Elsa's letters is inconclusive: she never once refers to the book Shklovsky is writing, although she does mention his famous essay on *Don Quixote*. Yet he mails everything he has written to her, and she indicates that she has received all his letters when she complains that her desk, purse, and apartment are overflowing with them! Since many of his letters refer to his epistolary novel, she must be aware that his letters are part of a book in the making.

Yet Elsa never hints that she sees either her letters or herself in literary terms; instead, she criticizes the lyricism and pathos that frequently infect Shklovsky's tone. One of the ways in which Shklovsky "breaks new ground" is by seizing on the concept of *"la chose littéraire"*: *Zoo* demonstrates that what one defines as literature depends on how it is framed. Elsa's personal letters are defamiliarized by being displaced from a private context to a public one; framed within the pages of a novel, they are raised to the status of literature. Derrida will exploit these same ambiguities in what he calls the "postcarded structure" of *The Post Card*, disrupting the categories of public/private, inside/outside, real/fictional. So dislocated are these categories in *Zoo* that one hardly knows what to call the writer of Elsa's letters— Elsa or Alya? It seems naive to call her Elsa but perverse to call her Alya. I would argue that the effect of such scrambling is to force the reader to make her own connections. The *mise en question* is the message; as in collage, each name has a dual function: "Elsa" refers to an external reality even as the compositional thrust undermines the very referentiality it seems to assert (*FM*, 49). Since what is lacking is an ordering guide telling us how to read, the novel compels a double reading. For purposes of clarity and exegesis, I have decided to call Shklovsky's beloved "Elsa" when referring to the letters she writes; in all other contexts I refer to her as "Alya," but I cannot overemphasize my dissatisfaction with such a solution, which is both imperfect and admittedly arbitrary.

Insofar as motives can be deduced from intrinsic evidence, Elsa and Shklovsky hardly share the same intentions for writing—quite the con-

45. Maria Isabel Barreño, Maria Teresa Horta, Maria Velho da Costa, *The Three Marias: New Portuguese Letters*, trans. Helen R. Lane (New York: Bantam, 1976); hereinafter cited parenthetically in the text as *TM*.

trary. Elsa's authentic letters provide a counterdiscourse to Shklovsky's: she invalidates the feminine stereotypes upon which he relies. Far from being the embodiment of the Eternal Feminine, Elsa is down to earth. Whereas Shklovsky portrays her as being as acquisitive and as materialistic as the Europeans, Elsa demonstrates that she is not nearly so status-conscious as Shklovsky imagines. She describes her apartment in Berlin as being "the sort of place you avoid if at all possible. My acquaintances from the Kurfürstendamm will not be casually dropping in!" (11).

Since he can only see her as the object of his desire, he never hints that she may have interests beyond dances, men, and shopping, but her own letters reveal her commitment to work, as when she explains what she misses about London: "the solitude, the measured life, the work from morning to night" (12). Each of these aspects contribute a far different impression of her: she is disciplined, she works hard, she likes to be alone. It is revealing that Shklovsky says nothing about her commitment to art and literature, although there is a certain mad logic—the logic of lover's discourses—in his repression of this information, for the lover solipsistically seeks to sustain the illusion that the beloved has no other existence, no other vocation besides loving him. "My whole life is a letter to you" (27), he proclaims. Although, in fact, he is much engaged in other activities, he nourishes the illusion that her life is dedicated solely to him.

Elsa is acutely aware of the social and political as well as the aesthetic milieu surrounding her. Whereas Shklovsky portrays her as being frivolous, she describes the abysmal social conditions in Berlin in 1923: "There is so much misery here that you can't put it out of your mind even for a minute" (12). Far from being narcissistic, she is compassionate to Shklovsky as well as to the multitudes. In contrast to his view of her pitilessness, she goes to considerable lengths to salvage a friendship with him: she assures him that she is not trying to hurt him and that, although she doesn't love him, "without you, my own, my dear, I would cry" (59). She kindly reminds him that "we still have much in common." The same letter reveals her own desires; she wistfully longs for youth and strength. Far from striving to break men's hearts, she yearns for a childlike capacity for happiness. Elsa mentions her shortcomings in several other letters. She even goes so far as to agree with him when he attacks her: "I know I'm good for nothing; no need to insist on that" (60). In her letter from Tahiti, she admits that "I have no sense when it comes to events and places; no idea of the number of inhabitants, or facts." Yet her descriptions of the water, the faces, and the people in Tahiti are quite wonderful, and she writes commandingly of "all this I know, see and feel" (76). She repeats this idea later: "Wherever I go, I know immediately what goes with what and who with whom" (101), implying that whoever goes with whom, she and Shklovsky do not go together, do not belong together, and she grows increasingly exasperated with his importunings.

Not only do her letters reveal an utterly different perspective about femininity in general and her character in particular, they reveal unattractive aspects of Shklovsky. Although he claims to be devastated by her rebuffs, she is well aware of his "amorous nature"; she shrewdly reveals that he loved many women before her and will love many after her. So much for female narcissism! Although she tries to be kind to him, his aggressiveness is wearing her out; she accuses him of doing "all you can to frighten me, to repel me" (15). He has become as demanding as a small boy, and she warns him:

> Don't write me only about your love. Don't make wild scenes on the telephone. Don't rant and rave. You're managing to poison my days. . . .
>
> You demand of me all my time. (15)

Elsa reacts against Shklovsky's egotism and obsessiveness first by trying to persuade him to talk of other things, such as books (another sign of her substantial intellectual interests), then by telling him frankly that "the momentum of your love frightens me; it's ghastly" (Let. 19). Elsa finally rebels against his possessiveness: "I need freedom—I refuse to account for my actions to anyone!" (15).

Above all, Shklovsky is jealous of Elsa's writing. First, the time she devotes to writing takes her away from him. Second, she writes about experiences that do not include him, like her trip to Tahiti. Third, he envies her style, ruefully noting:

> Writing comes easy to you.
>
> You don't know—and that's just as well—that many words are forbidden.
>
> Forbidden are words about flowers. Forbidden is spring. In general, all the good words are faint with exhaustion.
>
> I'm sick of wit and irony.

> Your letter made me envious.
>
> How I want simply to describe objects as if literature had never existed; that way one could write literarily. (84)

Couched in the guise of praise for her naiveté, Shklovsky is really criticizing her for not noticing clichés (flowers, spring, etc.). (In fact, her writing contains few clichés.) Although Shklovsky yearns to write as if literature never existed, he realizes how *quixotic* that desire is: one can only write in the wake of literature. Irony helps to defamiliarize the conventions of language, but it also distances the lover from the sincerity he wants to convey. The lover's double bind: however much he strives to avoid clichés, the very act of writing love letters turns him into one.

Elsa's most sustained critique of Shklovsky comes in the form of literary criticism: not only has he become a pest, but he doesn't even know how to write love letters:

> You claim to know how Don Quixote is made, but you certainly don't know how to write a love letter.
>
> And you're becoming more pesky all the time.
>
> When you write about love, you choke on your own lyricism and froth at the mouth. . . .
>
> On various pretexts, you keep writing about the same thing. Quit writing about HOW, HOW, HOW much you love me, because at the third "how much," I start thinking about something else. (101–2)

Reader-response criticism at its best! No matter how Shklovsky tries to mythologize Woman, Elsa's letters consistently thwart him. Her realistic assessment of her own charms includes the frank and objective revelation that "I'm no *femme fatale*" (31). What is most revealing about Shklovsky's obsession is how little it involves any desire to know the woman herself. Instead, he is obsessed with what Roland Barthes (echoing Lacan) will later call the lover's "Image-repertoire"; the beloved object is a mere projection of the lover's desire. Shklovsky's inability to perceive Elsa apart from his projection is especially ironic since the aim of defamiliarization is to make one *see*, to renew perception. But Shklovsky never does see her. She reproaches him for precisely that incapacity when she says, "One doesn't write love letters for his own satisfaction, since no real lover thinks of himself when he's in love" (102). Angry with him for violating her injunction,

Elsa sees no alternative but to terminate the correspondence; hence, this is her last letter. In its epigraph, Shklovsky attacks her false sincerity; he hopes readers never receive such letters as this, and he describes her tone as "truculent" (101).

Perhaps the most revealing aspect of their correspondence comes in Letter 19—the one prefaced by Shklovsky's injunction against reading it. In this letter, she recalls her wet nurse Stesha, and she thinks of Stesha's love for men; she gave herself freely and, as a result, was perpetually pregnant. Her whole life was circumscribed by love, pregnancy, childbirth, and wet-nursing. Although she asks, "[W]hat made me inflict Stesha on you?" the answer seems clear: she distinguishes between women who live solely for men and those who don't. She further distinguishes Woman (as mythical lover and mother) from *women*, in all their specificity and complexity—and attempts to prevent these differences from getting lost in translation. For her labor and her pains, Shklovsky crosses out this letter.

The juxtaposition of authentic letters with fictional ones is a genuine innovation in the genre of the love letter, although there are celebrated cases of authentic letters that were deemed fictional, like those of Héloise, and of possibly fictional letters that were defined as authentic, like *The Letters of a Portuguese Nun*.[46] The blurring of the boundaries of fiction and reality reflects Shklovsky's interest in the use of montage and collaboration, and shows the extent to which the illusion of authenticity can be manufactured by introducing real names and intimate acquaintances into a fictional narrative, a technique Barthes and Derrida will both repeat. Autobiography,

46. *Lettres portugaises (The Letters of a Portuguese Nun)* was published anonymously in France in 1669, ostensibly translated into French from Portuguese, but no Portuguese original has ever been found. For 300 years scholars have tried to identify the nun and the French chevalier who seduced her and to whom her letters are addressed. The translator was identified as Guilleragues, but in 1962 two scholars presented fairly persuasive evidence that Guilleragues actually wrote the letters and perpetrated the hoax to heighten their scandalous appeal. The issues of signature, authenticity, the differences between masculine and feminine writing, and the implications of the poststructuralist "death of the author" for feminist criticism resurfaced in the debate between Nancy K. Miller and Peggy Kamuf in *Diacritics* 12 (Summer 1982): 42–53. The debate over the authenticity of *Lettres portugaises* remains unresolved to this day. For the literary history of the debate, see Kauffman, *Discourses of Desire*, pp. 92–100; on Héloise's letters, see Kauffman, chap. 2.

Barthes reminds us, should be viewed as *auto-bio-graphy*. Shklovsky reinforces this view when he looks back retrospectively on his novel:

> For a long time now, what was cut from the heart has been borne away. I feel only pity for that past: the man that existed then.
>
> Now I have a hero, because the book is no longer written about me. I left him (my former self) in this book, as, in old-time novels, a sailor guilty of some offense was marooned on a desert island. (109)

Barthes echoes this strategy of self-distancing when he reflects in *Roland Barthes by Roland Barthes*, "It must all be considered as if spoken by a character in a novel."[47]

But if *Zoo* becomes endowed with a novelistic hero, it also has a heroine. The interpolated letters from Elsa authenticate the novel by shifting the focus away from Shklovsky's unrelenting obsessiveness with his image-repertoire. They are an antidote both to his lyricism and to his mystification of Woman. They simultaneously enlarge the text he is in the process of producing and undermine the stereotypes of femininity that he reproduces. When Shklovsky declares that "Alya" doesn't exist, that she is the realization of a metaphor, he means that she is a metaphor for an "alien people . . . an alien land" (103), like that of Berlin encircling the Russian diaspora. Yet he is simultaneously relying on an entire code which figures woman as alien *because* she is Woman, the Other. Not only does he declare that "she to whom I speak all my words is a foreigner" (69), but he insists, "Human women are incomprehensible" (24). Similarly, another man who has also been abandoned by a woman, asks him, "What do women need from us? What do they want?" (19). Like Freud, Shklovsky reinscribes Woman as the undiscovered country, the enigma. But just as Freud sought to define rather than to discover Dora, Shklovsky remains obsessed solely with Woman as metaphor in *Zoo*: he has declared her alien *avant la lettre*. Despite his attempts, the woman in the text remains, like the letter itself, legible—even under erasure.

Elsa's letters are dialogic in the sense that they are a dialogue with Shklovsky; they contribute myriad levels of intertextuality, contestation, and struggle. Most important, Elsa argues from an alternative *logic:* one

---

47. Roland Barthes, *Roland Barthes by Roland Barthes* (New York: Hill and Wang, 1977), p. i.

that resists his mythologizing, lyrical, and amorous impulses. She must find a way to write "as if literature doesn't exist" for reasons different from those Shklovsky acknowledges: literature is a major vehicle for disseminating and perpetuating the false stereotypes of Woman. *Zoo* becomes a contested site of a struggle for discourse: Elsa's resistance to metaphoric reduction exists in tension with Shklovsky's dizzying inventiveness in producing Woman. In this regard, Shklovsky anticipates Barthes and Derrida. As Alice Jardine asks, "While women are busy refusing the metaphors trapped in the chains of masculine desire, have the male philosophers found a "different/same" "femme-metaphor" for producing *new* images?[48]

Few critics in 1923 were more acutely aware than Shklovsky of the extent to which they were living in "a modern society [which] no longer nourishes itself with beliefs (as in the past) but with images."[49] Shklovsky's interests in cinema, photography, architecture, and art made him one of the first to declare war on the image by shocking us into a realization of its constructedness and by differentiating sign from the referent. Throughout *Zoo*, he insists that "art needs the local, the vital, the differentiated (just the word for a letter!)" (87). Although he fails to differentiate women from Woman, in narrative theory in general and epistolary theory in particular, *Zoo* breaks new ground. His theoretical experiments and generic innovations make *Zoo* a veritable allegory of reading in terms of personal, political, and aesthetic estrangement.[50] I turn now to another Russian emigré who passed through Berlin while Shklovsky was writing *Zoo*: Vladimir Nabokov.

48. Alice Jardine, "Pre-Texts for the Transatlantic Feminist," *Yale French Studies* 62 (1981): 220–36.

49. Roland Barthes, *Sollers écrivain* (Paris: Editions de Seuil, 1979), p. 89.

50. Since *Special Delivery* covers seventy-five years of literary history and places such emphasis on textual production, it seems fitting to note that, as the galleys went to press, the USSR dismantled communism, seventy-four years after the cataclysms Shklovsky recorded.

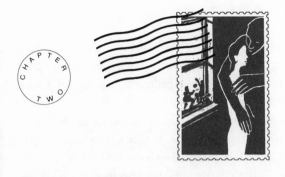

CHAPTER TWO

Framing Lolita: Is There a Woman in the Text?

EPISTOLARITY IN *LOLITA*

Like Shklovsky's *Zoo*, Vladimir Nabokov's *Lolita* (1955) combines lyric and satire, love and scholarship. Like *Zoo*, *Lolita* is a patchwork of fragmentary genres. Poems, jingles, advertisements, plays and filmscripts, literary criticism, newspaper articles, psychiatric and legal reports are mixed with vestiges of the diary, confessional, journal, and memoir. Nabokov follows Shklovsky in consciously dramatizing literary production. Just as Elsa Triolet's letters undermine Shklovsky's, *Lolita's* words and letters undermine Humbert's. *Lolita's* voice, however, is far more muted than Elsa's, despite the fact that an astonishing amount of writing, epistolary and otherwise, takes place in *Lolita:* Humbert writes "tortuous essays in obscure journals" on quixotic topics like "The Proustian Theme in a

Letter from Keats to Benjamin Bailey,"[1] willfully distorting chronology as well as plausibility. Humbert reads endless psychiatric reports on his neuroses; composes behavioral studies of fellow expeditionists in arctic Canada; writes, copies, then reconstructs a diary about his fifty days of connubial bliss with Charlotte. Letters are crucial to the plot: Charlotte confesses her love for Humbert in a letter; she dies while rushing to the mailbox with letters exposing Humbert's treachery; Mona Dahl's cryptic letter to Lolita contains vital clues to Quilty's identity; Lolita's letter enables Humbert to track her to Gray Star. The cumulative effect of this voluminous writing, particularly that of the specialists, is to impress upon us how little we know. Manuals and manuscripts, authorities and authors ranging from St. Augustine to Judge Woolsey are cited, but there seems to be an inverse relationship between writing and wisdom, as if the more specialized our language becomes, the less we perceive. That is especially true of Humbert's perception of Lolita: from beginning to end, she remains an enigma to him. For her, the rest is silence.

Specific letters are embedded in a larger generic framework that has often been overlooked, for Humbert's entire narrative owes much to epistolarity. Initially composed for use in his murder trial, it is a confession and an appeal. Legal language, direct addresses to the jury, invocations of legal precedents and case studies all reaccentuate one of the most ancient strains of epistolarity: the trial motif. In the *Heroides*, for example, the victimized heroine laments her fate, exposes her lover's treachery, exhorts the law to prosecute him, and dedicates herself to revenge. Héloise invokes the trial motif when she presents her grievances to Abelard, provides evidence of her wrongs, abjures Abelard to recognize the justice of her grievances and the allegiance he owes to her. Throughout, she remains defiantly unrepentant. The trial motif extends from *Clarissa, Jane Eyre*, and *The Turn of the Screw* to *Absalom, Absalom!*, where Rosa Coldfield obsessively weighs Sutpen's sins and finds him wanting.[2] Humbert's discourse is contested and contesting; he is the most eloquent witness for the defense and (occasionally) for

---

1. Vladimir Nabokov, *Lolita* (1955; reprinted New York: Berkeley Books, 1977), p. 18; hereinafter cited parenthetically in the text.

2. See Kauffman, *Discourses of Desire*, pp. 44–45, 77–78, 130–40, 201, 204–7, 269–73.

the prosecution. It is he who reminds us that "you can always count on a murderer for a fancy prose style"; it is he who condemns himself to prison, not for the murder of Quilty but for the murder of Lolita's childhood.

Despite such self-indictments, Humbert identifies with the poet and the madman; he thinks his excesses place him beyond the pale of ordinary society. His heightened sensitivity and refinement distinguish him from the vulgar multitudes. In this respect, it is significant that his closest analogue is another epistolary "hero": Werther. Werther, too, glorifies heart over head, passion over intellect, spontaneity over prudence, the individual over society. For Humbert as for Werther, the female object of adoration scarcely emerges as anything but a hazy abstraction, the mirror of the hero's narcissism as well as his desire. (Nabokov evokes Goethe's Lotte not only in the name Lolita but parodically in Charlotte Haze.) Werther reveals his narcissism when he confesses, "I coddle my heart like a sick child and give in to its every whim."[3] Humbert insists that acute sensitivity (rather than pedophilia) is what sets him apart from other people. He repeatedly reminds us of the "gentleness of my nature" (67); "the doe in me" (119); "my shyness, my distaste for any ostentation, my inherent sense of the *comme il faut*" (226). Both heroes claim that they yearn to be satisfied, as most people are, with modest contentment; both complain of the burden of having an exalted sensibility. "To be misunderstood," Werther observes, "is the miserable destiny of people like myself" (27).

That lonely destiny is what drives both Werther and Humbert to letter writing, but epistolary production, always a solitary endeavor, only increases their solipsism, a paradox of which both novelists are well aware. That paradox is what led Goethe to use the epistolary technique:

> When it came to the point . . . of my wishing to describe the weariness with which people often experience life without having been forced to such a dismal outlook by want, I hit upon the idea, as author, of expressing my feelings in letters. For this weariness, this disgust with life, is born of loneliness, it is the foster child of solitude. He who gives himself up to it, flees from all opposition. . . . Thus he is thrust back upon himself by the very things that should

3. Johann Wolfgang von Goethe, *The Sorrows of Young Werther*, trans. Catherine Hutter (New York: New American Library, 1962), p. 26; hereinafter cited parenthetically in the text.

serve to take him out of himself. If he ever does want to discuss it, then surely only in letters, for a written effusion, whether it be joyous or morose, does not antagonize anyone directly, and an answer filled with counterarguments gives the lonely man an opportunity to harden in his peculiarities and offers the inducement to become more obdurate.[4]

Goethe pinpoints the contestatory dialogic nature of epistolarity as well as its solipsism. Humbert "hardens in his peculiarities," using writing to become more "obdurate." Like Werther, Humbert composes himself as he writes, consciously creating a self and a prose style that blind as well as dazzle. "The artist in me has been given the upper hand over the gentleman." His rationale: "retrospective verisimilitude" (67–68). Werther's and Humbert's elegantly phrased celebrations of aesthetic and emotional excess disguise the most inordinate egotism. Each hero is infantile and vampiristic. Each sees his fate as unique and blames others for his failings, as when Werther asks, "Don't children try to grasp anything they can think of? And I?" (92). Humbert does not just lust after children, he identifies with them, even resorting to baby talk and using his childishness as an excuse for his crimes. The name Werther and Humbert each give to their egotism is Desire; the agent responsible for their actions is Fate. Each refuses to believe that he is culpable, despite the fact that Werther ruins Lotte's life by committing suicide (sadistically reminding her in his final letters that it was she who provided the weapons). Humbert kidnaps and drugs Lolita before having sex with her but excuses himself by complaining, "I was not even her first lover" (125). Werther tells himself that "my fate is unique. Consider all other men fortunate, I tell myself, no one has ever suffered like you. . . . I have to suffer much. Oh, has any heart before me ever been so wretched?" (95). Self-pity dominates Humbert's narrative, too: he insists that he "tried to be good," but "Never mind, never mind, I am only a brute, never mind, let us go on with my miserable story" (176).

The similarities between Goethe's novel and Nabokov's are structural as well as thematic. Like Goethe, Nabokov positions an obtuse editor as intermediary between the reader and the narrator. The editor's role is didactic. Unlike Werther and Humbert, William and John Ray are dull, practical men

---

4. Goethe, "Reflections on Werther," afterword in *The Sorrows of Young Werther*, pp. 139–40.

of common sense. (Ray even writes a scientific monograph on the topic, "Do the Senses Make Sense?"). Structurally, in each novel two triangular relationships are superimposed: that of hero, editor, and reader *of* the text parallels that of hero, rival, and beloved *in* the text. The Werther-Albert-Lotte triangle structurally mirrors the triangle of Humbert, Quilty, and Lolita. Nabokov depicts reading as a process of transference: just as Werther identifies with every lost lover, Humbert· identifies with Werther, Poe, and all other poets and madmen. (Similar identifications with Werther and Poe reverberate uncannily in Barthes and Derrida.)

By reinventing Werther in Humbert, Nabokov defamiliarizes not just the major codes of romantic love but the very roots of Romanticism. Yet, as with Goethe's gullible audience,[5] Nabokov's audience (unlike Nabokov himself) seems to have endorsed Humbert's self-presentation without a trace of irony. Lionel Trilling, for instance, proclaimed in reviewing the novel that *"Lolita* is about love . . . not about sex, but about love. Almost every page sets forth some explicit erotic emotion or some overt erotic action and still it is not about sex. It is about love. This makes it unique in my experience of contemporary novels."[6]

Humbert's narrative is a Nabokovian trap for unwary readers like Trilling, for critics can celebrate Humbert's role as lover only by minimizing his role as father. Yet paradoxically, only Humbert's role as father makes it possible to be Lolita's lover, since that is what gives him unmonitored access to the girl as her semi-legal "guardian."[7] Trilling is right to notice the overt erotic activity on every page, but wrong to conclude that the novel is about love, not sex. *Lolita* is not about love but about incest, which is a betrayal of trust, a violation of love. How have critics managed so consistently to confuse love with incest in the novel? My aim here is to show how—through a variety of narrative strategies—the inscription of the father's body in the text obliterates the daughter's.

5. For an account of Goethe's dismay at the public's identification with Werther, which culminated in a rash of suicides among young men, see ibid., pp. 130–53.

6. Lionel Trilling, "The Last Lover: Vladimir Nabokov's *Lolita*," *Encounter* 11 (October 1958): 9–19; hereinafter cited parenthetically in the text.

7. Humbert's legal rights as guardian are never notarized, but he exercises those "rights" nonetheless, threatening Lolita with reform school if she reveals their sexual relationship, and taking control of her inheritance following her mother's death.

LITERATURE AS SOCIAL CHANGE OR AESTHETIC BLISS

The first strategy involves the frame within which Humbert's narrative is placed between John Ray's foreword and Nabokov's afterword. John Ray, Jr., is the psychologist who reads Humbert's narrative for the message, the general lesson, the ethical impact: this cautionary tale "should," he pompously dictates, "make all of us—parents, social workers, educators—apply ourselves with still greater vigilance and vision to the task of bringing up a better generation in a safer world" (7). Yet everything conspires against Ray's exhortation. The issue of child abuse is obscured by Ray's professional self-advertisement, his pompous literary allusions, and his high-blown literary style. Nabokov not only parodies such seeming erudition through Ray's preface but pokes fun at readers who so simply correlate art with life. For "'old-fashioned' readers who wish to follow the destinies of the 'real' people beyond the 'true' story" (6), we learn in the preface what became of both Humbert and Lolita after Humbert ceased writing: he died of a heart attack and she died in childbirth. But readers curious about such matters belong at the bottom of the class, along with other dreary moralists, Freudians, and feminists who may murmur against the brutality of Lolita's treatment. As parody, then, the foreward acts as an injunction against the kind of reading that foregrounds social issues like child abuse.

Such readers will always miss the appeal of "aesthetic bliss," which Nabokov proposes as the appropriate response in "his" afterword:

> After doing my impersonation of suave John Ray . . . any comments coming straight from me may strike one—may strike me, in fact—as an impersonation of Vladimir Nabokov talking about his own book. . . . I am neither a reader nor a writer of didactic fiction, and, despite John Ray's assertion, Lolita has no moral in tow. For me a work of fiction exists only insofar as it affords me what I shall bluntly call aesthetic bliss. (282, 286)

Here, then, is the second strategy that explains why incest is overlooked: critics take Nabokov at his word. His wry disclaimer effectively throws sand in our eyes, for the fact is that the afterword is as thoroughly cunning an impersonation as John Ray's foreword. The "end," in other words, is as much a part of the fiction as the beginning. The afterword is a sham because it simply extends the Humbertian aesthetic manifesto, a detail that credulous readers fail to notice. The artifice of self-referential textuality extends through Nabokov's afterword: it is a trap for readers who pride themselves on their sophistication and their ability to distance themselves from "real life." It contributes as much to the text by way of irony and distortion as the spurious index at the end of *Pale Fire*.[8] Foreword and afterword are mirror images—distortions, displacements, impersonations that seduce us into reading Humbert's narrative in a way that minimizes the viewpoint of a bruised child and foregrounds Humbert's obsession. He is not obsessed with love but rather with his own body, as we shall see.

Foreword and afterword each direct us toward monologic readings that are mutually exclusive. The choice between John Ray's foreword (literature as a vehicle for social change) and Nabokov's afterword (literature as self-referential artifice) involve seemingly irreconcilable differences, and, since Ray is the butt of parody, readers seem willing to go to any length to avoid being identified with him. Parody thus acts as an injunction against a certain mode of referential reading.

The challenge for feminist criticism is thus to read against the grain, to resist Humbert's rhetorical ruses *and* Nabokov's afterword. Is it possible in a double movement to analyze the horror of incest by reinscribing the material body of the child Lolita in the text, and simultaneously to undermine the representational fallacy by situating the text dialogically in relation to other texts? Ironically, despite their commitment to using literature as a vehicle for social change, feminists also have a stake in dismantling the representational fallacy, for paradoxically the most misogynistic criticism of *Lolita* comes from critics who take the novel as a representation of real life. Trilling, for instance, begins by citing Humbert's "ferocity . . . his open brutality to women." Yet, Trilling continues:

> Perhaps [Humbert's] depravity is the easier to accept when we learn that he deals with a Lolita who is not innocent, and who seems to have very few emotions to be violated; and I suppose we *naturally* incline to be lenient towards a

8. The afterword, "On a book entitled *Lolita*," dated 12 November, 1956, is appended to every edition except the first, including over twenty-five translations. There are many precedents for discussing afterwords or appendices—some written many years later—as "integral" parts of novels: William Faulkner's *The Sound and the Fury* and *Absalom, Absalom!* come to mind. No afterword, however, can be relied upon as an answer to questions raised in a novel; instead, it makes the questions more problematic, as Nabokov's afterword to *Lolita* demonstrates.

rapist—legally and by intention H.H. is that—who eventually feels a death-less devotion to his victim! (14)

Yet far from finding rape and incest shocking, Trilling is only shocked that so few contemporary novels focus on "love." *Lolita*, he proclaims, is one of them, despite the fact that Humbert's greed is, in Trilling's own words, "ape-like."

Some feminist critics argue that only by reading referentially can one prevent the female subject from disappearing. By this logic, one would ex-pect critics who read *Lolita* as a representation of real life to pay considerable attention to Lolita, but, in fact, few have imagined what her victimization is like. Instead, they identify with the sensations Humbert records about his body by uncritically adopting his viewpoint. Thomas Molnar is repre-sentative:

> The central question the reader ought to ask of himself is whether he feels pity for the girl. Our ethical ideal would require that we look at Lolita as a sacrificial lamb, that we become in imagination, her knight-protector. Yet this is impos-sible for two reasons. One is very simple: before yielding to Humbert, the girl has had a nasty little affair with a nasty little thirteen-year-old. . . . Besides, she is a spoiled sub-teenager with a foul mouth, a self-offered target for lechers. . . . throughout, she remains an object perhaps even to herself.[9]

Molnar indicts Lolita for being a tease who "asks for it," and who deserves what she gets since she is "damaged goods." Both Trilling and Molnar casti-gate Lolita for being unknowable, but Humbert's failure to understand her demonstrates his obtuseness, not her inaccessibility. Indeed, despite his ag-gressive desire to know all, Humbert finally confesses that there are depths in her inaccessible to him (259).

Nor must one forget that Humbert is a notoriously unreliable narrator who lies to psychiatrists, deceives two wives, and otherwise takes elaborate precautions to avoid detection. In view of his unreliability, it is doubtful his claim that Lolita seduced him is true; more important, it is unverifiable, and credulous critics who read the novel as a reflection of life thus end up merely reifying codes that can be traced directly from literature, codes that—from the courtly love tradition to *Clarissa* to modern cinema—first idealize the

---

9. Thomas Molnar, "Matter-of-Fact Confession of a Non-Penitent," *Chronicles of Culture* 2 (January–February 1978): 11–13.

woman loved from afar and then degrade her by blaming her for her own rape and humiliation.

My reservations about referential readings, however, do not imply that the opposite emphasis on self-referential artifice is any more enlightened. Parody can serve to defamiliarize habitual modes of perception, as in *Zoo*, but it can also disguise strategies of appropriation, an aggressive will to power. Yet critics invariably excuse Humbert. Take Alfred Appel, who describes the novel as a "springboard for parody," adding: "Humbert's terrible demands *notwithstanding*, Lolita is as insensitive as children are to their *actual* parents; *sexuality aside*, she demands anxious parental placation in a too typically American way, and affords Nabokov an ideal opportunity to comment on the Teen and Subteen Tyranny."[10] Such passages rupture the critical stance that self-referentiality demands; when it comes to women, Appel seems to forget his main point that the novel is *not* realistic! In a now famous statement, Appel goes on to assert: "By creating a reality which is a fiction, but a fiction that is able to mock the reader, the author has demonstrated the fiction of 'reality,' and the reader who accepts these implications may even have experienced a change in consciousness" (120).

But before one can analyze a fiction that mocks the reader, or results in a change in consciousness, one needs to examine the kind of reader one has in mind. Humbert is not only an avid writer, he is an avid reader: of motel registers, class rolls, road signs, comics, even movie posters. His reading of Lolita is the model on which male critics rely—whether they read self-referentially *or* mimetically. And that is the source of their blindness: they fail to notice that Humbert is not only a notoriously unreliable narrator but that he is an unreliable reader, too. If he were not, he would have solved the mystery of Quilty's identity long ago. As it happens, he never does solve it; Lolita has to tell him. Like his heart, his powers of perception and his eyes are "hysterical unreliable organ[s]." A voyeur, he wants to see but not be seen. He wants to read, interpret, and write but not be analyzed by psychiatrists or "out-authored" by Quilty.

Despite his unreliability, feminist readers have the choice of either participating in their own "immasculation" by endorsing aesthetic bliss, or of

10. Alfred Appel, Jr., "*Lolita*: The Springboard of Parody" in *Nabokov: The Man and his Work*, ed. L. S. Dembo (Madison: Univ. of Wisconsin Press, 1967), p. 121; emphasis added; hereinafter cited parenthetically in the text.

demonstrating their humorlessness and frigidity. Judith Fetterly defines "immasculation" as the process by which "the female reader is co-opted into participation in an experience from which she is explicitly excluded; she is asked to identify with a selfhood that defines itself in opposition to her; she is required to identify against herself."[11] Consider the famous scene of Lolita on the couch with Humbert while he surreptiously masturbates and enjoins the reader to respond:

> I want my learned readers to participate in the scene I am about to replay; I want them to examine its every detail and see for themselves how . . . chaste, the whole wine-sweet event is. . . . What had begun as a delicious distension of my innermost roots became a glowing tingle . . . not found elsewhere in conscious life. . . . Lolita had been safely solipsized. . . . Suspended on the brink of that voluptuous abyss (a nicety of physiological equipoise comparable to certain techniques in the arts). . . . I crushed out against her left buttock the last throb of the longest ecstasy man or monster had ever known. (57–58)

This is a scene where the father's body is the site and the source of not only aesthetic bliss but literal orgasm; both come at the same time—if, that is— the reader is male. Lolita, however, is not so much "solipsized" as annihilated, as Humbert reveals while congratulating himself in the next scene:

> What I had madly possessed was not she, but *my own creation*, another, fanciful Lolita—*perhaps, more real* than Lolita; overlapping, encasing her; floating between me and her, and having no will, no consciousness—indeed no life of her own.
>
> The child knew nothing. I had done nothing to her. And nothing prevented me from repeating a performance that affected her as little as if she were a photographic image rippling upon a screen and I a humble hunchback abusing myself in the dark. (59; emphasis added)

Thus physical as well as aesthetic *jouissance* for Humbert requires psychic anesthesia or annihilation for Lolita. "Reader! Bruder!" Humbert exclaims, "I shall not exist if you do not imagine me" (119), is a man's appeal to male readers. The appeal disguises the fact that Lolita does not exist for Humbert precisely because he fails to imagine her except as a projection of his desire.

---

11. Judith Fetterly, *The Resisting Reader: A Feminist Approach to American Fiction* (Bloomington: Indiana Univ. Press, 1978), p. xii.

What the text mimes, then, is a bundle of relations between men, as clarified not only in the passage above but in the responses of critics like Trilling and Molnar. The incest taboo, as Lévi-Strauss (following Freud) reveals, has nothing to do with protecting the girl, and everything to do with ensuring that she functions as an object of exchange between men: "[I]t is the supreme rule of the gift . . . which allows [the incest taboo's] nature to be understood."[12] The scene in which Humbert masturbates with Lolita on his lap is a good example of how what is male is made to seem "universal." As Patrocinio Schweickart explains in discussing the implied authorial contract:

> For the male reader, the text serves as the meeting ground of the personal and the universal. . . . the male reader is invited to feel his *difference* (concretely, from the girl) and to equate that with the universal. Relevant here is Lévi-Strauss's theory that woman functions as currency exchanged between men. The woman in the text converts the text into a woman, and the circulation of this text/woman becomes the central ritual that establishes the bond between the author and his male readers.[13]

That male bond and identification with the male body help to explain further how incest can be mistaken for love. From the opening words, Humbert's body is a palpable presence: "Lolita, light of my life, fire of my loins. My sin, my soul. Lo-lee-ta: the tip of the tongue taking a trip of three steps down the palate to tap, at three, on the teeth" (11). "Lolita" is a word; Humbert is flesh: loins, tongue, palate, teeth. Humbert's obsession with his body is not just narcissistic but infantile; it is he who is marked by a preoedipal fascination with his own bowels, his digestion, his heartburn, his headaches, his blood pressure—and of course, his penis, that "pentapod monster" that feels like a "thousand eyes wide open in my eyed blood" (41). As he masturbates, he "entered a plane of being where nothing mattered, save the infusion of joy brewed within my body" (57). Thus, while exploiting his role as guardian to enforce the Law of the Father, Humbert also reverses it. He turns oedipali-

12. Claude Lévi-Strauss, *The Elementary Structures of Kinship* (1949; reprinted Boston: Beacon, 1969), p. 115.

13. Patrocinio P. Schweickart, "Reading Ourselves: Toward a Feminist Theory of Reading," in *Gender and Reading: Essays on Readers, Texts, and Contexts,* ed. Elizabeth A. Flynn and Patrocinio P. Schweickart (Baltimore: Johns Hopkins Univ. Press, 1985), pp. 31–62; hereinafter cited parenthetically in the text.

zation inside out, just as his "only grudge against nature was that I could not turn my Lolita inside out and apply voracious lips to her young matrix, her unknown heart, her nacreous liver, the seagrapes of her lungs, her comely twin kidneys" (151). She is the *femme morcélée par excellence*. The incestuous father-as-his-own-child: he feasts on the female body, sucking Lolita's flat breasts and "brown rose." In Lacanian terms, "Lolita" is little more than a signifier in Humbert's Image-repertoire, and Humbert's revealing allusion to her heart being "unknown" highlights how illusory his project (and his projections) are. Her sole function is to reflect and satisfy the body of the father. Initially, she has no reality for him except as the incarnation of his childhood love, Annabel Leigh; Lolita is little more than a replication of a photographic still. He wishes he had filmed her; he longs to have a frozen moment permanently on celluloid since he could not hold her still in life. She is thus the object of his appropriation, and he not only appropriates her but projects onto her his desire and his neuroses. Significantly, she only serves as a simulacrum when her nicknames—Lolita, Lo, Lola, Dolly—are used, for her legal name, Dolores, points too directly toward another representation—Our Lady of Sorrows—and thus to a higher law than man's. An abyss lies between the "Lolita" who is a purely imaginary product of Humbert's desire and the "Dolores" whose "guardian" is the source of her suffering.

READING DIALOGICALLY: *LOLITA'S* OTHER ANALOGUES

John Ray's foreword and Nabokov's afterword are diametrically opposed monologic readings. By exposing the weaknesses in such readings, one discovers what feminist criticism stands to gain by dismantling the representational fallacy. I should like to propose a dialogic reading, one that is both feminist and intertextual; one that releases the female body from its anesthesia and from Humbert's solipsism while simultaneously highlighting textual artifice. Nabokov, I would argue, is not writing in either the one mode or the other: he is writing a book that elides the female by framing the narrative through Humbert's angle of vision. He then comments indirectly on that framing device by references not to "real life" but to other literary texts. That the novel is an exercise in intertextuality, however, does not mitigate the horror of Lolita's treatment. Instead, it reinforces it. Among the multiple levels of intertextuality operating in the novel, four in particular deserve mention because they suggest the myriad ways in which the novel allegorizes Woman: the major poems in the courtly love tradition; certain stories and poems of Edgar Allan Poe, Henry James's *The Turn of the Screw*, and Charles Dickens's *Bleak House*.

The Handmaid's Tale, as we shall see presently, reveals that the effort to define Woman through binary oppositions (whore/madonna, victim/ devourer, witch/angel, etc.) has been a popular pastime through the ages. *Lolita* is, among other things, a compendium of definitions of Woman, in texts ranging from *Know Your Own Daughter* and *The Little Mermaid* to *Carmen* and *Le roman de la rose*. As in the courtly love tradition, Humbert moves from adoration to disillusionment when the beloved fails to measure up to his code of perfection. Like the knights who celebrated the chastity of the lady and the difficulty of their endeavors, Humbert boasts of his difficulties when he masturbates with Lolita on his lap. In contrast to his idealized "lady," "real" women are miserly, envious, fickle, loudmouthed, drunkards (like Rita, the drunk with whom Humbert lives after Lolita flees), or slaves to their bellies (like Valeria, the "brainless baba" who is Humbert's first wife). As he reveals when he insists that Lolita has no will or life of her own, Humbert denies not just what is womanly in Lolita—he denies what is human.[14] That is why he must insist that nymphets are demonic, and it is the myth of demonic children that ties the novel to James's *Turn of the Screw*.

Nabokov confesses, "My feelings towards James are rather complicated. I really dislike him intensely but now and then the figure in the phrase, the *turn* of the epithet, the *screw* of an absurd adverb, cause me a kind of electric tingle, as if some current of his was also passing through my own blood."[15] James said that he devised *The Turn of the Screw* as a trap to catch the "jaded, the disillusioned, the fastidious" reader—in other words, the reader who fancies himself or herself as being beyond sentimentality.[16] Similarly, so-

14. Frederick W. Shilstone, "The Courtly Misogynist: Humbert Humbert in *Lolita*," *Studies in the Humanities* 8 (June 1980): 5–10.

15. Appel, Jr., "An Interview with Vladimir Nabokov," in Dembo, *Nabokov*, pp. 19–44; emphasis added.

16. Henry James, *The Art of the Novel*, intro. Richard P. Blackmur (New York: Scribner's, 1934), p. 172. For a discussion of the tale as an elegiac reaccentuation of sentimental fiction, see Kauffman, *Discourses of Desire*, chap. 6.

phisticated readers of *Lolita*, avid to align themselves with "aesthetic bliss," fall into precisely the same trap by ignoring the pathos of Lolita's predicament. James said his subject was "the helpless plasticity of childhood: that *was* my little tragedy."[17] For Nabokov as for James, "plasticity" is the medium enabling one to create aesthetic bliss. But "plasticity" has other connotations: to mold, to form, to fix. The governess in *The Turn of the Screw* tries to arrest the children's development; the desire to "fix" things indeed is one of her motives for writing her retrospective narrative. She wants to frame time itself, just as Humbert desires "to fix the perilous magic of nymphets." In both texts—indeed throughout Poe and Dickens as well as James—how and what you see depends on the frame: James's governess anticipates Humbert by resorting to a fancy prose style to frame a murder.[18] "Aesthetic bliss" is a frameup. In both the governess's narrative and in Humbert's, silence, exile, and cunning lie in that gap between past and present and determine what inflection will be given to the murder of childhood. As Poe asks in *Lenore*, "How *shall* the ritual then be read?—the requiem how be sung / By you—by yours, the evil eye—by yours the slanderous tongue / That did to death the innocence that died and died so young?"[19]

To recognize that violence, one must first defuse the charge that any lament for the murder of Lolita's childhood is sheer sentimentality, a willful misreading of a novel meant to parody such attitudes. Lecturing at Cornell, Nabokov himself defused the charge, noting that Dickens's *Bleak House* deals "mainly with the misery of little ones, with the pathos of childhood— and Dickens is at his best in these matters."[20] Nabokov emphasizes the astonishing number of children in the novel—he counts over thirty—and says that "one of the novel's most striking themes" is "their troubles, insecurity, humble joys . . . but mainly their misery" (65). Their parents are

17. Henry James to Dr. Louis Waldstein, 21 October 1898, in *The Turn of the Screw*, ed. Robert Kimbrough (New York: W. W. Norton, 1966), p. 110.

18. For evidence that James's governess murders Miles, see Kauffman, *Discourses of Desire*, chap. 6.

19. Edgar Allan Poe, "Lenore," in *Poetry and Tales* (New York: Library of America, 1984), p. 69.

20. Vladimir Nabokov, *Lectures on Literature*, ed. Fredson Bowers, intro. John Updike (New York: Harcourt Brace Jovanovich, 1980), p. 83; hereinafter cited parenthetically in the text.

either "frauds or freaks" (69). And then he says something that will surprise contemporary readers:

> I should not like to hear the charge of sentimentality made against this strain that runs through *Bleak House*. I want to submit that people who denounce the sentimental are generally unaware of what sentiment is. . . . Dickens's great art should not be mistaken for a cockney version of the seat of emotion—it is the real thing, keen, subtle, specialized compassion, with a grading and merging of melting shades, with the very accent of profound pity in the words uttered, and with an artist's choice of the most visible, most audible, most tangible epithets. (86–87)

His allusion to "grading and merging of melting shades, with the very accent of profound pity," echo a poignant and revealing sentence about Lolita's temperament—that temperament to which critics like Trilling and Molnar claim no reader has access. After he overhears Lolita commenting that "what is so dreadful about dying is that you are completely on your own," Humbert realizes that "[b]ehind the awful juvenile clichés, there was in her a garden and a twilight, and a palace gate—dim and adorable regions which happened to be lucidly and absolutely forbidden to me, in my polluted rags and miserable convulsions, . . . living as we did, she and I, in a world of total evil" (259).

In his lecture on *Bleak House*, Nabokov goes on to contrast Skimpole, who *represents* a child, with the real children in the novel who are overburdened with adult cares and duties, like Charley, the little girl who supports all her little brothers and sisters. Dickens writes, "She might have been a child, playing at washing, and imitating a poor workingwoman." And Nabokov observes, "Skimpole is a vile parody of a child, whereas this little girl is a pathetic imitator of an adult woman" (86). The same is true of Humbert; like Skimpole, he imitates a child. It is Humbert, after all, who wants to play forever in his "pubescent park, in my mossy garden. Let them play around me forever. Never grow up" (22). It is Humbert who talks baby talk to Lolita—never she to him.[21] Thus, if parody serves as a "springboard," it can also be a "vile" screen for "total evil."

---

21. See James R. Pinnells, "The Speech Ritual as an Element of Structure in Nabokov's *Lolita*," *Dalhousie Review* 60 (Winter 1980–81): 605–21. Pinnells points out that in the speech rituals in *Lolita*, two realities come in conflict: average reality and Humbert's solipsism. Lolita

In contrast to Humbert's grotesque imitation of a child, Lolita is forced to imitate adult womanhood by performing "wifely" duties before she gets her coffee. In the very act of trying to fix her forever in childhood, Humbert not only stunts her growth but makes her old before her time. Her fate is presaged by Humbert's transactions with the whore Monique; he is briefly attracted to her nymphet qualities, but she grows less juvenile, more womanly overnight: only for a minute does "a delinquent nymphet [shine] through the matter-of-fact young whore" (24). The power of the image is one of the novel's dominant themes, for far from being in love with Lolita, Humbert is completely obsessed with the mental image he incessantly projects with random girls and women. From the moment he first masturbates on the couch, Humbert proceeds to turn Lolita into a whore, euphemistically alluding to her vagina as a "new white purse," and priding himself upon having left it "intact." By the time they reach the Enchanted Hunters Motel, he has begun paying her with pennies and dimes to perform sexually.

Father-daughter incest, as Judith Lewis Herman points out, is a relationship of prostitution: "The father, in effect, forces the daughter to pay with her body for affection and care which should be freely given. In so doing, he destroys the protective bond between parent and child and initiates his daughter into prostitution. This is the reality of incest from the point of view of the victim."[22] The victim's viewpoint in *Lolita* is elided, for rather than claiming any responsibility himself, Humbert defines his bribes as a "definite drop in Lolita's morals" (167). The fact that she ups the ante from fifteen cents to four dollars has been seen by misogynist critics as a sign that she was a whore all along. Humbert once again reveals his obsession with his own body and once again astutely sizes up readers' allegiances when he exclaims: "O Reader . . . imagine me, on the very rack of joy noisily emitting dimes . . . and great big silver dollars like some sonorous, jingly and wholly

---

is seldom allowed to speak in her own voice, but when she does, she effectively shatters Humbert's fantasies and exposes his lies, distortions, and duplicity. The best example of Pinnells's thesis is the scene at the Enchanted Hunters Motel, when Humbert speaks euphemistically about fathers and daughters sharing hotel rooms: " 'Two people sharing one room, inevitably enter into a kind—how shall I say—a kind—' 'The word is incest,' said Lo" (110–11).

22. Judith Lewis Herman, *Father-Daughter Incest* (Cambridge, Mass.: Harvard Univ. Press, 1981), p. 4.

demented machine vomiting riches; and in the margin of that leaping epi-lepsy she would firmly clutch a handful of coins in her little fist" (168).

Humbert implicitly assumes that his (male?) readers will identify solely with his sexuality and sensibility. Since he presents himself as a schlemiel, the comic urge to identify with him is almost irresistible. The hilarity, how-ever, is considerably undercut when we realize that Lolita is trying to accu-mulate enough money to run away—an escape Humbert thwarts by periodically ransacking her room and robbing her.

Nor can one ignore what materialist critiques of the novel expose: the rampant consumerism of postwar American society, a society that feeds on images rather than beliefs. Lolita is the ideal consumer: naive, spoiled, to-tally hooked on the gadgets of modern life, a true believer in the promises of Madison Avenue and Hollywood. Yet a materialist-*feminist* perspective en-ables one to see something seldom noted: Lolita is as much the object con-sumed by Humbert as she is the product of her culture. And if she is "hooked," he is the one who turns her into a hooker. She is the object of both his conspicuous consumption and concupiscence, as his voracious desire to devour her heart, liver, lungs, and kidneys demonstrates. When he sees a dismembered mannikin in a department store, Humbert comments vaguely that "it's a good symbol for something," and "Dolly Haze" (one of Lolita's many nicknames) comes more and more to resemble those mute, inanimate dolls on whose bodies consumer wares are hung. By the time of their final reunion in Gray Star, she has been so thoroughly prostituted that she as-sumes Humbert will only relinquish her rightful inheritance if she sexually services him in a motel.

What is most astounding about Ray's preface is that, despite his alleged interest in "reality," he says none of these things. He never once names in-cest; instead he refers to it as that "special experience" and insists that " 'of-fensive' is frequently but a synonym for 'unusual' " (7). While ostensibly reading Humbert's narrative as a "case history" and unctuously referring to its "ethical impact," he notes that, if Humbert had undergone psychiatric treatment, "there would have been no disaster; but then, neither would there have been this book" (7). Ray's disturbing statement reveals an utter disregard for Lolita's suffering. He effaces her entirely; "Lolita" is merely the title of a narrative by which he is "entranced." By thus focusing solely

on Humbert's "supreme misery," Ray becomes Humbert's dupe. In chart-
ing Humbert's quest, he replicates his crime. Is Lolita anywhere to be found
in the text?

IS THERE A WOMAN IN THE TEXT?

What effect does incest have on Lolita? The first act of coitus is rendered so
poetically as to camouflage what is being described; importantly, it is one of
the few passages depicting the sensations of Lolita's body rather than Humbert's. He describes it *as if* it were a painting: "a slave child [trying] to climb
a column of onyx . . . a fire opal dissolving within a ripple-ringed pool, a
last throb, a last dab of color, stinging red, smarting pink, a sigh, a wincing
child" (124). Aesthetic form distances us from Lolita's pain, diverting our
attention from content: Lolita is enslaved, bleeding, and in such pain that
she cannot sit because Humbert has torn something inside her. Humbert's
aesthetic response, however, cannot completely disguise the fact that with
this act Lolita's aborted childhood is left behind forever: she learns that her
mother is dead and realizes that she has nowhere else to go. In contrast to
conventional criticism, which divides the first part of the novel from the second part in terms of such dichotomies as illusion/reality or dream/night-
mare, all such framing devices invariably elide Lolita herself. Whether part
one focuses on Humbert's body and part two on his misery, Humbert remains the focus: his suffering, his sensations, his sex and sensibility. The
crucial dichotomy involves the shift in Humbert's role from Charlotte's
lover to Lolita's father, from artful lodger to evil guardian. Perhaps the
novel's most profound paradox is that Humbert cannot violate Lolita sexually until he assumes the societally sanctioned role of stepfather. The novel
systematically exposes the relentless familialism of American behavioral
science and psychology, with its obsessive insistence on "normalcy" in the
nuclear family. By conflating that familialism with the literary clichés of
romantic love, both ideologies are grotesquely defamiliarized.

John Ray's foreword is a parody of responses that might lead the reader
to inquire about the relation of fictional representations of incest to clinical
analyses. In that regard, it acts once again as an injunction, prohibiting the
reader from inquiring into "reality." But readers who defy that prohibition
discover that the novel is an uncannily accurate representation of father-

daughter incest. Not surprisingly, the clinical literature reveals that step-fathers are guilty of incest as often as natural fathers are. Carol Lynn Mithers points out: "Researchers estimate that as many as twelve to fifteen million American women have suffered incestuous abuse; about half of these cases involves fathers or stepfathers."[23] The overwhelming majority of children experience no pleasure in the act; and even later in life, as mature women, they are seldom able to enjoy sexual relations.[24] The fact that Lolita similarly feels nothing for Humbert is repeatedly presented as a black mark against her: "Never," Humbert confesses, "did she vibrate under my touch," and for this "crime," he dubs her "My Frigid Princess." And he realizes that "she was ready to turn away from [me] with something akin to plain repulsion" (152). But her response is not *akin* to repulsion, it *is* repulsion, and the difference is one of Humbert's characteristic strategies of evasion. Elsewhere, he describes their existence as a "parody of incest," but within the fictional framework the incest is literal, not parodic. Nabokov's framing device parodies Ray's reading of the novel as a case history, but he also ensures that we only think of one kind of case—that of obsessional love. The fact that he never mentions incest is no accident. Parody, which prohibits inquiry into "real cases," also prohibits us from asking, "Whose case is it, anyway?"

Humbert's jealousy, his tyranny inside the home balanced by his ineffectuality and obsequiousness outside it, the threats of reform school or punishment if Lolita reports him—these are all patterns of incest documented clinically as well as textually. To enjoy not Lolita but his fantasies, Humbert decides to "ignore what I could not help perceiving, the fact that I was to her not a boy friend, not a glamour man, not a pal, not even a person at all, but just two eyes and a foot of engorged brawn" (258). Humbert's exaggeration of the size of his penis may be male wish fulfillment or male penis envy, but in either case the exaggeration emphasizes male desire rather than the phys-

23. Carol Lynn Mithers, "Incest and the Law," *New York Times Magazine*, 21 October 1990, pp. 44, 53, 58, 62–63; see also Catharine A. MacKinnon, *Feminism Unmodified: Discourses on Life and Law* (Cambridge, Mass.: Harvard Univ. Press, 1987). MacKinnon argues that "one of two hundred of us, conservatively estimated, is sexually molested as a child by her father. When brothers, stepfathers, uncles, and friends of the family are included, some estimate that the rates rise to two out of five," p. 23. See also p. 197, below.

24. Herman, chaps. 5–7.

ical pain that the disparity between his physical proportions and Lolita's must cause her. The allusion to his eyes is revealing, for Humbert voyeuristically measures every aspect of Lolita's physical development. "Has she already been initiated by mother nature to the Mystery of the Menarche?" he asks (45).

Critics usually cite Humbert's obsessive scrutiny of Lolita's body as further evidence that the novel is a love story; instead, such obsessions are typical of father-daughter incest, signs not of overpowering love but of domination. Humbert spies on Lolita, monitors her every movement, subjects her to endless inquisitions about her whereabouts, her girlfriends, and potential boyfriends in a pattern common to incest. The father tyrannically controls the daughter's actions, is insanely jealous of boys, and strives to isolate her as much as possible from the rest of the world.[25] Humbert can only conceive of fatherhood tyrannically, as when he subjects Lolita to parental interrogations: Why has she missed two piano lessons? Who is she talking to when she disappears for twenty-eight minutes? His obsession with the names of all her schoolmates and acquaintances culminates in the crucial question he asks her in Gray Star about her rescuer/abductor's identity: "Where is he? . . . Come, his name?" (247). His dominant mode of discourse and of parenting is inquisitorial.[26]

Critics who condemn Lolita as wanton misunderstand the significance of Humbert's compulsion, for in philosophical terms it is he who is wanton rather than Lolita. As Harry K. Frankfurt explains, free will involves the freedom to have the will one wants. Those, like Humbert, who lack such freedom, are "wanton": "The essential characteristic of a wanton is that he does not care about his will. His desires move him to do certain things, without its being true of him either that he wants to be moved by those desires or that he prefers to be moved by other desires."[27] Humbert's sexual craving compels him to abuse Lolita, and while he insists that he does not want to be moved by such desires, he is never able to cease violating her sexually or psychically.

His mania for making Lolita reveal herself and respond to him demon-

25. Ibid., chap. 5.

26. Pinnells, pp. 612, 618.

27. Harry K. Frankfurt, "Freedom of the Will and the Concept of a Person," in *Free Will*, ed. Gary Watson (New York: Oxford Univ. Press, 1982), pp. 81–95.

strates that she is not—nor was she ever—"safely solipsized." The word he uses most frequently to describe his violation of her is "operation," but an operation in which Lolita is never really completely anesthetized either psychically or physically: "The operation was over, all over, and she was weeping . . . a salutory storm of sobs after one of the fits of moodiness that had become so frequent with her in the course of that otherwise admirable year!" (154). Her "sobs in the night,—every night, every night" (160), the moodiness that Humbert finds unfathomable, her powerlessness to escape him when she says, "Oh no, not again!"—all point to a despair that surpasses his powers of description—or so he claims. But from *The Sorrows of Young Werther* to *The Turn of the Screw*, guilty narrators have taken refuge in the ineffable: whatever they want to evade they claim is impossible to describe. The ineffable—like the inevitable (nicknamed "McFate" by Humbert)—is invariably an evasion. In one such passage, Humbert says that Lolita has "a look I cannot exactly describe—an expression of helplessness so perfect that it seemed to grade into one of rather comfortable inanity just because this was the very limit of injustice and frustration" (258).

Does such a statement imply that Humbert finally perceives the enormity of his crimes against Lolita? Not until Humbert is entrapped by Quilty does he begin to comprehend his injustice, for as Thoreau said, "How much more eloquently and effectively he can combat injustice who has experienced a little in his own person." Quilty "succeeded in thoroughly enmeshing me and my thrashing anguish in his demoniacal game. With infinite skill, he swayed and staggered, and regained an impossible balance, always leaving me with . . . betrayal, fury, desolation, horror and hate" (227). Quilty is the doppelganger, the figure traditionally presented not just as a double but as a brother, with whom one has the usual rivalry of siblings, according to Freud. As doppelganger, Quilty is the figure onto whom Humbert projects his guilt in an attempt to evade responsibility for the crime of incest. Freud suggests that the aim of the incest taboo is not to protect female children but to control male sexual rivalry. Lolita functions as the object of exchange between Quilty and Humbert, who are mirror images, locked in a Girardian triangle of mimetic desire.[28] Each wants what the

---

28. See René Girard, *Deceit, Desire, and the Novel: Self and Other in Literary Structure*, trans. Yvonne Freccéro (Baltimore: Johns Hopkins Univ. Press, 1965).

other wants: "[Quilty's] condition," says Humbert, "infected me" (271).[29] In pursuing Lolita, Humbert plays three roles: avenging father, jealous lover, and rival scholar. The latter role torments him most, for as Humbert embarks on his "cryptogrammic paper chase," he is indignant that Quilty "challenged my scholarship" in motel registers across the country; furious that Quilty's anagrams "ejaculate in my face" (228). While that is an experience Lolita probably shared in Humbert's hands, her perspective has no place in this confrontation of rivals. (That, indeed, is the problem with Girard's theory of mimetic desire: the female is always lost in translation.)[30]

In "The Springboard of Parody," Appel compares *Lolita* to Poe's "William Wilson," another "first-person confession by a pseudonymous narrator who fled in vain" from the Double who pursued him from school to school; like those doubles, "Humbert and Quilty are rivals in scholarship rather than love" (125). In their final confrontation, Humbert can no longer distinguish his own body from Quilty's: "I rolled over him. We rolled over me. They rolled over him. We rolled over us." Humbert describes the struggle as a "silent, soft, formless tussle on the part of two literati" (272). This competition between two second-rate talents disguises the fact that, even if they had been *first*-rate, their struggle would have been equally senseless, since it fails to undo the crimes against Lolita. Aesthetic bliss is not a criterion that compensates for those crimes; instead it is a dead end, meager consolation for the murder of Lolita's childhood. Conventional readings based on sin, confession, and redemption argue that Humbert exacts revenge be-

29. In *Totem and Taboo,* trans. James Strachey (London: Routledge and Kegan Paul, 1950), Freud states that

> anyone who has violated a taboo becomes taboo himself because he possesses the dangerous quality of tempting others to follow his example: why should he be allowed to do what is forbidden to others? Thus he is truly contagious in that every example encourages imitation, and for that reason he himself must be shunned.
>
> But a person who has not violated any taboo may yet be permanently or temporarily taboo because he is in a state which possesses the quality of arousing forbidden desires in others and of awakening a conflict of ambivalence in them. (32)

30. For feminist critiques of mimetic desire and male rivalry, see Michelle Richman, "Eroticism in the Patriarchal Order," *Diacritics* 6 (1976): 46–53; Mary Jacobus, "Is There a Woman in This Text?" *New Literary History* 14 (Autumn 1982): 117–42; and Toril Moi, "The Missing Mother: The Oedipal Rivalries of René Girard," *Diacritics* 12 (Summer 1982): 21–31.

cause Quilty broke Lolita's heart. But Humbert's vengeance is more egotistic: Quilty out-authored him. Quilty turned Humbert into a character in his script, which is precisely what Humbert does to Lolita. Armed with the tattered totemic photograph of his childhood love, Annabel Leigh, he "reincarnates" her image and superimposes it on Lolita. In his avid pursuit of immortality through art, he studies Poe's dictum that the death of a beautiful woman is "the most poetical topic in the world—and . . . that the lips best suited for such topic are those of a bereaved lover."[31]

Indeed, even in his last scene with Lolita, Humbert continues to interrogate her as if she were his legal possession, to interpret her as if she were a frozen image, a blank page. He is still talking *at* her. When she says that she would sooner go back to Quilty than leave now with Humbert, he writes, "She groped for words. I supplied them mentally (*"He* broke my heart. *You* merely broke my life") (254).[32] The narrative we read is an exercise in what Humbert calls "poetical justice"—but it is so only for himself, not for Lolita—although he never points this out. He writes simultaneously to set the record straight, to settle the score, and to ensure that the last word is his. But like all his other attempts to possess, to control, to fix, and to frame, this one, too, reveals his sterility and impotence—for while he has the last word on Quilty, John Ray has the last word on him. ("For better or worse, it is the commentator who has the last word," says Kinbote in *Pale Fire*.)[33] Humbert appropriates visibility, vulnerability, carnality for himself, and in so doing, he evacuates Lolita's body, turning it into a projective site for his neuroses and his narrative.

Humbert's notoriously poor circulation finally leads to coronary thrombosis; his heart proves to be as unreliable as his narrative is. His heart prompts him to declare that he has fallen in love forever, but he adds, "The word 'forever' referred only to my own passion, to eternal Lolita *as reflected in my blood*" (67; emphasis added). His is a closed circulatory system, sol-

31. Edgar Allan Poe, "The Philosophy of Composition," in *Essays and Reviews* (New York: Library of America, 1984), p. 19.

32. Clinical case studies help to explain Quilty's appeal for Lolita: incest victims tend to overvalue and idealize men, to seek out men who resemble their fathers (men who are older, or married, or indifferent to them), thereby compulsively reenacting the familiar pattern of exploitation and debasement. See Herman, chap. 2.

33. Vladimir Nabokov, *Pale Fire* (1962; reprinted New York: Berkeley Books, 1977), p. 12.

ipsistic and narcissistic. Like Goethe, Nabokov perceived that epistolarity was the perfect vehicle to mirror that claustrophobia. Humbert fathers nobody. Lolita only exists insofar as she can reflect him, magnifying his stature. "The refuge of art" for Humbert is the mirror of castration for Lolita, a polarity clearly exposed in her tennis game. Humbert appreciates it aesthetically: "[H]er form was, indeed, an absolutely perfect imitation of absolutely top-notch tennis . . . it had . . . beauty, directness, youth, a classical purity of trajectory" (211). But her form lacks—as does she herself—feeling, force, conviction, for she has no will to win. Sex with Humbert has taught her too well merely to mime, without enthusiasm.

By thus inscribing the female body in the text, rather than consigning it to the hazy and dolorous realm of abstract male desire, or letting it circulate as the currency of exchange between male rivals, one discovers that Lolita is not a photographic image, or a still life, or a freeze-frame preserved on film but a damaged child. This is what Humbert's own humiliation at the hands of Quilty enables him finally to perceive: the "semi-animated, subhuman trickster who had sodomized my darling" (269) turns out to be not Quilty but himself. Quilty is not far wrong to insist that Humbert is "a beastly pervert" and that he, Quilty, is "not responsible for the rapes of others" (271).

One crucial distinction is between Humbert the focus, trapped in chronological time, and Humbert the voice,[34] writing from jail, composing his death sentences: "Had not something within her been broken by me— *not that I realized it then!*—she would have had on the top of her perfect form the will to win" (212). If in part one his sole obsession is with his lust, he is in part two still utterly self-absorbed: his guilt and his misery are his themes: "*my* heart and *my* beard, and *my* putrefaction" (258). Humbert challenges the reader to prove to him that "in the infinite run it does not matter a jot that a North American girl-child named Dolores Haze had been deprived of her childhood by a maniac . . . (and if it can, then life is a joke), I see nothing for the treatment of my misery but the melancholy and very local palliative of articulate art" (258).

---

34. On temporal differences between narrative focus and voice, see Gérard Genette, *Narrative Discourse: An Essay in Method*, trans. Jane E. Lewin (Ithaca: Cornell Univ. Press, 1980), pp. 180–83, 206–7, 255.

The thirty-five-year sentence he imposes on himself for rape sounds harsh, but it actually lets him off the hook for other murders besides Quilty's: Lolita's death in childbirth and her stillborn baby's demise are anticipated as early as the first act of intercourse with Humbert when he feels "as if I were sitting with the small ghost of somebody I had just killed" (129). "Palliative," moreover, is yet another of Nabokov's Jamesian traps for the reader, for it can mean either to "lessen the pain without curing," or "to make appear less serious or offensive." Humbert is guilty on both counts, and while he takes refuge in the sham lyricism of articulating his shame, for Lolita the rest is silence.

Is there, then, a woman in this text—and in what sense is that question meant? For Shoshana Felman, it is allegorical:

> The allegorical question "She? Who?" will thus remain unanswered. The text, nonetheless, will play out the question to its logical end, so as to show in what way it *precludes* any answer, in what way the question is set as a trap. The very lack of the answer will then write itself as a different question, through which the original question will find itself dislocated, radically shifted and transformed.[35]

The feminist critic can expose the lack, the trap, and the frameup by reading symptomatically. She can dismantle the misogyny of traditional critical assessments of Lolita's "wantonness" by analyzing the precise nature of Humbert's craving. A feminist perspective thus shifts suspicion from Lolita to Humbert, for his organs—"heart," penis, eyes—expose his hysteria, treachery, and delusions. As Patrocinio Schwiekart explains, feminist criticism must pay attention to material realities in order to effect social change: "Feminist criticism . . . is a mode of *praxis*. The point is not merely to interpret literature in various ways; the point is to *change the world*" (39). But feminist theory also deconstructs language and signification, analyzing not just representations but the manifest and latent mechanisms of representation. On the one hand, feminist criticism can inscribe the female body in the text and, on the other hand, show how that textual body is *fabricated*—in both senses of the world—as a fiction and as a construct. One can unveil Lolita's viewpoint and simultaneously stress its verisimilitude—

---

35. Shoshana Felman, "Women and Madness: The Critical Phallacy," *Diacritics* 4 (Winter 1975): 2–10.

as opposed to its *veracity:* "Is it possible," Nabokov asks, "to imagine in its full reality the life of another, to live it oneself and transfer it intact onto paper? I doubt it . . . it can only be the verisimilar, and not the verifiable truth, that the mind perceives. . . . What we call art is, in essence, truth's picture window: one has to know how to frame it, that's all. "[36]

Framed between Ray's foreword and Nabokov's spurious afterword, Humbert's narrative fixes our attention on "love" as the vehicle for artistic immortality. Paradoxically, the more he mocks his own prose style, the more we notice its beauty and endorse the Humbertian aesthetic manifesto of "aesthetic bliss." By seeing how the framing of *Lolita* elides the issue of father-daughter incest, one shifts and transforms the questions, revealing how the father's sexuality is superimposed upon the daughter's body. The most eloquent testimony of the results comes from Lolita herself. In one of the few instances where she speaks in her own voice (which is as stark in its simplicity as Humbert's is baroque), she sends Humbert a brief letter from Gray Star: "I have gone through much sadness and hardship" (243).

The female subject need not disappear, despite poststructuralism's relativizing of relations between writer, reader, and critic, for the feminist critic can exploit that notion of relativity. Although Humbert's cunning aesthetic manifesto has been blithely endorsed by generations of critics, it is itself relative, which is why I have tried to defamiliarize it here. Since the foreword parodies case histories, we tend to forget that "representation *does* bear a relation to something which we can know previously existed."[37] Specifically, the incestuous father's tyranny is clinically verifiable in this novel. Nor does the subject's decentering invalidate the notion of agency: despite his insistence on *jouissance,* Humbert remains culpable. Deconstructive strategies, in fact, help to expose multiple frames of reference: the intertextual allusions to Dickens, Poe, and James (all dealing with the exploitation and death of children and childhood) undermine the purely aesthetic approach to the novel. Clinical studies of incest further expose Humbert's rhe-

---

36. Vladimir Nabokoff-Sirine, "Pouchkine ou le vrai et le vraisemblable," *La Nouvelle Revue Francaise* 48 (1937): 362–78, trans. Dale Peterson in "Nabokov's Invitation: Literature as Execution," *PMLA* 96 (October 1981): 824–36.

37. Michèle Barrett, "Ideology and the Cultural Production of Gender," in *Feminist Criticism and Social Change: Sex, Class, and Race in Literature and Culture,* ed. Judith Newton and Deborah Rosenfelt (London: Methuen, 1985), p. 70.

torical ruses. By combining feminist with deconstructive strategies, one discovers that the novel Trilling heralded as the greatest love story of the twentieth century in fact indicts the ideology of love and exposes literature's complicity in perpetuating it. The answer to the question, "Is there a woman in this text?" is no. But there was a female, one whose body was the source of crimes and puns, framed unsettlingly between the horror of incest and aesthetic *jouissance*, between material reality and antimimesis, between pathos and parody. That body was not a woman's; like Lolita's stillborn baby, it was a girl's.

Dangerous Liaisons: Roland Barthes's
A Lover's Discourse and
Jacques Derrida's The Post Card

I f *Lolita* enables us to see how to combine deconstructive strategies of decentering with a feminist critique of agency, Barthes and Derrida show what feminism stands to gain by questioning the connections between gender and identity. Shklovsky may keen the death of story, plot, and character in *Zoo*; *A Lover's Discourse* and *The Post Card* hammer the nails into the coffin. In multiple senses, *A Lover's Discourse* and *The Post Card* are wakes, simultaneously commemorating and contributing to the deaths of the author, of "Literature," and of the unitary subject. Both texts are archeological "desedimentations" of Western mythologies about literature and culture. Their aim is to stretch language to its limits and "beyond"—beyond the pleasure principle, beyond the narratable, beyond the constraints of genre and gender. Most remarkable of all: they try to go beyond totalizing theories—including even poststructuralism, on those occasions when it threatens to become potentially totalizing. Just as Shklovsky goes beyond Russian Formalism in *Zoo*, Barthes and Derrida expose the aporias of poststructuralism in these two texts. It is as if they unweave by night the theories they weave by day, a metaphor they each consciously invoke. Their projects overlap in numerous ways, but in this chapter I will focus soley on two major switch points (what Derrida calls "coup d'aiguillage"): (a) their strategies and motives for reaccentuating epistolarity, and (b) the ways in which Woman is "produced" in these texts. This double project distinguishes these two texts from all the rest of their work: nowhere else do they confront epistolarity so directly, while simultaneously miming and mining the *topos* of femininity so systematically.

THE PRODUCTION OF THE TEXT

Barthes's style in *A Lover's Discourse* is epigrammatic and aphoristic, reminiscent of Pascal's *Pensées*, La Rochefoucauld's maxims, La Bruyère's pithy paradoxes. His discourse is neither a scholarly exegesis, interpretation, or debate; instead, he invites readers to intervene in assembling and reassembling the text. His discourse is a dialogue with other texts and friends whose insights are memorialized in the margins. Whereas Barthes's style is conversational, allusive, and elusive, Derrida's is more consistently a meticulous deconstruction of Western metaphysics, philosophy, and psychoanalysis. His discourse is also dialogic, and it, too, is frequently conversational. But where Barthes is brief and genial, Derrida is exhaustive and (particularly where Lacan is concerned) combative. Both amorous discourses are paradoxically intimate and theoretical, autobiographical and fictive.

Since few would confuse Barthes's characteristic style with Derrida's, the similarities between these two amorous discourses are all the more startling. They both begin by defamiliarizing the production of the text. Barthes prefaces his fragments by explaining "How this book is constructed."[1] Whereas in *S/Z*, Barthes disassembles and reassembles the codes of the Symbolic, in *A Lover's Discourse* he performs a similar operation with/in the Imaginary.[2] He demonstrates that the most private and inviolate of

1. Roland Barthes, *A Lover's Discourse*, p. 3.

2. Stephen Heath, "Barthes on Love," *Sub-Stance* 37/38 (1983): 100–106. One must remember that the Imaginary is not simply the polar opposite of the Real; instead, all images (conscious and unconscious) are registered in the Imaginary, whether the images are actually perceived or imagined. Also crucial is the notion that the Imaginary is constituted by its rela-

emotions—love—follows certain codes and conventions; it is as carefully structured as language itself. His is an antiliterary text consisting of figures rather than characters. As in *Zoo*, these figures are

> non-syntagmatic, non-narrative . . . distributional but not integrative; they always remain on the same level: the lover speaks in bundles of sentences but does not integrate these sentences on a higher level, into a work; his is a horizontal discourse: no transcendence, no deliverance, no novel (though a great deal of the fictive). (*ALD, 7*)

A Lover's Discourse thus puts into practice Barthes's dominant theories: the text (as opposed to the "work") is open, fluid, nontotalizable. It is an activity, a performance; nothing can be resolved or reduced to a monologic whole. To resist such resolution, Barthes relies on an absolutely arbitrary order: the alphabet. His description of La Rochefoucauld's maxims applies equally to *A Lover's Discourse*, that "the language of the maxim always has a definitional and not a transitive activity; a collection of maxims is always more or less (and this is flagrant in La Rochefoucauld) a dictionary."[3] Barthes combines the static aspects of dictionary entries with the fluid aspects of epistolary spontaneity. He brilliantly manages to mime the epistolary fiction of writing-to-the-moment by making it look as if he has merely composed

---

tion to the image of a counterpart (*le semblable*)—*another who is me*—which helps to explain why Barthes and Derrida place such emphasis on the self-divisions of identity, alterity, counterparts, counterpoint (as in music), and dialogic exchange, as I discuss below. See J. Laplanche and J.-B. Pontalis, *The Language of Psychoanalysis*, trans. Donald Nicholson-Smith (New York: W. W. Norton, 1974), p. 210. Derrida finds far more to quarrel with in Lacan than Barthes does; his thesis in "Le facteur de la vérité" is that everywhere psychoanalysis looks, it finds itself. Responding to Lacan's analysis of Poe's "The Purloined Letter," Derrida argues that Lacan ignores the tale's frame of reference, specifically its relation to two other tales, which Derrida describes as Poe's "Dupin trilogy." Such omissions demonstrate the violence psychoanalysis does to literature in order to assert its own interpretations. Derrida nevertheless echoes numerous ideas from Lacanian psychoanalysis, sometimes miming them for his own purposes, as in the case of his allusions to the mirror stage, discussed below. The philosophical and psychoanalytic debate on love that commences with Lacan's seminar on the love letter in 1975 continues in Julia Kristeva's *Tales of Love* (1987). Although each theorist approaches the topic in entirely different ways, discussion of the full magnitude of those differences lies beyond the scope of my study. I do not devote separate chapters to Lacan and Kristeva because they do not exploit the genre of epistolarity in presenting their theories, in contrast to Barthes and Derrida who consciously represent the medium as the message.

3. Roland Barthes, "La Rochefoucauld: 'Reflections or Sentences and Maxims,'" in *New Critical Essays*, trans. Richard Howard (New York: Hill and Wang, 1980), p. 8.

"outbursts of language, which occur at the whim of trivial, of aleatory circumstances" (*ALD*, 3).

Derrida insists on the fictionality and specularity of his project, too. Like Barthes, he emphasizes the process of reading, the choices readers make, and their defiant, unruly desires:

> You might read these *envois* as the preface to a book that I have not written. . . . I do not know if their reading is bearable. You might consider them, if you really wish to, as the remainders of a recently destroyed correspondence. Destroyed by fire or by that which figuratively takes its place, more certain of leaving nothing out of the reach of what I like to call the tongue of fire, not even the cinders if cinders there are.[4]

The emphasis on desire is particularly notable because Derrida tacitly acknowledges that both the envois and readers are beyond authorial control: *if* they *wish* to, readers may view the letters as the remainder of a destroyed correspondence. To do so, Derrida implies, would be to enter into the fiction of the letters—indeed, the fiction of the entire epistolary tradition—which posits an authentic signature and an intrinsic correspondence between signifier and signified.

Throughout *The Post Card*, Derrida exploits the fiction of found letters, tantalizing the reader with descriptions of the letters that were censored or burned. He simultaneously makes the reader aware of what has been withheld and grateful for what remains. The technique highlights the extent to which epistolarity is written "under erasure" of one sort or another: internal or external censorship, postal inefficiency or political surveillance, or a sheer surplus of writing that nonetheless remains meager: "A correspondence: this is still to say too much, or too little. Perhaps it was not one (but more or less) nor very correspondent. This still remains to be decided" (*PC*, 3). These few words suggest asymmetry between Derrida's letters and his addressee's: neither the correspondence nor the emotions between the lovers seem matched in volume or intensity. These few words speak volumes, evoking the text's indeterminacy, his own lack of intentionality as letter writer, and his willingness to allow writing-to-the-moment to lead him to as

---

4. Jacques Derrida, *The Post Card: From Socrates to Freud and Beyond*, trans. Alan Bass (Chicago: Univ. of Chicago Press, 1980), p. 3; hereinafter cited parenthetically in the text as *PC*.

yet unknown discoveries. For the reader as well as the writer, the undecidable is the provenance of *The Post Card:* one searches in vain for answers to questions one knows are naive but which nonetheless arouse an unquenchable curiosity: Are we reading an authentic correspondence? Was there a real love affair? To whom are the letters addressed? If the addressee is female, who was Derrida's mistress? What *happened?*

Like *Zoo, The Post Card* is filled with retarding devices that consistently thwart the reader's expectations. Derrida frustrates the reader's desire for authenticity and intrigue; identity, after all, is not just unstable but finally undecidable. He stages—rather than answers—the questions, "Who is writing? To whom? And to send, to destine, to dispatch what? To what address?" (*PC*, 5) How is one to judge the sincerity and authenticity of the letter? These are the questions obsessively reiterated by Barthes as well.

Derrida and Barthes follow Shklovsky in defamiliarizing the underlying assumptions of representation by emphasizing how the text is assembled, painstakingly elucidating their principle of selection and organization. Barthes exploits the alphabet in order to break the stranglehold of hierarchies, binary oppositions, and discursive systems on the unconscious. These fragments of discourse cannot be resolved into a unitary, organic whole. Similarly, Derrida rigorously disapproves of the economy of sorting and the principle of selection that destines works for the archive. Playing on the traditional *avis au lecteur,* Derrida delivers a mock lecture:

> This is the way I name or accuse the fearful reader, the reader in a hurry to be determined, decided upon deciding (in order to annul, in other words to bring back to oneself, one has to wish to know in advance what to expect, one wishes to expect what has happened, one wishes to expect (oneself)). Now, it is bad, and I know no other definition of the bad, it is bad to predestine one's reading, it is always bad to foretell. It is bad, reader, no longer to like retracing one's steps. (*PC*, 4)

Not only is it "bad" to dislike retracing one's steps, it is *quixotic,* for reading is rereading, as the very word quixotic implies and as Barthes and Derrida amply illustrate in their rereadings of epistolary classics. They alternately chastize readers for bad habits and habitualization and recognize their complicity with unruly readers. "Ideally," says Barthes, "the book would be a cooperative: 'To the United Readers and Lovers'" (*ALD*, 5). They chastize themselves, too, since, as in all epistolary texts, they are both readers and writers. Not only are both texts exhaustive exercises in "close reading"; both offer a step-by-step representation of the "internal processes of the reading subject."[5] Only by proceeding step-by-step (the French word *pas* reverberates throughout *The Post Card*) can they demonstrate just how relative and fluid the roles are between writer, reader, and critic. "Proceeding step by step" is synonymous with writing-to-the-moment, which is of course the illusion one strives to maintain in epistolary texts; one marvels at how meticulously Barthes and Derrida manage to maintain it in their amorous discourses.

THE DECONSTRUCTION OF STORY AND PLOT

In "From Work to Text," Barthes describes the epistemological shift that undermined authorial privilege. Like Shklovsky before him, Barthes marvels at the profound transformation Einstein wrought in perception and epistemology. After Marx, Freud, and Einstein, we can only see history as narrative, and narrative as production. No new break has occurred since Marx and Freud; instead,

> for the last hundred years we have been living in repetition. What History, our History, allows us today is merely to slide, to vary, to exceed, to repudiate. Just as Einsteinian science demands that the relativity of the frames of reference be included in the object studied, so the combined action of Marxism, Freudianism and structuralism demands, in literature, the relativization of the relations of writer, reader and observer (critic). . . . Here then are these propositions; they concern method, genres, signs, plurality, filiation, reading and pleasure.[6]

That is an apt description of *The Post Card*, for it concerns method, genres, signs, plurality, filiation, reading, and pleasure, too; Derrida is equally obsessed with repetition, recuperation, and subjection to authority. The "postal principle" signifies a vast system of senders and receivers from whom reverence and revenues (stamps, taxes) are exacted, whose origins and destinations are monitored. Numerous double entendres illustrate the complexity of this system: the post is sentinel and a means of surveillance;

5. Frances Bartkowski, "Roland Barthes's Secret Garden," *Studies in Twentieth Century Literature* (Spring 1981): 133–46.

6. Roland Barthes, "From Work to Text," p. 156.

the mailman is a soldier and a factor in the system who guarantees its reliability and veracity ("Le facteur de la vérité"). The modern world of telecommunications signals the end of the epoch of letter writing, a metonymy
for the relativization of relations between author, reader, and critic. Authorial control, identity, and truth may be breaking down, but surveillance
is becoming increasingly sophisticated technologically. Derrida's thesis:
authority is a writing effect; the post, police, literature, philosophy, and
psychoanalysis work in tandem to buttress that authority. Although renun-
ciation is one of the most ancient of literary motifs, Derrida nonetheless
proclaims: "I have renounced literature, everything in it is a post and police
affair, finally, a police station affair" (PC, 144).

With a similar flourish, Barthes dissects the ideology of bourgeois individualism, while simultaneously showing how the novel reinforces it. He
does not just want to defamiliarize the novel as a genre, he wants to undermine realism by laying bare the devices of story, plot, and character:

> If you put the lover in a love story, you reconcile him with society because
> telling stories is a coded activity. Society tames the lover through the love
> story. I took Draconian measures so the book would not be a love story, so the
> lover would be left in his nakedness, a being inaccessible to the usual forms of
> social recuperation, the novel in particular.[7]

His Draconian measures include presenting a running dialogue in the margins, a rich web of intertextual allusions to his reading, music, and conversation with friends. His novel technique of citation exposes the pretensions of
scholarly exegesis (footnotes, bibliography, etc.). He is associative, anti-
linear, alogical. Like Derrida, he subverts our temptations to read for the
plot by insisting that "the language is fragmented, discontinuous, fluttering. . . . I constantly try to break up the construction of any story. . . . My
book is a discontinuous book that protests somewhat against the love story"
(GV, 285–86).

Forcing the question of what a "text" is by defamiliarizing the relation
of center to margin, inside to outside, is a gesture we have now come to recognize as characteristically Derridean, from Of Grammatology to Glas. His
letters begin and end at Oxford University's Bodleian Library where, in a

---

7. Roland Barthes, The Grain of the Voice: Interviews, 1962–1980, pp. 302–3; hereinafter
cited parenthetically in the text as GV.

thirteenth-century fortune-telling book, he first discovers Matthew Paris's illustration, now mass produced as a postcard. He is fascinated by Paris's audacious reversal of "proper" positions: Plato stands behind Socrates, who is seated at a scriptum, writing under the apparent dictation of Plato. The illustration signifies the arbitrariness of the seemingly "natural" order that places Socrates before Plato, presence before absence, speech before writing, an order enforced "from Socrates to Freud and beyond." Not only does Derrida subvert the conventions of citationality, he interrogates the entire notion of "beyond": what does *Beyond the Pleasure Principle* signify? Can one conceive of a *beyond* without relying on origins and endings? Rather than relying on classical narrative theory for answers, he draws upon classical mathematics' theory of sets, a theory of different types of infinities that have had a profound effect on computer languages and telecommunications.

Set theory attempts "to line up intuition with formalized, or axiomatized, reasoning systems."[8] One can see immediately why it would appeal to two theorists who are experimenting with "writing unprotectedly" in intuitive ways usually associated with femininity. Set theory can be seen as applying an ancient philosophical paradox, the Epimenides (or liar) paradox, to mathematics. Since Epimenides was a Cretan, his statement, "All Cretans are liars," displaces the dichotomy between true and false statements. In mathematics, similarly, "All consistent axiomatic formulations of number theory include undecidable propositions" (*GEB*, 17). Drawing on the mathematical figure of "Strange Loops" (similar to Möbius strips or labyrinths), Derrida turns the concepts of undecidability and self-referentiality back on literature, on philosophy, on writing and language itself. His entire project problematizes the relationship of figure to ground, making us aware of recursive figures—those whose ground can be seen as figures in their own right, as in the figure below (*GEB*, 67). "Exergue" in *Of Grammatology* is perhaps the best known deconstructive example of the mutual interdependence of figure and ground: that which is "out" of the work—the space around or below it—demonstrates how framing produces signification.

---

8. Douglas R. Hofstadter, *Gödel, Escher, Bach: An Eternal Golden Braid* (New York: Vintage, 1989), p. 20; hereinafter cited parenthetically in the text as *GEB*. In the discussion of set theory that follows, I am indebted to Hofstadter throughout.

Bertrand Russell's famous paradox regarding the problem that most sets are not members of themselves is also relevant: a set of walruses is not a walrus. Grelling's paradox is an audacious variant of Russell's: what happens when one substitutes adjectives for sets? If we divide adjectives into two categories—self-descriptive, like "pentasyllabic" and "recherche," and those which are not self-descriptive, such as "edible"—in which category would we place the adjective "non–self-descriptive"? (*GEB*, 20–22). Throughout *The Post Card*, Derrida exploits such paradoxes to expose the limits of genre: "(On the topic of my theory of sets and of the family romance, of the entire *set theory* that governs our paradoxes and enlarges us, each one aside from himself, beyond everything. We are beyond everything") (*PC*, 254). By linking the family romance to the theory of sets, Derrida puns on the fixity of Freudian theory; it is both self-referential and set in its ways, not easily displaced. (I shall return to the topic of the Oedipal masterplot.)

Set theory reveals the self's radical alterity: "one" is never wholly self-present; one is inevitably "beside oneself" in multiple senses, including, most notably, in the sense of self-reference. That same alterity applies to language, which is never self-present, fully where it means to be, yet wholly self-referential. Set theory examines the dilemma of distinguishing the identifiable from the self-identical. A metamathematics and a metalogics, set theory can be applied to any self-referential system which simultaneously governs while excluding itself (*GEB*, 23).

Genre is such a system. Set theory underlies Derrida's theory of genres, for what makes a genre distinct and definable are a set of identifiable recurring characteristics. But the trait that enables one to determine genre does not appear in genre itself. As he explains in "The Law of Genre," "the trait that marks membership inevitably divides."[9] Thus, as in set theory, genre

---

9. Jacques Derrida, "La loi du genre/The Law of Genre," trans. Avital Ronell, *Glyph* 7 (Spring 1980): 177–232; hereinafter cited parenthetically in the text as LG.

entails "a sort of participation without belonging—a taking part in without being part of, without having membership in a set" (LG, 206).

"The Law of Genre" is one motor that drives the narrative in *The Post Card*: literally, it is one of the papers Derrida is in the process of writing and delivering as he travels from conference to conference, mailing postcards wherever he goes. Particularly significant is the International Colloquium on Genre, held at the University of Strasbourg in July 1979, for *The Post Card* is filled with allusions to the conference. For example, Friedrich Kittler's "Writing into the Wind, Bettina," about Bettina von Arnim's correspondence with Goethe, is one of Derrida's leitmotifs, an annotated meditation from the archives about masculine fame and feminine desire. Their literal correspondence evokes Goethe's fictional one in *Werther*.[10] "The Law of Genre" sets the stage for Derrida's generic reaccentuation of epistolarity and enables him to stage the paradoxes of set theory. Epistolarity has certain definable traits, but "the epistle . . . is not a genre but all genres, literature itself" (*PC*, 48). "Literature" here includes psychoanalysis and philosophy, which Derrida reads as narratives, deconstructing their rhetorical tropes and underlying assumptions about truth, representation, and the individual subject:

> In the great epoch (whose technology is marked by paper, pen, the envelope, the individual subject addressee, etc.) and which goes shall we say from Socrates to Freud and Heidegger, there are sub-epochs, for example the process of state monopolization, and then within this the invention of the postage stamp and the Berne convention, to use only such insufficient indices. Each epoch has its literature (which in *general* I hold to be essentially detective or epistolary literature, even if within it the detective or epistolary genre strictly folds it back onto itself). (*PC*, 191)

While thus proclaiming the end of the postal epoch, *The Post Card* meticulously reinscribes all the traits that have marked it. Oscillating between valediction and performance, Derrida effectively defers its demise.

The Post Card sets a death sentence for epistolarity, but is composed of sentences that delay its execution, thus demonstrating that it is both paradigm and exception to the rule (law). Like set theory, which is folded into Derrida's theory of genre, epistolarity is a destabilized and destabilizing

---

10. Friedrich Kittler, "Writing into the Wind, Bettina" (paper delivered at the Colloquium on Genre, Strasbourg, 1979), in *Glyph 7* (Spring 1980): 32–69.

concept. Insofar as set theory "governs," it is a contract obeying certain rules of production. "Contract" signifies constriction, containment, legalities that bind. But set theory enlarges as well as contracts by enabling us to observe the law of the supplement at work.

THE DECONSTRUCTION OF CHARACTER AND IDENTITY

In order to deconstruct character and identity, Derrida and Barthes seize on the figure of the lover, since love has traditionally been viewed as epitomizing all that is unique, transcendent, and essential about individual subjectivity. One problem with the English translation of *Fragments d'un discours amoureux* is that, whereas the French title emphasizes the fragmentary and discursive aspects of the text, *A Lover's Discourse: Fragments* makes the lover, not discourse, primary. It suggests that we are reading the real sentiments of a lover named Roland Barthes. The book's reception shows how widespread this misconception was, for in numerous interviews Barthes was asked excruciatingly intimate questions, as if he were merely another so-called sexual authority, a French version of Dr. Ruth Westheimer or Ann Landers. Philippe Roger's questions, interviewing Barthes for *Playboy*, represent this naive approach to the Author:

> "Do you feel that heterosexual and homosexual lovers are in love in the same way?" "Were you in love when you wrote it?" "So, then, the lover who speaks is really you, Roland Barthes?" "For each figure in the book, one after the other, do you say: 'There I am?'" "Could we say that it's a book that is modestly militant on behalf of all lovers?" (*GV*, 303–5)

Roger has thoroughly misunderstood that Barthes's motive is to present the lover as a writing subject, not as a "real person"; his approach is structural, not sociological. Neither exegesis nor description, he calls his text a "simulation," which marks its distance from authenticity and sincerity. The fragments of discourse are *figures*:

> The word is to be understood, not in its rhetorical sense, but rather in its gymnastic or choreographic acceptation; in short, in the Greek meaning: σχῆμα is not the "schema," but, in a much livelier way, the body's gesture caught in action and not contemplated in repose: the body of athletes, orators, statues: what in the straining body can be immobilized. . . . The figure is the lover at work. (*ALD*, 3–4)

Derrida's readers are equally curious about the true identities ostensibly disguised in *The Post Card*, combing it for revelations about the author's habits, weaknesses, and private life. This cult of personality, one of the legacies of bourgeois individualism, preoccupies even those who are supposed to know better. At one conference, Derrida learns that Serge Doubrovsky has spread the rumor that Derrida is "in analysis":

> What truly fascinates me in this story is not the stupefying assurance with which they invent and drag out the sham, it's above all that they do not resist the desire to gain an advantageous effect from it (revelation, denunciation, triumph, enclosing. . . .) Who am I and what have I done so that this might be the truth of their desire? . . . This must signify something not negligible in the air of their times and in the state of their relation to what they read, write, do, say, live, etc. Especially if they are incapable of the slightest control at the moment of this compulsive invention. (*PC*, 203)

Despite poststructuralism's massive assault on representational systems, what this story reveals about the "air of the times" is that readers (even theorists) still have an avid appetite for autobiography, for true confessions, for revelations in the work about the author's life, and even texts like *The Post Card* which are specifically dedicated to thwarting those expectations are nonetheless enveloped by them.

Derrida pretends to placate the reader by signing his name, but by highlighting the fictionality of signatures and proper names he defies the authority vested in the postal system and psychoanalysis:

> Accustomed as you are to the movement of the posts and to the psychoanalytic movement, to everything that they authorize as concerns falsehoods, fictions, pseudonyms . . . you will not be reassured, nor will anything be the least bit attenuated . . . by the fact that I assume without detour the responsibility for these *envois*, for what remains, or no longer remains, of them, and that in order to make peace within you I am signing them here in my proper name, Jacques Derrida. (*PC*, 5–6)

Derrida's deconstruction of signature recurs throughout his work: the name is merely a common noun, never proper, never capable of identity with itself, always denaturalized. Signature is the last (and not the saving) remnant of referential identification—the final fiction and figment.[11] He adds a

---

11. See Jacques Derrida, *Signéponge/Signsponge*, trans. Richard Rand (New York: Columbia Univ. Press, 1984); see also Garrett Stewart, "Lit et Rature: 'An Earsighted View,'" *Lit* 1, nos. 1–2 (December 1989): 1–18.

footnote and date, simulating authenticity while invalidating all that he has just seemed to guarantee: "I regret that you [tu] do not very much trust my signature, on the pretext that we might be several" (PC, 6). He is indeed "several"; his voice(s) mix conflicting tones and undermine conflicting traditions. His opening gambit is an unspoken gloss on the Epimenides paradox, for by relegating sincerity, authenticity, and identity to the realm of undecidability, he places the reader in an impossible situation. While seeming to acquiesce to the reader's desire for identity, presence, being, and truth, he parodies those desires at every turn. Authority is a writing effect sustained by signature, masking the ruses, plots, and poses of language itself.

Neither love nor signature—two fundamental elements heretofore presumed to be inviolate and unique—provide any clues to identity. Character is not intrinsic but literary, a compendium of all one has read. La Rochefoucauld is never far from mind, especially the famous maxim Barthes quotes: "Some people would never have been in love, had they never heard love talked about" (ALD, 136). From Writing Degree Zero to A Lover's Discourse, Barthes's motto remains larvatus prodeo: "The one who says 'I' in the book is the I of writing" (GV, 285). Like writing and signing, passion, too, is performative:

> Passion is in essence made to be seen: the hiding must be seen: *I want you to know that I am hiding something from you*, that is the active paradox I must resolve: *at one and the same time* it must be known and not known: I want you to know that I don't want to show my feelings: that is the message I address to the other. *Larvatus prodeo*: I advance pointing to my mask: I set a mask upon my passion, but with a discreet (and wily) finger I designate this mask. (ALD, 42–43)

Derrida exploits the same paradox for the same reasons: to reveal and conceal, to lay bare the devices of writing while covering his tracks, to censor traces of the forbidden while leaving it legible. That is why he stresses "what remains." The epistle, as Poe's "Purloined Letter" illustrates, is both private and public, hidden in plain sight. Repetition and reproduction further undermine the claims of uniqueness, of origins and originality. Not only does Derrida depict Socrates and Plato as copyists, but both he and Barthes allude to Bouvard and Pecuchet, and see themselves as copyists, too:

> My letters are too knowing (stuffed epistles) but this is in order to "banalize" them, to cipher them somewhat better. And then in any event, I no longer

know whom I wrote this to one day, letters are always post cards: neither legible nor illegible, open and radically unintelligible. (*PC*, 79)

Since they see themselves as scribes of reproduction and banal ideas, *Tristram Shandy* again comes to mind, as does Barth's "The Literature of Exhaustion": the sense of belatedness is the legacy that extends from Socrates to Freud, from Sterne to Flaubert, Joyce, and Shklovsky. As Barthes noted, the fact that "for the last hundred years we have been living in repetition" results in the compulsion to repeat. One can say the same for the entire sum of knowledge; like the history of love, it is a repetitive copy of desire. Barthes and Derrida are all too aware that even *that* insight isn't original— La Rochefoucauld beat them to it: "There is only one love, and a thousand copies of it."

THE ROLE OF THE ADDRESSEE

Once story and plot, character and identity are deconstructed, what becomes of the addressee? To whom do Barthes and Derrida address their discourses? The identity of the receiver is as undecidable as the identity of the sender, because both rely on conceptions of Being that were already interrogated by Nietzsche (another giant who makes them aware of their belatedness). Like truth, Being is a metaphor, the metaphoricity of which has been forgotten, denied, or repressed. Just as one never writes precisely what one intends, one can never determine the writing's reception, destination, or destiny. As Barthes says to his addressee:

> Hence I cannot give you what I thought I was writing for you—that is what I must acknowledge: the amorous dedication is impossible (I shall not be satisfied with a worldly or mundane signature, pretending to dedicate to you a work which escapes us both). The operation in which the other is to be engaged is not a signature. It is, more profoundly, an inscription: the other is inscribed, he inscribes himself within the text, he leaves there his (multiple) traces. (*ALD*, 79)

Like Derrida, Barthes subverts the signature; the other's traces in the text are the result of the dispersal of signifying components. In "Les morts de Roland Barthes," Derrida uncannily says almost the same thing about Barthes himself and about Barthes's effect:

> Roland Barthes contemplates us (looking into each of us, and each of us can say that his thought, his memory, his friendship is meant only for us). We do

not do what we want with his gaze, even though each of us disposes of it in our own way, according to our place and history. What we do is in us but not ours; we don't dispose of it as we would dispose of a moment or a part of our interiority.[12]

Derrida goes on to speak of the means by which one inscribes an other in "that rapport without rapport" (LMRB, 287). That, too, is an apt description of the relationship of *The Post Card* to *A Lover's Discourse:* the very dispersal of effects (unconscious as well as conscious) makes the impact far more pervasive than any mere study of influence could encompass. Like Barthes, Derrida signals the presence and absence of multiple addressees throughout his discourse. He stresses the fictionality and radical alterity of the addressee when he reflects on the whole problematic of being, presence, giving, and sending in relation to Heidegger:

> *Geschick* is destiny . . . I like that this word also says address, not the address of the addressee, but the skill of whoever's turn it is, in order to pull off this or that, chance too somewhat . . . like an *"envoi"* . . . which . . . does not send this or that, which sends nothing that is, nothing that is a "being," a "present." Nor to whoever, to any addressee as an identifiable and self-present subject. (*PC*, 63)

As Derrida reiterates throughout his work, one cannot undertake a critique of Western metaphysics without dragging along the whole system with it; nor can one write a history of genre or of the postal system without reinscribing it at the same time. This is why the words "send," "sort," "destiny," and "determination" are so fraught with signification in *A Lover's Discourse* and *The Post Card:* they are overdetermined in every possible relay (linguistic, philosophical, psychoanalytic, economic, political, sexual, technological). Every missive and message is a postscript (a P.S., like the initials of Plato and Socrates) to the already written; every reading is a rereading, a fact that, combined with each writer's internal self-divisions, further distances the writer from the addressee:

> By no longer treating the posts as a metaphor of the *envoi* of Being, one can account for what essentially and decisively occurs, everywhere, and including language, thought, science, and everything that conditions them, when the postal structure shifts, *Satz* if you will, and posits or posts itself otherwise.

12. Jacques Derrida, "Les morts de Roland Barthes," *Poétique* 47 (1981): 269–92; hereinafter cited parenthetically by page number as LMRB; my translation.

This is why this history of the posts, which I would like to write and to dedi-
cate to you, cannot be a history of the posts: primarily because it concerns the
very possibility of history, of all the concepts, too, of history, of tradition, of
the transmission or interruptions, goings astray, etc. (PC, 66)

As with genre, one cannot write a history of any "sort" without addressing the theoretical issues surrounding the very notions of sorting (as
type, classification, selection, representation) and of history (as narrative,
production, and representation). This is why at every turn Barthes and
Derrida announce the impossibility of the very projects in which they are
engaged. That is why it is difficult to disentangle the different threads of
their respective projects, even though they meticulously enumerate the
painstaking steps of their procedures. What Derrida says of Barthes reveals
his own strategy, too:

As he often does, Barthes is in the process of describing his progression
[cheminement], also of accounting for what he does in doing it (what I called
his [musical] notes). He does it in cadence, in measure and by measure, with a
classic sense of measure, as well. He marks the stages (or he may underline, to
emphasize and maybe play point against point or point against study: "at this
point in my research").[13]

All writing partakes of the dialogism which makes the voice interior and ex-
terior simultaneously, and, in all, the unconscious continues to "insist."
That means that it insistently asserts itself, in slips of the tongue, the pen,
and in various other manifestations of daily psychopathology. Miming the
epistolary technique of writing-to-the-moment, Derrida remarks, " 'I' begins again with a reprosuction (say, I just wrote reprosuction: have you noticed that I make more and more strange mistakes)" (PC, 27). The love letter
is addressed to the self, to one's multiple interior others, and to the loved
object. It is also addressed to literature. They each write of and to literature
in order to displace the false canonical hierarchies that relegate love letters to
the margins of discourse. It is important to note that while they address this
devaluation, they cannot automatically redress it; displacement is not the
same as reversal. Far from proclaiming that what was marginal shall now
become central, they demonstrate that discursive practices are not so mal-

---

13. Ibid., pp. 274–75, quoting Barthes's La chambre claire, p. 55; my translation.

leable. They nevertheless defamiliarize the habits of thinking that praise scholarship over love, center over margin, conscious over unconscious. Marginality is what makes their discourses necessary, as Barthes explains on the first page:

> The necessity for this book is to be found in the following consideration: that the lover's discourse is today *of an extreme solitude*. This discourse is spoken, perhaps, by thousands of subjects (who knows?), but warranted by no one; it is completely forsaken by the surrounding languages: ignored, disparaged, or derided by them, severed not only from authority but also from the mechanisms of authority (sciences, techniques, arts). Once a discourse is thus driven by its own momentum into the backwater of the "unreal," exiled from all gregarity, it has no recourse but to become the site, however exiguous, of an *affirmation*. That affirmation is, in short, the subject of the book which begins here. (*ALD*, 1)

Theirs is a Nietzschean affirmation of joy-in-becoming, of all impulses that defy systemization. Conscious of the traditional devaluation of the letter as an aesthetic, critical, or theoretical medium, they choose it *precisely* to expose the assumptions upon which that devaluation rests. Derrida ridicules the prejudices of an unnamed French scholar who maintains that the Sophists resorted to letter writing because they were incapable of creating great art. To Derrida, such scholars

> not only allege that they know how to distinguish between the authentic and the simulacrum, they do not even want to do the work, the simulacrum should point itself out, and say to them: "here I am, look out, I am not authentic!" . . . what above all throws them off the track in their hunt is that the epistolary simulacrum cannot be stabilized, installed in a certain place, and especially that it is not necessarily, and completely, intentional. If the imposture were perfectly organized, there would always be some hope, a principle, a point of "departure," a partition would be possible. There would be a chance to follow the thread. But there it is, one never knows, the part of the unconscious is itself never properly determinable, and this is due to the postcarded structure of the letter. (*PC*, 89)

Derrida chooses the postcard because it resists manipulation; its borders cannot be discounted; its telegraphic style is not easily deciphered; and it is already so devalued that false inflation is impossible. (He notes that in Europe, as opposed to the United States, postcards are considered second-

class mail [*PC*, 185].) He writes "on" postcards in a double sense: he applies a
pen to their surface, and he writes about them:

> Why prefer to write on cards? . . . Because . . . it resists manipulations; and
> then it limits and justifies, from the outside, by means of the borders, the indi-
> gence of the discourse, the insignificance of the anecdoque [*sic*]. (*PC*, 21–22)

Polyglot puns, portmanteau words, and citations—woven into the text
or literally in the margins of *A Lover's Discourse*—dramatize the complex
processes by which they both write to and of literature. Some idea evokes a
chance remark, a literary allusion, a theoretical formulation which they
then weave into their discourses. This technique subverts the dichotomy
between center/margin and enables them to simulate spontaneous writing-
to-the-moment. They purposely eschew the traditional form of scholarly
notation so that, as in *Zoo*, the reader is forced to perceive scholarship and
love as being side-by-side, interwoven in a fabric of intertextuality.

One of Barthes's specific addressees is *The Sorrows of Young Werther*;
one of Derrida's is *Finnegans Wake*. *A Lover's Discourse* evolves from a
seminar Barthes taught on Goethe's novel; he reminds the reader that lovers
once comported themselves à la Werther, complete with blue coats and
yellow vests, committing suicide in the name of love (*ALD*, 128). Why is
such behavior improbable in the twentieth century? Not because the power
of the image has been diluted; its power in the electronic age of telecommunications is stronger than ever. Not because lovers no longer desire.
What has changed are our attitudes about love and death. Why, he asks, has
no one written a history of tears? Tears are powerful signifiers in lover's discourses: they guarantee the authenticity of the sentiment, they are material
signs of the heart's intentions, manifested in the body's responses.[14]

> Since when is it that men (and not women) no longer cry? Why was "sen-
> sibility," at a certain moment, transformed into "sentimentality"? . . . (A
> Nietzschean problem: How do History and Type combine? Is it not up to the
> type to formulate—to form—what is out of time, ahistorical? In the lover's
> very tears, our society represses its own timelessness, thereby turning the
> weeping lover into a lost object whose repression is necessary to its "health."

14. Signs of physical pain (either tears or blood) frequently blot the lover's letters in the
Heroides, The Letters of a Portuguese Nun, and *Clarissa;* see Kauffman, *Discourses of Desire,*
pp. 36–38, 152–53, 315–16.

In Rohmer's film *The Marquise of O,* the lovers weep and the audience giggles.) (*ALD,* 180–81)

Barthes historicizes desire by recording contemporary society's repressions, without nostalgically romanticizing the past. Instead, he insists that the lover cannot be separated from his historical milieu; if love copies the book, the book it copies remains historically specific, historically determined. Our attitudes about death have changed as dramatically since Goethe's day as our attitudes about love. Barthes highlights the gulf between the epoch of the man of feeling and our own when he comments on Gide's response to Werther: it takes so long for Werther to die that Gide, in his impatience, is tempted to push him right into the grave (*ALD,* 219). For Goethe's Werther, death is a transcendent experience, promising eternal union with the beloved, but for Gide it is void of transcendent meaning. As Garrett Stewart observes,

> After the "death of the novel" and the deconstruction of its fictive language, how does the human fact of death retain its power in narrative art? Losing ground as subject, death tends to renew itself as formal issue, modality of narration as much as motif. . . . Postmodernism draws much of its charge from this short-circuitry.[15]

The chasm between Goethe and Gide is signified by their radically different perspectives on love and death. Barthes does not exhume Werther to bridge that chasm but to mark the historical differences between the eighteenth century and the twentieth. Discussing what he calls the "mourning for mimesis," Stewart observes:

> Since the rise and decline of the traditional novel, the phenomenon of death remains among the few fictional beneficiaries of a decentered vision. Death fills the power vacuum at the center by shifting emphasis from its formerly glimpsed function as sheer terminus to its role as the disclosed ground of all figuration, the void beneath every device. In this way death underwrites all utterance without becoming party to any new lease on presence which speech might wish to inscribe and secure. (*DS,* 316)

Stewart demonstrates how to reconcile poststructuralist decentering without abandoning the notions of agency and voice. His ideas shed more light

---

15. Garrett Stewart, *Death Sentences: Styles of Dying in British Fiction* (Cambridge, Mass.: Harvard Univ. Press, 1984), p. 315; hereinafter cited parenthetically in the text as *DS.*

on the significance of the plural in Derrida's "Les morts de Roland Barthes": the disappearance of the author can be transformed into an analysis of utterance without necessarily endorsing the fictions of signature and presence.

Death is omnipresent in Derrida's address to *Finnegans Wake*: he seizes in Joyce motifs which he compulsively reiterates in *The Post Card*. One motif is the anxiety of influence: how does one write in the wake of Joyce's *Wake*, with its multiple languages, its circular structure, its erudition aimed at keeping scholars busy for three hundred years? One mourns, because even if the proper name is a common noun, it still exacts a tax, homage, payment:

> [*T*]*he anxiety of influence* is born then in that in order to take a given course, in order to transmit or transfer a given message, you must in advance pay for the stamp. . . . The payment due does not fall only to the dead who are dead but to their name. (*PC*, 200)

One pays homage: Derrida visits Joyce's tomb, commenting (perhaps ruefully, perhaps with awe), "He has read all of us—and plundered us, that one. I imagined him looking at himself posed there—by his zealous descendants I supposed" (*PC*, 148). One mimes: *The Post Card*, too, is designed to confuse scholars, compelling them to "rush in with eyes closed" (*PC*, 77). One explicates: Derrida elaborates on the meaning of HCE, Shem and Shaun in *Finnegans Wake*. One makes connections: between Earwicker-Issy and Freud-Sophie. One dreams: recording one's own fall, just as a fall from a ladder leads to Finnegan's death. One identifies: "James (the two, the three), Jacques, Giacomo Joyce—your *contrefacture* is a marvel, the counterpart to the *invoice: 'Envoy: love me love my umbrella'*" (*PC*, 238). As always, the puns rely on multiple sounds and literary allusions in multiple languages: *contrefacture* and "counterpart" are connected to "counterfeit" (what all fiction, all writing, all naming is), as well as to *le facteur de la vérité; invoice* (reminding us of the debt the dead exact) evokes "envois" as well as "envoy"; Derrida sees himself as an envoy, carrier (courier) of signification from Joyce to his readers; Giacomo Joyce is a portmanteau word suggesting Joyce's Italian years and carrying James to Jacques aurally; the umbrella is a phallic symbol to Freud. *The Post Card* is a *traumscript* of Derrida's reading of Joyce: a transcript, trauma, script (predestined, already written), combining the scraps of dreams, sounds, visions, language: "a scrap copy of scrapped paths" (*PC*, 177). It is Derrida's "*perverformance*"

(*PC*, 136) of polyglot puns; he is the picaresque professor following in and retracing Joyce's steps (*pas*), quixotically writing in the awareness that he can at best but limp behind.

Limping and running are antic activities throughout Derrida's letters; at one point, a genuine injury causes him to limp, which is but a symptom of the psychic injury already inflicted by his obsession with all sorts of legs, legacies, and "couriers." The latter signifies both messenger, courier, and mail, and is linked etymologically to *courir*, to run. Barthes points to the same antic exertion on the part of the lover:

> *dis-cursus:*—originally the action of running here and there, comings and goings, measures taken, "plots and plans." . . . So it is with the lover at grips with his figures: he struggles in a kind of lunatic sport, he spends himself, like an athlete; he "phrases," like an orator; he is caught, stuffed into a role, like a statue. The figure is the lover at work. (*ALD*, 3–4)

Derrida sees the comedy in his predicament, too; he confesses that "this satire of epistolary literature had to be farci, stuffed with addresses, postal codes, crypted missives, anonymous letters, all of it confided to so many modes, genres, and tones" (*PC*, back cover). Both would endorse Shklovsky's invocation of Charlie Chaplin, of circuses, and zoos as metaphors for the lover's state, and both are aware of the incongruity of the lover's position, his post. At one point Derrida even says, "Now I have fallen from my flying trapeze" (*PC*, 198). Their discourses are what Joyce would call an "outragedy of poetscalds! Acomedy of letters!"[16] Spouting sentiments that they know are outrageously outmoded as tragedy, they resort instead to tragicomedy. If they cannot generate either the scalding heat or light of past geniuses, they can at least simulate. Derrida laments:

> I resemble a messenger from antiquity, a bellboy, a runner, a courier of what we have given one another, barely an inheritor, a lame inheritor, incapable even of receiving, of measuring himself against whatever is his to maintain, and I run, I run to bring them news which must remain secret, and I fall all the time. (*PC*, 8)

That Joyce himself, writing in the wake of Homer, suffered the same anxiety is scant consolation; instead, it merely reinforces their shared sense of

16. See Shari Benstock, "The Letter of the Law: *La carte postale* in *Finnegans Wake*," *Philological Quarterly* 63 (1984): 163–86, and "From Letters to Literature: *La carte postale* in the Epistolary Genre," *Genre* 18 (Fall 1985): 257–95.

belatedness, of never being able to *catch up*. The desire to catch up compels one to repeat, but the inability to catch up (to arrive at one's destination) is one of the vagaries of desire, which fuels the repetition compulsion. What Alan Bass says of Freud's inheritors is equally true of Joyce's: "Freud's legacy binds his heirs to stay on the go" (*PC*, xxiii).

The recursive paradoxes of set theory again provide the paradigm: How does one recount the impossibility of writing in Joyce's wake when the *Wake* ceaselessly recounts the difficulty, the impossibility of its own telling? One thinks of Shklovsky's admiration for *Tristram Shandy*, which of course Joyce also admired. An *envois* is supposed to sally forth, but if Derrida and Barthes are limping inheritors, how can they send anything but a reflection, a reproduction of the already written? Every reading is a rereading and a rewriting; every repetition is repetition with a difference (différance). Barthes and Derrida take up Shklovsky's novelistic experiment with de-familiarization and apply it to poststructuralism, unsettling the logocentric assumptions of Russian Formalism in the process. With every new voice that comments on the text (or creates a new contribution to the genre), the entire analysis has to be refigured. The result: suspension of all beginnings and endings; decentering of subject, writer, reader, and genre. Just as Derrida adds his voice to *Finnegans Wake*, he imagines how critics of *The Post Card* would be affected if first they were told that the key word was *arrive*, then later that it was *do*:

> The text then sees itself transfigured by this, they would have to reread every-thing. . . . And if another voice in the same book says: everything is con-noted in *do* . . . look back over the entire scansion (not the *das* as in *fort/da* or *derrida*, but also the most trailing, drawling *dos*, like *derrière les rideaux* [behind the curtains], then it would be necessary to go through everything once more, which is one more book. And if another voice comes to add that everything was calculated . . . to sing the play of the *pours* [fors] and the (long) *às* [tos], and that the entire book is *pour toi* [for you], but for this very reason dedicated to "to" ["à"], devoted to the dative, by chance then they can always run. And everything would be done so that they might run: never oblige them to stop, except to catch their breath. (*PC*, 78)

Derrida's polyphonic puns compel one to hear as well as to read; the multi-valent voices in the text compete with the voices of competitive critics at-tempting to have the "last word" about it. One cannot overestimate the significance of the fact that *A Lover's Discourse* and *The Post Card* are not written *on* literature but *to* [à] literature; the dedication to the dative (*PC*, xiii) is a subtle displacement that makes all the difference. Specifically, it enables them to abandon the fiction of authoritative interpretation. Instead, they can record the comic antics of pedants running to and fro (a motif dear to Nabokov's heart as well as to Shklovsky's). The dedication to the dative shakes epistolarity from the moorings that date, location, and the identities of sender and addressee have traditionally provided. Derrida's puns shake reference from its moorings, too; they defamiliarize representation; they give us an "earsighted view."[17] As Derrida demonstrates here and throughout his work, the best simulacrum is the one that disproves its own validity, transgressing the boundaries of model and image, figure and ground.[18]

THE PRODUCTION OF WOMAN

The concept of the simulacrum is crucial to the production of Woman, for Barthes and Derrida see Woman as a writing effect rather than an intrinsic essence. Insofar as their discourses attempt to "write from the place of Woman," what is that place, and how is Woman conceived? Do they invent a new conceptual space, named "Woman," or do they merely reinscribe outworn stereotypes? What are the implications of using Woman as a rhetorical *topos* and figure?

Before one can assess their representations of the feminine, one has to know what is being represented, which entails a reconsideration of genre. They choose the epistle because from the *Heroides* to Héloise, from *Letters of a Portuguese Nun* to *Clarissa*, it has traditionally been considered the feminine mode par excellence. Derrida describes his project as a "fiction," one that consciously parodies "epistolary or detective literature (from the Philosophical Letters to the Portuguese nun, from the *liaisons dangereuses* to Milena)" (*PC*, 179). He mimics the disorder of the Portuguese nun's rhetoric since, in the seventeenth century, to write "à la Portugaise" meant

17. See Stewart, "Lit et Rature: 'An Earsighted View,'" pp. 1–18.

18. See esp. "Plato's Pharmacy," in *Disseminations*, trans. Barbara Johnson (Chicago: Univ. of Chicago Press, 1981); see also Gayatri Spivak, "Love Me, Love My Ombre, Elle," *Diacritics* 14 (Winter 1984): 19–36.

specifically to be carried away by passion, irrationality, and disorder.[19] Just as the nun laments, "I no longer know who I am or what I am doing," Derrida echoes,

> I no longer know what I am doing, and how I am "scratching," if I am erasing or writing what I am "saving." I no longer know which complicity to count on. . . . You have taken back your name. You have taken mine and I no longer know who I am. Your wife, of course, but what does that mean now? (PC, 229)

I'll return to Derrida's comic disruption of gender categories presently. For the moment, I want to point out similar allusions to the *Portuguese Letters* in Barthes's text. In her last letter, the nun's epiphany comes when she writes, "I discovered that it was not so much you as my own passion to which I was attached; it was remarkable how I suffered while struggling with it even after you had become despicable to me through your wretched behavior."[20] Barthes admits that

> it is my desire I desire, and the loved being is no more than its tool. I rejoice at the thought of such a great cause, which leaves far behind it the person whom I have made into its pretext. . . . And if a day comes when I must bring myself to renounce the other, the violent mourning which then grips me is the mourning of the image-repertoire itself: it was a beloved structure, and I weep for the loss of love, not of him or her. (ALD, 31)

Letters of a Portuguese Nun is a crucial antecedent for Barthes and Derrida because of the myriad ways it reproduces the fictiveness of epistolary production. The lover and addressee constitute a double-edged interiority: from the very first paragraph, the nun refers to her grief, "imaginative as it is" (339). Writing fuels imagination which fuels desire; the purpose is to keep the circuit of desire open long after the beloved has ceased to matter.

Derrida similarly exploits the ambiguities of address when he asks, "When I call you my love, my love, is it you I am calling or my love? You, my love, is it you I thereby name, is it to you that I address myself?" (PC, 8). This query is both an echo and an analysis of the first words of *Letters of a*

---

19. See Kauffman, *Discourses of Desire*, pp. 92–98.

20. *Lettres portugaises, Valentins, et autres oeuvres de Guilleragues*, ed. Frédéric Deloffre and J. Rougeot, p. 62; hereinafter cited parenthetically in the text; my translation.

Portuguese Nun, for *tutoiement* is self-reflexive as well as being a familiar form of address to the beloved. It signals from the outset the self-divisions of identity and the insistence of the interior voice. The nun's first words exploit this ambiguity:

> Consider, my love, how extremely lacking you have been in foresight. You have been betrayed, miserable one, and you have betrayed me with false hopes. A passion on which you have built so many prospects for pleasure can give you now nothing but mortal despair, equalled only by the cruelty of the separation which causes it. (339)

Although the nun seems to be addressing the chevalier who seduced and abandoned her, her primary addressee is interior, for it is *she* who has lacked foresight; it is she who has been betrayed by false hopes. Blurring of the boundaries between interior/exterior, self/other, subject and object recurs throughout Barthes's and Derrida's discourses.

The *Letters of a Portuguese Nun* is a crucial antecedent for Barthes and Derrida for other reasons: it has been the focal point in a three-century debate about the relationship of signature to authenticity, of feminine versus masculine writing styles, and of identity's foundation in gender. Many critics (including La Bruyère, Laclos, Stendhal, Sainte-Beuve, and Rilke) insisted that only a woman could have written in a style so passionate, disordered, and vehement. The letters had such a phenomenal impact on both sides of the English Channel that to write "à la Portugaise" became a veritable code for a certain style of writing-to-the-moment, at the height of passion and distress. Barthes and Derrida would also be aware of the researchers' discoveries in the early 1960s which seemed to prove definitively that—far from being the spontaneous overflowing of powerful feelings in a woman's hand—the letters were written by a man. Although the dispute is far from settled, Barthes and Derrida are less interested in its resolution than in its symbolic significance. Thus to argue that Barthes and Derrida write "from the place of Woman," one must acknowledge that that place is unlocatable, unstable, oscillating. Elsewhere, Derrida defines the place of Woman as a "non-place"; to write from it or in it is to situate oneself in the realm of the undecidable.[21] Although interpretation, desire, destina-

---

21. Jacques Derrida, *Spurs/Eperons*, trans. Barbara Harlow (Chicago: Univ. of Chicago Press, 1979), pp. 111–13, 119–21; see also Spivak, p. 23.

tions also may be undecidable, they do not have the same equivalence. Woman has a special status; Derrida's deconstructive project of invagination represents Woman as a destabilizing force who makes propriation, property, propriety, and paternity undecidable. This project has an apocalyptic and utopic aspect, as Derrida explains elsewhere. He seems to echo Shklovsky's praise for the painter who was not bad, though saccharine; just as Shklovsky instantly amends the statement by reflecting that the painter was probably a good painter because of the saccharine quality, Derrida reflects that Woman,

> because she is a good model, she is in fact a bad model. She plays at dissimula-
> tion, at ornamentation, deceit, artifice, at an artist's philosophy. Hers is an
> affirmative power. And if she continues to be condemned, it is only from the
> man's point of view where she repudiates that affirmative power and, in her
> specular reflection of that foolish dogmatism that she has provoked, belies her
> belief in truth.[22]

The equivocal punning illustrates how intransigent binary thinking is: truth/artifice, woman/man, deny/affirm, lie/truth. Derrida and Barthes consciously strive to denaturalize gender, to defamiliarize metaphor, and to undermine the assumptions of Western metaphysics by exposing its reliance on binary oppositions. By approaching the feminine as a writing effect, the multiplicity of signifiers creates chains of supplements without origin or end.

Barthes also exploits the traditional associations of the feminine to solitary waiting, weaving, and writing. Just as the Portuguese nun transforms the chevalier's absence into "an ordeal of abandonment," Barthes notes:

> Historically, the discourse of absence is carried on by the Woman: Woman is
> sedentary, Man hunts, journeys: Woman is faithful (she waits), man is fickle
> (he sails away, he cruises). It is woman who gives shape to absence, elaborates
> its fiction, for she has time to do so; she weaves and she sings; the Spinning
> Songs express both immobility (by the hum of the Wheel) and absence (far
> away, rhythms of travel, sea surges, cavalcades). (*ALD*, 14)

Having defined Woman's mythic place, Barthes proceeds to situate himself in it. He is the One Who Waits: he waits for the telephone to ring; he waits in cafes; he waits in hotels, filled with anxiety. Like the Portuguese nun, he turns his role as lover into a vocation; his behavior and dress become ascetic.

22. Ibid., pp. 67–68.

"I shall chasten my body: cut my hair very short, conceal my eyes behind dark glasses (a way of taking the veil)" (*ALD*, 33). As victim, as sufferer, he thus assumes the feminine posture: he tries to make his beloved feel guilty by "representing his unhappiness"; he accentuates his pathos. (The code of pathos is perhaps the single most gender-inflected of all codes, as Barthes suggests in *S/Z* when La Zambinella appeals to Sarrasine on "her" knees, arms outstretched.)[23] Barthes would argue that, rather than seeing men as masculine or women as feminine, gender is situational, structured by differential relations. Even when the lover is male (as in *Werther*), whenever the situation involves passion, especially in its etymological sense of suffering, he is feminized:

> In any man who utters the other's absence *something feminine* is declared: this man who waits and who suffers from his waiting is miraculously feminized. A man is not feminized because he is inverted but because he is in love. Myth and utopia: the origins have belonged, the future will belong to the subject *in whom there is something feminine*. (*ALD*, 14)

Barthes traces the *topos* of femininity from Werther to Proust to Rohmer; the figures he finds range backward and forward in literary history, and by reenacting the repertoire he takes his place as a fictional character, consciously "novelized" as well as feminized. This is not an act of appropriation, since the feminine, as we have seen, is marked specifically by its disruption of the proper, propriety, and property. Nor is it an act of nostalgia, or some weird kind of womb envy. Those clichés reveal how deeply ingrained the habit is of assuming that gender is the foundation of identity.

As the peripatetic professor in *The Post Card*, Derrida seems to fulfill the "masculine" role of being constantly in motion. But he simultaneously assumes the stereotypically passive feminine role. He is mobile and immobile simultaneously, seizing every opportunity on the train to be *en train d'écrire en genoux*; his knees are his lap-top desk. "Genoux" in French sounds like "je nous," as in "Je nous écrit" (one part of "To Speculate" is entitled "I Writes Us" [*PC*, 273]). The purposeful polyphony of "genoux/je nous" exploits the ambiguity of the lover as "several"; he plays different roles, has several functions, and speaks in different voices. "Je nous" also signifies the ways in which the lovers are (or desire to be) united (sexually,

23. Roland Barthes, *S/Z*, pp. 168–69, 195.

emotionally, intellectually) "I" am "myself," but "I" am also in "you" and a part of "us." The subject-object division divides each of us from ourselves as well as from each other; like language itself, each of us is irreparably self-divided.

Derrida effects a perceptible displacement in the stereotyping that identifies the male as active and the female as passive. Despite his travels, his role is feminine: like Barthes, he, too, is the One Who Waits. Just as Shklovsky writes under an injunction not to speak of love, Derrida laments numerous interdictions: the Law of the Father, the entire system by which the "postal principle" interdicts desire, and the beloved's determination to end the affair:

> You terrify me, you are bad for me, when will I cease to be afraid of you, of the entire picture that you send me back? I don't even know if I desire it. Perhaps I would no longer love you, and yet I don't love you, not you, to the extent that I am afraid and to the extent that, as I am doing here, on the eve of this return from which I fear the worst, I am writing under your threat. (PC, 38)

By passively waiting to learn the outcome of his lover's "determination," Derrida "accepts" the feminine role. She acts, he receives; she decides, he acquiesces. His repeated refrain is "J'accept," which parallels what Barthes calls "the non-will-to-possess." Indeed one of Barthes's and Derrida's major motives for writing from the place of the feminine is to subvert the phallic dominance that orders and tyrannizes discourse from Socrates forward. This is why Barthes's discourse has so many allusions to Zen, Tao, and to the Nietzschean notion of the non-will-to-possess: "I let desire circulate within me . . . to let come (from the other) what comes, to let pass (from the other) what goes; to possess nothing, to repel nothing: to receive, not to keep, to produce *without appropriating*" (ALD, 232–34; emphasis mine). The feminine signifies not just the undecidability of ownership but the relinquishment of all designs of mastery and competition. To ask whether the amorous discourses of Barthes and Derrida succeed or fail is to participate in the very logic they strive to circumvent, the logic that divides all activity into win/lose, victory/defeat/, vanquisher/victimized. Barthes observes that

> the world subjects every enterprise to an alternative; that of success or failure, of victory or defeat. I protest by another logic: I am simultaneously and contradictorily happy and wretched; "to succeed" or "to fail" have for me only contingent, provisional meanings (which doesn't keep my sufferings and my

desires from being violent); what inspires me, secretly and stubbornly, is not a tactic: I accept and I affirm, beyond truth and falsehood, beyond success and failure; I have withdrawn from all finality, I live according to chance (as is evidenced by the fact that the figures in my discourse occur to me like so many dice casts). (*ALD*, 22–23)

Derrida has the same reasons for poking fun at the antics of scholars scurrying to interpret everything in terms of *arrive* or *do*. He, too, emphasizes chance, fortune, and gambling, in references ranging from Matthew Paris's fortune-telling book to his obsession with numerology. "Jacques sept," for instance, sounds identical to "J'accept"; as with "Giacomo Joyce," Derrida shows how language aurally as well as ontologically enacts its own slippages. He is fascinated with origins and apocalypse, even as he deconstructs them, along with all first and last things, including the origins and endings of the epistolary genre and of love affairs. He makes much of the fact that his first and last names each have seven letters, and relates that to the seventh book of Plato and the number seven in the Book of the Apocalypse. "Sept" also sounds like the "set" of set theory, the paradigm of his entire epistolary project (*PC*, xiv, xv, xxvii). More generally, he examines the implications of accepting the beyond—of destiny, of good and evil, of the pleasure principle. "Du Tout" may be Derrida's attempt to take step after step "beyond the abyssal limits of theoretical production where reading and writing, fact and fiction, become undecidable. And this postscript ['Du Tout'] shows either that he could not do it at all, or how those steps relate to the 'all' of psychoanalysis."[24] Just as language is singular in its resistance to singularity, Derrida's and Barthes's achievements resist definition in terms of success or failure. Their aim is precisely to posit a (feminine) alogic, one whose asymmetry renders the outcome of all competition and rivalry (Socratic, Platonic, Oedipal, Freudian, etc.) undecidable.

Since gender is commonly perceived as the fundamental attribute of identity, one of the main ways that Barthes and Derrida subvert attempts to read their discourses autobiographically is by undermining gender categories. At some points, Barthes refers to his lover as male, but he often resorts to a variety of strategies to avoid identification by gender—a difficult feat, given the nature of the French language. Instead of referring to the addressee

24. Spivak, p. 34.

as "he" or "she," he frequently refers to "the loved object," in order to remind us repeatedly that the addressee has been objectified in the lover's
Image-repertoire. He emphasizes the specularity of the lover's Imaginary
processes for the same reason; what the lover perceives is a projection of internal obsessions, neuroses, desires. The technique resembles that in *Roland
Barthes*, where he sometimes refers to "I" and sometimes to "he"; from the
first page forward, he mandates that what follows "must be considered as if
spoken by a character in a novel." In *A Lover's Discourse*, as he explains to
Philippe Roger:

> I was careful to de-emphasize the sexual difference. Unfortunately, French is
> not a language that makes this kind of thing very easy. "The beloved object"
> has the advantage of being an expression that doesn't take sides on the sex of
> *whom one loves*. . . . The beloved is inevitably an object, is not experienced at
> all as a subject. "Object" is the right word, because it indicates the depersonal-
> ization of the beloved. (*GV*, 293)

Derrida frequently exploits the same ambiguity in *The Post Card* by using
indirect objects without antecedents, as in his use of the word "lui," which
can refer either to him or her (*PC*, xxiv). At some points, he uses feminine
pronouns when referring to the beloved, but elsewhere he repudiates the notion that his letters are addressed to a woman: "To reach the conclusion . . . that I am certainly writing to a woman . . . would be as daring, in
your case, as using it to infer the color of your hair" (*PC*, 79). "Envois" forces
readers to recognize the extent to which they project the binary oppositions
writer/reader and man/woman into the reading process:

> *La séance continue*, how do you analyze that? I'm talking grammar, as al-
> ways, is it a verb or an adjective? These are the right questions. For example, (I
> am saying this in order to reassure you: they will believe that we are two, that
> it's you and me, that we are legally and sexually identifiable, unless they wake
> up one day) in our languages. . . . Now all possible accidents might happen in
> the interval that separates the subject (who says I) and his attribute. By saying
> *I* only, I do not unveil my sex, I am a subject without a sexual predicate, this is
> what had to be demonstrated about "S is p," this is the performance. (*PC*,
> 178–79)

When gender is undecidable, the entire psychoanalytic structure which
erects Oedipus as the master trope is displaced. Barthes's and Derrida's discourses demonstrate that whether one invokes the Imaginary processes of

identification, or the Symbolic processes of differentiation, one is oedipalized in either case. Whether viewed as a family crisis or as a structure in which mother and father are replaced by institutions functioning as Mother and Father, it is difficult to go beyond the oedipalizing constraints of Western thought.[25] That is why Derrida places so much emphasis in the "au-delá," the "beyond" in his subtitle. Barthes, too, explores the possibility of living beyond the father's law, beyond all law. "The great problem," says Barthes, "is to outplay the signified, to outplay law, to outplay the father, to outplay the repressed—I do not say to explode it, but to outplay it."[26] Paradoxically, psychoanalysis was the first "science" both to explore that possibility and to repress it.[27] As long as sexuality is kept within narcissistic, oedipal, and castrating coordinates, it will always be subject to repression (D&G, 351); to displace those coordinates, Barthes and Derrida exploit a libidinal economy that oscillates between male and female, heterosexuality and homosexuality. Says Derrida: "I owe it to you to have discovered homosexuality, and ours is indestructible. I owe you everything and I owe you nothing at all. We are of the same sex" (PC, 53).

Their discourses, however, are not merely celebrations of transgression. One cannot simply step outside the entire discursive apparatus of lack, castration, law, cure. Nor does transgression become a reality simply by formulating a wish. Instead, they consistently reveal their own entrapment in discursive systems that define by dividing and differentiating. They formulate (directly and indirectly) a dialogic series of fragmentary philosophical questions, a mode that has its own venerable tradition, dating from the Socratic dialogues to the Questions of Love formulated in the literary salons

25. Gilles Deleuze and Félix Guattari, *Anti-Oedipus: Capitalism and Schizophrenia*, trans. Robert Hurley, Mark Seem, and Helen R. Lane (Minneapolis: Univ. of Minnesota Press, 1983), p. 82; hereinafter cited parenthetically in the text as D&G. Barthes alludes specifically to his reading of *Anti-Oedipe* in *Roland Barthes by Roland Barthes*, trans. Richard Howard (New York: Hill and Wang, 1977), p. 100.

26. Quoted by Susan Sontag, ed., "Writing Itself: On Roland Barthes," *A Barthes Reader* (New York: Hill and Wang, 1982), p. xxxi.

27. On psychoanalysis's repressive as well as liberating potentialities, see Deleuze and Guattari, chaps. 2 and 4; Gayle Rubin, "The Traffic in Women," in *Toward an Anthropology of Women*, ed. Rayna Reiter (New York: Monthly Review Press, 1975), pp. 157–210; Mary Jacobus, "Is There a Woman in This Text?" pp. 117–42; and Jacqueline Rose, *Sexuality in the Field of Vision* (London: Verso, 1986), pp. 80–81, 101–3.

of seventeenth-century Paris: How might we envision a "beyond" that is social, utopic, post-Freudian, and postrepresentational? What might desire be like, if we could separate it from the Oedipus complex? How might we stimulate desiring-production in the unconscious? What role(s) does the feminine play in desiring-production? Their discourses can perhaps best be described as provisionary, speculative responses (rather than answers or solutions) to the following questions:

> How to produce, how to think about fragments whose sole relationship is sheer difference—fragments that are related to one another only in that each of them is different—without having recourse either to any sort of original totality (not even one that has been lost), or to a subsequent totality that may not yet have come about? It is only the category of multiplicity, used as a substantive and going beyond both the One and the many, beyond the predicative relation of the One and the many, that can account for desiring-production: desiring-production is pure multiplicity, that is to say, an affirmation that is irreducible to any sort of unity. (D&G, 42)

The passage illuminates their motives for refusing to resolve their discourses into a unified whole, their resistance to all reductive systems, and their valorization of paradox, fragmentation, contradiction, and multiplicity. It also explains their repeated allusions to "desiring-production," by which I mean the activity of the unconscious, which cannot be contained, assimilated, or censored. Derrida describes the unconscious in a continuous process of production:

> Trrrr goes the machine on which I am preparing in sum the critical apparatus of our loveletter in order to take them away in advance from every center of, as they say, genetic criticism. Not a sketch will remain to uncover the traces. Trrrr, *je trame*, I weave, *je trie*, I sort, I treat, I traffic, I transfer, I intricate, I control, *je filtre*, I filter. (PC, 232)

At many points, it almost seems as if Derrida's text is a duet with *A Lover's Discourse*, for Barthes says, "I spin, unwind, and weave the lover's case, and begin all over again (these are the meanings of the verb μηρύομαι, (*meruomaī*): to spin, to unwind, to weave)" (ALD, 160). That they both figure the unconscious as feminine is hardly a new idea when we consider the etymology of "hysteria." They evoke Penelope at her loom, unweaving by night what she weaves by day, as well as Arachne the spider, weaving her intricate web. Derrida's allusion to "transfer" refers of course to psychoana-

lytic transference; "traffic" similarly suggests Freud's discussion of "'associative traffic' apropros of hysteria and hypnosis" (an allusion repeated by
Barthes) (*ALD*, 90). Thus, for both theorists, the production of Woman is
intricately interwoven with the production of psychoanalysis. Their amorous discourses are experiments in delirious writing, in writing hysteria, discourses of the Other.

Lacan (whose seminar on the love letter precedes the publication of
Barthes's text and Derrida's) haunts both their texts and is evoked directly
and indirectly in numerous allusions. In this seminar, Lacan elaborates his
theory that, to man, woman is a symptom. He defines "symptom" as "that
something which dallies with the unconscious."[28] To constitute a symptom,
the patient must believe in it:

> In the life of a man, a woman is something he believes in. . . . Anyone
> who comes to us with a symptom, believes in it.
>
> If he asks for our assistance or help, it is because he believes that the
> symptom is capable of saying something, and that it only needs deciphering.
> The same goes for a woman, except that it can happen that one believes her
> effectively to be saying something. That's when things get stopped up—to
> believe *in*, one believes *her*. It's what's called love. . . . Hence the common
> saying that love is madness. (*FS*, 168–70)

Both Derrida and Barthes use their discourses to reflect on the processes of
the mirror stage, that stage of development when, according to Lacan, the
infant first perceives the subject/object dichotomy and establishes a specular
image of ideality, unity, and harmony from which she or he feels alienated.
Lacan maintains that life becomes an endless quest for supplementary signifiers to fill a lack that by definition cannot be filled. Like Shklovsky,
Barthes and Derrida echo the Freudian theory that all our cultural products
are constructed on the way to love. All three would further agree that love is
a destination at which we never arrive, no matter how many letters we send
in advance. The love letter is thus a metonym of the fort-da game: just as
Ernst acts out (if not masters) his anxiety over his mother's departure by
miming it (gone/here), the love letters of Barthes and Derrida reproduce

28. Jacques Lacan, "Seminar of 21 January 1975," in *Feminine Sexuality*, ed. Juliet Mitchell
and Jacqueline Rose (New York: W. W. Norton, 1982), p. 168; hereinafter cited parenthetically
as *FS*.

that oscillation of presence/absence, mastery/powerlessness; they both consciously mime Ernst's motives and desires.

The extent to which Derrida and Barthes identify with Ernst and his game is startling, for each situates himself as the infant. *Infans* means the one who lacks speech; the infant is trapped between the needs of the body and the demands of speech. He needs because he is in the body; he demands when he enters speech, the realm of the Symbolic. Desire is the lack, the gap that lies between need and demand. Barthes reflects,

> Absence is the figure of privation; simultaneously, I desire and I need. Desire is squashed against need: that is the obsessive phenomenon of all amorous sentiment.
>
> ("Desire is present, ardent, eternal: but God is higher still, and the raised arms of Desire never attain to the adored plenitude." The discourse of Absence is a text with two ideograms: there are *the raised arms of Desire*, and there are *the wide-open arms of Need*. I oscillate, I vacillate between the phallic image of the raised arms, and the babyish image of the wide-open arms.) . . .
>
> *I invoke* the other's protection, the other's return: let the other appear, take me away, like a mother who comes looking for her child. (*ALD*, 16–17)

In stressing oscillation, Barthes evokes Lacan's description of the "fluttering" motion of the infant: one cannot fix on any one motion or response and define it as paradigmatic of the mirror stage in its entirety. It is a destabilized point and perception, one that comes and goes in fits and starts. Desire is "squashed of all need"; since one is no longer a child, one is able to fulfill one's physical needs oneself. In amorous discourses, however, lovers nevertheless revert to infantile demands, irrational needs. Thus Werther is as jealous as a two-year-old when Lotte divides a cake at one point, an orange at another—not because he is starving but because he does not want Lotte's attention distracted, nor does he want to share her with others (*ALD*, 111, 145).

Barthes's fascination with eating in *Werther* is uncanny, for in the epistolary tradition male lovers invariably have voracious appetites, ranging from Lovelace (in contrast to Clarissa, who ceases to eat) to Humbert. Werther longs to devour Lotte; Humbert yearns to swallow Lolita's kidneys, lungs, liver. Barthes and Derrida allude repeatedly to the same voracity. Barthes compares the tantrums the lover stages to "the Roman style of vomiting: I tickle my uvula . . . I vomit (a flood of wounding arguments), and then, quite calmly, I begin eating again" (*ALD*, 207). Derrida not only illuminates the psychoanalytic implications of this desire but links it to epistolary production:

> The letter "interiorized" in whatever mode (sucked, drunk, swallowed, bitten, digested, breathed, inhaled, sniffed, seen, heard, idealized, taken by heart and recalled to whoever, or on the way to being so, *en voie de l'être*) . . . the letter that you address yourself . . . then can not arrive at its destination. . . . This is the tragedy of myself, of the ego, in "introjection": one must love oneself in order to love oneself, or finally, if you prefer, my love, in order to love. (*PC*, 195)

Derrida puns here on *envois, en voie,* and *en voix.* In loving, one wants to introject the other; introjection is the process in analysis by which the patient transposes objects and their inherent qualities from "outside" to "inside" himself. It is concretely expressed in the oral mode: "expressed in the language of the oldest—the oral—instinctual impulses, the judgment is: 'I should like to eat this,' or 'I should like to spit it out'; it is in contrast to 'incorporation,' which applies to what one takes into the body; 'introjection' refers to what one takes into the psyche."[29]

Another key process and motive in these texts involves identification, which is related to introjection. Derrida "identifies" with Matthew Paris's postcard of Socrates and Plato; elsewhere he identifies with Socrates and compares his beloved to Plato, finger raised, tyrannically dictating to him (*PC*, 38). He also identifies with the Wolfman. When the Wolfman dies on 7 May 1979, Derrida writes:

> A little bit of me is gone. Had I told you that I am also Ernst, Heinele, Sigmund, Sophie, and HAlberstAdt. . . . This is the story that I write myself, *fort:da.* . . . question concerning the Wolfman: does an "incorporated" letter arrive at its destination? And can one give to someone other than oneself, if to give, *the* giving must also be introjected? Have we ever given ourselves to each other? (*PC*, 194–95)

That question, which haunts all lovers, brings us back to the obsession with possession, and with the contradictions inherent in "je nous." What one desires from the beloved is total incorporation and introjection, but if one's desires were granted, what would one be receiving that was authentic or

---

29. J. Laplanche and J.-B. Pontalis, *The Language of Psychoanalysis,* pp. 229–30.

unique? Or that differentiated the lover from oneself? Barthes shares this obsession with the vagaries and paradoxes of positioning in the amorous structure; he, too, demonstrates how the personality is constituted and specified by a series of identifications, some of which come from life, some from literature. Literature works by the same transferential system as psychoanalysis:

> Werther identifies himself with the madman. . . . As a reader, I can identify myself with Werther. Historically, thousands of subjects have done so, suffering, killing themselves, dressing, perfuming themselves, writing as if they were Werther (songs, poems, candy boxes, belt buckles, fans, colognes à la Werther). A long chain of equivalences links all the lovers in the world. In the theory of literature, "projection" (of the reader into the character) no longer has any currency: yet it is the appropriate tonality of imaginative readings: reading a love story, it is scarcely adequate to say I project myself; I cling to the image of the lover, shut up with this image in the very enclosure of the book. (*ALD*, 131)

Humbert's identification with Werther, discussed in Chapter 2, is also relevant here. Just as Werther identifies with Heinrich, the madman within the novel, Goethe's contemporaries identify with Werther, Barthes identifies with Werther and Heinrich, and readers identify with Barthes, who addresses his book to "the United Readers and Lovers." He mocks commodity culture, which manufactures candy, buckles, fans, colognes in imitation of Werther (and eventually turns *A Lover's Discourse* into a bestseller). Commodity culture is a desiring-machine; it simultaneously tantalizes, manufactures, and withholds what one desires. ("Mass culture is a machine for showing desire: here is what must interest you, it says, as if it guessed that men are incapable of finding what to desire by themselves" [*ALD*, 136–37].) One cannot get "beyond" the mirroring; one cannot keep from being "reduced to a certain personality" (*ALD*, 130). Like Derrida's postal system, with its circuits of delivery and return,

> the structure has nothing to do with persons; hence (like a bureaucracy) it is terrible. It cannot be implored—I cannot say to it: "Look how much better I am than H." Inexorable, the structure replies: "You are in the same place, hence you are H. No one can *plead* against the structure." (*ALD*, 130)

By stressing psychoanalysis, I may seem to have digressed from discussing the production of Woman, but the psychoanalytic process of identification provides a clue to the fascination with the *topos* of femininity. One way to account for Barthes's and Derrida's shared interest in producing Woman is to argue that their shared emphasis on identification enables them to work through the paradoxes of structure and system. They write as Héloise and Mariane (the Portuguese nun) because the feminine is the already written. The already written has been installed in the same place in which they find themselves.

With that insight in mind, one can see the motif of "catching up" and the repetitive miming of the fort-da game as an aspect of the production of a subject. One loves one's own ego identification.[30] It is one's own ego that one loves when one is "in love," one's own ego realized in the Imaginary. The subject is a production—multiple, unfinished, in process. Paradoxically, while the subject is produced in language, language ceaselessly divides it. The Symbolic is the term for the constitutive division; the Imaginary the term for these effects of subject identity, for the very props of subjectivity in which the individual I seeks reflection as a totality, and coherence. Love, Barthes suggests, is the catching up of the Symbolic in the Imaginary.[31] This helps to explain why, in the absence of the beloved, the lover plays with language:

> Absence persists—I must endure it. Hence I will *manipulate* it: transform the distortion of time into oscillation, produce rhythm, make an entrance onto the stage of language (language is born of absence: the child has made himself a doll out of a spool, throws it away and picks it up again, miming the mother's departure and return: a paradigm is created). Absence becomes an active practice, a *business* (which keeps me from doing anything else); there is a creation of a fiction which has many roles (doubts, reproaches, desires, melancholies). This staging of language postpones the other's death. (*ALD*, 16)

Barthes and Derrida both record their desire not just for the lost mother, but for preoedipal verbal states, which are figured as maternal in the Imaginary. Derrida alternately fantasizes about suckling the breast and having the capacity to breast-feed. At times he associates the mother with language itself; he is the devouring, vengeful son of a phallic mother: "Our mother language sucks everything, the dirty vampire, I'll get her back for it" (*PC*,

---

30. Heath, p. 101.
31. Ibid., p. 102.

228). Elsewhere, he sexualizes the operation he performs in and on language, referring to it as "this whore of a language" (PC, 158) and throwing himself

> onto language like a feverish virgin ("wait till you see what I'll do to her") who still believes that the tongue can be taken on, that things can be done to her, that she can be made to cry out or can be put into pieces, penetrated, that one can inscribe one's claws in her as quickly as possible before the premature ejaculation. (PC, 184)

The last two words signal a comic diminishment of the grandiose fantasies in the rest of the passage. They also circle back to the repetition compulsion. Any "ejaculation" of victory over language is always premature because it has already been anticipated, written, and thus defeated in advance. Conversely, laments about language's intractability, its ineffability, are also repetitions. Language is both a *fort-da* game and a self-reflexive comment on *fort-da*. It is an "old lady" whom to Derrida remains "impenetrable, virgin, impassive, somewhat amused, all-powerful. . . . One day I heard her . . . mock their infantile compulsion: to believe that they violated everything by breaking the two in order to throw the pieces far away, and then to yell loud [*fort*], very loud" (PC, 184). Derrida's identifications extend from Earwicker's desire for Issy in *Finnegans Wake* to Freud's desire for the mother/daughter Sophie. Desire underwrites narrative: Plato projects his desire to have his will written in Socrates's dead hand, just as Freud engages transferentially with his patients' desires. Writing prolongs and extends transferential relations: the introjection and projection of needs, demands, and desires results in a "reconstituted nearness." Just as Barthes comments on "the pleasure of the text," when we are enclosed in it, Derrida lays bare his strategy in writing *The Post Card* when he says

> ([I] enclose myself in a book project, to deploy all possible ruses and a maximum of consciousness, intelligence, vigilance, etc., while remaining, in order to remain (as you said to me one day) enclosed in this puerile (and masculine) enclosure of naiveté, like a little boy in his playpen, with his construction toys. That I spend the clearest part of my time taking them to pieces and throwing them overboard changes nothing essential in the matter. I would still like to be admired and loved, to be sent back a good image of my facility for destruction and for throwing far away from me these rattles and pieces of tinkertoy), finally you will tell me why I still want this, and in a certain way for you, in

order to prepare in your absence what I will give you on your return, at the end
of time. *(PC, 51)*

Barthes's and Derrida's production of the feminine is sometimes associated with what is "puerile (and masculine)"; both participate in a larger
strategy of "desiring-production." They want to reproduce the vicissitudes
of psychic life, the process by which the unconscious is continually producing desires, fantasies, identifications that transgress all boundaries. Rather
than channeling their desires into prescribed modes of oedipalization, they
want to simulate and stimulate the free play of genres and genders.

FEMINIST CRITIQUES OF BARTHES AND DERRIDA

Some critics have misunderstood what desiring-production is and how it
functions in the realms of fantasy where all imaginings are permissible. Perhaps because at many points Derrida specifically refers to the addressee by
using feminine pronouns, some feminists have blithely assumed that there
is a real woman in the text whose identity is suppressed. They have thus
indicted him for silencing her. As Shari Benstock comments: "[H]e stole her
voice, consumed it in his own desire . . . she is robbed of name, signature,
personality, gender, body, voice."[32] Alicia Borinsky, similarly, protests,
"The woman who has generated the conflict and received the letters is obliterated."[33] Such responses wrongly assume that *The Post Card* has a single
addressee and that she is an identifiable woman. Through such responses,
these critics sentimentalize victimized Womanhood. Focusing single-
mindedly on gender, they overlook the implications of genre, for amorous
discourse is *always* an effort to bury the beloved (male or female) with/in
language: its sheer volubility smothers the beloved object—whether the object is male or female. Rosa Coldfield in William Faulkner's *Absalom,
Absalom!* is a good example of the feminine enactment of this impulse: she
buries Sutpen (or, more accurately, reburies him, since he is already dead)
beneath an avalanche of voluble grievances over ancient wounds. Rosa's dis-

32. Benstock, "The Letter of the Law: *La carte postale* in *Finnegans Wake*," pp. 182–83.

33. Alicia Borinsky, "No Body There: On the Politics of Interlocution," in *Writing the
Female Voice: Essays on Epistolary Literature*, ed. Elizabeth C. Goldsmith (Boston: Northeastern Univ. Press, 1989), pp. 245–56.

course represents a specific type of complaint, which Barthes defines as the Loquela: "the flux of language through which the subject tirelessly rehashes the effects of a wound or the consequences of an action: an emphatic form of the lover's discourse" (*ALD*, 160).[34] Barthes emphasizes that the beloved, objectified by the lover's fixation on his own discourse, inevitably seems to disappear:

> If you were only the dedicatee of this book, you would not escape your harsh condition as (loved) *object*—as god; but your presence within the text, whereby you are unrecognizable there, is not that of an analogical figure, of a fetish, but that of a force which is not, thereby, absolutely reliable. Hence it doesn't matter that you feel continuously reduced to silence, that your own discourse seems to you smothered beneath the monstrous discourse of the amorous subject. (*ALD*, 79)

Just as the author is a fiction, Woman, like the simulacrum, is a concept that disproves its own validity and defies the boundaries of model and image. The letter is a metonym for the beloved's body; letter writing simulates the lover's voice (*en voix*) speaking to the beloved. As Barthes notes:

> Language is a skin: I rub my language against the other. It is as if I had words instead of fingers, or fingers at the tip of my words. My language trembles with desire. The emotion derives from a double contact: on the one hand, a whole activity of discourse discreetly, indirectly focuses upon a single signified, which is "I desire you," and releases, nourishes, ramifies it to the point of explosion (language experiences orgasm upon touching itself); on the other hand, I enwrap the other in my words, I caress, brush against, talk up this contact, I extend myself to make the commentary to which I submit the relation endure. (*ALD*, 73)

Derrida similarly describes amorous discourse as a site of sensuous production, comparing the texture of language to the sensuousness of flesh, corps to corpus. Evoking Barthes's "the figure is the lover at work" (*ALD*, 4), Derrida echoes: "This is my body, at work, love me, analyze the corpus that I tender to you, that I extend here on this bed of paper, sort out the quotation marks from the hairs, from head to toe" (*PC*, 99).

These two passages reveal the extent to which Derrida's and Barthes's discourses are dedicated to desiring-production as an activity in and of the

---

34. On Rosa Coldfield's lover's discourse, see Kauffman, *Discourses of Desire*, chap. 7.

unconscious. They also serve to reveal inescapable contradictions in the theoretical foundations of poststructuralism, contradictions Derrida and Barthes consciously mean to accentuate. For example, Derrida's entire deconstructive project seeks to displace the hierarchies that idealize speaking over writing and presence over absence, yet the traditional love letter is by definition a lament for the beloved's absence; if the beloved were present, one would not need to write. The *je crois te parler* motif, then, reinscribes the very dichotomies Derrida theoretically seeks to displace. He dramatizes these contradictions when he confesses,

> You are the only one to understand why it really was necessary that I write exactly the opposite, as concerns axiomatics, of what I desire, what I know my desire to be, in other words you: living speech, presence itself, proximity, the proper, the guard, etc. I have necessarily written upside down—and in order to surrender to Necessity. (*PC*, 194)

Although such confessions seem to go against the grain of deconstruction, Derrida reminds us that the "confession" may be spurious; it may merely be one of the things, along with dates, signatures, titles, and references that he "abuses." The confession recalls the paradoxes of set theory; like Epimenides's Cretan lie, Derrida's confession relies on an irreducible doubleness; it is that which disproves its own validity, and thus cannot be relied upon as a model of sincerity, authenticity—or even of deconstructive strategy. The recording of that which resists one's theories, that contradicts one's axioms, that turns all the tranquil categories of genre and gender upside down is precisely the activity of desiring-production. Deleuze and Guattari's description of the subject in the process of desiring-production is an apt corollary to Barthes's and Derrida's project:

> [He] has his own system of co-ordinates for situating himself at his disposal, because, first of all, he has at his disposal his very own recording code, which does not coincide with the social code, or coincides with it only in order to parody it. The code of delirium or of desire proves to have an extraordinary fluidity. It might be said that the schizophrenic passes from one code to the other, that he deliberately *scrambles all the codes*, by quickly shifting from one to another, according to the questions asked him, never giving the same explanation from one day to the next, never invoking the same genealogy, never recording the same event in the same way. (D&G, 15)

Throughout their discourses, Barthes and Derrida demonstrate the extraordinary fluidity of the codes of delirium and of desire. They are "feminized" through rhetoric that reproduces the disorder and delirium of the epistolary heroine. Hysteria is a writing effect in a double sense: one writes to record one's hysteria, and writing augments it at every turn. Delirium permits the unspeakable to be spoken: irrationality, paranoia, vengeance, and obsession are all made legible. The amorous discourses of Barthes and Derrida are "dialogic" in that their interior voices resist all systems and all logic and substitute another value—insistent, infantile, and preternaturally self-reflexive. Barthes reflects:

> I am mad to be in love, I am not mad to be able to say so, I double my image: insane in my own eyes (I know my delirium), simply unreasonable in the eyes of someone else, to whom I quite sanely describe my madness: conscious of this madness, sustaining a discourse upon it. (ALD, 120)

Another paradox: if one is "mad" or "possessed," can one simultaneously be self-possessed? Can one "know" one's delirium? These lovers are possessed by love, by knowledge, by acute self-consciousness, despite their lack of belief in a "self." Derrida confesses that he writes to

> get rid of delirious images. You know them better than I, which is what always will prevent me from being delivered of them, you were there before me. . . .
> And then I am not writing falsely knowledgeable letters in order to keep me from the delirium which possesses me, I am writing delirious letters, knowledge walls them up in their crypt and one must know crypts, delirious letters on the knowing letters that I make into cards. I summon them to appear, that's all. (PC, 96).

Derrida compares the cryptic messages on postcards to crypts, which contain remains, just as he reminds us at the outset that what we are reading may be the remainder of a correspondence. He describes crypts as being both inside and outside nature: they highlight the significance of death while disguising its content.[35] The postcard performs a similar function: it signifies desire while disguising its content.

Like Barthes waiting in the hotel, Derrida suffers numerous apprehen-

---

35. What Derrida says in The Post Card about crypts is exhaustively elaborated in "Fors," his preface to Le verbier de l'homme aux loups, by N. Abraham and M. Torok (Paris: Flammarion, 1977).

sions: he fears that the affair will end badly; he worries about numerous miscommunications, flaws in the postal system, and misinterpretations. "It's not that you are absent or present when I write to you but that I am not there myself when you are reading," as if his presence and the immediacy of speech could ward off misunderstandings. Even while invalidating the illusion of full presence, he inscribes a certain nostalgia for it. (Whether he really feels this nostalgia or is simply memorializing its traces remains undecidable.) Like Barthes, he wants to defamiliarize these illusions in order to expose their force and signification.

Derrida's fears are fulfilled when the letter he sends "poste restante" goes astray; as in Poe's "Purloined Letter," the fate, contents, and significance of the lost letter become one of the major switch points in the text, and the source of numerous quarrels with his lover. His motive for highlighting this interpolated tale (whether he invented it or whether it really happened cannot be determined) is to demonstrate that the letter can always *fail to* reach its destination. The vicissitudes of the unconscious are less traceable and tractable than (in his view) Lacanian psychoanalysis will admit. To Derrida, there are more pathways, prevarications, and detours than are dreamt of in Lacan's philosophy. Barthes does not share Derrida's view of Lacan, nor is he interested in using *A Lover's Discourse* to prove Lacan wrong. Nevertheless, he comments on the tendency of dominant discourses (including psychoanalysis) to turn into authoritative prescriptions:

> The several systems which surround the contemporary lover offer him no room (except for an extremely devaluated place): turn as he will toward one or another of the received languages, none answers him, except in order to turn him away from what he loves. Christian discourse, if it still exists, exhorts him to repress and to sublimate. Psychoanalytic discourse (which, at least, describes his state) commits him to give up his Image-repertoire as lost. As for Marxist discourse, it has nothing to say. If it should occur to me to knock at these doors in order to gain recognition *somewhere* . . . for my "madness" (my "truth"), these doors close one after the other; and when they are all shut, there rises around me a wall of language which oppresses and repulses me—unless I *repent* and agree to "get rid of X." (*ALD*, 211)

Like Héloise and the Portuguese nun, Barthes refuses to "repent," to let himself be recuperated by any of the socially sanctioned systems which might "cure" him of his "addiction." He is nonetheless aware that he cannot replace those sanctioned systems with any positivistic belief, which is why "truth," even if it *feels* like his own, must be defamiliarized with quotation marks. Contemporary society's rhetoric of normative health, its positivistic faith in determining whether one loves "too much"; its guarantees of "cures" for "addictive" "dysfunctions" is the new mythology, the new religion—one that belies the regimented, behavioristic bent in society's approach to subjects, all of which Derrida and Barthes resist.

Since no discursive system sanctions the lover's discourse, Barthes and Derrida produce an endless chain of supplements. It is precisely because the language of love is impossible that Derrida and Barthes have chosen it: not to co-opt it, not to make it conform to societal norms, but to perform it—with all the irresolvable contradictions that entails. Derrida's allusion to Necessity above echoes Barthes's explanation of what makes his book a necessity: the lack of models, the lack of a language of and for love in the modern world.

Although some feminists have misunderstood the role and function of Barthes's and Derrida's amorous discourses, I am not implying that their discourses are faultless or intrinsically feminist. Feminist appropriations of deconstruction do not require a wholesale endorsement. Instead, they imply a reciprocal critique—what I shall call a strategy of infidelity—for, as with Shklovsky and Nabokov, in the process of producing Woman, Barthes and Derrida frequently reinscribe traditional stereotypes of femininity. For instance, associating Woman with the relinquishment of mastery (as in Barthes's "non-will-to-possess") is an idealization. Ironically, the traditional love letter negates such idealizations. Instead of victimized or wisely passive heroines, one finds remarkably cunning assertions of mastery: Héloise's unrepentant desire is accompanied by a virtuoso display of her erudition in philosophy and theology. Richardson's Clarissa refuses to be a passive victim; instead, she refutes her persecutors point by point and exercises her will, particularly in her last will and testament. In *The Turn of the Screw*, the governess masterfully attempts to usurp the Master's authority and to fix the one "true" meaning of her tale, exonerating herself for murder in the process.[36]

36. On the assertions of mastery and aggression by Héloise, Clarissa, and the governess in James's *The Turn of the Screw*, see Kauffman, *Discourses of Desire*, chaps. 2, 4, and 6, respectively.

Absence of mastery (over meaning, language, interpretation) does not mean that the effects of power are absent or invisible. Barthes and Derrida sometimes overlook the irreducible difference that gender makes economically, sexually, and politically. The celebration of multiplicity has its dangers. Myra Jehlen warns that the celebration of plural sexualities may result in women disappearing altogether:

> [T]he claim of difference criticizes the content of the male universal norm. But beyond this, it represents a new understanding that if the other is to live, it will have to live as other, lest the achievement of integration be crowned with the fatal irony of disappearance through absorption.[37]

Despite certain limitations, *A Lover's Discourse* and *The Post Card* are particularly notable for the ways in which they try to come to terms with otherness without merely absorbing it. Disappearance need not be indissolubly associated with deconstruction, for in these texts numerous strategies are presented to preserve alterity, to make legible that which is threatened by erasure in the dominant discursive structures. To wrest identity away from its grounding in gender, Barthes and Derrida exploit the paradoxes of set theory: gender roles entail "a sort of participation without belonging—a taking part in without being part of, without having membership in a set" (LG, 206). The same strategy can be exploited to prevent women from being assimilated into the category Woman. As Lacan observes, that is the whole point of set theory:

> *The* woman can perfectly well be delineated, since it is all women, as you might say. But if women are "not all"? Then if we say that *the* woman is all women, it is an empty set. The advantage of set theory, surely, is that it introduced a measure of seriousness into the use of the term "all." (FS, 168)

Despite his manifold differences from Lacan, Derrida is striving for that same measure of seriousness in his use of "all" throughout *The Post Card*, perhaps most notably in "Du Tout." Derrida and Barthes open up a space that feminists should be urged to keep from closing again, for if feminism

37. Myra Jehlen, "Against Human Wholeness: A Suggestion for a Feminist Epistemology" (unpublished paper presented to the Columbia Univ. Seminar on Women and Society), cited in Naomi Schor, "Dreaming Dissymmetry: Barthes, Foucault, and Sexual Difference," in *Men in Feminism*, ed. Alice Jardine and Paul Smith (New York: Methuen, 1987), pp. 109–10, 275n.23.

and theory have taught us anything, they teach us how seamless the act of recuperation can become.

Ironically, some strategies for dealing with these dilemmas in feminist criticism can be found in Derrida's own work, for he struggles with the same issues when he confronts the scene of writing in the wake of Barthes's death. In "Les morts de Roland Barthes," he uses musical analogies to illustrate the dilemma; the relationship between one's own voice and the voice of the other (Barthes) is comparable to that of a pianist accompanying a soloist:

> Two infidelities, one impossible choice: on the one hand saying nothing that one must attribute to oneself alone, to one's own voice; to remain silent or at least have oneself accompanied or preceded by the voice of the friend, in counterpoint. In consequence, to content oneself to cite, in fervent friendship or homage—also by approbation—to accompany that which returns, more or less directly, to the other; to give him the word, to efface oneself before it, and in front of him. But this excess of fidelity would finish by saying nothing, and by exchanging nothing. It turns back to death. It returns there; it restores death unto death.
>
> On the other hand, in avoiding all citation, all identification, even all *rapprochement*—so that he who addresses himself to Roland Barthes or speaks of him may truly come from the other, from the living friend—one again risks making him disappear, as if one could add death to death, and so indecently pluralise it. What remains is simultaneously to make and not make the two [impossible] choices—to correct one infidelity by the other. From one death another: is that where the trouble lies which compelled me to begin with a plural?(LMRB, 276–77)

Derrida is faced with the impossible choice of, on the one hand, attributing nothing to Barthes's voice, of limiting himself to citing Barthes's texts. By so doing, he would be faithful to poststructuralist theories of decentering and relativizing the relation of author, reader, and critic. But such fidelity is excessive; not only would it say nothing, it would exchange nothing. This emphasis on the importance of a transformative economy is vital to both the Derridean and the Barthesian projects. The opposite choice is to avoid all citation of and all identification with Barthes, to avoid all allusion to the friend still very much alive in Derrida's memory, but that would have the effect of making Barthes disappear, thus adding yet another death to the "deaths" of Roland Barthes.

The use of the plural "deaths" reveals Derrida's anxiety confronted with such questions; one sign of his attempt to work through that anxiety lies in the revelation of the *cheminement*—the tracing of the working-through process—here. I've taken that as my model in this study, trying to work through the conflicts and contradictions between feminism and deconstruction without foreclosing either one. One strategy entails resistance to genre itself: confronted with an occasion in which the genre of eulogy insistently asserts itself, Derrida refuses to eulogize Barthes; he refuses to reduce him to the conventional. Death in the plural marks the metonymic chain of signifiers which multiply ceaselessly: the deaths of author, of the mother, of literature itself. That multiplicity does not detract from or mitigate the literal death of Roland Barthes. Multiplicity, in fact, signals the extent to which death defies representation. The advent of modernity, Derrida observes, commences with finding literature impossible (LMRB, 276). Barthes echoes this view when he observes (in an analogy full of significance for feminist criticism) that modern literature has been playing a "dangerous game with its own death." Modern writing "is like that Racinean heroine who dies upon learning who she is, but lives by seeking her identity."[38] Not only is that another way of figuring the feminine, but it has important implications for feminist investigation: rather than imposing consensus, feminist criticism is poised to forestall the death that comes with positiveness. (Dostoyevsky: "Positiveness is the beginning of death.") Feminist criticism lives by continuing to seek its identity, by seeing identity as a process—that, indeed, has long been one of its strengths. By exposing the intractability of language, one prevents language from closing itself off, embalming itself.

Feminist criticism faces the same challenge today. Indeed, Derrida's multiple dilemmas in confronting Barthes's death are a parable of the dilemmas feminist criticism has been confronting in the last decade: How to engage poststructuralist theory without losing sight of the material body? What does it mean to be constituted as a subject in and of language? In and by institutions? Which texts (and which ideologies) survive and why? What material and economic conditions contribute to their survival or their demise? If "positiveness is the beginning of death," how is feminist criticism going to avoid becoming either a passing fashion or worse—the new ortho-

---

38. Cited in Stewart, p. 389n.1.

doxy? A feminist appropriation of the infidelity Derrida proposes above may provide a possible strategy: we can be unfaithful to formulations that we may subsequently find inadequate. In *Discourses of Desire*, for example, I remark at one point: "I have tried to expose the devaluation of the sentimental as another form of repression, with ramifications as serious at the end of the twentieth century as sexual repression was at the end of the nineteenth."[39] I now see that the valorization of the sentimental has led in directions I couldn't have predicted—although perhaps I should have been able to predict them. Specifically, I don't believe in "women's ways of knowing" or "Sentimental Power," yet I unwittingly became a party to such idealizations in the passage above.[40] A conscious strategy of rejecting one's own postulations if they are subsequently found wanting is one way for feminist criticism to keep from embalming itself. Far from striving for consensus, we learn most from the ruptures, limitations, and contradictions in our own thought. We can also consciously highlight the ways in which our desires may be in conflict with the theoretical stances we endorse, as Derrida does when he confesses that the very act of writing *"Envois"* defies all the axiomatics of deconstruction.

Derrida's dilemma is that he wants to remember Barthes without merely eulogizing him; he wants to pay homage and acknowledge his debt while simultaneously marking his difference. Since feminists' debt to Barthes and Derrida has been incalculable, we, too, can acknowledge it without losing sight of the grounds of difference. The new conceptual space Derrida and Barthes have opened has utopic possibilities, as Gayatri Spivak explains, for it "is concerned with forging a practice that recognizes its condition of possibility in the impossibility of theoretical rigor, and that must remain apocalyptic in scope and tone, 'render delirious the interior voice which is the voice of the other in us.'"[41] This passage, quoting from Derrida's

39. Kauffman, *Discourses of Desire*, p. 316.

40. See Mary Field Belencky, Blythe McVicker Clinchy, Nancy Rule Goldberger, Jill Mattuck Tarule, *Women's Ways of Knowing: The Development of Self, Voice, and Mind* (New York: Basic Books, 1986), and Jane Tompkins, "Sentimental Power: *Uncle Tom's Cabin* and the Politics of Literary History," in *Sensational Designs: The Cultural Work of American Fiction, 1790–1860,* (Oxford: Oxford Univ. Press, 1985).

41. Spivak, "Love Me, Love my Ombre, Elle," p. 25, quoting from Derrida's "Of an Apocalyptic Tone Recently Adopted in Philosophy," trans. John P. Leavey, *Semeia* 23 (1982): 63–

"Of an Apocalyptic Tone Recently Adopted in Philosophy," further illuminates "Les morts de Roland Barthes": the voice of Barthes is the voice of the
other in Derrida, *in all its alterity*. Spivak's statement above does not repudiate the value of theoretical rigor, nor does it relegate theory to some realm of
so-called masculine discourse. Instead, it emphasizes the partiality and pro-
visionality of one's theoretical constructs. It further suggests how to retain a
sense of "living as other," of sustaining a sense of alterity that resists
absorption.

Feminism and deconstruction are mutually indebted and benefit from a
mutual reciprocity, despite the insistence of some feminist critics on sustaining the (false) dichotomy between "male" theory and feminist criticism.[42]
Some male critics have enforced the same dichotomy, as Spivak observes:

> It is surely significant that, even today, the men who take to him take every-
> thing from him but his project of re-naming the operation of philosophy with
> the "name" of woman. Although sexual relations of reproduction are still cru-
> cial in every arena of politics and economics—and the tradition of love letters
> has been the most powerful ideological dissimulation of those relations, such
> letters continue to be considered merely frivolous in a world of bullets and
> starvation. Although Derrida is using them as texts for interpretation and
> suggesting their complicity with the objective tradition of intellectual dis-
> course, they can still be dismissed as a mark of bourgeois individualism. . . .
> If, however, we academic women of the First World observe Derrida's minuet
> with the epistles of love, we might learn that sexuality, "the woman's role," is
> not in simple opposition to "real politics," and that a vision that dismisses a
> man's conduct in love as immaterial to his "practical" stands would not be able
> to see the generally warping legacy of masculism. . . . This, I think, is why

97. Spivak quotes the same passage slightly differently in "Can the Subaltern Speak?" in
Marxism and the Interpretation of Culture, ed. Cary Nelson and Lawrence Grossberg
(Urbana: Univ. of Illinois, 1988), pp. 271–313, when she says:

> To render thought or the thinking subject transparent or invisible seems . . . to hide
> the relentless recognition of the Other by assimilation. It is in the interest of such cau-
> tions that Derrida does not invoke "letting the other(s) speak for himself" but rather
> invokes an "appeal" to or "call" to the "quite-Other" (*tout-autre* as opposed to the self-
> consolidating other), of "rendering delirious that interior voice that is the voice of the
> other in us."

42. E.g., Elaine Showalter, "Critical Cross-Dressing: Male Feminists and the Woman of
the Year," pp. 130–49; Jane Tompkins, "Me and My Shadow," pp. 121–39.

Derrida reads great men's letters and writes about them as he writes about their "serious" work.[43]

By defamiliarizing the arbitrary oppositions between "serious" scholarship and love letters, between theory and practice, Barthes and Derrida reframe the questions. One need not choose—indeed, it is not even a question of choosing—between language and experience, deconstruction and psychoanalysis, poststructuralism and materialism, for we are already implicated in these competing discourses and institutions. We are simultaneously in language *and* the body, the "disreal"[44] and the material. Feminist criticism can mark the vicissitudes of psychic life without ignoring the material conditions of real women around the globe. One can deconstruct the ruses of identity and desire, while simultaneously analyzing their impact on material bodies and material conditions. To see how such a double movement is enacted in women's writing, we turn now to Doris Lessing's *The Golden Notebook*, which shifts the entire frame of reference toward global politics and apocalypse.

43. Spivak, "Love Me, Love my Ombre, Elle," p. 35.

44. Barthes defines "disreality" [déréalité] as the "sentiment of absence and withdrawal of reality experienced by the amorous subject, confronting the world" (*A Lover's Discourse*, p. 87).

Women's Productions

The Golden Notebook:
Anna Wulf's Schizoanalysis

oris Lessing's *The Golden Notebook* (1962) is a pivotal text in several crucial ways, for my focus shifts from the "Production of Woman" by male writers to "Women's Productions." Chronologically, Lessing's novel follows seven years after the publication of *Lolita*, fifteen years before *Fragments d'un discours amoureux*. It may seem as if I am perversely disrupting chronology in order to dichotomize male versus female texts, but instead my aim is to defamiliarize these dichotomies, for Lessing's stylistic innovations have much in common with Shklovsky, Barthes, and Derrida. Rather than reinforcing the dichotomies between male/female, theory/fiction, or theory/practice, her novel decenters such binary oppositions. Her techniques are illuminated by—and in some ways anticipate—developments in poststructuralist theory. She historicizes desire by examining fascism's capacity to make subjects desire their own subjection. Looking forward, Lessing not only heralds the feminist movement but predicts the paradoxes feminism eventually has to confront in global politics.

The novel looks backward as well as forward: it is a retrospective narrative that meticulously lays bare the processes of retrospection, with special emphasis on how the past is distorted by lies and nostalgia. In this sense, it dramatizes the theoretical strategy of infidelity discussed in my last chapter, for the narrator constantly criticizes her own earlier views, selves, and history, exposing her suspicion and infidelity toward both linguistic and historical narrative constructs. In terms of genre, the novel displays the same Janus-like ability: it functions as remembrance by reaccentuating traditional notebook, diary, and letter fiction. It functions as prophecy by predicting the demise of the realist novel and by exposing the genre's inadequacies. *The Golden Notebook* fulfills Shklovsky's prediction that "factography," a new form based on fragmentary notebooks that combine literature, news reports, and cinematic techniques, would emerge in the twentieth century as the ideal model for integrating form and content. Like *Zoo,* the novel might be defined as "historiographic metafiction," for it is simultaneously parodic and prescient; it analyzes the impact of actual historical characters and events on the twentieth century.[1]

One may, nevertheless, question its inclusion in a study of epistolary fiction, since notebooks may at first seem substantially different from letters. Notebooks, after all, appear to be written for the self rather than being mailed to someone else. As Janet Altman observes,

> What distinguishes epistolary narrative from . . . diary novels . . . is the desire for exchange. In epistolary writing the reader is called upon to respond as a writer and to contribute as such to the narrative. . . .
>
> To a great extent, this is the epistolary pact—the call for response from a specific reader within the correspondent's world.[2]

Instead, I would argue that the "specific reader within the correspondent's world" can be one of the writer's multiple selves. The exchange the writer desires may be with one (or more) of those selves, for epistolary narrative frequently fragments the self, and defamiliarizes the premises which have

---

1. Linda Hutcheon defines "historiographic metafiction" in "The Post-Modern Ex-Centric: The Center That Will Not Hold," in *Feminism and Institutions: Dialogues on Feminist Theory,* ed. Linda Kauffman, p. 158n.1; hereinafter cited parenthetically in the text as PME.

2. Janet Gurkin Altman, *Epistolarity: Approaches to a Form* (Columbus: Ohio State Univ. Press, 1982), p. 89; hereinafter cited parenthetically.

led us to conceive of it as fixed, unified, and coherent. From *Letters of a Portuguese Nun* to *The Post Card*, we have seen that letter fiction can be as intensely oriented toward internal as toward external exchange; it frequently takes the form of multiple interior dialogues. Notebooks, conversely, are not solely internal. Dostoyevsky's *Notes from Underground*, for example, is clearly a model for Lessing precisely because it is dialogic: the older narrator addresses his youthful self, the "Gentlemen" whom he detests (but whose approbation he desires), and various other representatives of his mediated desire. Indeed, it is precisely because Dostoyevsky's novel so perfectly embodies his theories of dialogism that Mikhail Bakhtin devotes so much attention to it in *Problems of Dostoyevsky's Poetics*. Even when notebooks are addressed solely to the "self," that self—as *The Golden Notebook* demonstrates so meticulously—is multiply divided between past and present, between younger and older selves, between roles, functions, insights, moods, and experiences. The desire for exchange is the motor that drives the narrative. Like letters, then, these notebooks depend on dialogic contestation. Like letters, these notebooks strive to create the illusion of immediacy in writing. That spontaneity is mediated by an editor as frequently in notebooks as in letters, a device exploited in *The Golden Notebook* as well as in *Notes from Underground, Zoo, Lolita,* and *The Handmaid's Tale*. Letter and notebook are both self-reflexive modes, and both combine unreliable with reliable narration. H. Porter Abbott nevertheless describes the common distinction between diary and letter in terms similar to Altman's:

> The crucial issue is not the existence or nonexistence of an addressee but the degree to which the addressee is given an independent life and an active textual role in the work. After a certain point the illusion of a hermetic seal is broken. . . . The term "diary" evokes an intensity of privacy, cloistering, isolation, that the term "letter" does not. From our point of view, the strategic decision that the author makes is not the decision to have periodic entries in letter form or in diary form, but the decision to create cumulatively the effect of a consciousness thrown back on its own resources, abetted only by its pen.[3]

I would argue, however, that Lessing has it both ways: she presents an acutely self-reflexive consciousness in Anna Wulf, *and* gives the ad-

3. H. Porter Abbott, *Diary Fiction: Writing as Action* (Ithaca: Cornell Univ. Press, 1984), pp. 10–11; see also pp. 9, 12, 109–24, 125, 144–45, 147, 154, 158, 159, 168, 174, 185, 207–22; see also Lorna Martens, *The Diary Novel* (Cambridge: Cambridge Univ. Press, 1985), pp. 233–45.

dressee(s) "independent life and an active textual role"—including those addressees that are fragments of herself. The most dramatic example of this double movement is Saul Green, whose textual role is (hyper)active, but who, I will argue, is nonetheless solely a projection of Anna's self-reflexivity. The notebooks simultaneously allow Anna to divide experience into disparate segments for disparate addressees, and to return obsessively to interrogate the same topics from different angles. All four notebooks deal in different ways with memory, nostalgia, idealism, cynicism, and sexuality, but Anna's "others" are so different that she has distinct writing styles and even different penmanship in her various notebooks; although all entries are written by her, the cumulative effect is like reading the letters of multiple correspondents in the classic epistolary novel. Literal letters, moreover, proliferate throughout the novel: Anna corresponds with her agents about transforming her novel *Frontiers of War* into a film; Charlie Themba's letter alerts her to his descent into madness; Ella corresponds with desperate strangers, who write to the advice column in the magazine which employs her; Anna corresponds with the comrades who send manuscripts to a Communist publishing house. Despite the proliferation of writing, the drive to communicate is insatiable; writing marks the gap between selves, between correspondents, between language and experience, between the conscious and the unconscious.

Anna Wulf, the novelist-heroine, is usually described as undergoing a schizophrenic "breakdown" and recovering her "identity" with the novel's "resolution." Since her illness results in a paralysis of will and a writing block, the evidence of her "cure" is that the novel commences with her novella, "Free Women." Such narratives of illness reinforce the message that society cannot be changed; the individual can only heal herself. Fiction thus remains reified as a tragic representation of life, life conceived of as a universal and unchangeable tale of individual sickness and recovery.[4]

Such readings recuperate the novel within the conventions of bourgeois individualism, the very conventions it was Lessing's aim to dismantle. As

---

4. For critiques of such readings of contemporary American fiction as reflections of the ideology of bourgeois individualism, see Richard Ohmann, "The Shaping of a Canon: U.S. Fiction, 1960–1975," *Critical Inquiry* 10 (September 1983): 199–223; see also Judith Newton and Deborah Rosenfelt, *Feminist Criticism and Social Change: Sex, Class, and Race in Literature and Culture* (New York: Methuen, 1985), pp. xv–xxxix.

Joan Didion pointed out in 1971, for nearly twenty years Lessing produced "a torrent of fiction that increasingly seems conceived in a stubborn rage against the very idea of fiction."[5] Lessing's rage is directed against fiction's immemorial role in reinforcing the ideology of the unified, autonomous bourgeois subject. One of the ways that she combats that ideology is by drawing on the theories of R. D. Laing regarding schizophrenia and psychopolitics. Despite the fact that Laing is sometimes viewed merely as a countercultural guru, it is difficult to underestimate his influence, for, in Juliet Mitchell's words, he "places our assumed ideology before our eyes."[6] His analysis of madness and civilization was part of a concerted theoretical movement to lay bare the devices of socialization and repression. Rather than defining schizophrenia as an individual pathology, Laing analyzed its social roots, which he saw as inextricably related to the entire family nexus. His extensive interviews with families reveal the extent to which the so-called schizophrenic is the product of a disturbing network of familial relations. By allowing schizophrenics to speak in their own voices and by listening to their perspectives, Laing discovered that many were simply fighting for the right to exist. Their families unconsciously selected them to act out the impossible contradictions—the "double binds" that the family refused to confront collectively or individually. He concludes in The Politics of Experience that "there is no such 'condition' as 'schizophrenia,' but the label is a social fact and the social fact a political event."[7] Laing's lucid insistence on the connection between the social and the political— especially where medicine, "madness," "normality," and socialization are concerned—had an enormous impact on Lessing.

That impact can be seen in The Golden Notebook, The Four-Gated City (1969), and Briefing for a Descent into Hell (1971); even a novel as recent as The Fifth Child (1988), where familial discord allegorizes societal doom, suggests a residual debt. Far from dealing solely with an individual's

5. Joan Didion, "Briefing for a Descent into Hell," New York Times, 14 March 1971, pp. 1, 38, 39; reprinted Critical Essays on Doris Lessing, ed. Claire Sprague and Virginia Tiger (Boston: G. K. Hall, 1986), pp. 192–96.

6. Juliet Mitchell, Psychoanalysis and Feminism: Freud, Reich, Laing and Women (New York: Random House, 1975), p. 273; hereinafter cited parenthetically in the text as PF.

7. R. D. Laing, The Politics of Experience (1967; reprinted New York: Ballantine Books, 1968), p. 121; hereinafter cited parenthetically in the text as PE.

schizophrenia, all of these novels relate that psychic dissolution to the disintegration of society. Like Laing, Lessing saw Marxism and Freudian psychoanalysis "as the twin poles of a failed radicalism at the heart of British culture."[8] But far from merely complementing Laing, her fiction consistently modifies his theories. For example, Lessing followed Laing in repudiating orthodox Freudian ego psychology, which disseminates the ideology of normality, universality, and integration of identity. Ego psychology maintains that the ego is embattled by the libidinal id, the disapproving superego, and an intractable reality. Ego psychologists equate the ego with the self; the ego must protect its identity from all invasions. In literary analyses, ego psychologists emphasize the substance of literature rather than literature as a system of signification. They assume that the literary text, like the ego, is "naturally" meaningful.

But Lessing goes beyond Laing by approaching the ego as the source of libidinal energy; it thus displaces the id and is conceived of as a linguistic construct articulated in an unconscious discourse. In contrast to Laing's emphasis on family roles, Lessing approaches those roles as positions in language; articulation of these relations constitutes mental functioning. The ego is merely one among other products of this operation; it does not control the overall process, nor is it "naturally" or intrinsically meaningful. In contrast to ego psychology, *The Golden Notebook* represents the ego not as a thing but as an effect of a linguistic operation, inscribed in a psychic discourse that is constantly oscillating, destabilizing.[9]

Lessing's other major departure from Laingian theory involves women. Laing's intense scrutiny of the family frequently focused on mother-child relationships, but he did not analyze those relationships as a reflection of patriarchal society. Lessing focuses specifically on how society makes women sick. She experiments with the notion of woman-as-writing-effect à la Barthes or Derrida, but she is also interested in the material conditions of female subjectivity. Her novel is a feminist negotiation, critically written against the grain of orthodoxies of the Right as well as the Left. Not only

8. Jacqueline Rose, *Sexuality in the Field of Vision*, p. 88.

9. For further elaboration of the differences between what has become known as the "French Freud" and Freudian ego psychology, see Robert Con Davis, "Depth Psychology and 'The Scene of Writing': Jung and Freud," in *Contemporary Literary Criticism* (New York: Longman, 1986), pp. 217–24.

does she challenge the orthodoxies of the Freudian psychoanalytic establishment, but she challenges the premises of British Marxists in the late 1950s and early 1960s who found the unconscious, feminism, and subjectivity equally irrelevant.[10] Lessing's challenge to the concept of the unitary psyche has important implications for feminism, because—far from viewing subjectivity as an individual matter—she situates subjectivity within a political context. She thinks groups like the British Communist party are wrong to dismiss problems of subjectivity as trivial or irrelevant to collective politics. Lessing simultaneously contributes to feminism by demonstrating how to avoid the misguided emphasis on individualism and by translating female subjectivity from the individual to the collective sphere.

Lessing further departs from Laing concerning the relationship of language to the unconscious, for Laing's emphasis on the family nexus tended to efface the function and the value of the unconscious as a system, and to efface language's significance in that system. As Juliet Mitchell points out: "[If] the unconscious as a distinctive system is discounted, words too must vanish. With his denial of the unconscious, Laing must deny that anything particular happens to the schizophrenic words—they are intelligible by the processes of consciousness" (*PF*, 264). By contrast, much of the power of *The Golden Notebook* comes from Lessing's recording of unconscious processes in association with linguistic experiments. She describes the vicissitudes of psychic life, and focuses on the raw matter that is put into language in the process of "schizoanalysis." This emphasis on raw matter is where epistolarity comes in, for in *The Golden Notebook* schizoanalysis is the theory, epistolarity the practice. For Lessing, schizoanalysis is a theory of the representation of the unconscious. Schizoanalysis views the unconscious as being radically indeterminate or "schizophrenic," which means that any fixed determination of it imposed by linguistic or social codes distorts and misrepre-

10. Rose describes the fraught relationships between Marxism and psychoanalysis in British culture, noting that, even while *New Left Review* was publishing the research of David Cooper and R. D. Laing, it failed to recognize the radical anti-empiricist potential of psychoanalysis: "After 1968 *New Left Review* published Althusser's famous article on Lacan and one article by Lacan, but for the most part the commitment to psychoanalysis was not sustained even by that section of the British Left which had originally argued for its importance" (87). One exception to the general blindness among Leftist intellectuals was Juliet Mitchell, as Jacqueline Rose argues in *Sexuality in the Field of Vision*, pp. 83–89.

sents it. [11] Schizoanalysis is opposed to orthodox Freudian psychology on every ground: where the latter emphasizes negation and constriction, schizoanalysis substitutes a Nietzschean affirmation of the unconscious in all its multiplicity; it is in a constant state of "desiring-production." This is the term Gilles Deleuze and Félix Guattari use in *Anti-Oedipus: Capitalism and Schizophrenia*, first published in French in 1973. I want to read Lessing in light of Deleuze and Guattari, first because they initially build on the theories of R. D. Laing, whom they call "the most revolutionary of the antipsychiatrists" (D&G, 360). Indeed, despite many differences between the French and the English movements, Gilles Deleuze and Félix Guattari are often referred to as the R. D. Laing and David Cooper of French antipsychiatry. [12] Second, the rationale for Lessing's departures from Laingian theory are illuminated when read in light of the subsequent critiques of Laing in *Anti-Oedipus:*

> At the very moment [Laing] breaks with psychiatric practice, undertakes as-
> signing a veritable social genesis of psychosis, and calls for a continuation
> of the "voyage" as a process and for a dissolution of the "normal ego," he
> falls back into the worst familialist, personological, and egoic postulates.
> (D&G, 360)

How Lessing avoids these traps will be part of the chapter's focus. In contrast to what Deleuze and Guattari call the "oedipalized territorialities" of Family, Church, School, Nation, Party, and the Individual—institutional apparatuses which all enforce repressive "normalization"—schizoanalysis celebrates " 'deterritorialized' flows of desire, the flows that have not been reduced to the Oedipal codes and the neuroticized territorialities" (D&G, xvii). Just as the theorists in the antipsychiatry movement sought to develop a materialistically based analysis of the kinds of breakthroughs recorded among some schizophrenics, Lessing's novel is a fictional record of similar breakthroughs. I shall read *The Golden Notebook* as a fictional exploration of some of the theoretical propositions in the new discourse of antipsychia-

---

11. Norman Holland, "Schizoanalysis: The Postmodern Contextualization of Psycho-analysis," in *Marxism and the Interpretation of Culture*, ed. Cary Nelson and Lawrence Grossberg (Urbana: Univ. of Illinois Press, 1988), pp. 405–16; see also Sherry Turkle, "Psychoanalysis as Schizoanalysis: Antipsychiatry," in *Psychoanalytic Politics: Freud's French Revolution* (New York: Basic Books, 1978).

12. Sherry Turkle, *Psychoanalytic Politics: Freud's French Revolution*, p. 83.

try beginning to emerge in the late 1950s and early 1960s. By splitting Anna's "self" into multiple "others" through the act of writing in her note-books, the notebooks become performances of and by her interwoven "indi-vidualities." The aim is not only to free desiring-production but to demonstrate that the unconscious is as influenced by social, economic, and political realities as by individual "neurosis." Schizoanalysis is a "politics of experience" in Laing's terminology; Deleuze and Guattari call it a "politics of desire." The question of whether psychoanalysis is or can be political has been hotly disputed for some time. Lessing's interest in the utopian poten-tial of the "political unconscious" suggests how the unconscious can be polit-icized indirectly, as *The Golden Notebook* so exhaustively documents.[13] By contextualizing the novel in this fashion, one not only learns to read Lessing a little better but to better comprehend the profoundly radical implications of her political project.

One point cannot be overemphasized: Lessing is not romanticizing madness or idealizing schizophrenia. Instead, by shifting the emphasis away from the individual's "abnormality," Lessing exposes the arbitrariness of society's systematic labeling and policing of difference. Indeed, how to de-fine "the individual" is the question that underlies most of the debates in *The Golden Notebook*, whether one thinks of politics or aesthetics. The schizoanalytic project is to free political action from all monolithic systems. The aim is to establish a politics based not on the individual's rights but one that defines the individual as the product of power.[14] Whether to focus on individual rights or on institutional and structural power relations is one of the questions that divides so-called bourgeois feminists from materialist and poststructuralist feminists. Lessing, I would argue, was pointing the way to-ward the reconceptualization of subjectivity thirty years ago, for she situ-ates the subject as a product of power relations, whether one turns to the

13. See Fredric Jameson, *The Political Unconscious: Narrative as a Socially Symbolic Act* (Ithaca: Cornell Univ. Press, 1981); Jacqueline Rose discusses the political impact of psycho-analysis on feminism in *Sexuality in the Field of Vision*; see also Elizabeth Weed, ed., *Coming to Terms: Feminism, Theory, Politics* (London: Routledge, 1989); *Between Feminism and Psy-choanalysis*, ed. Teresa Brennan (London: Routledge, 1989); and Turkle, *Psychoanalytic Politics*.

14. Michel Foucault, "Preface," *Anti-Oedipus*, p. xiv. Foucault suggests that a good subtitle for *Anti-Oedipus* is *Introduction to the Non-Fascist Life*, p. xiii.

black notebook, devoted to Anna's past in Africa and the commercial transactions attending her best-selling novel of those years, *Frontiers of War*; or
to the red one, about her involvement with the British Communist party
from 1950 to 1954; or to the yellow one, a novel about her love affair with
Michael; or to the blue one, which reflects her insights in the writing present
and which "tries to be a diary."

The epistolary mode of writing-to-the-moment enables Lessing to represent schizoanalysis in process, for epistolary texts are schizoid experiments par excellence. "Schizo," it is important to note, does not mean "split
in two"; it merely means, "split, divided, or fragmented"; Lessing consistently defamiliarizes and subverts binary oppositions by multiplying them,
just as the notebooks multiply and flow into one another. Each notebook
focuses on the years 1950–57, but they shift backward and forward in time,
oscillating between the topical and the timeless, between chronicles of historical events, reveries, dreams, fantasies, ideas for fiction, stylistic experiments. Instead of striving for unity, Lessing's motto (as in *Zoo, A Lover's
Discourse*, and *The Post Card*) is "production for production's sake." The
notebooks record a process of schizoanalytic experimentation, the outcome
of which is undecidable. Dreams, desires, plots, and "personalities"—
human and nonhuman—are ceaselessly produced without resolution and
narrative closure. As in Derrida's *The Post Card*, she purposely produces a
text that resists compartmentalization; every critic must concede the partiality of his or her analysis at the outset. My discussion thus focuses on four
major matrixes of production in the notebooks: sexuality, psychoanalysis,
global politics, and the dismantling of the realistic novel.

SEXUALITY, SEXUAL POLITICS, AND THE DISPLACEMENT OF IDENTITY

The bedroom is one of the most dangerous places in our society. . . . When
sex comes in the door, love flies out the window. Men are afraid of women and
women have good reason to be afraid of men. If I hazarded a guess as to the
most endemic, prevalent anxiety among human beings, including fear of
death, abandonment, loneliness—nothing is more prevalent than the fear of
one another. . . . The Greeks called it *anthropophobia*, the fear of human
beings. We are afraid of ourselves for good reason. We are an endangering

species and the only species whose primary danger is from ourselves. Men and women are a danger to each other.[15]

Like many epistolary lovers before her, Anna writes in the absence of the beloved, compulsively analyzing the break-up of her five-year affair with Michael. But in contrast to traditional heroines, Lessing's does not focus single-mindedly on her sexual passion. Instead, Anna is acutely aware of how inextricably constrained the relationship was by social forces. Michael is a Jewish emigré from Prague whose background embodies "the history of Europe in the last twenty years."[16] His family's murder by the Nazis and the murder of his Communist friends by other Communists have destroyed something in him. He simultaneously needs and resents Anna because history has not scarred her as it has him.

Lessing's London is nevertheless a city torn asunder, devastated by the destruction of the Second World War. England is striving for political stabilization and economic reconstruction, a return to "normality." But it is impossible to smooth over the cracks in the socioeconomic edifice; the schisms of class and gender are greater than ever. In Anna's novel, *The Shadow of the Third*, Ella and Paul are fictional shadows of Anna and Michael. Ella envisions the present as a series of discontinuous breaks with the past; she sees Paul as being torn in two by the disparity between his working-class background and his present status as a psychiatrist:

> There can't be any connection at all between how you live now and the way your parents lived. You must be a stranger to them. You must be split into two parts. That's what this country is like. You know it is. Well I hate it, I hate all that. I hate a country so split up that—I didn't know anything about it until the war and I lived with all those women. (189–90)

Living in a community of women raised Anna's consciousness. The war changed women's status: while it brought destruction to Europe, it necessitated the creation of a national workforce of women. While the men were away, the women discovered autonomy through communal living with other women. But all that ended with the Allies' victory. The emphasis on

---

15. R. D. Laing, "The Lies of Love," interview with Richard Leviton in *East/West: The Journal of Natural Health Living* 17 (September 1987): 36–42.

16. Doris Lessing, *The Golden Notebook* (New York: Simon and Schuster, 1962; reprinted New York: Bantam Books, 1981), p. 132; hereinafter cited parenthetically as *GN*.

home and family heralds a return to conservative values: women who worked in factories are barred from employment and encouraged to marry; day-care centers are shut down; mother and child are touted as the "ideal couple." Patriarchal ideology closes in again. Juliet Mitchell maintains, "It is doubtful whether praise of the patriarchal family has ever, since its hey-day in the mid-nineteenth century, been as rampant as in the years of the cold war" (PF, 228). Amid that abrupt transition in social relations, Anna is struggling to reconcile her past with her present, and—as a single mother who is economically independent—she realizes that she is living a life that most women have never had before, in a particular historical moment of acute social, sexual, and psychic division.

The deep divisiveness between men and women is depicted (at least in part) as being the result of splitting off despised parts of themselves and projecting them onto their partners. Rather than recognizing their partners as separate entities, they only see them as projections of their own anxieties and fears. In *The Shadow of the Third*, Anna splits her experience with Michael into fictional fragments which she can analyze but cannot sum up. The novella's title has multiple meanings. First, it demonstrates that what we call "the individual" actually refers to multiple individualities, unconscious as well as conscious. It also refers to Paul's "negative self," the "compulsive self-hating womaniser" (208). Rather than understanding this part of himself, Paul projects it onto Ella, accusing her of heartlessness and promiscuity. Ella's own insecurities compel her to internalize Paul's definitions; she unconsciously plays the role he assigns her. The title also refers to Ella's role as the mistress in the triangle, but it evokes Paul's wife as well, whom Ella idealizes. The wife's shadow is always present whenever Paul leaves Ella's bed to go home. Paul himself becomes the shadow after he abandons her—he is simultaneously present and absent in her consciousness. Being abandoned dramatically alters Ella: insecure, dependent, and terrified, *she* becomes a mere shadow of the competent, independent woman she had been when she met Paul five years earlier. Yet Anna is acutely aware of Ella's collusion in this self-destructive metamorphosis, for Anna writes:

> Paul gave birth to Ella, the naive Ella. He destroyed in her the knowing, doubting, sophisticated Ella and again and again he put her intelligence to sleep, and *with her willing connivance*, so that she floated darkly on her love for him, on her naivety, which is another word for a spontaneous creative faith. (211; emphasis added)

This is a crucial passage in decentering the subject and romantic ideology. Whereas Ella endorses romantic love without reservation, Anna is ambivalent about its virtues, and Lessing exposes its ruses. The ideology of romantic love has given the novel in general and the epistolary novel in particular its raison d'être through the centuries. In Chapter 3 we saw how Barthes takes "Draconian measures" to keep *A Lover's Discourse* from being a love story, to prevent reconciling the lover with society; he wanted the lover to be "a being inaccessible to the usual forms of social recuperation, the novel in particular."[17] Lessing, too, takes "Draconian measures," including presenting a continuum of attitudes toward romantic love ranging from total validation and dependence on love (Ella and Marion) to complete nihilism (Saul). Lessing's aim is to write against the grain by providing abundant evidence of the crippling effects of romantic love, whether one turns to the red, black, yellow, or blue notebooks. The passage above is also crucial because Ella's metamorphosis exemplifies one of the major tenets of schizoanalysis: identity is not fixed but, instead, is only momentarily defined by the states through which she passes—loving or hateful, creative or destructive. What we call "the individual" is, in fact, a series of individualities. If there is any "center," it is unlocatable, constantly oscillating between soaring ascents and plunging falls (D&G, 21).

If in one sense Paul "gives birth" to Ella, in another sense Anna "gives birth" to Saul Green. Saul is the catalyst for Anna's most intense metamorphoses; with him she participates in a violent process of splitting and projecting multiple selves, multiple "others." Few critics have noticed that Saul does not "exist" and that oversight has led to numerous misconceptions about the novel.[18] Rather than being a full-dimensional character, Saul is

17. Roland Barthes, *The Grain of the Voice: Interviews, 1962–1980*, pp. 302–3.

18. The few critics who share my view of Saul as Anna's projection include Evelyn J. Hinz and John J. Teunissen, "The Pieta as Icon in *The Golden Notebook*," *Contemporary Literature* 14 (Fall 1973): 457–80. I disagree, however, with their comment that Saul "is not a flesh and blood character but a projection of a maddened imagination upon a normal, healthy, and good-natured male named 'Milt' who appears in the final section of *The Golden Notebook*." Since this section is Anna's last installment of "Free Women," I would argue that Milt is no more a "flesh and blood character" than Saul is. Saul and Milt are both Anna's creations. Joseph Hynes, in "The Construction of *The Golden Notebook*," *Iowa Review* 4 (1973): 100–113, maintains that Saul "exists," but he argues that Saul and Anna

> are the same self (selves), psychologically. . . . each recognizes the possibility of a cured self in the mirror that is the other; separately, however opposed they are, each is attracted to the evil extremes of insanity and indifference. . . . they could not name

imaginary; he appears during Anna's schizoanalytic descent. To emphasize
that he is a projection of Anna's unconscious, I will refer to "him" as "Saul,"
by which I mean Anna-as-Saul. One sign that "Saul" does not exist is that
Anna's interactions with him are so formulaic. She enacts every possible
combination of male versus female stereotype: sexual stud versus possessive

---

each other's free-imprisoned identities had they not *become* each other in a very real
manner of speaking.

As insightful as Hynes's analysis is, I think he overemphasizes the importance of a "cure," a
notion Lessing represents as illusory. Roberta Rubenstein, in "Doris Lessing's *The Golden
Notebook*: The Meaning of its Shape," *American Imago* 32 (1975): 40–58, maintains that the
great difference between Saul Green and Milt discloses the extent of Anna's disintegration and
of her psychological projection. Like Ella, Saul Green is an invention—a fictional alter ego
through whom Anna lives out her deepest problems. The evidence of Saul's status as a "fiction" is clear from the relationships among the yellow, blue, and golden notebooks and the
final "Free Women" section. Similarly, in *The Novelistic Vision of Doris Lessing* (Urbana:
Univ. of Illinois Press, 1979), Rubenstein observes:

As the angle of distortion increases during the course of her breakdown, Saul's function
as a projection of her own inner schism also increases, so that his independent existence
as a "character" narratively equivalent to Molly or Tommy becomes more problematic. . . . he participates in that blurring of the distinctions between "reality" and "fiction," one of the consistent subversions of narrative convention upon which the novel
depends. (104–5)

Claire Sprague notes that Lessing's "rich exploration of female doubles has few precedents . . . [her] exploration of female/male selves is equally bold. The Anna/Saul predecessors are also few: Poe's Roderick and Madeline Usher, Emily Brontë's Cathy and
Heathcliff, Woolf's Clarissa Dalloway and Septimus Smith. Other examples will be hard to
find, for opposite sex doubles are even more rare in clinical literature than they are in literature. . . . Anna's 'others' are at once real and not real"; see "Doubles Talk in *The Golden
Notebook*," in *Critical Essays on Doris Lessing,* ed. Claire Sprague and Virginia Tiger, pp. 56–
57. Here again I would argue that Heathcliff and Septimus are full-dimensional characters,
whereas Saul is solely a projection.

I am aware that Saul Green is modeled upon Clancy Sigal, a writer with whom Lessing had
an affair. Rather than undermining my thesis, however, this knowledge reinforces it, for Sigal
and Lessing experimented with hallucinogenic drugs aimed at inducing schizophrenic states,
under the guidance of R. D. Laing. Moreover, if psychoanalysis has taught us anything, it is
that real life models do not necessarily correspond to the narratives invented about them.
Clancy is to Saul as "normal reality" is to LSD; he may have provided Lessing's donnée, but
his representation in the novel is utterly fractured, subsumed into her larger schizoanalytic
project.

It should be clear by now that Lacan also helps us read Lessing better, for Saul's function
parallels the Lacanian Imaginary, which relies on the image of the counterpart (the specular
ego—*another who is me*). Far from merely being opposed to the real, the Imaginary registers
all images (real or imagined, conscious or unconscious). See J. Laplanche and J.-B. Pontalis,
The Language of Psychoanalysis, p. 210.

lover, rebellious son versus manipulative mother, all-powerful father versus little girl, sadist versus masochist, egomaniac versus egoless martyr, frightened child versus nurturing parent. The sheer repetition of these trite roles makes romantic love less seductive and exposes its delusions. These roles are compendiums of Anna's unconscious—her past, dreams, desires, frustrations, narcissistic wounds—and her reading. Of one dream, Anna writes,

> I was playing roles, one after another, against Saul, who was playing roles. It was like being in a play, whose words kept changing, as if a playwright had written the same play again and again, but slightly different each time. We played against each other every man-woman role imaginable. . . . It was like living a hundred lives. (603–4)

Lessing accentuates the function of the repetition-compulsion, which (as Barthes and Derrida similarly demonstrate) is always repetition with a difference. (Freud was fond of quoting Heraclitus: "You shall not go down twice to the same river.") Significantly, Anna's roles are played *against*, not *with* her masculine counterpart. "Saul" is, among other things, a projection of her anger against men: against Paul, the dead lover who was the first ever to arouse her sexually; against Max Wulf, the husband with whom she was frigid; against Michael, who leaves her.

Yet Anna is no mere victim. She is responsible for her actions; she wanted to believe in the ideology of love above all else, whether it paralyzed her or not, which is why she places such emphasis on the fact that Paul put Ella's mind to sleep "with her willing connivance." Anna looks back on another phase of her life and writes: "I was a woman terribly vulnerable, critical, using femaleness as a sort of standard or yardstick to measure and discard men. Yes . . . I was an Anna who invited defeat from men without even being conscious of it" (480). Elaine Showalter and Ellen Morgan have argued that Lessing's heroines do not take responsibility for their feelings,[19] but Anna's confessions refute this critique, for she is acutely aware that she chooses men who will rob her of will and power, men with whom she can play the role of masochist: "I was looking for men who would hurt me. I needed it," she says (626). In retrospect, Lessing's emphasis on Anna's responsibility seems particularly prophetic; she was emphasizing women's

---

19. Elaine Showalter, *A Literature of Their Own: British Women Novelists from Brontë to Lessing* (Princeton: Princeton Univ. Press, 1976), pp. 311–12; Ellen Morgan, "Alienation of the Woman Writer in *The Golden Notebook*," in *Doris Lessing: Critical Studies*, p. 63.

collusion in their own oppression long before many feminists were willing to confront this unpleasant issue. Anna searches for men who will consciously act out a hostility which is but a projection of her own self-loathing; that self-loathing results in her willful self-enslavement to men, as she points out: "No one does anything to me, I do it to myself" (622).

That self-loathing is intimately related to her body and her sexuality, as she reveals while recording her last schizoanalytic descent, when her body suddenly becomes so alien and repulsive to her that it reminds her of a spider:

> all clutching arms and legs around a hairy central devouring mouth. . . . My wet sticky centre seemed disgusting, and when I saw my breasts all I could think of was how they were when they were full of milk, and instead of this being pleasurable, it was revolting. . . . For the first time, the homosexual literature of disgust made sense to me. (612)

A far cry from either *Our Bodies, Ourselves* or from celebrations of female sexuality in *écriture féminine*! Yet perhaps the most significant element of Anna's terrifying experience is its literariness. She can even identify the genre to which it belongs: the homosexual literature of disgust. She thus reaccentuates Shklovsky's motif of the conventionality of literature, and anticipates Barthes's and Derrida's efforts to expose the ubiquitousness of literary codes. In contrast to the male theorists, however, she chooses to shock us by deromanticizing one of culture's most sacred icons: the female body. Such techniques of distortion and the shocking defamiliarization of the body and the text are necessary to the task of schizoanalysis, which is to dismantle what has blithely been called the "normal" ego.

Anna's experience has all the characteristics that Laing describes as typical of the schizophrenic voyage: it moves from outer to inner, from life to a kind of death, from a going forward to a going back, from outside (postbirth) to the womb (prebirth). Jesse Watkins's schizophrenic voyage in Laing's *Politics of Experience* recounts the same regression Anna undergoes: he experiences a sense of relation to all things, from the lowest forms of animal life to the highest. Although the process is terrifying, once he loses his ego, he discovers "the enhanced significance and relevance of everything" (PE, 150). Anna strives for the same sense of connection when she plays "the game," a creative effort to situate her "self," her room, city, country, and continent in relation to the planet in order to "reach what I wanted, a simultaneous

knowledge of vastness and of smallness." Lessing, like Laing, believes that
only at the point of breakdown can something new enter, something that
transforms our perceptions and enables us to see the relation of politics to
personal malaise. Anna wants to tear the social fabric, to create a schism
through which what is genuinely new in her particular historical moment
can emerge. She believes in cracks, gaps in the personality,

> like a gap in a dam, and through that gap the future might pour in a different
> shape—terrible perhaps, or marvellous, but something new. . . . Sometimes
> I meet people, and it seems to me the fact they are cracked across, they're split,
> means they are keeping themselves open for something. (473)

Laing uses almost identical language when he reflects that "what we call
'schizophrenia' was one of the forms in which, often through quite ordinary people, the light began to break through the cracks in our all-too-
closed minds" (*PE*, 129). Significantly, in the passage above when Mrs.
Marks asks Anna if she has met the kind of person she is describing, she
says no. Not only is this further proof that "Saul" is a projection, but in
one sense she has already invented his prototype, in her fictional outline
about an unpossessive woman who turns into a jealous jailor when she falls
in love, while watching herself becoming possessed by a personality which
is not her own (461). Elsewhere she imagines a plot about a man and a
woman "both at the end of their tether. Both cracking up because of a deliberate attempt to transcend their own limits. And out of the chaos, a new
kind of strength" (467).

Until it happens, Anna does not know what she is trying to open her
"self" to: "Saul's" visitation. That visitation turns out to be an inscription
of language, for in contrast to Anna's stammering and her linguistic paralysis in her waking life, "Saul" is all language:

> I, I, I, I . . . shot out, spewed out, hot aggressive language, words like bul-
> lets. . . . It was as if a machine, tuned or set by a mechanic to stop briefly at a
> sound from outside, stopped, checked itself mechanically, mouth, or metal
> opening already in position to ejaculate the next stream of I I I I I I. . . . words
> spattering against the walls and ricochetting everywhere, I I I, the naked ego.
> (628–29)

In this remarkable passage, Lessing depicts the ego as a boundary concept
whose limits she violates, delimits, strips of its territoriality. Anna and
"Saul" are multiple voices, "ideologues in conflict," without resolution or

closure.[20] The schizoanalytic process of opening herself to the invasion of these "others" frees artistic production, for after every descent—not *with* but *as* "Saul"—she goes directly to her notebooks to record these unfathomable, unnameable experiences, thus freeing the flows of language and desire. In this sense, her notebooks are letters *to* "Saul," as well as being written *by* "Saul" at those times when she feels entirely submerged in that alien personality.

"Man" and "woman" are as unnameable as experience is. As Deleuze and Guattari point out, neither man nor woman are "models" of anything; they are not clearly defined categories, essences, or entities; instead, they are vibrations, "schizzes," flows—what Laing calls "knots."[21] Because the unconscious is always producing flows of desire, Deleuze and Guattari call it a "desiring-production machine." This helps explain why the image of a flow recurs repeatedly in the novel: Anna records the flows of lovemaking; her menstrual flows, the flows of blood in political purges; the flows of words in newspapers, the ways happiness flows into her and leaks out again; the flows of one "personality" into another. Observations that belong in one notebook repeatedly flow into others. Hard as she tries, it proves to be impossible to partition her thoughts on sexuality, politics, literature, and economics. Deleuze and Guattari maintain that political economy (the flows of capital and interest) and the economy of the libido (the flows of desire) are one and the same economy, for there is no way of delimiting the boundaries between their interlocking effects in the unconscious. In Lessing, social production cannot be arbitrarily divided from desire production; libidinal economy is no less objective than political economy, and the political is no less

20. On the novel as the genre uniquely suited for dialogic contestation among "ideologues," see Mikhail M. Bakhtin, *The Dialogic Imagination*, pp. 259–422. In Russian, "ideology" means an idea system. Every word reveals the speaker's ideology; therefore every speaker is an "ideologue" and every utterance an "ideologeme" (p. 429).

21. Deleuze and Guattari, pp. 360–62; see also R. D. Laing, *Knots* (New York: Pantheon, 1970), a good example of dialogic interweaving and contestation, which shows how utterly entwined is the gordian knot of social intercourse, unspoken communication, hostility, aggression, misrecognition, and slippages in meaning and intention. Lacan obviously comes to mind; not only do Deleuze and Guattari build on Lacan's critique of theories of the ego, but in his final works Lacan attempted to break through "common-sense" language and "common-sense" notions of the self by drawing increasingly on mathematical models of psychoanalytic theory and new topological symbolizations such as knots. See Turkle, chap. 6.

subjective than the libidinal (D&G, 24–26, 28, 171, 355–56). They are part of the same interlocking system, the same mechanisms of production and dissemination. Objective/subjective, political/libidinal, conscious/unconscious: these are the same dichotomies Shklovsky, Barthes, and Derrida break down (albeit in dramatically different ways) in their amorous discourses. Lessing's aim, like that of poststructuralism, is to demonstrate that both gender and authority are writing effects, and to expose the mechanisms of surveillance and subjection that keep them in place.

"Saul" is thus described as machine-like, not because his "masculinity" makes him inhuman but because of the machine-like quality of production in Anna's unconscious. Male and female are merely unstable, decentered designations, interlocking and metamorphosing as "Saul" and Anna play out roles that encapsulate her compulsions and obsessions: "Saul and I were two unknown quantities, two forces anonymous, without personality. It was as if the room held two totally malignant beings" (631). At the beginning of her schizoanalytic descent, Anna misidentifies this malignancy as a solely male characteristic. Naming it the "principle of joy-in-spite, destruction, or malice," she recognizes it in Charlie Themba, de Silva, and Nelson, and dreams of it as a figure that is

> anarchistic and uncontrollable . . . with a jerky cocky liveliness . . . it menaced not only me, but everything that was alive, but impersonally, and without reason . . . [it] took shape in an old man, almost dwarf-like. (477)

In Anna's subsequent dreams, however, the figure is either sexless or combines male and female traits. Anna realizes that with the appearance of this malicious dwarf in her unconscious, one of her desires has been fulfilled: she had wanted an experience outside the Oedipal boundaries of family, myth, and tragedy, and this dwarf, embodying the principle of joy-in-destruction, is that experience. Terrified, she realizes that

> if the element is now outside of myth, and inside another human being, then it can only mean it is loose in me also . . . [This] is the beginning of something I must live through. Or: This emotion, which I have not felt before, is not the alien I believed it to be. It will now be part of me and I must deal with it. (479)

One of the most fascinating aspects of schizoanalysis is that it involves the recognition not just of multiple individualities but of transgender experiences. Anna sometimes dreams that the figure "had a great protruding penis sticking out through his clothes, it menaced me, was dangerous, because I knew the old man hated me and wanted to hurt me" (562). At other times, she becomes "instantly the old man, the old man had become me, but I was also the old woman, so that I was sexless. I was also spiteful and destructive" (563). Anna's breakthrough comes when she identifies this principle as part of herself (her "selves"), and strives to transform it into something creative, to tap its vitality for her own creativity. She learns to dream the dream "positively," which does not mean that she imposes a happy ending but that she realizes that "madness and sanity," "male and female" are boundary concepts which have hardened into prescriptive behavioral formulas that are socially and politically repressive. When Anna dreams the dream for the last time, "Saul" is a projection of her own capacity for emotional cannibalism and outright evil:

> There was no disguise anywhere. I was the malicious male-female dwarf figure . . . and Saul was my counter-part, male-female, my brother and my sister, and we were dancing in some open place, under enormous white buildings, which were filled with hideous, menacing, black machinery which held destruction. But in the dream, he and I, or she and I, were friendly, we were not hostile, we were together in spiteful malice. There was a terrible yearning nostalgia in the dream, the longing for death. We came together and kissed, in love. It was terrible, and even in the dream I knew it. . . . it was the caress of two half-human creatures, celebrating destruction. There was a terrible joy in the dream. (594–95)

Nostalgia and nihilism merge here in Anna's desire for self-obliteration, quiescence, death.[22] Her dream has the uncanny logic of the theater of cruelty. Where previously Anna could only see her difference from "Saul," now she identifies him as a part of her: he is a projection of *her* naked ego, her malice, her spitefulness, her destructiveness, her death instinct. The recognition hardly sounds positive, much less joyful, but it frees Anna from the passive role of victim persecuted by men, or by any (O)ther monolithic or external enemy.

Thus, far from losing their identities, as some feminists fear, women stand to gain much from the subversion of gender categories. By seeing herself as male and female, Anna breaks out of the narcissistic, Oedipal, and

22. Patrocinio P. Schweickart discusses the twin evils of nostalgia and nihilism as well as the novel's dialectical structure, in "Reading a Wordless Statement: The Structure of Doris Lessing's *The Golden Notebook*," *Modern Fiction Studies* 31 (Summer 1985): 263–79.

castrating coordinates which constrict sexuality, for until those coordinates are dismantled, sexual repression will remain in force (D&G, 351). Lessing's subversions of sexual identity resemble those of other writers who have experimented with schizoanalysis: Nijinsky writes in his diary: "I am husband and wife in one. I love my wife. I love my husband." Artaud proclaims, "I, Antonin Artaud, am my son, my father, my mother, and myself. . . . I don't believe in father / in mother, / got no papamummy" (D&G, 77, 15, 14). In *The Post Card*, similarly, Derrida writes to his beloved, "We are of the same sex, and this is as true as two and two are four" (*PC*, 53). Elsewhere, he calls himself his beloved's "twin sister" (*PC*, 129). By displacing identity's traditional foundations in sexuality, Lessing anticipates the poststructuralist experiment Michel Foucault proposes:

> [W]e need to consider the possibility that one day, perhaps, in a different economy of bodies and pleasures, people will no longer quite understand how the ruses of sexuality, and the power that sustains its organization, were able to subject us to that austere monarchy of sex, so that we became dedicated to the endless task of forcing its secret, of exacting the truest of confessions from a shadow.
>
> The irony of this deployment is in having us believe that our "liberation" is in the balance.[23]

Repudiating the false dichotomy of male/female as an either/or concept, Lessing replaces it with "either . . . or . . . or" (D&G, 70). Indeed, she anticipates deconstruction by debunking all binary oppositions: "Men. Women. Bound. Free. Good. Bad. Yes. No. Capitalism. Socialism. Sex. Love" (44). The motif of the shadow of the third reveals how consistently dialogical Lessing's strategy is throughout the novel, for the "shadow of the third" effects a perceptible displacement of all dichotomies, even such seemingly ingrained ones as those related to sexuality and gender.[24] Lessing

---

23. Michel Foucault, *The History of Sexuality*, vol. I, trans. Robert Hurley (New York: Vintage, 1980), p. 159.

24. Schweickart describes Lessing's strategies as "dialectical" (see n. 22 above), as does Betsy Draine, *Substance under Pressure: Artistic Coherence and Evolving Form in the Novels of Doris Lessing* (Madison: Univ. of Wisconsin Press, 1983), chap. 4; and Annis Pratt, "The Contrary Structure of Doris Lessing's *The Golden Notebook*," *World Literature Written in English* 12, no. 2 (1973): 150–60. I see the novel as being more *dialogical* than dialectical; it inscribes alternatives to logic, synthesis, and resolution. See n. 46 below.

writes against the grain of psychoanalysis precisely to open up circulation of the sexualities and other economies which orthodox psychoanalysis is supposed to repress.

PSYCHOANALYSIS AND ITS DISCONTENTS

The second major matrix for Anna's productivity is her experience in psychoanalysis, which commences on 10 January 1950. She attacks the orthodox psychoanalytic establishment for its conservatism: it is "traditional, rooted, conservative, in spite of its scandalous familiarity with everything amoral" (5). One source of her frustration is that she is a specific woman in a particular historical moment, but her Jungian analyst interprets Anna's neurosis in terms of fairy tales, tragedies, and myths. This seems incongruous to Anna, who is acutely aware of modernity: the atrocities of the modern world, the repressions that conspire to crush one's spirit, the inhumanity among nations as well as among friends and lovers. Not only does she disagree with her analyst's Jungian interpretations, she feels that society in general pigeonholes her between the theories of Freud and Marx. The latter's name sounds like her analyst's, Mrs. Marks, who dogmatically marks and labels her according to Greek mythology: " 'You're Electra,' or 'You're Antigone,' and that was the end, as far as she was concerned" (5). Mrs. Marks consistently "misses the mark" with such interpretations, and Anna protests against her analytic tautologies:

> I'm tired of the wolves and the castles and the forests and the priests. I can cope with them in any form they choose to present themselves. But I've told you, I want to walk off, by myself, Anna Freeman.
>
> . . . I'm convinced that there are whole areas of me made by the kind of experience women haven't had before . . . I'm living the kind of life women never lived before. . . . I want to be able to separate in myself what is old and cyclic, the recurring history, the myth, from what is new, what I feel or think that might be new. (471–73)

The name "Anna Wulf" is itself a compendium of authorized discourses and literary allusions: in addition to echoing Joyce's Anna Livia, it evokes Freud's daughter, Anna; his patient, Anna O.; Virginia Woolf; and Freud's Wolfman, who is not only obsessed with fairy tales and wolves but who (like Anna) dreams of wolves (470). Anna's name, moreover, is a palindrome; like the entire novel, it ends where it begins. Anna is striving to free desiring-production from the universal mythologizing and essentialism of orthodox psychoanalysis. She wants to break out of the "Oedipal territorialities" and to situate psychoanalysis in a specific social and historical matrix. Like the patient of Laing's who suffered from a delusion that an atomic bomb was inside her head,[25] Anna insists that her terrifying dreams of nuclear holocaust are not analogous to ancient wars with crossbows; that her negotiations with film moguls about adapting her novel to film are not equivalent to Lesbia's bartering with wine merchants. She criticizes the intellectual primitivism of Mrs. Marks's Jungian interpretations, since they rely on myth, folklore, and the reduction of the collective to the infantilism of individual childhood experience. Mrs. Marks insists that "the details change, but the form is the same," but Anna disagrees: "What really pleases you, what really moves you, is the world of the primitive" (469). (Since Mrs. Marks has a collection of primitive art in her office, Anna's critique hits the mark.) Lessing represents orthodox psychoanalysis as being completely unequipped to grapple with modernity, much less postmodernity. Mrs. Marks accords a sanctity to art and the artist which Anna finds nauseating, since art, like psychoanalysis, is seldom the means of moral regeneration that Anna thinks it should be. She is critical of the fundamental bases of psychoanalysis—the limits, taboos, and injunctions which are allegedly responsible for her neurosis. Her protests alone do not make those taboos disappear, but the schizophrenic journey she undergoes shifts the entire frame of reference away from individual neuroses and toward the social genesis of psychosis; from unresolved Oedipal conflicts to global politics and repression.

In contrast to psychoanalysis, the aim of schizoanalysis is to enable the subject to strip himself of "all anthropomorphic, and other armoring, all myth and tragedy, all existentialism; to perceive what is nonhuman in man: his will and forces, transformations and mutations" (D&G, xx). That is why Anna dreams of the crocodile: whereas in dreaming of the dwarf she ceases to be female, in dreaming of the crocodile, she ceases to be human. Not accidentally, her first dream of the crocodile coincides with her last session with Mrs. Marks. In the dream, she performs in a lecture hall or art gallery, presenting the audience with a basket containing a precious object, which (like

25. R. D. Laing and A. Esterson, *Sanity, Madness and the Family: Families of Schizophrenics* (New York: Penguin Books, 1970), p. 75.

Keats's "well-wrought urn") signifies her own writing. But the audience consists of businessmen and brokers, capitalists who lavish her with money while ignoring her work. When she opens the casket she finds—rather than a thing of beauty—ugly fragments of global destruction: bits of earth from Africa, the flesh of war casualties in Korea, a gun from Indochina, a Communist party badge from a Soviet prisoner. Suddenly, a crocodile of jade and emeralds materializes; its tears turn into diamonds.

The dream reflects Anna's guilt about the money she made on *Frontiers of War*, her first novel, which falsified the painful reality of existence in Africa by reducing it to a bourgeois love story. By focusing on interracial love, it was all the more sensationalistic, therefore false. Anna's dream also reflects her obsession with fragmentation: confronted with the atrocities of the twentieth century, Anna believes art not only evades but distorts. Purely aesthetic responses are as hypocritical as "crocodile tears." The transformation of the tears suggests the end of Anna's emotional frigidity and creative paralysis; the movement from freezing to flowing anticipates the circulation of all sorts of flows of desire in the novel.

Anna's paralysis reflects the fate of intellectuals in the modern world: surrounded by instruments of surveillance and subjection in government, education, technology, and the media, the language of intellectuals, historians, and journalists suffers from abstraction, evasion, and outright falsification. Anna feels paralyzed because she cannot capture the plenitude of experience in language, whereas the media blithely reduce causal relationships to clichés, heedless of complexity or veracity. The dream critiques capitalism as a machine that benefits from the wars, traumas, and territorial skirmishes symbolized by the fragments of flesh and earth. Anna laughs spitefully in the dream, because she figures out how to thwart the capitalists who run the "culture industry" by taking over the modes of production herself. She transforms the diamond crocodile from bejeweled commodity into menacing monster. Following the logic of the dream, this transformation is apt because diamonds are the chief cause for exploitation of black workers in Africa. She also turns the tables on "the money-people" who consistently turn the writer into a commodity by hacking up her novels for film and television; they take pleasure in destroying the text and the writer in the process. Anna's writing in general and this dream in particular lay bare the devices of production and consumption, exposing capitalism's corruption in the multinational arena.

Since the dream follows directly after Anna's departure from Mrs. Marks, it constitutes a repudiation of orthodox psychoanalysis, which serves the interests of capitalism every bit as much as the "money-people" who exploit the writer. Henry Miller protests, "The analyst has endless time and patience; every minute you detain him means money in his pocket. . . . Whether you whine, howl, beg, weep, cajole, pray or curse—he listens. He is just a big ear minus a sympathetic nervous system."[26] No wonder then that in terminating analysis, Anna feels a malicious, spiteful satisfaction in breaking out, which she associates with the "winking, sardonic snout" of the crocodile in her dream. Seeing her reflection in a window, she recognizes a "small, pale, dry, spiky woman, with a wry look . . . which I recognized as the grin on the snout of that malicious little green crocodile in the crystal casket" (253).

In this passage, the novel's debt to *Notes from Underground* is perhaps most pronounced, for Anna shares the underground man's spitefulness, capriciousness, and refusal to be ruled by the "laws of nature," or by the behaviorists who treat human desires like piano keys. Anna's Dostoyevskian grin comes from her conviction that Mrs. Marks never succeeded in constricting the desires and drives in Anna's unconscious, or in routing her social and political obsessions into Oedipal contortions. The analyst's traditional role, Laing notes, is—like the colonist's—to mystify and obfuscate his true ends, that of using his power to control others (*PE*, chaps. 2–4). Deleuze and Guattari expand on Laing's insight: "Oedipus is always colonization pursued by other means, it is the interior colony . . . even here at home, where we Europeans are concerned, it is our intimate colonial education" (D&G, 170). Anna resists that colonization, insisting instead on taking the misery and madness of the world into account in a materialist-based politics of experience.

GLOBAL POLITICS AND THE SOCIAL GENESIS OF PSYCHOSIS

[The structuralists] search for their structures in culture. As for myself, I look for them in the immediate reality. My way of seeing things was in direct relationship to the events of the times: Hitlerism, Stalinism, fascism. . . . I was

26. Henry Miller, *Sexus* (New York: Grove Press, 1965), pp. 429–30.

fascinated by the grotesque and terrifying forms that surfaced in the sphere of the interhuman, destroying all that was held dear until then.[27]

Throughout *The Golden Notebook*, Lessing investigates the same phenomenon that so many other intellectuals have grappled with (including Laing, Reich, Deleuze, Guattari, as well as Alice Walker and Margaret Atwood): how to account for the rise of Hitler, Mussolini, and the appeal of fascism. What makes the masses desire their own subjection? What accounts for the fascism within us? The crocodile, indigenous to Africa and prime target for capitalist exploitation, is Lessing's symbol for the massive paranoia of the world's despots. (Charlie Themba and Joseph McCarthy are more localized versions of the paranoid styles of Hitler and Stalin.) Lessing consistently links psychic disintegration to social psychosis. In the dream in which Anna is lying in dark water beneath a tiger cage, for instance, "the depths of the water under me had become dangerous with monsters and crocodiles, and things I could scarcely imagine, they were so old and so tyrannous" (615). Her words uncannily echo those of Jesse Watkins, whose account of his schizophrenic breakdown is tape-recorded by Laing:

> I had a feeling . . . that I was more—more than I had always imagined myself, not just existing now, but I had existed since the very beginning . . . from the lowest form of life to the present time, and that that was the sum of my real experiences, and that what I was doing was experiencing them again. . . . I had this sort of vista ahead of me as though I was looking down . . . not *looking* so much as just feeling—ahead of me was lying the most horrific journey. (*PE*, 108)

The schizophrenic process is a voyage of initiation, a transcendental experience in the loss of the Ego. In order to overcome her desire for self-destruction, Anna has to find some way to shift from being "sunk in subjectivity" to experiencing the copresence of others around the globe. That is why she reviews her African past, because it helps distance her from the oedipalizing constraints of Western thought. While Laing disengaged himself from the familialism of psychoanalysis by focusing on the Orient (D&G, 95), Lessing concentrates on Africa, where the Oedipus myth's configurations are defamiliarized and defamilialized. As Deleuze and Guattari remark:

27. Witold Grombrowicz, *L'herne*, no. 14, p. 230, cited by Deleuze and Guattari, pp. 97–98.

It is strange that we had to wait for the dreams of colonized peoples in order to see that, on the vertices of the pseudo triangle, mommy was dancing with the missionary, daddy was being fucked by the tax collector, while the self was being beaten by a white man. It is precisely this pairing of the parental figures with agents of another nature, their locking embrace similar to that of wrestlers, that keeps the triangle from closing up again, from being valid in itself, and from claiming to express or represent this different nature of the agents that are in question in the unconscious itself. (D&G, 96)

The images in Anna's dreams about her African experience juxtapose the interlocking repressions of oedipalization and colonization. At one point, Anna tries to evoke other figures who have struggled for collective causes; she thinks of Mr. Mathlong and wonders what it must have been like "to be a black man in white-occupied territory, humiliated in his human dignity. I tried to imagine him, at mission school, and then studying in England" (597). But she cannot imagine him, precisely because he symbolizes a kind of dignity and detachment to which Anna no longer has access. She tries to conjure up images of sanity like Mathlong, but instead she dreams of madness. She remembers receiving a letter from the African nationalist Charlie Themba, whose small spiky figure resembles both the crocodile and Anna herself:

I became [Themba]. . . . It was as if he stood there slightly to one side of me, but part of me, his small spiky dark figure . . . looking at me. Then he melted into me. I was in a hut, in the Northern Province, and my wife was my enemy, and my colleagues on the Congress, formerly my friends, were trying to poison me, and somewhere out in the reeds a crocodile lay dead, killed with a poisoned spear, and my wife, brought by my enemies, was about to feed me crocodile flesh, and when it touched my lips I would die, because of the furious enmity of my outraged ancestors. (592–93)

In the course of her breakdown, Anna comes to feel with a certainty that will never leave her that the underlying reality of her time is war, brought on by the madness of paranoid despots. Whether one thinks of Joseph McCarthy's witch hunts or Joseph Stalin's clinical madness, the social genesis of psychosis is everywhere apparent. Anna has been betrayed by Stalin and the Communist party; her American friends have been persecuted by McCarthy's hysteria; her Eastern European friends have been hung in Prague and Hungary. She is sickened by her epiphany. Neither literature

nor art nor moments of individual happiness can assuage her acute consciousness of living in a terrible century, for she sees

> the world with nations, systems, economic blocks, hardening and consolidat-
> ing; a world where it would become increasingly ludicrous even to talk about
> freedom, or the individual conscience. . . . I was experiencing the fear of war
> as one does in nightmares, . . . knowing, with my nerves and imagination,
> the fear of war. . . . the real movement of the world towards dark, hardening
> power. . . . I felt this, like a vision, in a new kind of knowing. And I knew that
> the cruelty and the spite and the I, I, I, I of Saul *and of Anna* were part of the
> logic of war; and I knew how strong these emotions were, in a way that would
> never leave me, would become part of how I saw the world. (567, 588–89;
> emphasis mine)

Rather than depicting man as aggressor and woman as victim, in this passage
Lessing portrays aggression as a force that transcends gender; the naked ego
is as powerful a force in women as in men. It is one thing, she suggests, for
women to comply to their own suffering; it is quite another to be responsible
for the oppression of others. Women's awareness of their complicity is also
one of the hallmarks of epistolarity in *The Color Purple* and *The Handmaid's Tale*, as we shall see presently. Celie's confession that she urged
Harpo to beat Sophia is a milestone in her moral development. Offred confesses her participation in the barbaric rites devised by the Gileadeans:
salvaging and hanging adulterous handmaids. Like them, Anna first acknowledges her complicity in the cruelty and spite, then searches for forms
of political action that resist power and paranoia, fascism and repression—
whether in Africa, China, Korea, Indochina, Europe, or the United States.

Anna searches obsessively for some distillation of the truth in books,
journals, or newspapers. She papers her walls with newspaper stories precisely because these pieces of print are unassimilable; they convey nothing
of the urgency or the menace of global crises. Whether she reads of the
slaughter of Koreans, Africans, Communists, of the Rosenbergs' electrocu-
tion, or of atom bomb tests, she cannot conjure up a sense of the tragic reality of such events. Rather than failing to imagine these things, she has lost
the ability to make words *match* her imagination, with the result that the
meaning becomes more terrible as the gulf between meaning and language
widens. When the threat and the desire for extinction are strongest in Anna,
she envisions another split in herself, between the self that desires extinction and the observing ego which tells her that she is sunk in subjectivity,

sunk in herself and her own needs. This critique of subjectivity and of the individual's obsession with private emotions is one of Lessing's major motifs. It is this critique of subjectivity which led her to distance herself from feminists who heralded the novel as a manifesto about the "sex war," and who read it solely as a clarion call to women's liberation. Lessing confessed her disappointment at the novel's reception to Florence Howe:

> When *The Golden Notebook* came out, I was astonished that people got so emotional about that book, one way or another. They didn't bother to see, even to look at, how it was shaped. . . . What I'm trying to say is that it was a detached book. It was a failure, of course, for if it had been a success, then people wouldn't get so damned emotional when I didn't want them to be.[28]

Lessing's objections seem all the more pertinent with the passage of time, especially in light of recent exhortations by some feminists to return to personal criticism.[29] Lessing, in contrast, was aware that the personal is not simply equivalent to the political; that celebrating the emotions cannot substitute for collective action. Long before global politics became part of feminisms's agenda, she insisted on situating women's struggle in relation to other emancipatory struggles around the globe; from that perspective, she predicted that eventually "the aims of Women's Liberation will look very small and quaint" (*GN*, "Introduction," ix). Anna's notebooks simultaneously reflect her boredom with her emotions and her irritation at being trapped in them nonetheless. She creates a fictional heroine Ella, in an attempt to distance herself from her own subjectivity; Ella, in turn, debunks her feelings rather than idealizing them when she complains, "How boring these emotions are that we're caught in and can't get free of, no matter how much we want to" (318). Schizoanalysis has been described in terms that uncannily echo her words: its function is "to break the holds of power and institute research into a new collective subjectivity and a revolutionary healing of mankind. For we are sick, so sick, of our *selves!*" (D&G, xxi). Schizoanalysis thus involves the transformation of a chaotic, destructive individual consciousness into a vital, creative, and collective force. The aim is

---

28. Florence Howe, "A Talk with Doris Lessing," *Nation*, 6 March 1967, pp. 311–13; see also "A Conversation with Doris Lessing (1966)," in *Contemporary Literature* 14 (Autumn 1973): 418–36.

29. For example, Jane Tompkins, "Me and My Shadow," and Barbara Christian, "The Race for Theory," in *Gender and Theory: Dialogues on Feminist Criticism*, ed. Linda Kauffman, pp. 121–39, 225–37, respectively.

to cultivate a sense of the copresence of others *in their otherness,* to cultivate a sense of difference rather than identity. (The emphasis on difference explains why Derrida similarly emphasizes the irreducible alterity of the "quite-other" [*tout-autre*].)[30] As the result of her collaborative descent with/as "Saul," Anna's individual subjectivity gives way to a collective subjectivity: in her dreams, she becomes an Algerian torturer, a French soldier, a Chinese peasant woman. She wakes, "a person who had been changed by the experience of being other people." She reveals that her voyage has not been solely *with* Saul—or, more accurately—*as* Saul; instead,

> if there were a tape recorder of the hours and hours of talk in that room, the talk and the fighting and the arguing and the sickness, it would be a record of a hundred different people living now, in various parts of the world, talking and crying out and questioning. (623)

This insight leads her to reveal further how utterly "Saul" has been an interior projection, and to question the implications of such a transformation for society at large: "If a person can be invaded by a personality who isn't theirs, why can't people—I mean people in the mass—be invaded by alien personalities" (623). Schizoanalysis wants precisely this sort of relation to the outside, this imaginative experiencing of other people, without attempting to assimilate or colonize them. It is one alternative to waging war by maintaining the category of otherness, based on the boundaries of nation states, political allegiances, racial identity, or religious intolerance. Lessing thus provides an answer to the question Susan Bordo poses:

> To deny the unity and stability of identity is one thing. The epistemological fantasy of *becoming* multiplicity—the dream of limitless multiple embodiments, allowing one to dance from place to place and self to self—is another. What sort of body is it that is free to change its shape and location at will, that can become anyone and travel everywhere? If the body is a metaphor for our locatedness in space and time and thus for the finitude of human perception and knowledge, then the postmodern body is no body at all.[31]

30. Jacques Derrida, "Of an Apocalyptic Tone Recently Adopted in Philosophy," trans. John P. Leavey, *Semeia* 23 (1982): 63–97; see also Gayatri Spivak, "Can the Subaltern Speak?" in *Marxism and the Interpretation of Culture,* ed. Cary Nelson and Lawrence Grossberg (Urbana: Univ. of Illinois Press, 1988), p. 294.

31. Susan Bordo, "Feminism, Postmodernism, and Gender-Scepticism," in *Feminism/Postmodernism,* ed. Linda J. Nicholson (New York: Routledge, 1989), p. 145.

Lessing demonstrates that reconceptualizing the body does not erase its materiality; instead, her postmodern experiment situates the body in the widest possible network of social, political, and global interconnections, and strives simultaneously to inscribe the specificities of those other historical bodies—Chinese, Korean, Algerian, Russian. Schizoanalysis is a mode of artistic production that rejects divisions and pyramidal hierarchization, and instead urges us to develop action, thought, and desires by proliferation, juxtaposition, and disjunction. In Lessing's view, such a complex and ambitious project cannot be accomplished in the conventional novel.

LESSING'S CRITIQUE OF THE REALISTIC NOVEL

The whole world is being shaken into a new pattern by the cataclysms we are living through: . . . I write all these remarks with exactly the same feeling as if I were writing a letter to post into the distant past: I am so sure that everything we now take for granted is going to be utterly swept away in the next decade.

(So why write novels? Indeed, why! I suppose we have to go on living *as if* . . .) (Doris Lessing, *GN*, "Introduction," viii–ix).

Among the many dilemmas confronting the writer is how to transform raw material in all its multiplicity into a novel that doesn't lie with every word. In the preface, Lessing says that the structure of the novel is a wordless statement about the novel form (xiv). Thus, like the other epistolary texts in my study, the novel is a work of literary criticism as well as fiction. Her "wordlessness" speaks volumes. She contrasts the great philosophical novels of ideas with journalistic novels; she parodies numerous genres and styles of writing; she relentlessly exposes the inadequacy of fiction. The lament in language for what language cannot describe is another hallmark of the novel's epistolary indebtedness. Lessing shares Derrida's acute awareness of writing in Joyce's wake: not only does she name her heroines Anna and Molly after Anna Livia and Molly Bloom, but she painstakingly records the rhythms of the body over the course of one day, ranging from Anna's desire to make love to the onset of menstruation. Writing after the fiftieth anniversary of Bloomsday, Anna records everything she thinks, feels, and does on 15 September 1954, the day her lover leaves her and she leaves the Communist party:

It was as if I, Anna, were nailing Anna to the page. Every day I shaped Anna, said: Today I got up at seven. . . . Yet now I read those entries and feel nothing. I am increasingly afflicted by vertigo where words mean nothing. . . . They have become, *when I think*, not the form into which experience is shaped, but a series of meaningless sounds, like nursery talk, and away to one side of experience. Or like the sound track of a film that has slipped its connection with the film. *When I am thinking* I have only to write a phrase like "I walked down the street," or to take a phrase from a newspaper "economic measures which lead to the full use of . . ." and immediately the words dissolve, and my mind starts spawning images which have nothing to do with the words. . . . then the words swim and have no sense and I am conscious only of me, Anna, as a pulse in a great darkness, and the words that I, Anna, write down are nothing, or like the secretions of a caterpillar that are forced out in ribbons to harden in the air. (476)

In this passage, Lessing draws attention both to the process of writing-to-the-moment and of reading in order to dramatize the shifting temporalities, individualities, and states through which Anna passes. Words are a mere residue of all the sensations, emotions, stimuli that are constantly being absorbed consciously and unconsciously. That residue is neglible, compared to what is left out. Nevertheless, Anna fears that the breakdown of language signifies the onslaught of psychic disintegration: "If I am at a pitch where shape, form and expression are nothing," Anna thinks, "then I am nothing" (477). Anna is protesting against the ways in which the subject is sutured into discourse without benefit of identity; protesting against the self's finding a language so as to find a self in that language.[32] Lessing's interest in this

32. See Garrett Stewart, "Catching the Stylistic D/rift: Sound Defects in Woolf's *The Waves*," *ELH* 54, no. 2 (Summer 1987): 421–61. Woolf's stylistic devices are particularly interesting in light of Lessing's homage to Woolf, signaled by naming her heroine Wulf. Molly Hite, in *The Other Side of the Story* (Ithaca: Cornell Univ. Press, 1989), points out that

Woolf's writing and her writing practices may have had more influence on Lessing than scholars have yet been able to document; for instance, the "degeneration" of the notebooks into collections of newspaper clippings is suggestively reminiscent of the notebooks of clippings that Woolf assembled during the years in which she was preparing to write *Three Guineas*. (87)

Hite's valuable study appeared as I was making my final revisions. There are notable similarities in our emphases, although we disagree about Saul Green's function (see Hite, pp. 96–102) and about the role of transgender experiences in the novel.

psychic state and in wordless statements parallels Laing's observation that "at the point of nonbeing we are at the outer reaches of what language can state" (*PE*, 40). She has long been interested—in novels ranging from *The Golden Notebook* to *The Four-Gated City* to *Briefing for a Descent into Hell*—in subjects who communicate without words.[33] Yet, in contrast to Laing, Lessing refuses to repudiate the unconscious, choosing instead to represent the vicissitudes of psychic life in linguistic experiments. Just as Anna searches for a schism in society and in the personality through which something new might be poured, so in discourse, too, she is searching for a pulsional break, a breakthrough of phonic play into the chain of symbolic or discursive continuity.[34] Hence the emphasis on words swimming together in the darkness. When her notebooks overlap, when she loses the capacity to compartmentalize topics into black, red, yellow, and blue, language itself begins to disseminate, multiply, flow. This is not a failure but an achievement, accompanied by Anna's recognition that there is no absolute truth, no untainted idealism, no origin or end that is all-encompassing. There is no stasis; all structures participate in incessant and dynamic interaction.

The stylistic experiments and new way of perceiving that Lessing described in 1962 involves what we would now identify as the deconstructive theory of supplements, for the novel testifies to the plenitude of writing. If one views "Free Women" as the novel's "center," then the rest of Anna's writing must be viewed as marginal, supplementary: letters, notebooks, plot synopses, plot outlines for future fiction. But Lessing dismantles the very notion of a center through discontinuous narration that is associative, nonlinear, inconclusive. She subverts the conventional novel by exposing its reductiveness on the one hand, and on the other hand by juxtaposing voluminous "supplementary" writings.

In many respects, Lessing's novel seems uncannily to fulfill Viktor Shklovsky's prophecies about the evolution of the genre: he predicted that a new literary form based on facts recorded in fragmentary notebooks would

33. Margaret Drabble, "Doris Lessing: Cassandra in a World under Siege," *Ramparts* 10 (February 1972): 50–54.

34. Stewart, speaking of Woolf, p. 421. In contrast, Elizabeth Abel, "*The Golden Notebook*: 'Female Writing' and 'The Great Tradition,'" in Sprague and Tiger, pp. 101–7, wrongly identifies Anna's writing with *écriture féminine* and argues that Saul is a real character whose masculine writing should be contrasted with Anna's feminine writing.

emerge by fusing the literary and the nonliterary. *The Golden Notebook* is what Shklovsky would call "factography"—a combination of journalism, essays, cinematic techniques, and other nonliterary forms. Like Shklovsky, Barthes, and Derrida, Lessing pushes the novel as a genre beyond its limits, and simultaneously criticizes those limits by showing how the genre is framed—in tradition, in literary criticism, in the media. Like Shklovsky, Lessing acts on a new perception of text as production, and of history as narrative. Anna's paralysis derives from her sense that language reduces the complexity of all emotions, experiences, and ideals. Her strongest emotions and whole epochs of both her personal existence and modern history are "buttoned up" to form a narrative with beginning, middle, and end. The very act of making a story is, in Anna's view, a falsification and an evasion. One of "Saul's" functions, as one of Anna's "others," is to critique her writing, a role anticipated by Anna's own earlier harsh criticisms of *Frontiers of War*. "Saul" is a projection of the political Anna, who becomes so troubled by the lies in the Communist Party that she begins to stammer. Her stammer is one sign, like Irma's injection or the Wolfman's ticktock, of desire pounding away in the unconscious, "speaking" what cannot be said (D&G, 54). As in so many epistolary narratives from Shklovsky's forward, Anna is obsessed with exile and writes under an injunction. The injunction never to challenge the official party line by protesting against some patently absurd cliché compels Anna to split off her speech onto "Saul," so that she can criticize its oscillations between sentimental clichés, "stock from the liberal cupboard," and revolutionary clichés, "stock from the marxist cupboard." Further evidence that "Saul" is her projection is revealed in the dream in which he is the "projectionist"; he is her internal critic, challenging her in a "jaunty, practical, jeering, a commonsensical voice" by asking whether the emphasis she has put on her experience is "politically correct." This is why she compares the disjunction of words and experience to a sound track out of sync with a film reel. The necessity of being "politically correct" fills Anna with "the nausea of being under strain, of trying to expand one's limits beyond what has been possible" (619). She is paralyzed by the institution of language as a discourse of otherness and by her awareness that all officially sanctioned discourse is a form of power, devoted to policing what can be said, thought, felt, dreamt. Alice Walker and Margaret Atwood will be haunted by similar nightmares of linguistic and material repression.

As Derrida will do later, Lessing acknowledges her debt to James Joyce, but her gender gives the issues of belatedness and the anxiety of influence an entirely different slant. Despite her Joycean ambition to defamiliarize cultural taboos, she discovers that when *women's* bodily habits are described, male and female readers alike are repelled:

> When James Joyce described his man in the act of defecating, it was a shock, shocking. Though it was his intention to rob words of their power to shock. And I read recently in some review, a man said he would be revolted by the description of a woman defecating. I resented this; because of course, what he meant was, he would not like to have that romantic image, a woman, made less romantic. (340)

Lessing's novel is an antiromance, one that attempts to expose the underlying hypocrisy in the traditional inscription of femininity, which she sees as indissolubly linked to the ideology of romantic love, the ideology disseminated so successfully in novels and love letters through the centuries. Romance and sentimentality disguise the concrete operations of economic and political power, a deception in which love letters play a crucial role, as Gayatri Spivak observes: "Sexual relations of reproduction are still crucial in every arena of politics and economics—and the tradition of love letters has been the most powerful ideological dissimulation of those relations."[35] But Anna goes on to confess that she herself finds menstrual smells distasteful, and even though she has set herself the task of writing about everything of which she is conscious, and of trying to be conscious of everything, there will always be an inevitable gap between authorial intention and reader response, even when the reader is the writer herself:

> Whereas to me, the fact I am having a period is no more than an entrance into an emotional state, recurring regularly, that is of no particular importance; I know that as soon as I write the word "blood," it will be giving a wrong emphasis, and even to me when I come to read what I've written. And so I begin to doubt the value of a day's recording before I've started to record it. (340)

Such confessions of failure are acknowledgments that we enter a preexisting language system that is aswarm with names and connotations beyond the control of author, reader, and even author-as-reader. Her self-doubt and sense of defeat reinforce Anna's paralysis and help to explain why she is torn

35. Gayatri Spivak, "Love Me, Love my Ombre, Elle," p. 35.

between her desire to write a novel about women of her time and her desire
to write a political novel. Among her "others," political figures like Mr.
Mathlong reproach her for "scribbling" about such "trivial topics as
women's issues" in the midst of Africa's crisis; unable to resolve this conflict
between the personal and the political, she initially writes nothing. Another
reason why the dream in which "Saul" is the projectionist is so crucial is that
it marks her growth and enables her to dream political dreams, like the one
about being a soldier fighting the French, holding a rifle in the moonlight on
a dry hillside in Algeria:

> Anna's brain was working in this man's head, and she was thinking: Yes I shall
> kill, I shall even torture because I have to, but without belief. Because it is no
> longer possible to organise and to fight and to kill without knowing that new
> tyranny arises from it. Yet one has to fight and organise. (600–601)

This dream further illuminates "Saul's" function, for the novel produced
from this projection (with Saul as projectionist) is classified as "Saul's
novel," but it is actually written by Anna. Not only does it incorporate all
the details of her abiding political preoccupations, but it is structured around
polar political responses that she herself experiences: at one pole, a French
prisoner of the Algerians is tormented by a sense that "he never had a
thought, or an emotion, that didn't instantly fall into pigeon holes, one
marked Marx and one marked Freud. His thoughts and emotions were like
marbles rolling into predetermined slots" (643). His jailor and torturer, the
Algerian soldier, has the opposite problem: he never thinks what is expected; he is totally spontaneous, undirected. These two poles—overdeter-
mination and spontaneity—are aspects of Anna herself. The novel ends
with the French prisoner and Algerian soldier seeing *themselves* as
projections of each other. Ironically, they are both executed by the authorities for communing with one another and for breaking free of their prescribed roles. Their recognition of their affinities is deemed treasonous, since
war and destruction rely on maintaining a rigid set of differences—political,
geographical, religious, racial. Lessing thus vividly illustrates just how irre-
vocable the definition of the individual as the product of power is.

Anna thus authors far more than the first sentence of the Algerian
novel, for this denouement incorporates one of her earliest recurrent
dreams: of prisoners on a firing line who exchange places (351). The novel
crystallizes the two poles of Anna's political dilemma, but it gives no indica-

tion of the raw material that went into it, for it is Anna who feels that her every emotion is predetermined and pigeonholed; it is Anna, conversely, who knows that she does not feel what she is expected to feel about God, State, Law and Order. The Algerian novel contains no trace of Anna's other major obsession about being a possessive woman and a prisoner of sex, but that obsession is reiterated wordlessly in the Algerian jailor–French prisoner relationship. Some critics cite the Algerian novel as evidence that "Saul" must be a full-dimensional character, since the plot synopsis is written in "his" handwriting, but we have already seen how many of Anna's notebooks are written in a variety of hands—all hers. Furthermore, Anna does not say that *Saul* later published the novel but that "this short novel was later published and did rather well" (643). In other words, Anna is author of not one but four short novels in *The Golden Notebook:* "Free Women," *Frontiers of War, The Shadow of the Third,* and "Saul's" political novel. Roberta Rubenstein notes that "the outline of the novel . . . written by Anna through her alter ego of Saul Green—is the fiction that springs her loose from her own fragmented introspection."[36] This schizoanalytic splitting enables her to put her individual subjectivity in perspective and to confront her distaste for the bourgeois novel. Lessing's own comments about the novel's construction illuminate her method:

> When I wrote *The Golden Notebook,* I deliberately evoked the different levels to write different parts of it. To write the part where two characters are a bit mad, I couldn't do it, I couldn't get to that level. Then I didn't eat for some time by accident (I forgot) and found that there I was, I'd got there. And other parts of *The Golden Notebook* needed to be written by "I's" from other levels.[37]

Lessing's aim is to dismantle realist fiction through discontinuous narration that is associative, nonlinear, inconclusive. With the exception of "Free Women," and "Saul's" novel, everything else is an unbounded text; her weaving of memory, dream, history, and desire all appear uncircumscribed by considerations of length, logic, consistency, rationality.

36. Roberta Rubenstein, *The Novelistic Vision of Doris Lessing: Breaking the Forms of Consciousness* (Urbana: Univ. of Illinois Press, 1979), p. 105.

37. Roy Newquist, "Interview with Doris Lessing," in *A Small Personal Voice,* ed. Paul Schlueter (New York: Knopf, 1974), p. 60.

There is no frame of reference that can be cited as the source of truth, origin of being, authority for writing in the novel. Instead, she anticipates Barthes and Derrida by drawing attention to the act of framing, enframing in order to expose authority as a writing effect. The pressure to write and the impossibility of writing are simultaneously articulated. By affirming the value of wordless communication and presymbolic discourse, Anna is paradoxically freed to put words on paper. The sheer voluminousness of the notebooks testifies wordlessly to the value—and indeed the inevitability—of the supplement—another idea central to the Barthesian and especially the Derridean project. Anna periodically rereads what she has written, makes marginal emendations, modifies earlier insights, criticizes her prose, and thus acts as both writer and addressee as she makes "correspondences" between earlier and later selves, ideas, styles. She is both "inside" and "outside" the text in ways reminiscent of the experiments of Shklovsky, Barthes, and Derrida. This experiment is a way of surmounting one of the main limitations of the conventional novel, since what she finds unreproducible in art is the physical texture of life and the flow of movement. She consciously captures the flow of desires, ideas, intensive states by reproducing acts of composition and recomposition in the notebooks, even miming the hastiness of composition with spelling errors, slash marks, and emendations. Indeed, as in *Zoo*, Lessing crosses out material in the notebooks, but leaves it visible nonetheless.[38] Epistolary texts are invariably written under erasure; the texture of experience is serial rather than linear; the associations are aleatory rather than calculated. In the very act of forming a conclusion, the conventional novel distorts experience, for—as Derrida also demonstrates—one cannot know what one's destiny or destination will turn out to be. The sense of an ending is a falsification, as Anna remarks:

> As soon as one has lived through something, it falls into a pattern. . . . And the pattern of an affair . . . is seen in terms of what ends it. That is why all

---

38. Sprague, "Doubles Talk," notes that the reader is privy to such crossed-out material as her long entry on 15 September 1954; the black lines, typescript, musical symbols, interlocking circles, asterisks, doodling, brackets, "speak to the excisions that falsify in published writings," p. 55. John Carey, in "Art and Reality in *The Golden Notebook*," *Contemporary Literature* 14 (Autumn 1973): 437–56, also discusses the careless spelling and punctuation, which give the impression of hasty, unrevised and unedited writing.

this is untrue. Because while living through something one doesn't think like that at all. . . . Literature is analysis after the event. (227–28)

Lessing's strategy for subverting that analysis-after-the-event is to construct the novel so that the story is "over" when we read the first words. But as we read, we are unaware that everything we read has already occurred, that it has been ordered and rearranged by Anna the editor. The same technique informs *The Handmaid's Tale*: not until we read the historical note do we realize that what we took for epistolary immediacy was actually subject to an editor's mediation. *The Golden Notebook*, however, is more circular: when the women part in the last lines of "Free Women 5," we are brought back to "Free Women 1," which commences with their reunion. Some critics call this a "sleight of hand," arguing that "Free Women" is not a satisfactory resolution to the dilemmas the novel poses.[39]

By focusing on the editor's role in epistolary production, however, different criteria of value emerge. One has only to think of *The Sorrows of Young Werther*, *Notes from Underground*, *Zoo*, *Lolita*, *A Lover's Discourse*, *The Post Card*, and *The Handmaid's Tale* to see how the epistolary editor problematizes the dichotomies between fiction/reality, inside/outside, lies/truth, character/author, past/present, self/other. We have seen how John Ray's preface alters our perception of *Lolita*: interpretation depends on how the text is framed. We shall shortly investigate authorship in *The Handmaid's Tale*; should it be read as a narration in the present by the handmaid, or as a reconstruction by a historian some 150 years later? Multiple framing and embedding devices thwart interpretation of Lessing's novel, too. As editor, Anna is her own harshest critic—not only of her prose but of her earlier selves and her earlier writings. This strategy is epistolary, for her earlier selves are veritable addressees, as alien to her now as actual correspondents would be. Of her love affair with Michael, for example, she notes that "any intelligent person could have foreseen the end of this affair from its beginning. And yet I, Anna, . . . refused to see it" (211). Elsewhere she looks back on her immaturity in Africa and comments that, at that phase of her life, she viewed other people merely as reflections of her own needs.

Such techniques of prolepsis and analepsis contribute to the texture of

39. Martens, *The Diary Novel*, p. 242.

supplementarity in the novel. They also testify to a radical reconceptualization of subjectivity, one inseparable from global politics. As a young woman, the emotions Anna anticipated having in later life never materialize; conversely, as she looks back, she cannot believe that she was so idealistic, so naive. She is paralyzed by the complexity of memory, too: how can she trust the accuracy of her memory? How can she know whether what she now remembers is what was most important? Anna now would certainly record different things from the Anna then. Temporal disruptions further undermine the notions of a fixed, unified, coherent self. "Free Women" is not meant to resolve the problems of unity, identity, totality; quite the contrary. It dramatizes the insolubility of those dilemmas. Neither the novella, nor the final golden notebook, in which Anna resolves to "put all of herself," nor even the novel The Golden Notebook in its entirety resolve the dilemmas they each present. Instead, she dismantles the dichotomies between Literature ("Free Women") and writing (the notebooks, letters, parodies, plot outlines, etc.); between outside/inside the text, between center/margin, between origin/supplement. Like the Derridean notion of a fold, a pli in the text, Lessing calls "Free Women" an "envelope" for the rest of the novel.[40] No "envelope" can fully contain the novel any more than a postmark can. The novel demonstrates that the whole itself is a product, nothing more than a part alongside other parts, which it neither unifies nor totalizes. Her aim was to try to produce fragments whose primary relationship was one of difference, without recourse to a totalizing origin. I think Lessing purposely constructed "Free Women" as the least interesting segment of the novel in order to expose the limitations of realism—a daring feat. "Free Women" illustrates how what Richard Ohmann calls "the illness story" enforces the ideology of bourgeois individualism; it reduces the mass of experience (social, sexual, historical, economic, political) solely to a matter of individual health or illness. The implied message is that one cannot change society, only oneself.[41] As Lessing notes in the preface,

> "Free Women" as a summary and condensation of all that mass of material, was to say something about the conventional novel, another way of describing the dissatisfaction of a writer when something is finished: "How little I have

40. Florence Howe, "A Conversation with Doris Lessing," p. 428.
41. Ohmann, "The Shaping of the Canon of U.S. Fiction," pp. 212–19.

managed to say of the truth, how little I have caught of all that complexity; how can this small neat thing be true when what I experienced was so rough and apparently formless and unshaped." (*GN*, "Introduction," xiv)

Since the novella is about failure, it is ironic that it even fails to live up to its title, since neither Anna nor Molly are free from the constraints of their society. As Schweikart points out, the novella is "about two women who gradually realize that they are not free, that they really cannot be free."[42] The title can be seen as either an ironic statement, or as a command to "Liberate Women" (like "Save the Whales"). In any case, it is a closed text, a purposeful parody of realistic fiction. "Free Women" is to *The Golden Notebook* as Balzac's "Sarrasine" is to Barthes's *S/Z*. It is certainly not the novel Anna aspired to write, one that is philosophical, that creates a new order and a new approach to representation. Instead, Lessing makes a shambles of domestic "women's fiction" in the same way that Shklovsky makes a shambles of *La nouvelle Héloise*. The novella consists of melodramatic scenes of domestic strife and intrigue worthy of television soap operas. "Free Women" might also be described as Lessing's *Anti-Oedipus*: she parodies the Oedipus myth by substituting the wimpy Tommy for the mythical hero; Tommy plays the role of the truth seeker. He attempts suicide to avoid becoming the person he is destined to become. After blinding himself, he takes up with his stepmother.[43]

Parody, it is worth remembering, is the form that, according to Shklovsky, usually presages the beginning of a new form. Parodies, which are frequently means of protesting against the "thinning of language against the density of experience" (302), abound in *The Golden Notebook*.

---

42. Schweickart, "Reading a Wordless Statement," p. 274. Hite points out that men are the chief beneficiaries of Molly's and Anna's "freedom"; "free" simply means sexually "available," p. 61.

43. Vivien Leonard, in "Free Women as Parody: Fun and Games in *The Golden Notebook*," *Perspectives on Contemporary Literature* 6 (1980): 20–27, describes Lessing's parodic use of Oedipus as a way of nailing down patriarchal society's embodiment of the destructive principle. The idea is suggestive, but one should not therefore conclude that Lessing idealizes women in contrast to men. Hite describes Tommy as being "represented as becoming a parody of the self-limited human being. . . . Tommy's backward metamorphosis from a complex and deeply engaged young man to a singleminded and therefore coherent personality constitutes a fable pointing up how other characters are also self-maimed, self-blinded" (*The Other Side of the Story*, p. 73).

Anna critiques even her dreams for their "quality of false art, caricature, illustration, parody" (228–39); Lessing parodies the "romantic tough school of writing," women's magazine stories, and Communist party manifestos. She even parodies the notebook as a mode, inscribing all the clichés she can think of in a spurious journal of a young man in Paris: "The best die young"; "At thirty, I shall kill myself"; "A woman of the streets offered me one of her nights, for love"; "Time is the river"; "Art is the mirror of our betrayed ideals" (435). Like Shklovsky, Nabokov, Barthes, Derrida, Walker, and Atwood, Lessing exploits the epistolary form to mirror and mimic the culture's received ideas. Parody's distortions expose the culture's clichés and delusions, the debasement of literary codes, the exhaustion of genres, and the underlying ideologies that keep them in circulation.

Anna parodies her own novel, *Frontiers of War*, when she writes a plot synopsis for a film producer, dividing her synopsis and his response into two columns in her notebooks (another way of folding the margins in on the "center"). She even composes parodic reviews of the novel, which—like the "authentic" reviews, overlook what Anna sees as the "terrible lying nostalgia [in] every sentence" (63). In retrospect, she finds the novel repugnant because it deals so exclusively with individual problems, and as such it affirms the status quo in literature and society rather than offering a paradigm for collective action and social change.

Like the two soldiers in Anna's ["Saul's"] political novel, Molly and Anna in "Free Women" are split facets of Anna the author, trying to find a language with which to describe the paradoxes of her time. (Dostoyevsky's description of his underground narrator as a "paradoxicalist" comes to mind again.) But "Free Women" conveys none of the compulsion, terror, or savagery of Anna's experience with schizoanalysis that comes from splitting off part of herself in the creation called "Saul," nor does the novella convey any of the exhilaration of transgressing the boundaries of genre and gender. Anna's most complex parody involves "Saul," for every interaction between "Saul" and Anna in her unconscious is a parody of the sexual power struggle, combining myriad male/female roles: when "Saul" takes the role of the aggressive naked ego in Anna's unconscious, then Anna becomes the passive, wounded sufferer, all "weak soft sodden emotion, the woman betrayed. Oh boohoo, you don't love me. . . . Oh boohoo, and my dainty pink-tipped forefinger pointed at my white, pink-tipped betrayed bosom . . . I began to weep weak, sodden whisky-diluted tears on behalf of womankind" (630). In other words, Anna is aware that she has assumed a literary posture: Wounded Femininity. (Lessing, moreover, sometimes felt that the feminist movement resorted to the same literary stereotype of victimized Woman-hood, which she did not see as an effective means of political activism.) "Saul," similarly, is depicted as the stereotypical Hollywood stud because, as Anna's projection, he is a compendium of all the books she has read and all the movies she has seen which encode masculinity: "all balls and strenuous erection." When she first thinks of the idea of a jealous woman acting as her lover's jailor, she wonders if she read this somewhere (461). "Saul" is a literary figure because she figures him as literature: he is the American Communist party member, political exile, slum schoolboy, Jewish intellec-tual, writer of the great American epic, Hemingway macho man, neurotic child. Like Tommy, Nelson, and de Silva before him, "Saul" is one of the many facets of Oedipal mother-fixation. Whenever Anna is strong, calm, and nurturing, "Saul" is the weak, hysterical, rebellious little boy. This helps to explain the final exchange between them when "Saul" says, "Ise a good boy"; he speaks "out of literature . . . mawkishly, in parody," and then comments, "We can't either of us ever go lower than that" (640–41). The debasement is not of character (since "Saul" is a fragment of Anna); rather it is a debasement of literary form, one that recalls Shklovsky's similar technique of distortion through devaluation of content. Like Shklovsky's, Lessing's novel also parodies the codes of conventional love-as-passion. Anna is aware that she has reached the most debased, clichéd writ-ing style she can imagine. In her dream with "Saul" as projectionist, she is able to perceive that her imagination has been dulled by dead plots as well as by dead metaphors, for when "Saul" challenges her to reproduce a sixteen-year-old girl from her African past, what emerges are all the clichés from women's magazines. "Saul" is sadistically delighted that Anna "could not prevent these words from emerging" (619), because the tendency of lan-guage to repeat clichés and received ideas justifies Anna's repudiation of *Frontiers of War* as well as her subsequent repudiation of writing. In a pas-sage that echoes Shklovsky's warnings about how habitualization devours perception, Anna discovers that stale language inevitably emerges when one relies solely upon the familiar: "I was unable to distinguish between what I had invented and what I had known, and I knew that what I had invented was all false. . . . The material had been ordered by me to fit what I knew, and that was why it was all false" (619–20).

This epiphany signals one of her major breakthroughs, because previously she was unable to confront "that Anna who will read what I will write. Who is this other I whose judgement I fear; or whose gaze . . . is different from mine when I am not thinking, recording and being conscious" (351). The "other I," is, of course "Anna-as-Saul," the internal judge and critic who enables her to experiment with the unknown and untried process of schizoanalysis. The aim of schizoanalysis is to record desiring-production, and that production is stimulated by the semiotic codes and flows that the unconscious mind absorbs incessantly. As Anna's voluminous writings testify, the schizophrenic has her own system of recording, her very own recording code which only coincides with the social code in order to parody it, as she parodies it here (D&G, 15). This helps to explain why Lessing was disappointed that readers became so "damned emotional" about the novel: they persisted in reading representationally, when her purpose was to expose the representational fallacy through parody and distortion.

Since Anna believes that film is better than fiction at capturing the physical flow of life, it is no surprise that her final dream unreels like a film. Film-making is the perfect medium for desiring-production: it is a collaborative art form, one which transposes negative and positive images. Like Lessing's novel, film is serial rather than linear. The notion of a desiring-*machine* illuminates the many mechanical metaphors Lessing employs, ranging from Anna's sense of shifting gears to her "switching off the machine." Anna collaborates with "Saul," her negative image, trying to retrieve and preserve something of the tremendous flow of words, ideas, images unreeled in the vast archives of the unconscious. She even pastes in productions by other hands, thus contributing to the quality of montage in the novel. When one recalls Shklovsky's novel *The Third Factory* (about early Russian cinema), as well as his collaboration with Eisenstein, it seems uncanny that Lessing praises early Russian films as offering a better model for production than novels can offer; her novel in its entirety has been compared to Cubist painting (another of Shklovsky's theoretical interests) and to Eisenstein's montage film technique. [44] Through schizoanalysis, Anna is able to split away the familiar from the unfamiliar, to experience the "grotesque and terrifying

44. Barbara Bellow Watson discusses Lessing's Cubist and cinematic technique in "Leaving the Safety of Myth: Doris Lessing's *The Golden Notebook,*" in *Old Lines, New Forces: Essays*

forms that surfaced in the sphere of the interhuman, destroying all that was held dear until then" (D&G, 97–98). Schizoanalysis entails a going back, a revisiting one's past in slow motion, to see it for the first time. In her dream:

> Patches of the film slowed down for long, long stretches while I watched, absorbed, details I had not had time to notice in life. . . . the film was now beyond my experience, beyond Ella's, beyond the notebooks, because there was a fusion, and instead of seeing separate scenes, people, faces, movements, glances, they were all together. . . . a rock stood glistening while water slowly wore it down, or a man stood on a dry hillside in the moonlight. . . . Or a woman lay awake in darkness, saying No, I won't kill myself, I won't, I won't. (634–35)

This is a classic statement of the schizophrenic voyage, for as Laing explains, numerous patients describe the same journey from temporal movement to a standstill; in the process, one experiences one's relation to everything else (*PE*, 128). The journey is characterized by the movement from mundane time to eonic time, evoked here in the image of water on a rock. That image also signifies the kind of endurance that has eluded Anna: it enables her to experience imaginatively the patience, fortitude, and courage that survival requires. Anna's vision of the man in the moonlight provides the kernel for the first sentence for "Saul's" political novel. It also helps her to see that courage does not consist of the kind of epic heroism one finds in novels; instead, Anna suddenly understands for the first time that heroism consists of a small painful will to endure despite all the injustice and cruelty of existence; it consists of the courage to be a "boulder-pusher," even if one never sees mountains move. Lessing's vision of collective subjectivity parallels what Deleuze and Guattari call "molecular analysis," which is "analysis of the smallest elements which exist as subversive [revolutionary] potential."[45]

---

on the *Contemporary British Novel, 1960–70*, ed. Robert K. Morris (Cranburg, N.J.: Associated University Presses, 1976), p. 14; Sydney Janet Kaplan compares Lessing's montage technique to Eisenstein's films in "The Limits of Consciousness in the Novels of Doris Lessing," in L. S. Dembo and Annis Pratt, ed. *Critical Studies of Doris Lessing* (Madison: Univ. of Wisconsin, 1974), p. 123. Sprague and Tiger, in their introduction to *Critical Essays*, compare the novel to "the experience of seeing all at once the three hundred or so works Van Gogh created in that one year at Arles" (10).

45. Interview with Félix Guattari, *Diacritics* 4 (Fall 1974): 38–41; see also *Anti-Oedipus*, chap. 4.

Another tenet of schizoanalysis is underscored by Anna's epiphany: the unconscious is intimately related to the real, stimulated as much by the social as by the libido. Desire is not based on lack, nor is desiring-production based on fantasy. On this point, Deleuze and Guattari disagree with Lacan; they maintain that

> If desire produces, its product is real. If desire is productive, it can be productive only in the real world and can produce only reality. Desire is the set of *passive syntheses* that engineer partial objects, flows, and bodies, and that function as units of production. The real is the end product . . . desiring-production is one and the same thing as social production. . . . Thus fantasy is never individual: it is *group fantasy*—as institutional analysis has successfully demonstrated. (D&G, 26, 30)

By "institutional analysis," Deleuze and Guattari allude to the La Borde Clinic's efforts in the late 1950s to deal collectively with the issues of psychoses and with the political analysis of desire by placing previously privatized aspects of analysis (transference, fantasies, desire) in an institutional framework. Their work transforms these analytical concepts so that transference comes to be seen as institutional, fantasies as collective: *"desire is a problem of groups and for groups"* (D&G, 30).[46] Although they go much further than Laing, the relevance of his theory of the social genesis of psychosis is clear. This emphasis on desire as a *problem* for groups illuminates Lessing's depiction of her growing disillusionment with the Communist party on the one hand, and the rise of McCarthyism on the other hand. Such groups have what Deleuze and Guattari call a "molar" constitution; they view things in terms of monolithic, totalizing, global coercion, and subjugate people accordingly. Schizoanalysis is thus a counterdiscourse, one that

46. Deleuze and Guattari find much to praise in Lacan, particularly regarding his separation of Freudian theory from biologism, but they do not share his view that lack lies at the root of desire:

> [T]he traditional logic of desire is all wrong from the very outset: from the very first step that the Platonic logic of desire forces us to take, making us choose between *production* and *acquisition*. From the moment that we place desire on the side of acquisition, we make desire an idealistic (dialectical, nihilistic) conception, which causes us to look upon it as primarily a lack: a lack of an object, a lack of the real object. (25; see also 27n.)

Their view of desire is thus closer to that of Derrida, who in *The Post Card* similarly critiques the limitations of both Lacanian psychoanalysis and the Platonic logic of desire. The passage further illuminates why Lessing's strategy is dialogic rather than dialectical. See n. 24 above.

inevitably involves participation in history: one hallucinates and raves history (D&G, 334, 340–45).

Lessing's portrait of communism in general and Anna's paralysis in particular seem to fulfill Shklovsky's prophecy in the 1920s that the insistence on establishing an official Marxist-Leninist aesthetic would stultify all avant-garde experiments. Just as Lessing takes revenge on the orthodox psychoanalytic establishment in her parody of Tommy, she takes revenge on the Communist party in her send-up of officially sanctioned fiction. The novels that comrades submit to the Communist publishing company are politically correct but contrived and banal. Lessing parodies the style in which they wax eloquent about the glories of the party. In the accompanying cover letters, however, the aspiring novelists confess their struggles to believe in the party and to survive. They recount the obstacles, pain, and frustrations they must surmount in order to write. By juxtaposing these different levels of discourse, Lessing pays homage to the letter as the traditional testament of authenticity and sincerity, for in contrast to the hackneyed prose in each comrade's fiction, the letters testify to the heroism and force of will of each correspondent. Initially overwhelmed by the disjunction between language and feeling, Anna eventually comprehends what an achievement a "small painful endurance" is. The letters in *The Golden Notebook* are significant contributions to the utopian vision of collective subjectivity that Anna is striving to articulate.

Elaine Showalter is thus wrong when she argues that Lessing will "have to face the limits of her own fiction very soon if civilization survives the 1970s. . . . Either she will have to revise her apocalyptical prophecies (like other millenarians), or confront, once again, the struggling individual."[47] Lessing demonstrates that it is precisely such "either/or" thinking that is dangerous; it is precisely the ideology of the individual that may lead to apocalypse, for the individual cannot be confronted in isolation, separated from the complex matrix of global politics. Moreover, perhaps only the threat of annihilation commands our serious attention for any length of time—a suspicion that Margaret Atwood develops in *The Handmaid's Tale*. As Marion Vlastos observes, "Given that so much contemporary literature portrays humanity's terrible adjustment to its own future destruction, it

47. Showalter, *A Literature of Their Own*, p. 313.

seems that the *least* criticism can do is be equal to the sense of apocalypse in the art it analyzes"; D. J. Enright concurs: to dismiss the notion of apocalypse as a "gimmick" is "to participate in the blindness that both Lessing and Laing warn against."[48]

Whether the myth of unity pertains to fiction or to the individual, Lessing thus dismantles it, substituting multiplicity as a formal mode and a political potentiality. This is why she presents so many more story lines in the novel than she actually develops; she is dramatizing the supplementarity of language *and* of experience. In any given exchange, numerous levels of communication are going on simultaneously, which is why she resorts at several points to the technique of using asterisks in order to delineate separate threads in a given conversation—a device Laing also employs in interviewing schizophrenic patients. (This technique also anticipates the kind of deconstructive experiment Barthes performs on Balzac's "Sarrasine" in *S/Z*.) Lessing celebrates multiplicity when she informs us that the final, golden notebook is a collaboration between "Saul" and Anna. When Anna declares that she will put all of herself into one book, she is not saying that she is now whole, cured, unitary; she is saying that rather than sustaining the fiction that she and "Saul" are different entities, she will write in a way that makes their relation as facets of her sel(ves) clear. She thus anticipates Barthes's and Derrida's experiments with desiring-production, for whether one deconstructs Anna's multiple others, the notebooks' multiple discourses, or the novel's multiple stories,

> [i]t is only the category of multiplicity, used as a substantive and going beyond both the One and the many, beyond the predicative relation of the One and the many, that can account for desiring-production; desiring-production is pure multiplicity, that is to say, an affirmation that is irreducible to any sort of unity. (D&G, 42)

The novel demonstrates that the end of the book is the beginning of writing—literally, the last words of "Free Women" make us return to the first words and see them for the first time. The "end" of the conventional novel is the beginning of experimental writing—the outcome of which is

48. Marion Vlastos, "Doris Lessing and R. D. Laing: Psychopolitics and Prophecy," *PMLA* 91 (March 1978): 345–58; D. J. Enright, "Shivery Games," *New York Review of Books*, 31 July 1969, pp. 22–24; cited in Vlastos, p. 258n.

undecidable. The outcome cannot be evaluated in terms of the dichotomies that have been dismantled in the process of writing: success/failure, unified/fragmented, whole/split. The structure of the novel enacts the schizophrenic voyage of breakdown and breakthrough: the end returns us to the beginning, just as after the voyage "in," one reverses the movement and returns from inner to outer, from death to life, from going back to going forward, from standstill to temporal movement. But no repetition is the same; it is a return trip with a difference; everything has changed. We cannot return to the first sentence of the novel with our preconceptions about form, structure, plot, and character intact; the novel and its structure have been utterly defamiliarized and reassembled.

Lessing's novel is a complex negotiation between feminism, Marxism, and psychoanalysis. Although her debt to Laing is everywhere apparent, she is dramatizing rather than repudiating unconscious production. In so doing, she anticipates the theoretical formulations of Deleuze and Guattari by linking linguistic experimentation to unconscious processes. Like all letter writers, Anna Wulf writes to her others, revealing both the reductiveness of language and its supplementariness; its intractability and its plenitude. The four major matrixes of her productions are sexuality, psychoanalysis, global politics, and the novel genre. By linking the theory of schizoanalysis to the practice of epistolarity, Lessing shows how the Imaginary can serve the real; how desiring-production functions in the unconscious, in society, and in literature simultaneously. She liberates "what was present in art from its beginnings, but was hidden underneath aims and objects, even if aesthetic, and underneath recordings or axiomatics; the pure process that fulfills itself, and that never ceases to reach fulfillment as it proceeds—art as 'experimentation'" (D&G, 370–71). Although Deleuze and Guattari overlook her, hers is, like Artaud's and Burroughs's, an authentically postmodern experiment. Like Deleuze and Guattari's, Lessing's "work, since at least 1972, as science and fiction, has had a perhaps inevitable aura of futurity." Like them, she is one of the "faithful and vigilant keepers of the future."[49] Alice Jardine warns that the work of Deleuze and Guattari "represent the efforts of new kinds of male bodies attempting, not always successfully, to invent new

---

49. Alice Jardine, speaking solely of Deleuze and Guattari, in *Gynesis: Configurations of Woman and Modernity* (Ithaca: Cornell Univ. Press, 1985), pp. 209, 223.

kinds of subjectivities . . . it is, of course, up to women not to disappear from that space of exploration."[50] One of the limitations of Jardine's study, however, is that she devotes scant space to women novelists who *do* experiment with new kinds of bodies and new subjectivities, as Lessing does here. Betsy Draine, in contrast, compares Lessing to Barth, Barthelme, Beckett, Coover, Cortázar, and Robbe-Grillet, noting:

> with this novel, the writer who once held "the view that the realist novel, the realist story, is the highest form of prose writing; higher than and out of the reach of any comparison with expressionism, impressionism, symbolism, naturalism, or any other ism" . . . suddenly and emphatically rejects both the conventional novel and the modernist novel as models for her own. . . . In this new and powerful identity, Lessing reshapes the form of the novel, giving it a postmodern order.[51]

The Golden Notebook grapples with postmodernity by inscribing a politics of desire, a collective utopian vision of the correspondences between one's others and all others around the globe. The novel's attempt to dismantle the representational fallacy by pushing both psychoanalysis and fiction beyond their conventional boundaries makes it a tour de force. Lessing is in the vanguard of those acting upon a new understanding of history as text and of writing as production; she leads the way in imagining a plural history of diverse writing practices that are specific to a particular time and place, and she tries to conceptualize a politics that reflects a nonrepresentational view of writing. In Alice Walker's *The Color Purple*, the construction of otherness is racial as well as sexual; Africa and America are again represented— this time through the eyes of the colonized rather than the colonizers.

---

50. Ibid., p. 223. Since the sole woman writer in Jardine's study is Marguerite Duras, one is tempted to add that one danger of women disappearing is if feminist critics consistently ignore them! In this regard, Elaine Showalter's and Barbara Christian's critiques of poststructuralist feminists are not entirely unjustified. See Showalter, "Critical Cross-Dressing: Male Feminists and the Woman of the Year," pp. 130–49; and Christian, "The Race for Theory," in *Gender and Theory*, ed. Linda Kauffman, pp. 225–37.

51. Draine, pp. 69–70, 196n.4.

Constructing Otherness:
Struggles of Representation
in The Color Purple

There are many ways to be "colonized." Alice Walker's *The Color Purple* (1982) depicts multiple forms of colonization by juxtaposing Celie's story with Nettie's: both sisters are colonized as blacks in America, and Nettie describes the colonization of the Olinkas in Africa. Yet, within each society, black women are doubly "colonized," treated as chattel by black men at home and abroad. With *The Color Purple, Special Delivery*'s angle of vision shifts from Doris Lessing's urban England to the rural southern United States, from a white to a black woman's perspective. Where the economic independence of Anna Wulf enables her to experience a kind of life women have never had before, Celie would be considered a member of the peasant class (if Americans were willing to relinquish the myth of a classless society). The twenty years between publication of *The Golden Notebook* and *The Color Purple* were marked by the Civil Rights movement, the march on Washington, the assassinations of Medgar Evers, Malcolm X, Martin Luther King, Jr., John and Robert Kennedy, Vietnam, the bombing of Cambodia, murders of college war protesters at Kent, Jackson, Augusta, Berkeley, and Santa Barbara, the rise of the counterculture, the Black Power movement, Watergate, the women's movement, Reaganism and the rise of the New Right—these are but a few signposts. Where Lessing's novel forewarns that the emerging feminist movement must not reduce the political to the personal, twenty years later Walker coins the term "womanist" to include women of color in feminist movement.[1]

The novel is a distinctive addition to epistolary tradition: not only is it different from all the other texts in my study, but it is the first known epistolary novel by an African-American, male or female. The novel's generic debt to slave narrative and to Zora Neale Hurston further illuminates Walker's achievement. Multiple forms of enslavement link Celie's story to Nettie's; their letters expose the mechanics of colonization at home and abroad. Slavery's scars, poverty's brutality, centuries of racism, and the repression of African-American history are haunting legacies in these pages.

Steven Spielberg's 1986 film adaptation elides these legacies. It also erases both the "womanist" and lesbian subversiveness in the novel. By turning it into a black pastoral, a black version of "The Waltons," he restores the dominant (white, bourgeois, male) ideology, a distortion that foregrounds the question of the artist's function in commodity culture—one of the abiding preoccupations throughout *Special Delivery*. Indeed, art seems to imitate life in this regard, for the fate of Walker's novel in the hands of Spielberg and Hollywood seems to parallel Lessing's parody in *The Golden Notebook* of the film industry's hatchet job on Anna's novel, *Frontiers of War*; there, too, complex issues of racial tension and injustice were whitewashed, sentimentalized, reduced to a bourgeois story of individual problems.

1. Walker uses the word "womanist" to distinguish between a white feminist and a black feminist or feminist of color. From the black folk expression of mothers to female children "You act womanish," i.e., like a woman. Usually referring to outrageous, audacious, courageous or *willful* behavior. Wanting to know more and in greater depth than is considered "good" for one. Interested in grown-up doings. . . . Responsible. In charge. *Serious.* . . . *Also*: A woman who loves other women, sexually and/or nonsexually. Appreciates and prefers women's culture, women's emotional flexibility (values tears as natural counterbalance of laughter), and women's strength. Sometimes loves individual men, sexually and/or nonsexually. Committed to survival and wholeness of entire people, male *and* female. Not a separatist, except periodically, for health.
(*In Search of Our Mothers' Gardens* [San Diego: Harcourt Brace Jovanovich, 1983], pp. xi-xii; hereinafter cited parenthetically in the text as *ISMG*)
Following bell hooks, I use the phrase "feminist movement" rather than *the* feminist movement; the latter signifies the monolithic, white, middle-class movement that hooks critiques. See *Feminist Theory: From Margin to Center* (Boston: South End Press, 1984).

While Lessing strives to dismantle the representational fallacy, Walker must confront an oppressed race's need for positive images, literary precursors, and visions of unity, consensus, community. Where Lessing painstakingly depicts the decentering of the human subject, Walker's novel suggests that perhaps one must first have the opportunity to be constituted *as* a subject before one can endorse such decentering. Similarly, in seeming contrast to the Barthesian "death of the author,"[2] Walker straightforwardly confesses her "need" for such authors as Zora Neale Hurston; in discovering her work, "a kind of paradise was regained" (*ISMG*, 83–84). What she values most in Hurston's novels is their representation of "racial health; a sense of black people as complete, complex, undiminished human beings" (*ISMG*, 85). Where Derrida finds himself visiting James Joyce's magnificent grave in *The Post Card*, Walker discovers that Hurston is buried in a weed-infested cemetery without so much as a grave marker; she sets about ordering one herself. Far from endorsing Derrida's notion of belatedness and the anxiety of influence, Walker at one point calls herself Zora's niece, because "as far as I'm concerned, she *is* my aunt—and that of all black people as well."[3]

Walker was nevertheless attacked by critics who disapproved of *The Color Purple's* representation of blacks, particularly of black men. Ishmael Reed charged that her distorted depiction of black men created divisiveness in the black community. In his view, Walker "sold out" to the white feminist establishment, epitomized by Gloria Steinem and *Ms. Magazine*, publishers of Walker's early work. Feminism is thus a crucially contested site, paradoxically erased by such admirers as Steven Spielberg and attacked by black male critics like Reed and Stanley Crouch. As Deborah McDowell points out, "Walker has been the object of the most savage, sustained, and partisan attack (primarily for *The Color Purple*) and the lightning rod for these reviewers' hostility to feminism." McDowell also points out that such attacks ignore the long and distinguished history of black feminism, which emerges from the material existences of black women in America and precedes the resurgence of [white] feminist activism in the late 1960s.[4]

2. Roland Barthes, "The Death of the Author," *Image/Music/Text*, trans. Stephen Heath (New York: Farrar, Straus and Giroux, 1977), pp. 142–48.

3. Alice Walker, "Looking for Zora," *In Search of Our Mothers' Gardens*, pp. 93–116.

4. As I was completing revisions on *Special Delivery*, I discovered Deborah E. McDowell's fine essay, "Reading Family Matters," in *Changing Our Own Words: Essays on Criticism*,

The Color Purple remained controversial throughout the 1980s, first upon publication of the novel (which won the American Book Award and a Pulitzer Prize); then again when the film appeared in 1986; and finally in the pages of scholarly books and journals which appeared by the decade's end. My focus on "struggles of representation" has three connotations. First, the significance of the struggle to achieve representation as a black woman writer. Second, the function and meaning of literary representation to those debating The Color Purple's merits. Third, I shall discuss the relevance of the representational fallacy (so clearly rejected by the male authors in the first part of my study, as well as by Doris Lessing), to authors who write in the awareness of centuries of silencing. As we shall see presently, that includes Margaret Atwood in The Handmaid's Tale as well as Alice Walker.

EPISTOLARY PRECURSORS

A poor, black, barely literate epistolary heroine seems to defy novelistic realism, which may be why The Color Purple is the only epistolary novel to date in African-American literature.[5] Celie's letters are nevertheless firmly rooted in epistolary tradition, for like Héloise, the Portuguese nun, and Clarissa, she appeals to God for succor and solace. An addressee who is absent, silent, or incapable of replying is one of the distinguishing characteristics of epistolarity; if God were present, Celie would not need to write. The letter is thus a tangible measure both of the heroine's isolation and of her desperate need to communicate. Race is nevertheless an irreducible difference between Walker's novel and epistolary predecessors, for initially Celie can only envision her Maker as a white patriarch, punishing her for crimes she did not commit but for which she nonetheless feels guilty. She is a

---

Theory, and Writing by Black Women, ed. Cheryl A. Wall (New Brunswick, N.J.: Rutgers Univ. Press, 1989), pp. 75–97; see also p. 226n.17; hereinafter cited parenthetically in the text as RFM.

5. Melvin Dixon, Ride Out the Wilderness: Geography and Identity in Afro-American Literature (Urbana: Univ. of Illinois, 1987), p. 104; Henry Louis Gates, Jr., states, "We do not have, before The Color Purple, an example of the epistolary novel in the black tradition of which I am aware," in "Color Me Zora: Alice Walker's (Re)Writing of the Speakerly Text," in The Signifying Monkey: A Theory of African-American Literary Criticism (New York: Oxford Univ. Press, 1988), p. 244; hereinafter cited parenthetically as SM.

cursed "daughter of Ham," victim of a racist biblical rhetoric as well as of an implacable social order.

As so often in epistolary narratives ranging from *Zoo* to *Clarissa* to *The Handmaid's Tale*, Celie's writing springs from an injunction: after her presumed father rapes her, he warns, *"You better not never tell nobody but God. It'd kill your mammy."*[6] His is the first voice the reader hears in the text; it carries all the weight of the father's law. The theme of incest ties the novel to *Lolita*, but in contrast to the lyricism of Humbert Humbert's aesthetic description of the act from a male point of view, when described by an uneducated, poor black girl who is raped, battered, and terrorized, incest is stripped of romanticism. Like Doris Lessing and Margaret Atwood, Walker depicts the institution of language as a discourse of otherness: the father's injunction demonstrates that discourse is a form of power; those who have the power continually police what can be said, thought, and written. The fact that Celie initially writes to God because she takes her father's words literally reveals both her innocence and her pathos. The discourse of pathos characteristically borrows from the discourse of other genres, as Mikhail Bakhtin points out in tracing the discourse of pathos back to pre–seventeenth-century trial literature, but I have argued elsewhere that these traits can be found as early as the *Heroides*.[7] The discourse of pathos in Celie's letters give the reader the impression of immediacy and sincerity; there does not seem to be any distance, guile, or artifice in her writing. As Bakhtin notes, the discourse of pathos "is fully sufficient to itself and to its object. Indeed, the speaker completely immerses himself in such a discourse, there is no distance, there are no reservations. A discourse of pathos has the appearance of directly intentional discourse" (*DI*, 394). When Celie writes, "~~I am~~ I have always been a good girl. Maybe you can give me a sign letting me know what is happening to me" (11), she reveals her thinking processes as they unfold in the act of writing, for although she cannot articulate it in grand abstractions, she is asking God to explain the nature of evil and injustice. She won-

6. Alice Walker, *The Color Purple* (New York: Simon and Schuster, 1982), p. 11; hereinafter cited parenthetically in the text. Clarissa's parents forbid her to write; her father persecutes her before she leaves him, repudiates her afterward, and curses her in the hereafter. See Kauffman, *Discourses of Desire*, pp. 129–35.

7. Mikhail Bakhtin, *The Dialogic Imagination: Four Essays*, pp. 394–95; hereinafter cited parenthetically as *DI*; see also Kauffman, *Discourses of Desire*, pp. 44–47.

ders why she has been chosen to be persecuted, and what she has done to deserve it. The shift from "I am" to "I have always been" good reflects her fear that she is somehow responsible for her rape, although she would probably not even define the act as "rape." Her inability to express these fears, her powerlessness, and the nonjudgmental, reportorial style in which we learn of her suffering all give the novel its particular pathos. Such pathos is one of distinguishing characteristics of the traditional epistolary novel, one that links Celie to Ovid's heroines, Héloise, and Clarissa. [8]

Walker's depiction of the fate of women under patriarchy also recalls such epistolary predecessors as *Clarissa*. In both novels, wives and daughters are chattel, terrorized by implacable fathers. Celie's presumed father hands Celie (along with other "property" like a cow) over to a brutal husband, just as Mr. Harlowe plans to hand Clarissa to the repulsive Solmes, in order to consolidate the Harlowes' status and land holdings. For both heroines, the "traffic in women" results in the deformation of bodily development: after producing two children by the time she is fifteen, Celie stops menstruating, a selling point stressed by her father when he tells her prospective husband that he "can do everything just like you want to and she ain't gonna make you feed it or clothe it" (18). One must remember that Clarissa, like Celie, was not only a victim of rape but was possibly impregnated as a result. The possibility of life struggling to develop in her womb while she starves herself to death gives Richardson's novel a particular pathos and horror. As in *Clarissa*, Celie's letters recount an unfolding moral development and spiritual epiphany utterly at odds with religious doctrine; both heroines forcibly confront the differences between letter and spirit, church dogma and faith.

Marjorie Pryse is thus wrong when she maintains that Walker merely "pays lip service to the eighteenth-century roots of the [epistolary] genre,"[9] for Walker's indebtedness is pervasive. However, her reaccentuation points up differences that are even more dramatic than the similarities, for one can never forget that Celie is poor and black as well as female. Moreover, these differences cannot be conflated: the problems that arise from poverty over-

8. On pathos in the *Heroides*, Héloise's letters, and *Clarissa*, see Kauffman, *Discourses of Desire*, chaps. 1, 2, and 4, respectively.

9. Marjorie Pryse, "Introduction: Zora Neale Hurston, Alice Walker, and the 'Ancient Power' of Black Women," in *Conjuring: Black Women, Fiction, and Literary Tradition*, ed. Marjorie Pryse and Hortense J. Spillers (Bloomington: Indiana Univ. Press, 1985), p. 1.

lap with, but are not the same as, those arising from racism; the sexual tyranny inflicted by men (black and white) is related to racial persecution, but it is not equivalent to it. Far from being equivalent, race, class, and gender are irreducible as material differences and as sources of suffering. *The Color Purple's* relationship to the epistolary tradition is thus dialogic, for Walker simultaneously reaccentuates the traditional genre and transforms it by fusing it with another genre. As Bakhtin points out:

> Novelistic pathos . . . always works in the novel to restore some other genre, genres that, in their own unmediated and pure form, have lost their own base in reality. In the novel a discourse of pathos is almost always a surrogate for some other genre that is no longer available to a given time or a given social force. (*DI*, 394)

In *The Color Purple*, the genre that is no longer available, the genre that Walker restores, is a uniquely African-American form of literary production: the slave narrative.

SLAVE NARRATIVES AS GENERIC PREDECESSORS

All the major motifs that dominate slave narratives can be found in Celie's letters: forced labor, beatings, sexual assaults which result in pregnancy and which lead to the abduction and selling of children. Critics have sometimes charged that Celie's initial passivity is too extreme to be plausible,[10] but Walker's allusions to slave narratives remind us that for those enslaved, merely to survive was a form of resistance. This explains why Celie says at one point, "I don't know how to fight. All I know how to do is stay alive" (26). Nonetheless, slaves attempted to sabotage the system in numerous ways, large and small. For instance, many narratives record the slave's surreptitious attempts to get an education, something both Celie and Nettie fight hard for, because like slaves, they are consumed with "the desire to know" (124).[11] Reading and writing were "crimes" punishable by death, for

10. For example, Trudier Harris, "On *The Color Purple*, Stereotypes, and Silence," *Black American Literature Forum* 18, no. 4 (Winter 1984): 155–61.

11. My analysis of the novel's debt to slave narratives is itself indebted to Calvin Hernton, *The Sexual Mountain and Black Women Writers* (New York: Doubleday, 1987), chaps. 1 and 2; hereinafter cited parenthetically. For first-person accounts of the slave experience, see Gerda Lerner, ed., *Black Women in White America* (New York: Pantheon, 1972); see also

these acts might enable slaves to forge written passes allowing them to move from one plantation to another, or to plot insurrection, or to escape to the North.

Slave narratives invariably recount the slave's growing obsession with escape and the journey to freedom. Such transformations sometimes take the form of a great awakening and are providential in tone and plot. In addition to describing the wondrous things seen and discoveries made on the journey, the slave resolves to lift others out of the chains of ignorance and bondage. In the *Narrative of Frederick Douglass* (1845), for example, Douglass emphasizes the role of Providence and claims the right to interpret his own life (*TTFS*, 97–105). Nettie's letters to Celie memorialize these generic features of slave narratives, for once she escapes from her family, she describes the wonders of the North, the excitement of Harlem, her discovery of the manifold achievements of black people throughout history. Her resolution to spread the gospel continues the tradition of "moral uplift" found in slave narratives. Her letters resemble journalistic reports, another feature of both slave narratives and black autobiography.[12] In contrast to traditional epistolary texts which focus claustrophobically on the heroine's private emotions, the setting in *The Color Purple* is panoramic; it encompasses the social, political, economic, and global arena. Since geographical mobility was usually reserved for men, slave narratives tended to reproduce cultural definitions of masculinity;[13] Walker appropriates the genre first by giving one epistolary heroine (Nettie) the power to roam far and wide, and the other (Celie) the acumen to succeed in business.

By fusing epistolarity—the genre traditionally associated with

The American Slave: A Composite Autobiography, 12 vols., ed. George P. Rawic (Westport, Conn.: Greenwood Press, 1977); and John W. Blassingame, *Slave Community*, 2d ed. (New York: Oxford Univ. Press, 1979). On the slave narrative as an art form, see John Sekora and Darwin T. Turner, eds., *The Art of Slave Narrative: Original Essays in Criticism and Theory* (Macomb: Western Illinois Univ. Press, 1982); and William L. Andrews, *To Tell a Free Story: The First Century of Afro-American Autobiography, 1760–1865* (Urbana: Univ. of Illinois, 1986); hereinafter cited parenthetically as *TTFS*.

12. Elizabeth Fox-Genovese, "To Write Myself: The Autobiographies of Afro-American Women," in *Feminist Issues in Literary Scholarship*, ed. Shari Benstock (Bloomington: Indiana Univ. Press, 1987), pp. 161–80; hereinafter cited parenthetically.

13. Valerie Smith, *Self-Discovery and Authority in Afro-American Narrative* (Cambridge, Mass.: Harvard Univ. Press, 1987), p. 34; hereinafter cited parenthetically.

women's voices, feelings, and textual production—with slave narrative, Walker thus transforms both genres.[14] To say that the relationship between the two genres is "dialogic" means not merely that there is a dialogue between them but that the juxtaposition reveals an entirely different economy and *logic*. By reaccentuating the distinguishing characteristics of a traditionally feminine genre like epistolarity, Walker demonstrates how dramatically genre can be transformed by an African-American historical consciousness. Conversely, she uses the slave narrative to dramatize the modern condition of women, demonstrating that black women are still enslaved by their gender nearly a century after gaining emancipation as a race. Walker further combines two distinct types of slave narratives: the criminal-confessional and the conversion narrative. In the first type, the slave confesses to forbidden desires that are "crimes," like the yearning for freedom; slavery is presented as a system of benevolent controls. Conversion narratives similarly tend to rob the slave of free will, by emphasizing that all suffering leads to a heavenly reward (Smith, 12–13). Walker invokes both types: at various points Celie confesses her crimes, some real (like urging Harpo to beat Sophia) and some imagined. Elements of the conversion narrative abound: speaking of her husband's brutality, Celie confesses, "Sometimes Mr. ____ get on me pretty hard. I have to talk to Old Maker. But he my husband. . . . This life soon be over . . . Heaven last all ways" (47). She thus unwittingly endorses the Protestant ideology of life as sacrifice, a pilgrim's progress through a vale of tears to a heavenly reward. Patriarchal white religion justifies the oppression of blacks and women by endorsing and encouraging such passive martyrdom. In the process of composition, however, Celie slowly discovers how to eradicate her conception of God as a vengeful white patriarch, and to replace that crippling ideology with her own conception of divinity. Walker thus subverts and transforms both the confessional and conversional types of slave narrative. The process of epistolary composition enables us to see how Celie wrests language from those who would persecute and silence her. One cannot overemphasize the

14. On women's voices in epistolary fiction, see Kauffman, *Discourses of Desire*; and *Writing the Female Voice: Essays on Epistolary Literature*, ed. Elizabeth Goldsmith (Boston: Northeastern Univ. Press, 1988), particularly Carolyn Williams's "'Trying to Do without God': The Revision of Epistolary Address in *The Color Purple*," pp. 273–86; hereinafter cited parenthetically.

connection of dialogism to dialogue, for Walker places a high premium on oral communication; one marvels at the variety and vitality of African-American speech on every page. By fusing the slave narrative with the epistolary genre, Walker creates a dialogic hybrid, uniquely "womanist" in form—one that connects the individual to collective history, orality to textuality, gender and genre to race.

Although Calvin Hernton argues that the writing of letters in the novel is incongruous because it is too much of a departure from the slave narrative (29), writing is an act of specifying, a defiant testimony to Celie's growing ability to comprehend the injustice of her fate and to rebel against it. From Frederick Douglass's narrative forward, literacy has been a vital source of liberation and salvation. It is the only thing that keeps Celie from being "buried" alive (26). Walker reproduces the epistolary convention of writing-to-the-moment, complete with errors and crossings-out, in order to represent Celie's rebellion in process. The slow evolution of Celie's historical consciousness is accompanied by changes in her style as she masters reading and writing. It is a necessary struggle: she must first wrest the alphabet if she is to wrest mastery from the forces that oppress her by defining her as poor, black, and ugly, good for nothing but sex and labor.[15] Celie's writing, like her quilting, is "piecework," written (one assumes) in small snatches of random segments in the course of her daily labors. It conforms to the "four-page formula" Susan Willis describes in contemporary black women's writing: it is short, anecdotal storytelling and "partakes of the rhythm of daily life as it evolved in an oral agrarian culture."[16]

Theorists of the novel—particularly Shklovsky and Bakhtin—repeatedly emphasize the significance of orality in narrative. Orality is crucial in Bakhtin's definition of the novel as a genre that captures the living mixture of speech patterns. His theories of dialogism shift the paradigms of novel

15. Robert B. Stepto defines the "Afro-American canonical story or pregeneric myth" as "the quest for freedom *and* literacy," *Afro-American Literature: The Reconstruction of Instruction*, ed. Dexter Fisher and Robert B. Stepto (New York: Modern Language Association, 1979), p. 18.

16. Susan Willis, *Specifying: Black Women Writing the American Experience* (Madison: Univ. of Wisconsin Press, 1987), p. 14; hereinafter cited parenthetically. *The Handmaid's Tale* is written with the same brevity, which suggests further close parallels between her latter-day slave narrative and epistolarity. See chap. 6 below.

studies from seeing to hearing; this is why he consistently relies on such musical metaphors as polyphony and orchestration in describing novelistic language and technique. Despite their manifold differences in other respects, Shklovsky and Bakhtin both see the novel as the only genre capable of absorbing many other genres, including poetry, drama, nonfiction, newspaper reports, legal documents, letters, and songs, like the Stevie Wonder song that Walker uses as her opening epigraph. Epistolary and slave narratives place similar emphasis on oral discourse, albeit for different reasons. The epistolary heroine typically invokes the *je crois te parler* motif, attempting to bring the addressee to consciousness by writing, and nurturing the illusion that writing simulates speaking. As Nettie writes,

> But always, no matter what I'm doing, I am writing to you. Dear Celie, I say in my head in the middle of Vespers, the middle of the night, while cooking. Dear, dear Celie. And I imagine that you really do get my letters and that you are writing me back: Dear Nettie, this is what life is like for me. (144)

Orality in slave narratives is often a matter of life and death. Since slaves seldom had privacy, they developed a coded language that whites could overhear but not decipher. Some slave narratives were transmitted orally to sympathetic transcribers. Although the transcriber's interventions frequently distorted the slave's meaning and intention,[17] the narratives often retain phonetic spellings, ungrammatical constructions, musical rhythms, and spiritual allusions. Remarkably polemical debates over what an "authentic" black voice would or could "sound" like when represented in print have been part of the African-American tradition since its inception.[18] The African-American vernacular can be found throughout *The Color Purple*. The vibrancy of Celie's written expression comes from its proximity to speech; dialogism, after all, signifies the living mix of voices, the particular utterances of specific individuals in a concrete historical moment.[19] The

17. Mae G. Henderson discusses the relationship of orality to textuality and the editorial distortions that "contaminate" the slave's text in "(W)Riting *The Work* and Working the Rites," in *Feminism and Institutions: Dialogues on Feminist Theory*, ed. Linda Kauffman, pp. 10–43; see also George Cunningham's response to Henderson, "In No Man's Land: Writing Gender and Race," pp. 44–54.

18. See Henry Louis Gates, Jr., *The Signifying Monkey*, pp. 170–72.

19. See Caryl Emerson, "The Outer Word and Inner Speech: Bakhtin, Vygotsky, and the Internalization of Language," *Critical Inquiry* 10 (December 1983): 245–64.

orality of Celie's writing remains in her phonetic spelling, her syntax, grammar, speech patterns, and her use of proverbs, repetition, and antithesis.[20] Her vivid imagery, folk idioms, humor, and musical rhythms are equally memorable. The alternation of letters between Celie and Nettie suggests the call and response (lead and chorus) of African music, Negro spirituals, and the blues. The interpenetration of written and musical "texts" is yet another aspect of the novel's dialogism, ranging from church hymns to songs by Stevie Wonder, Bessie Smith, Billie Holiday, and the blues sung by Shug and Mary Agnes.[21]

No discussion of orality would be complete without mentioning Zora Neale Hurston, for she audaciously invents the "speakerly text" and captures the "living mix of voices" of the black folk community. The drama of the telling (sometimes called the diegetic aspect of narrative) takes on a life of its own, and the performance is so dazzling that it seems to eclipse the mimetic aspects. Henry Louis Gates, Jr., defines *Their Eyes Were Watching God* (1937) as the first African-American text designed to mime oral narration. He demonstrates how mimesis is transformed into diegesis in her novel, and notes Hurston's particular brilliance in rendering the collective community's thoughts and speech through free indirect discourse. He makes the provocative suggestion that *The Color Purple* may be Alice Walker's love letter to Hurston. Where Hurston creates a "speakerly text" in *Their Eyes were Watching God*, Walker's Celie "writes her speaking voice" in her letters. *The Color Purple* is "in a direct line of descent from *Their Eyes Were Watching God*, in an act of literary bonding quite unlike anything that has ever happened within the Afro-American tradition. . . . Walker rewrites Hurston's narrative strategy, in an act of ancestral bonding that is especially rare in black letters."[22]

20. Valerie Babb, "*The Color Purple:* Writing to Undo What Writing Has Done," *Phylon* 37, no. 2 (Summer 1986): 107–17. Babb argues that the written word traditionally obliterates oral cultures, but the epistolary genre can be seen as an exception to that rule, since it strives to sustain the *je crois te parler* motif.

21. Deborah E. McDowell, "'The Changing Same': Generational Connections and Black Women Novelists," *New Literary History* 12, no. 2 (Winter 1987): 281–302; hereinafter cited parenthetically as CS. For a vernacular theory of the blues, see Houston A. Baker, Jr., *Blues, Ideology, and Afro-American Literature* (Chicago: Univ. of Chicago Press, 1984).

22. See Henry Louis Gates, Jr., "Zora Neale Hurston and the Speakerly Text," pp. 170–216; and "Color Me Zora: Alice Walker's (Re)Writing of the Speakerly Text," in *The Signifying Monkey*, pp. 243–44.

The Color Purple is thus an intricate patchwork of different novelistic codes and genres. Walker once observed that "the truth about any subject only comes when all the sides of the story are put together, and all their different meanings make one new one. Each writer writes the missing parts to the other writer's story. And the whole story is what I'm after" (*ISMG*, 49). That illuminates her rationale for developing the dual structure of alternating letters between Celie and Nettie. Nettie's letters revise Celie's personal history: the man who raped her is not her father; therefore, her children are not her siblings. Celie is bequeathed both a material inheritance and a cultural inheritance, neither of which she would have discovered without Nettie's correspondence.

The quest for wholeness, however, is constantly in danger of being subverted, for one of epistolarity's central motifs concerns the transience of correspondence; letters are repeatedly lost, withheld, seized, misdirected, or misplaced. In this respect, the fate of individual letters parallels the fate of a lost African-American history.[23] Epistolary transmission involves deferrals, delays, and reroutings in the dissemination of the letters, which, like speech, are fragile, fallible, unreliable. The failure to communicate is paradoxically endemic in epistolary transmission; silence, absence, and loss are omnipresent threats. This explains why Nettie never receives Celie's letters and why the reception of Nettie's letters is so long deferred. By the time Celie discovers the cumulative bundle of Nettie's letters in Albert's trunk, they have come to constitute an epistolary novel in miniature. That discovery signals another hallmark of epistolarity: the story of the making of the book—a trait that ties the novel to *Zoo*, *Lolita*, *A Lover's Discourse*, *The Post Card*, *The Golden Notebook*, and *The Handmaid's Tale*.[24] The discovery of the letters also provides Celie with her greatest spiritual crisis: torn between her love for her sister and the desire for revenge, she has to restrain herself from cutting Albert's throat. Shug helps Celie to focus on creativity rather than destruction, to keep "a needle and not a razor in my hand" (137). In addition to sewing and writing, her creativity finds another outlet: she shifts from letter writing to editing, as she puts Nettie's letters in chronological order, arranging the material just as she arranges patches of

23. Babb, p. 14.

24. See Bernard Duyfhuizen, "Epistolary Narratives of Transmission and Transgression," *Comparative Literature* 37 (Winter 1985): 1–26.

quilt so that it forms a coherent pattern. Indeed, the structure of epistolary fiction seldom emerges until all the pieces are put together to form correspondences as well as a correspondence.

CONSTRUCTING OTHERNESS BY GENDER AND TRIBE

The juxtaposition of the sisters' letters enables us to analyze the mechanics of colonization at home and abroad. Doubling and repetition reveal an underlying symmetry: woman is to man as black is to white. But the analogy is complicated considerably when one recognizes the interlocking systems of oppression: white women persecute black women; black women are oppressed by black men as well as by whites; and black missionaries contribute to the colonization of black Africans, who in turn were once complicitous in enslaving the ancestors of the black missionaries. By examining these interlocking forms of colonization, one discovers the mechanics of constructing "the Other."[25]

It is one thing to argue that *The Color Purple* reaccentuates the genre of slave narrative; it is another to insist that Celie herself is a slave. Yet her condition precisely parallels the process by which one is first enslaved and then constructed as "other." What is that process? In *Slavery and Social Death,* Orlando Patterson describes the rituals of initiation which the acquisition of a slave entailed, complete with identifying marks of enslavement.[26] Celie's initiation ritual takes place when she is raped: she is initiated into her new "status" in the household as her mother's surrogate in sex as well as in labor. The function of the slaveowner's ritual is to obliterate the slave's previous bond, and Celie's rape has similar effects, permanently alienating her from her mother, who dies cursing her. Celie is put in the impossible position of being accused of her own rape *and* of her mother's death. She is forced to conspire in her own oppression, an ambiguous moral position that links her to Harriet Jacobs in *Incidents in the Life of a Slave Girl* (1860), where Jacobs can only fight the sexual advances of her master by taking another

25. I was led to consider the mechanics of the constitution of the Other after reading Gayatri Spivak's "Can the Subaltern Speak?"

26. Orlando Patterson, *Slavery and Social Death* (Cambridge, Mass.: Harvard Univ. Press, 1982), pp. 51–62; hereinafter cited parenthetically as *SSD*.

white man as a lover. Celie's dependence on her oppressor is direct and personal, but it is a "fictive kinship." Throughout the old South, similarly, slavemasters encouraged slaves to call them "Big Pappy," or other terms that emphasized their paternalism and "benevolence." Such "fictive kinship" simultaneously reenforced the master's authority and the slave's alienation. Slaves were viewed as illegitimate children—loyal but lazy, humble but chronic liars (*SSD*, 63, 95). This "heritage" suggests why Celie's presumed father warns her husband that she tells lies. (It also protects him should she reveal the incest.) Although reviewers criticized Walker for miraculously "releasing" Celie from incest by transforming the presumed father into a stepfather, the device of a stepfather makes the reader keep the abiding power and authority—as well as the psychic damage— of fictive kinship in mind. Moreover (as Humbert's brutality demonstrates in *Lolita*), the fact that the rapes are committed by a stepfather is hardly a "release" from incest (see p. 71 above); the scars of rape and the betrayal of childhood remain indelible for the victim.

Religion proved invaluable in advancing slavery. In the second half of the nineteenth century, the conversion from Protestant to revivalist fundamentalism occurred, which celebrated piety and obedience, stressed conversion as a sudden spiritual transformation, and emphasized salvation's rewards in the hereafter. This religious revival provided slaves with some sense of dignity, but it also buttressed the slaveholder's authority and control (*SSD*, 73–76). Cornel West explains how the ideology of institutionalized religion justified racism:

> The Judeo-Christian racist logic emanates from the biblical account of Ham looking upon and failing to cover his father Noah's nakedness and thereby receiving divine punishment in the form of blackening his progeny. Within this logic, black skin is a divine curse owing to disrespect for and rejection of paternal authority.[27]

Black women are doubly cursed, according to this logic, since their femaleness links them to Eve, another traitor. Celie's stepfather falls back on the myth of innate female depravity by beating Celie for dressing "trampy," then raping her. Significantly, slavery was viewed as a substitute for death

---

27. Cornel West, "Marxist Theory and the Specificity of Afro-American Oppression," in *Marxism and the Interpretation of Culture*, p. 22; hereinafter cited parenthetically.

but not as a pardon; instead, it was more like a "conditional commutation. The execution was suspended only as long as the slave acquiesced in his powerlessness" (*SSD*, 5). Celie confronts the same stark alternatives: she can either "play dead" by passively submitting to the men who "own" her, or she can end up dead like many of the other women in the novel: her mother; the daughter Celie believes is murdered; the wife of Nettie's beau, who is murdered by her lover. Sheer survival is no small feat.

Nevertheless, rather than sentimentalizing victimized Womanhood, Walker, like Lessing, depicts her heroine's collusion in the oppression of others. When Harpo asks Celie how to make Sophia obey him, Celie advises him to beat her, because she envies Sophia's spunk. Eventually, Celie's betrayal gnaws on her conscience; she knows she has sinned against her spirit. The scene where Sophia confronts her marks the beginning of Celie's transformation, for she must confront her own rage. She discovers that numbness has masked her rage: "Every time I got mad, or start to feel mad, I got sick. Felt like throwing up. Terrible feeling. Then I start to feel nothing at all" (47). With that acknowledgment, Celie begins to overcome her isolation. The first step toward autonomy, as in *The Golden Notebook*, is to recognize her complicity in oppression.

Walker repeatedly demonstrates how complex relations become when the oppressed are oppressors themselves. Black men are victims of racism, but they sometimes become tyrants within the one small realm they can control—the home. They conspire to deprive women of all they possess, including their sexuality and the issue of their own bodies—a procedure that will be repeated in *The Handmaid's Tale*. (In the film, Celie's stepfather stands in the doorway of his house as Celie gives birth; he then takes the baby and disappears.) By portraying sexism as a form of slavery at home and abroad, Walker exposes women's oppression as a transhistorical phenomenon that is always already predetermined.

The African setting repeats the same structural duality that informs the scenes in Georgia: one form of colonization encircles another. The Olinka are colonized by white Europeans, but their women—subjected to patriarchal tribal beliefs—are doubly colonized. Since girls are devalued from birth, the Olinka see no reason to educate them. Tashi tries desperately to please her father "all her young life . . . never quite realizing that, as a girl, she never could" (153). The husband has the power to decide whether his wife lives or dies, and "if he accuses her of witchcraft or infidelity, she can be killed" (153). A husband may take multiple wives, and all the women do his bidding. As in *The Handmaid's Tale*, women may not look at men directly or speak unless spoken to. In societies like that of the Olinka, one's status depends on the number of protectors one has. Thus, rather than seeking freedom and autonomy from the tribe, one seeks to consolidate one's ties to it, for a protective network helps to prevent becoming enslaved (*SSD*, 27). That is why the Olinka view Nettie as "an object of pity and contempt," because she is a woman without a man—unprotected, uncared for, alone.

To understand the paradoxical position of black missionaries in Africa, one must review the history leading up to slavery and the ideology that was subsequently developed. Before slavery, Africans were viewed as potential partners in commerce with the Europeans, who shrewdly recognized their economic dependence on the Africans. By the eighteenth century, Europeans had developed an ideology to justify the slave trade; Africans were represented as superstitious, subhuman, innately depraved.[28] In the United States, similarly, proponents of slavery initially defended it as vital to maintaining an agrarian economy; only after the rise of the Abolitionist campaign did slavery's supporters develop a systematic theory of racial inferiority to justify the institution.[29] Two other discourses besides Judeo-Christianity buttressed European domination and exploitation of African peoples, as Cornel West explains:

> [1] [A] scientific racist logic . . . undergirded by Cartesian notions of the primacy of the subject and the preeminence of representation, and buttressed by Baconian ideas of observation, evidence, and confirmation that promote and encourage the activities of observing, comparing, measuring and ordering physical characteristics of human bodies. . . . Within this logic, the notions of black ugliness, cultural deficiency, and intellectual inferiority are legitimated by the . . . authority of science. [2] The psychosexual racist logic arises from the phallic obsessions, Oedipal projections, and anal-sadistic ori-

28. Abdul JanMohamed, *Manichean Aesthetics: The Politics of Literature in Colonial Africa* (Amherst: Univ. of Massachusetts, 1983), pp. 7–8; hereinafter cited parenthetically as *MA*.

29. See Smith, p. 21; and George M. Frederickson, *The Black Image in the White Mind: The Debate on Afro-American Character and Destiny, 1817–1914* (New York: Harper and Row, 1971).

entations in European culture that endow African men and women with sexual prowess; view Africans as either cruel, revengeful fathers, frivolous, carefree children, or passive, long-suffering mothers. . . . Within this logic, Africans are walking abstractions, inanimate things or invisible creatures. For all three white supremacist logics, which operate simultaneously in the modern West, Africans personify degraded otherness, exemplify radical alterity, and embody alien difference. (22–23)

Such ideologies place black American missionaries in Africa in the late nineteenth and early twentieth centuries in a paradoxical position. On the one hand, they are thrilled to discover their African heritage, anxious to learn about the culture from whence their ancestors may have sprung, as Nettie's letters testify. They are also eager to teach the Olinka new ways and to share their own devout Christianity with them. The Olinka, however, are indifferent. To them, the missionaries are like flies on an elephant's hide. The missionaries make tremendous personal sacrifices to help the Olinka, but the tribe remains ungrateful. They have no interest in discussing slavery, or their ancestors' complicity in it. Samuel despairs over their indifference:

> The Africans don't even *see* us. They don't even recognize us as the brothers and sisters they sold. . . . We love them. We try every way we can to show that love. But they reject us. They never even listen to how we've suffered. And if they listen they say stupid things. Why don't you speak our language? they ask. Why can't you remember the old ways? (210)

The Olinka cannot comprehend how the collective memory of a race was systematically obliterated by slave traders, who disrupted villages, dislocated families when transporting them to America, and brutalized the Africans sold into slavery. Nor can they comprehend the linguistic estrangement which is the condition of exile in the New World. Since African-Americans are robbed of their personal and collective history, forced to forsake their old language and forcibly deprived of all remnants of their previous culture, it is no wonder that they cannot remember the old ways. Samuel laments that where the Africans should see an identity between themselves and him, they see only difference. They hold tenaciously to their old beliefs and customs, literally engraving them on the faces of the young so that future generations will not forget.

The younger Olinka are nevertheless completely willing to abandon their heritage; they are eager to embrace the new ways and to acquire the material goods the colonists have brought, "bicycles and British clothes. Mirrors, and shiny cooking pots. They want to work for the white people in order to have these things" (207). Their materialism makes Samuel despair, but Samuel fails to recognize his own role in destroying the very culture he is ostensibly committed to saving, literally and spiritually. He does not see Christian indoctrination as a form of imperialism or an act of arrogance. His blindness as a man highlights Nettie's insight as a woman: having firsthand experience of colonization by her gender, she perceives what Samuel does not: how it feels to be defined as "other" by members of one's own race. It is thus Nettie, not Samuel, who perceives that "even the picture of Christ . . . looks peculiar here" (147). Later, she confesses that she would like to leave worshippers free to imagine their own deity, a desire that parallels Celie's growing spiritual imagination and emancipation at home.

Whereas in European society, otherness is determined by class status and gender, in colonial society, race is the determining factor. That does not minimize the importance of class and economics, but no matter how much wealth an Olinka tribesman acquires, he will always be viewed as inferior by the colonist (*MA*, 7–8). Colonists can appropriate the tribe's land, destroy their villages, and force the villagers to work the very land they formerly owned. Missionaries differ from the colonists in these respects, but they are not innocent, as Samuel's story of his Aunt Theodosia's medal from Belgium's King Leopold reveals. When she proudly shows it to W. E. B. Du Bois, he rebukes her: the medal is "a symbol of your unwitting complicity with this despot who worked to death and brutalized and eventually exterminated thousands and thousands and thousands of African peoples" (210).

Nor is education an innocent activity, for the acquisition of literacy, so important to Celie's individual liberation at home, is an important phase of cultural domination abroad. In Africa, Nettie points out, "[m]y education began," by which she means that she learned to follow the strict rules of grammar, expository prose, to master "the King's English," in order to teach it to the tribe. Critics of the novel who find her prose stilted overlook Walker's motives for making her writing so stylized.[30] Mastery of proper

30. To Hernton, Nettie's letters "sound too much as if they were written during the nineteenth century by, say, Charlotte Forten Grimke. . . . [It] sounds too much like the stylized

English was so crucial an instrument of colonization that " 'English literature' was born, as a school and college subject, not in England but in the
mission schools and training colleges of Africa and India. . . . The primary
emphasis falls . . . on linguistic standardization and conformity."[31]
Nettie's formal education abroad bleaches the color and life out of the black
folk English that characterizes Celie's.[32] Nettie disseminates not just literacy but literariness in Africa; her English is far closer to textuality than to
orality. In contrast to Celie's graphic colloquial descriptions of her body and
her literal, straightforward descriptions of her emotions, Nettie's language
is as formal as eighteenth-century epistolary prose, even when she describes
her passion for Samuel: "Passion soon ran away with us. I hope when you
receive this news of your sister's forward behavior you will not be shocked or
inclined to judge me harshly. . . . I was transported by ecstasy in Samuel's
arms"[33] (210–11). Nettie and her missionary colleagues have a dual mission:
(1) to teach reading and writing, and (2) to compile a written record of the
Olinka oral culture. These dual intentions seem mutually contradictory, for
the oral culture is in danger of becoming extinct as a result of the influx of
the very people who have come to preserve it. Conversely, without literacy,
it is much more difficult for an oral culture to preserve its history and to
resist the colonizer's racist constructions. Abdul JanMohamed argues that
literacy's function is to disrupt the process of "structural amnesia" among
colonized peoples (*MA*, 280). Nettie's structural function in the novel, then,

---

rendering of a middle-class romantic-heroine-do-gooder," pp. 29–30. McDowell finds
Nettie's letters "lackluster and unengaging" and compares them to the prose in Frances
Harper's morally uplifting *Iola Leroy*, a novel that disseminates the ideology of domesticity
and the cult of true womanhood. See "'The Changing Same,'" pp. 284, 292, 294. Carolyn
Williams, in contrast, astutely explains that

> Nettie's voice seems to relate to Celie's voice as theory relates to practice (Nettie theo-
> rizes the practice of epistolary introspection which Celie begins) or as the explicit com-
> mitment to "uplift" (127) relates to the pure experience of racism. . . . In relation to
> Celie's voice, the lack of "color" in Nettie's voice may be seen as its point, spelling the
> losses as well as the gains of education, uplift, universalism. (285n.8)

31. *Rewriting English: Cultural Politics of Gender and Class*, ed. Janet Batsleer, Tony
Davies, Rebecca O'Rourke, Chris Weedon (London: Methuen, 1985), p. 23.

32. Walker prefers the term "black folk English" to "dialect," which in her view has racist
connotations. See Gloria Steinem, "Do You Know This Woman? She Knows You: A Portrait of
Alice Walker," *Ms.* (June 1982): 35–37, 89–94.

33. McDowell, " 'The Changing Same,' " p. 294.

is to embody a double marginality: as a woman, she is the colonized; as a missionary, she aids the colonizer. She is the pivot on which the question of orality versus textuality turns in the African scenes. The doubleness and duplicity in her roles reveal another facet of dialogism, for as Bakhtin explains, one always appropriates a preexisting language system:

> [T]he word in language is half someone else's. . . . It exists in other people's mouths, in other people's contexts, serving other people's intentions: it is from there that one must take the word, and make it one's own. . . . Language is not a neutral medium that passes freely and easily into the private property of the speaker's intentions. . . . Expropriating it, forcing it to submit to one's own intentions and accents, is a difficult and complicated process. (*DI*, 293–94, 276–77)

Walker's hybrid blending of epistolary and slave narrative is uniquely suited to reproduce that process *as process*. Whether one thinks of the levels of colonization to which the Olinka are subjected, or of Celie's attempt to write in defiance of her father's injunction, Walker's novel is a meticulous representation of the tensions that arise from estrangement from and in language.

WALKER'S VISION OF HISTORY AND UTOPIA

Like the reconstruction of the African-American heritage, Walker's vision of history and utopia involves a collective transformation of all levels of society—personal and political, familial and racial, local and global. Walker describes *The Color Purple* as a "historical novel," but she views history from the bottom up and reconstructs it to reflect the voices of the oppressed, the disenfranchised, the silenced. If, as Susan Willis argues, "the wellspring of revolution is the rebellion of the peasant class" (127), Walker depicts the revolt of those among the most oppressed within the American peasant class: black women. "History," she argues, "starts not with the taking of lands, or the births, battles, and deaths of Great Men, but with one woman asking another for her underwear" (*ISMG*, 356). Rebellion consists of small concrete acts in everyday life:

> *The real revolution is always concerned with the least glamorous stuff.* With raising the reading level from second grade to third. With simplifying history

and writing it down (or reciting it) for the old folks. With helping illiterates fill out food-stamp forms—for they must eat, revolution or not. (*ISMG*, 135)

The emphasis on specific kinds of suffering in concrete conditions is one of the things that Walker never forgets. Since the so-called rise of the novel has traditionally been associated with epistolary fiction,[34] the effect of Walker's juxtaposition of the epistolary genre with slave narratives is to undermine traditional literary history and to reconstruct it, too. Slave narratives, after all, radically undermine the bourgeois myth of progress by showing the barbarism that underlies antebellum Southern "civilization," with its three interrelated obsessions: cotton, slaves, and the cult of chivalry. That is the lesson Walker tries to convey when she recounts her visit to Flannery O'Connor's house, built by slaves who made the bricks by hand in blistering heat:

> O'Connor's biographers are always impressed by this fact, as if it adds the blessed sign of aristocracy, but whenever I read it I think that those slaves were some of my own relatives, toiling in the stifling middle-Georgia heat, to erect her grandfather's house, sweating and suffering the swarming mosquitoes as the house rose slowly, brick by brick.
>
> Whenever I visit antebellum homes in the South, with their spacious rooms, their grand staircases, their shaded back windows that, without the thickly planted trees, would look out onto the now vanished slave quarters in the back, this is invariably my thought. I stand in the backyard gazing up at the windows, then stand at the windows inside looking down into the backyard, and between the me that is on the ground and the me that is at the windows, History is caught. (*ISMG*, 47)

History, for Walker, is intensely personal; just as she describes Zora Neale Hurston as aunt to her and all black people, here, too, she vividly imagines those slaves as her own relatives. As with Lessing's Anna Wulf, Walker posits multiple individualities to encompass the broad sweep of individual consciousness in historical perspective. Walker arrests History and indicts it. The "me" who gazes from the windows is finally permitted to traipse through the house owned solely by whites through the centuries; she lives in the present, postsegregation South. The "me" on the ground represents not just the past but all that has vanished of the history of her people in that

---

34. See, for example, Ian Watt, *The Rise of the Novel.*

past. In such moments, history cannot lie by glossing over the material facts of oppression.

Literary history is equally deceptive: it traditionally represents reality from the point of view of those "upstairs," a gesture initially repeated by some white feminist literary critics, as if all that was needed to make the picture more accurate was the inclusion of a lady rather than a gentleman at the window. In *The Female Imagination,* Patricia Meyer Spacks justified her exclusion of women of color by confessing her reluctance to construct theories about experiences she had not had.[35] Walker comments, "Spacks never lived in nineteenth-century Yorkshire, so why theorize about the Brontës?" (*ISMG,* 372). Walker insists that we need white and black women critics, creative writers, and historians whose vision is revolutionary rather than reactionary or liberal. She reconstructs history by recording the sweat and agony of those who built the frame and erected the monuments of "civilization"—the poor, illiterate, and dispossessed blacks for whom "progress" is nonexistent.

Shug is the catalyst for the dawning of Celie's historical consciousness, for it is Shug who first detects Nettie's hidden letters and helps Celie to reassemble her personal and collective past. Together they construct a positive identity for Celie which repudiates the views of Celie's father, husband, minister, and stepchildren. They repeatedly emphasize that this is a process of reconstruction, a willful intervention. Like Anna Wulf before and Offred after her, Celie must first find a language in order to invent a self in that language. Shug teaches Celie how to turn destructive impulses into creative ones, how to channel grief and rage into a new vocation. The motif of rebirth is most pronounced when Celie tells Mr. _____ she is leaving him to go to Memphis with Shug and that his dead body is just the welcome mat she needs to "enter into the Creation" (181). Her "emancipation proclamation" prompts Sophia to inform Harpo that he is not the father of their youngest child, which leads Squeak to insist on having a singing career. One act of defiance triggers another, which testifies both to the collective nature of political rebellion and to the cooperation among women, as they make arrangements to care for one another and for their children while they pursue their separate destinies. Celie overcomes her isolation by joining a com-

35. Patricia Meyer Spacks, *The Female Imagination* (New York: Knopf, 1975), p. 5.

munity of women who form their own protective network of empowerment. Walker achieves this in a scene of high comedy, purposely turning the ideology of romantic love into farce. Tears of hilarity roll down the women's faces when Grady solemnly warns Celie that if she keeps acting up, she may not be able to get another man. "Aint they something?" (182) Shug laughs. The heteroglossia of the novel reminds us that one of the most effective ways to ridicule patriarchy is through comedy. Significantly, the entire scene of rebellion takes place at the dinner table, firmly inscribed within domestic space.

This space is transformed in economic as well as feminist terms, for Celie turns her home into her workplace when she begins making pants. Previously, all the products of her labor were consumed immediately: the house she cleans gets dirty; the food she cooks gets eaten. By sewing, she shifts to a mode of production that emphasizes exchange rather than use value. Walker's vision of the return to the homestead and the creation of the cottage industry of sewing is unquestionably utopian, but it is not so far-fetched as some critics have maintained. The South provides cheap agricultural as well as textile products, and the artisanal economy that Celie develops represents an alternative to the dominant exploitive modes of production (Willis, 159–63).

The novel is a conservative as well as a progressive genre, and novelists inevitably collude in the very ideology they set out to resist.[36] Celie's pro-

---

36. Recent studies of the novel's collusion with the dominant ideology include Joseph Allen Boone, *Tradition/Counter Tradition: Love and the Form of Fiction* (Chicago: Univ. of Chicago Press, 1987); Lennard J. Davis, *Resisting Novels: Ideology and Fiction*; Michael McKeon, *The Origins of the English Novel* (Baltimore: Johns Hopkins University Press, 1987); Hazel V. Carby, *Reconstructing Womanhood: The Emergence of the Afro-American Woman Novelist* (Oxford: Oxford Univ. Press, 1987); Abdul R. JanMohamed, *Manichean Aesthetics: The Politics of Literature in Colonial Africa*; and Houston A. Baker, Jr., *Blues, Ideology and Afro-American Literature*. I discovered Molly Hite's "Romance, Marginality, Matrilineage: *The Color Purple*," in *The Other Side of the Story: Structures and Strategies of Contemporary Feminist Narrative* after my manuscript was completed; Hite suggests that Walker exploited the conventions of romance rather than realism because "unlike the genre of realism, the genre of romance is recognized as highly conventional, so that its ideological implications are easier both to underscore and to undermine" (p. 107). Hite invokes Northrop Frye's classifications in comparing Celie's world to the green world of romance; coincidentally, I delivered a paper on the formal and structural organization of the novel, using Frye's archetypal categories on 21–22 February 1986, at a symposium on "Black, White and *The Color Purple*," Univ. of North Carolina Program in the Humanities, Chapel Hill.

gress from victimization to success as a pantsmaker and businesswoman could be seen as a black feminist version of the Horatio Alger myth. Celie, the proud owner of a home and a business, is reunited with her family, with the scars of incest erased—or so the argument goes. But the happy ending does not invalidate the novel's artistic achievement; instead, it reaccentuates its generic roots. Where tragic epistolary novels like *Clarissa* end with the heroine's death, comic ones end with reunions among the correspondents whose separation made writing necessary in the first place. Generic precedents can also be found in slave narratives. From *The Life of Olaudah Equiana, or Gustavus Vassa, the African: Written by Himself* (1789) onward, the economics of slavery is one of the major motifs in the plot. Vassa's economic shrewdness enables him to secure his freedom and to survive thereafter. Slaves had to master the mercantile system in order to set themselves free and to free their families. They had to shift paradigms, to learn how to exploit the exchange value of money rather than being exchanged themselves.[37] Since such shrewdness is traditionally attributed solely to males, slave narratives reinforced the dominant culture's patriarchal bias; by showing Celie's transformation into a savvy businesswoman, Walker subverts that bias by shifting the gender paradigm as well as the economic paradigm.

Celie gains control of her sexuality as well as her labor when she meets Shug. Far from being depicted as a sin, lesbianism is a natural extension of the love women share for one another. Barbara Smith discusses the novel's origins in fable to explain how Walker is able to make it seem natural and ordinary for women to fall in love with each other, unencumbered by homophobia.[38] The sexual relationships in the novel consistently subvert the hierarchy of a binary male/female pair by introducing a third party: the first triangle consists of Celie, Mr. _____ , and Shug, which creates rivalry not between the women but between Celie and her husband. Eventually, their mutual love for Shug enables them to achieve a kind of reconciliation; Albert breaks free of the gender roles that warped his personality and even

37. Baker, *Blues, Ideology, and Afro-American Literature*, pp. 31–39.

38. Barbara Smith, "The Truth That Never Hurts: Black Lesbians in Fiction in the 1980s," in *Wild Women in the Whirlwind: Afra-American Culture and the Contemporary Literary Renaissance*, ed. Joanne M. Braxton and Andrée Nicola McLaughlin (New Brunswick, N.J.: Rutgers Univ. Press, 1990), pp. 213–45.

returns to sewing. Similarly, the initial rivalry between Sophia and Mary Agnes eventually gives way to cooperation between the two women who love Harpo. The third triangle—Nettie, Samuel, and Corinne—follows a similar pattern: Corinne finally conquers her jealousy and her lack of faith, although her health is irremediably undermined before she does so. M. Teresa Tavormina links the three sets of triangular relationships to the quilting pattern known as "Sister's Choice." Susan Willis's insight about three-women households in Toni Morrison's novels also illuminates Walker's novel: "these are societies that do not permit heterosexuality as it articulates male domination to be the determining principle for the living and working relationships of the group, as it is in capitalist society."[39] Moreover, neither these relationships nor the lessons learned from them ever become static. For example, when Shug runs off with Germaine, Celie has to learn all over again how to keep from being destroyed by jealousy, how to find inner resources of contentment, and how to love Shug without possessing her; as a result, Shug eventually returns.

While undermining the ideologies of romantic love and compulsory heterosexuality, Walker also subverts the Western concept of the family. Her alternatives to the bourgeois family interrogate the premises of patriarchal possessiveness and property ownership. Nettie writes, for example, that the American and African Missionary Society seems like a family, or "like family might have been, I mean" (121). Adam and Olivia similarly flourish in an extended family. Like sexuality, paternity ceases to be a proprietary matter. For example, even though no one knows who Henrietta's father is, the entire community cares for her, men and women alike. As Christine Froula observes,

> Henrietta . . . is a crucial figure in the novel. Though Harpo tries to claim her
> as his sixth child, she is nobody's baby . . . nonetheless, Harpo, Albert, and
> everyone else feel a special affection for "ole evil Henrietta" . . . in Walker's
> recreated universe, the care of children by men and women without respect to

39. The center of "Sister's Choice" is a nine-patch square. This is one of the patterns the women are sewing in the novel. See M. Teresa Tavormina, "Dressing the Spirit: Clothworking and Language in *The Color Purple*," *Journal of Narrative Technique* 16, no. 1 (Winter 1986): 220–30; see also Willis, p. 106.

proprietary biological parenthood is an important means of undoing the ex-
ploitative hierarchy of gender roles.[40]
It is also a means of undoing the relentless familialism and the oedipal stranglehold on the psyche, demonstrating (as in *The Golden Notebook*) that individual psychic life is grounded in a broadly social, historical, and economic
rather than a strictly familial matrix of determinations. As with the self,
Walker represents the family as a construction rather than as an inviolable
reflection of innate or essential characteristics.

Walker's concept of religion also repudiates essentialism and emphasizes the constructedness of belief systems. Her utopian vision is a religious
affirmation of a spirit unifying humanity. Given the racism of institutionalized religion, she is acutely conscious that such faith is a hard-won achievement as well as a construction. Walker laments that her parents "even
today, . . . can never successfully picture a God who is not white, and that is
a major cruelty, but their lives testify to a greater comprehension of the
teachings of Jesus than the lives of people who sincerely believe a God *must*
have a color and that there can be such a phenomenon as a 'white' church"
(*ISMG*, 18). Celie's faith is hard won, too. She undergoes a profound spiritual crisis when she decides that God must be deaf and blind to permit such
suffering in the world, and she rebels against His indifference by ceasing to
write to Him. She concludes that he is a man "just like all the other mens I
know. Trifling, forgitful and lowdown" (176). But Shug helps her to see the
narrowness of her original conception of God as a white patriarch. By defamiliarizing society's received ideas of divinity and learning how to see
anew, she discovers that it lies within her power to reinvent God. She reconstructs divinity, under Shug's guidance, as the principle of creation and love
in the universe: "Next to any little scrub of a bush in my yard, Mr. _____'s
evil sort of shrink" (179).[41] God has no race or gender, nor is he the property
of any single church, as Shug says: "Any God I ever felt in church I brought
in with me. And I think all the other folks did, too. They come to church to

40. Christine Froula, "The Daughter's Seduction: Sexual Violence and Literary History,"
Signs 11 (Summer 1986): 621–44.

41. Carolyn Williams discusses Celie's spiritual transformation in "'Trying to Do without
God.'"

share God, not find God" (176). Nettie arrives at a similar awareness in
Africa. She writes to Celie every Christmas and Easter as a way of affirming
both the birth and resurrection of Jesus and of affirming her faith in her
eventual reunion with her sister, but her concept of religion transcends traditional rituals, for she, too, is a utopian dreamer who dreams of founding a
church free of all idols and sectarianism.

Despite all signs to the contrary, despite letters announcing Nettie's
death, Celie never ceases to believe that Nettie is alive; her communion with
a sister whom others believe has perished parallels her communion with the
God whom she thought had forsaken her. Her letters enable her to make
what is absent (Nettie and God) present. Once she understands that God
dwells within her, she resumes writing to her new conception of God, thank-
ing a spirit who dwells in all things, people, and places. Shug's lessons are all
dialogic: Celie's dialogue with Shug substitutes an alternative logic for
church doctrine and dogma. Their discussions of spirituality resemble the
call-and-response technique of Negro spirituals in a way that affirms God's
presence in their souls, a dramatic contrast to such monologic sermons on
sin and depravity as the one to which Stephen Dedalus is subjected in *Portrait of the Artist as a Young Man*. Rather than indoctrinating Celie with a
sense of her own evil and worthlessness, many of Shug's "sermons" are
firmly rooted in the comic vein, as when Celie complains that it is hard to
quell her murderous impulses. Shug admonishes, "Hard to be Christ
too. . . . But he manage. . . . Thou Shalt Not Kill, He said. And probably
wanted to add on to that, Starting with me. He knowed the fools he was
dealing with" (134). While Stephen Dedalus is forcibly pressured to confess
his own abjectness and to endorse orthodox Catholic doctrine, Shug teaches
Celie the black woman's unique feat of "conjuring," which resembles Anna
Wulf's efforts in *The Golden Notebook* to achieve a collective subjectivity that
enables her to perceive the copresence of others and to affirm their alterity:

> You have to git man off your eyeball, before you can see anything a'tall. Man
> corrupt everything. . . . He on your box of grits, in your head, and all over the
> radio. He try to make you think he everywhere. Soon as you think he every-
> where, you think he God. But he ain't. Whenever you trying to pray, and
> man plop himself on the other end of it, tell him to git lost. . . . Conjure up
> flowers, wind, water, a big rock. (179)

Walker invokes the type of slave narrative that relies on conversion, but she
also subverts it; rather than submitting to orthodox religion, Celie hereti-

cally substitutes nature for man as symbol of religious omnipresence and grandeur.

Walker reaccentuates these generic characteristics and simultaneously transforms them in a double gesture of historical specifying and utopian dreaming. By historical specifying, I mean that Walker accurately represents the vitality of religion in the material existences of rural Southern blacks, a point she makes again and again in her novels and essays. In *In Search of Our Mothers' Gardens*, for example, she refers to "black women whose spirituality was so intense, so deep, so *unconscious*, that they were themselves unaware of the richness they held" (*ISMG*, 231–32). By utopian dreaming, I mean that Walker recognizes the revolutionary potential of faith. Jesus, after all, was the greatest of utopian dreamers, which is what Walker meant when she said that her parents understood Jesus' teachings better than most white churchgoers. Walker understands the enormous political impact of religion among blacks in the South. Indeed, no one can overlook the impact of evangelical Protestantism on African-Americans, whether one thinks of the NAACP, the National Black United Front, the Southern Christian Leadership Conference founded by Reverend Martin Luther King, Jr., or Reverend Jesse Jackson's People United to Save Humanity. Rather than espousing mere assimilation in white society, these organizations developed concrete strategies to adapt Protestantism to the cause of social justice. Cornel West argues that these emancipatory visions are religious; as a result, he urges African-Americans to appropriate the subversive potential of Christianity and other religions "for counterhegemonic aims."[42] Walker's utopian vision is rooted in a comprehensive understanding of Christianity's radical potential; she combines that vision with a comprehensive rewriting of African and American history from a counterhegemonic perspective.

STEVEN SPIELBERG'S *THE COLOR PURPLE*

The controversy over the film adaptation of Walker's novel centered on the issues of representation: Who speaks for the black race? How shall blacks be represented? Numerous conferences, panels, and colloquia were organized around such topics as "Will *The Color Purple* Destroy the Color Black?"

42. West, p. 28nn.20 and 25.

(Hernton, 31). Protesting against the depiction of black men as brutal, the Coalition against Black Exploitation carried pickets asking, "Are white producers trying to destroy black men?" Oprah Winfrey's Sophia was attacked as a perpetuation of the Aunt Jemima stereotype. Although the film was nominated for eleven Academy Awards, it won only one, a slight that was alternately attributed to the racism of the Academy and to the racism of the film.

In numerous reviews of the film, critics treated the novel as synonymous with the film. Darryl Pinckney compares Celie's people to the Waltons, noting that the lush greenery of the countryside makes it clear that Spielberg's Georgia is not far from Oz.[43] Pinckney maintains that

> Walker's literary clichés meet so well with Spielberg's visual clichés because both are derived from the same stereotypes. Ridiculous pickaninnies, stern matriarchs, big brutes, noble sinners, feeble-minded ladies, together with a host of other conveniently desexualized images, have been part of the American popular imagination since the abolitionist movement, and it is not so much that Spielberg has revived these stock types as that he has reminded us of how present these heirlooms of folly still are, how quickly and comfortably summoned, how great the pressure is to conform to the familiar, the recognizable. (20)

Protests against the film were particularly vehement because critics were aware that millions who would never read the book would see the movie. The film unquestionably flattens out the novel's ambiguities and complexities. One of the things that is entirely lost in translation is the notion of epistolarity, and with it the slow evolution of Celie's coming-to-historical-consciousness. Epistolarity is always a difficult genre to translate cinematically; François Truffaut's *Story of Adele H.* is one of the few films which admirably captures obsessional epistolary writing on film, and Stephen Frears's *Dangerous Liaisons* manages brilliantly to capture the claustrophobia of the epistolary universe among the aristocracy in eighteenth-century France. Ironically, the fate of Walker's novel fulfills the fate Lessing's Anna Wulf predicted for *Frontiers of War*: the complexity of the plot is reduced to the most sensationalistic common denominator; a simple resolution to complex ethical and political dilemmas is found; novel and

43. Darryl Pinckney, "Black Victims, Black Villains," *New York Review of Books* 34, 29 January 1987, pp. 17–20; hereinafter cited parenthetically.

novelist alike become market commodities. (The lead article in the *People* magazine issue on the controversy over the film is devoted to reporting the salaries of producers and top stars like Spielberg and Whoopi Goldberg, who plays Celie.)[44]

The film also disassociates Walker's utopia from politics and history. Michele Wallace notes that the audience responded to the film as if it were a comic *Birth of a Nation:* Shug "seems less the embodiment of the black female blues spirit than some ahistorical hybrid of the Cotton Club and the Ziegfeld follies. . . . Sophia is the epitome of the woman with masculine powers" in the book, cinematically transformed with Harpo into "the reincarnation of Amos and Sapphire; they alternately fight and fuck their way to a house full of pickaninnies."[45] The film erases such historical aspects of the novel as the allusions to the Harlem Renaissance, the Black Nationalist and African Missionary movements, lynchings in the South in the 1920s, and the onslaught of the Second World War. While the brutality of black men remains intact, the film presents it as if it were wholly inexplicable, unrelated to white racism, poverty, or oppression. The scene in which Celie is shaving Mr. _____ is juxtaposed with African scarification rituals, replete with jungle tom-toms and dancing, as if to suggest that the violence of blacks is so deeply ingrained "in the blood" as to be an innate menace. Yet the film elicited powerful responses: when Celie holds the razor to Mr. _____'s throat, the audience in Chapel Hill, North Carolina, where I saw it began chanting, "Do it! Do it! Do it!" A white man in the front row had the opposite reaction: he stood up, confronted the audience, and urged people to walk out, as he proceeded to do.

The result of Spielberg's effacement of politics and history is, inevitably, a fantasy of wish fulfillment. The very fact that the film ever got made is supposed to be a tribute to white liberalism, but at every point the message it conveys is racist. To take but one example: in the novel, when Shug initiates Celie sexually, she urges her to touch her clitoris. In the film, Shug urges Celie to smile. The stereotype of the happy-go-lucky black inevitably comes to mind. As Shelby Steele points out,

Black Americans have always had to find a way to handle white society's pre-

44. *People,* 10 March 1986, pp. 32–42.

45. Michele Wallace, "Blues for Mr. Spielberg," *Village Voice* 31, 18 March 1986, pp. 21–26.

sumption of racial innocence whenever they have sought to enter the American mainstream. Louis Armstrong's exaggerated smile honored the presumed innocence of white society—I will not bring you your racial guilt if you will let me play my music. Ralph Ellison calls this "masking"; I call it bargaining. But whatever it's called, it points to the power of white society to enforce its innocence. I believe this power is greatly diminished today. Society has reformed and transformed—Miles Davis never smiles.[46]

But the ways in which Spielberg alters the novel by reinscribing the ubiquitous smile shows that the power of white society to enforce its innocence has not diminished as much as Steele thinks. Spielberg, after all, has made a career out of celebrating the childlike innocence of white Americans, whether one thinks of E.T., Close Encounters of the Third Kind, or the Indiana Jones films.

This particular scene is also sexist. "Smile, Miss Celie," Shug insists repeatedly, despite the fact that Shug knows Celie is repeatedly beaten by her husband. Michele Wallace asks, "Am I the only woman for whom such a demand recalls all those endless childhood-into-adulthood requests to smile, just smile?" (24). Spielberg's transformation of Celie's discovery of her clitoris into a scene where she first shows her teeth is an unsettling juxtaposition, one that evokes the vagina dentata. Lesbianism is apparently so threatening that Spielberg distorted the novel's plot: a redemption scene is written for Shug, in the church where her father forgives her for her "sins" and she shows him a wedding ring to certify her "normal" heterosexuality. Hernton calls this "the biggest capitulation of patriarchy, the most dastardly cop-out in the film, and the most blatant reversal of what happens in the novel."[47] Through such distortions, the film consistently eradicates feminism, for there is no hint that the rebellion of women is a political act, or that their achievements are feminist. Spielberg does not permit anything to dull the glory of individual innocence or individual industry. Entirely lost in the film is any sense of the collective feminist consciousness which women are first denied, and which they later struggle valiantly to sustain. Whereas the novel both subverts and reinforces the culture's dominant ideology, the film

46. Shelby Steele, "I'm Black, You're White, Who's Innocent?" Harper's 276, no. 1657 (June 1988): 45–53.

47. Hernton, p. 30. See also Wallace, pp. 21–26.

recuperates all the novel's subversive potential by transforming it into an "entertainment."

Just as numerous critics made no distinction between the film and the novel, they also failed to distinguish between Spielberg and Walker. Walker is just the most recent of a long series of successful black female artists to be the target of envy and resentment among black male critics and writers. The attacks range from antifeminism to homophobia: Tony Brown was so incensed that he refused to read the book or see the movie, which did not prevent him from labeling its defenders "frustrated Black women, closet homosexual men; closet lesbians; and meddling white people" (Hernton, 33–34). Pinckney slyly links his review of the movie and the novel to a discussion of Ishmael Reed's *Reckless Eyeballing,* a novel about a black playwright who, after being "sex-listed," writes a play about militant black women in order to regain favor. While Pinckney concedes that "the premise is a little nasty, even for Reed," he praises Reed's novel while criticizing Walker for playing it safe, "given the acceptability of feminism" (18–20).

But if feminism is so "acceptable," why is there so much resistance and hostility? At least since Langston Hughes's attack on Zora Neale Hurston, in which he commented that some wealthy white people "paid her just to sit around and represent the Negro race for them . . . to many of her white friends, no doubt, she was a perfect 'darkie,'"[48] numerous critiques by African-American men of the work of black women suggest that feminism is anything but safe. When Ntozake Shange's *For Colored Girls Who Have Considered Suicide/When the Rainbow Is Enuf* (1975) appeared, Stanley Crouch wrote, in language reminiscent of Nathaniel Hawthorne's complaint about the "damn mob of scribbling women," that whites were "promoting a gaggle of black female writers who pay lip service to the women's movement while supplying us with new stereotypes of black men and women." A similar furor arose when Michele Wallace's *Black Macho and the Myth of Superwoman* appeared three years later. Both women were attacked for degrading black men, mocking the family, creating divisiveness in the black community—the very same charges that were leveled against Walker in the

---

48. Langston Hughes, *The Big Sea: An Autobiography* (New York: Hill and Wang, 1963), pp. 238–39.

1980s.[49] In view of her own success and the resentment it inspired, Walker's response to an essay in the 1979 March/April issue of *Black Scholar* by Dr. Robert Staples on "The Myth of Black Macho: A Response to Angry Black Feminists" is prescient. She told blacks to look around if they did not believe there was sexism in the black community. She tells the editors to try to suppress their envy over the success of Shange and Wallace and to judge their work on its own merits. They rejected Walker's letter as being "too personal and too hysterical" to publish (*ISMG*, 320–35).

Hernton points out that those who complain about the depiction of black men in the novel and the film have little comment on the frequency of wife battering, child molestation, and incest within the black community. Indeed, it is as if there is a conspiracy to deny the reality of these occurrences in the name of presenting a united front of black virtue to the public (Hernton, 34). The internal pressure among marginalized groups to present images of harmony and consensus is unquestionably intense, and the desire to create positive representations is clearly a reaction to the enormous weight of centuries of racism. At the end of the nineteenth century and the beginning of the twentieth, the texts of Frances E. W. Harper, Pauline Hopkins, and Emma Dunham Kelley consciously set out to elevate the image of blacks in the public eye; their literary texts paralleled the movement of black club women whose motto was "Lifting as We Climb." Rather than resulting in literature that was more complex or realistic, yet another myth developed,[50] for it is unrealistic to think that complex textual representations can be produced which avoid confronting the very conflicts among blacks that arise from poverty and oppression. Moreover, as Hortense J. Spillers points out, blacks must be liberated from the crucifixion of needing to be perfect; it is time to resist the fetish of self-integration, unity, purity.[51]

49. Crouch's comment and the discussion of Wallace's book are cited in Hernton, pp. 42–45. Hernton calls Shange's play and Wallace's book the two straws that broke "the billy goat's back" and says that "Hell broke loose."

50. McDowell, "'The Changing Same,'" p. 284.

51. Hortense J. Spillers, "The Habit of Pathos" (paper delivered at International Conference on Feminist Critical Practice and Theory, Dubrovnik, Yugoslavia, 8–14 May 1988). Spillers also notes that the African-American literary community feels compelled to tell a unified story rather than experimenting with postmodern techniques of disruption and fragmentation.

I said at the outset that "struggles of representation" had three connotations in my chapter: first, the black woman writer's struggle to achieve representation in the marketplace and for posterity; second, the debates about what aesthetic representation is or should be; and third, the relevance of the representational fallacy. The distinctions among these connotations frequently disappears in the heat of debate. Regarding the first category, Alice Walker identifies with Zora Neale Hurston because she understands how miraculous it is that Hurston's work has survived and that Hurston ever managed to create it in the first place:

> What is amazing is that Zora, who became an orphan at nine, a runaway at fourteen, a maid and manicurist (because of necessity and not from love of the work) before she was twenty—with one dress—managed to become Zora Neale Hurston, author and anthropologist, at all. (*ISMG*, 90–91)

Where this first category is concerned, then, one can never forget the material conditions of production and the historical specificity of the author. As "author-function,"[52] the name "Hurston" functions to remind readers of the accidents of history, the vagaries of fate that can lead to obscurity in an unmarked grave. In this context, it is vital to preserve the signature, as Walker insists: "*We are a people. A people do not throw their geniuses away.* And if they are thrown away, it is our duty *as artists and as witnesses for the future* to collect them again for the sake of our children, and, if necessary, bone by bone" (*ISMG*, 92). As Offred suggests in *The Handmaid's Tale*, "Context is all." Offred records her narrative in *The Handmaid's Tale* for the same identical reason: to serve as a witness for the future; to memorialize the spirits, voices, and bodies of the regime's dissenters and its victims.

Such action, however, does not preclude drawing attention to the ways "the author-function" serves to reinforce authorial privilege and to buttress ideology. Walker is equally fascinated with these facets of Hurston: how she managed to construct herself as author; how that construction differed from such authors as Richard Wright, among others. Wright's self-construction as author and his theory of representation are diametrically opposed to Hurston's. Henry Louis Gates suggests that Hurston sees Wright as central

52. The term is Michel Foucault's in "What is an Author?" in *Textual Strategies*, ed. Josué Harari (Ithaca: Cornell Univ. Press, 1979), pp. 149–60.

to "the sobbing school of Negrohood who hold that nature somehow has given them a low down dirty deal";[53] his naturalism is based on a theory of representation that her lyricism repudiates. As Gates explains:

> The Hurston-Wright debate, staged not only in the lyrical shape of *Their Eyes Were Watching God* (1937) against the naturalism of *Native Son* (1940) but also in reviews of each other's books, turns between two poles of a problematic of representation—between what is represented and what represents, between the signifier and the signified. Theirs are diametrically opposed notions of the internal structure of the sign, the very sign of blackness. (*SM*, 182)

Walker is not naive about what "the author-function" is or how it works. Had she merely wanted to idealize Hurston, she wouldn't take pains to criticize her autobiography, which she calls "the most unfortunate thing Zora ever wrote" (*ISMG*, 91). Instead, she exposes its effects: falseness, unctuousness, bitterness. Hurston's later work was similarly marred: it became "reactionary, static, shockingly misguided and timid" (*ISMG*, 89). Just as Walker refuses to idealize the black race in her fiction, in her prose she refuses to succumb to the weight the author-function exerts toward idealization.

To turn to my second category, the function and meaning of representation, Hurston's conception of representation is radically antimimetic. Walker is aware of this delicious paradox: the same author who Walker takes such pains to memorialize, Hurston, herself took great pains to disperse the authorial voice, to highlight diegesis over mimesis. Walker goes further: she mimes that dispersal by effacing her own voice in *The Color Purple* through epistolary narration. That brings me to the third connotation of "representation," the representational fallacy. Far from repudiating representation, Walker—like Hurston before her—endorses it and enacts it throughout *The Color Purple*. Walker believes that one must have the opportunity to be constituted as a subject before one can endorse the decentering of the human subject. The novel portrays the process by which Celie slowly constitutes herself—specifically as a writing subject. But it simultaneously demonstrates the necessity of multiple *decenterings*: of institutionalized religion,

53. Zora Neale Hurston, "How It Feels to Be Colored Me," *The World Tomorrow*, 1928; reprinted in *The Norton Anthology of Literature by Women*, ed. Sandra Gilbert and Susan Gubar (New York: W. W. Norton, 1985), p. 1650.

of compulsory heterosexuality, of the ideology of romantic love, of the oedipal stranglehold on the family.

Nor does Walker have any nostalgia for the concept of a center. By combining slave narrative with epistolarity, Walker not only subverts both genres, she also decenters literary history, forcing readers to reconsider the gaps and omissions in previous constructions of the rise of the novel. Her hybrid novel further combines the seemingly contradictory modes of romance with elements of the documentary nonfiction novel.[54] Like the other authors in my study, she has invented a historiographic metafiction—one that relies on self-conscious parody while simultaneously inscribing actual historical characters and events.[55]

As a feminist literary critic, I see literature as a nonexpository theory of practice, a means of making different discourses interrupt each other dialogically in order to initiate a crisis.[56] That is also a good description of Walker's technique in *The Color Purple*. Rather than insisting on either the centrality or the death of the subject, she dramatizes its situatedness; her characters occupy a range of "subject positions" in their discursive practices and in history. After demonstrating how race, identity, class, religion, nationality, and gender have been constructed, she illustrates how these arbitrary and crippling classifications might be reconstructed. As in so many of the other epistolary texts in *Special Delivery*, Walker purposely blurs the boundaries between "inside" and "outside," between margin and center, when she dedicates the novel "To the Spirit: without whose assistance neither this book nor I would have been written." Just as Celie concludes many letters with the affirmation of "Amen," Walker's valedictory is, "I thank everybody in this book for coming"; she signs her last words "A. W., author and medium." Like Derrida's apostrophes in *The Post Card*, Walker's dismantle the mystique surrounding the author, intentionality, and signature; she disperses herself as the medium through which myriad voices make themselves heard. An orchestra of polyphonic voices, ranging from

54. See Barbara Foley, "History, Fiction, and the Ground Between: The Uses of the Documenting Mode in Black Literature," *PMLA* 95, no. 3 (May 1980): 389–403.

55. See Linda Hutcheon, "The Post-Modern Ex-Centric: The Center That Will Not Hold," p. 158n.1.

56. This is the approach suggested by Gayatri Chakravorty Spivak, in *In Other Worlds: Essays in Cultural Politics* (New York: Methuen, 1987), p. 241.

Stevie Wonder's songs to Negro spirituals, testifies to the novel's hetero-glossia. An example of historical specifying and utopian dreaming, her dialogic method exposes the invisible work of ideology and reveals the complicated interactions of collusion and colonization. These issues are also central in Margaret Atwood's *The Handmaid's Tale*; like Walker, Atwood traces the intersections between orality and textuality, history and utopia in a radical re-visioning of biblical prophecy and apocalypse.

CHAPTER SIX

Twenty-first Century Epistolarity
in *The Handmaid's Tale*

A woman's life is all like the act of giving birth; a solitary, painful, furtive act.—*The Three Marias: New Portuguese Letters*

*T*he Handmaid's Tale would seem to have little in common with *The Color Purple*. Walker's southern agrarian setting seems closer to the nineteenth century than to the twentieth; even Celie's successful business at the end remains a cottage industry centered in domestic space. *The Handmaid's Tale*, set in an urban center under siege, is more evocative of the twenty-first century than the twentieth, especially where science, technology, and surveillance are concerned. Where Celie is black, uneducated, and initially unskilled, Offred is a white, educated, former librarian at what seems to have once been Harvard. Yet both novels focus on slavery—psychic, sexual, and political—and both draw upon slave narratives to enhance the epistolary genre. Where Celie's skin color marks her as a victim of racism for life, Offred's red costume visibly signifies her caste and sexual status; each novel demonstrates how arbitrary yet rigid society's racial and gender classifications are. Although their strategies and

221

techniques are vastly different, Atwood shares Walker's interest in rewriting patriarchal discourse in general and the Bible in particular. Like Celie, Offred is struggling to resist the cultural amnesia that her oppressors systematically instill; she must find ways to invent a counterdiscourse to resist the crippling effects of subjection and enslavement. Where Walker focuses on the psychic effects of colonization among Africans abroad and African-American women at home, Atwood focuses on the colonizing impulse in North America—an obsession that pervades all her prose and poetry, beginning with *Survival: A Thematic Guide to Canadian Literature* (1972). In both women's novels, racial resettlement and the specter of genocide loom large. Genocide is a historical reality for Celie's ancestors, a dystopian portent for Offred's contemporaries.

Set in Cambridge before the year 2000, *The Handmaid's Tale* depicts the aftermath of a paramilitary coup by right-wing fundamentalists who establish a theocracy in the United States, renamed the Republic of Gilead. Born in the 1960s, the heroine is old enough to remember her feminist mother's activism but young enough to be recruited into surrogate motherhood in the new regime. Toxic wastes, nuclear accidents, and epidemics like AIDS have so decimated the population that reproduction is compulsory: the surrogates, called handmaids, are dressed in red habits and veils and assigned to aging childless couples among the regime's military elite. The narrator is stripped of her previous identity and given the name "Offred," a patronymic composed of the possessive preposition and the first name—in this instance, Fred—of each commander whom she services.

The novel seems at first to have little in common with epistolary literature, since letter writing will presumably become extinct in the age of telecommunications and technological wizardry. (That is why Derrida declares that *The Post Card* marks the end of the epistolary genre and the postal epoch.) But Atwood transports the dominant motifs of epistolarity into the twenty-first century by transforming the heroine's "letter" into a tape recording from the 1990s, recorded randomly from memory and purposely scrambled to avoid discovery. In shifting from letter to tape cassette, the medium changes, but all the salient generic conventions of epistolarity remain intact. The novel's re-presentation of speech is a reconstruction several times removed, for Offred's discourse is muted, mediated, and modified by the interventions of time and technology, and by a masculine interpretation appended to her own speech. Her tapes are unearthed and reconstructed in 2195 by a male archivist whose written transcript is the narrative we read. Postmodernism is stamped on the text as indelibly as the postmark of epistolarity is, for the representational status of writing and the voice of authority are decentered by Atwood's juxtaposition of two entirely different texts, one masculine and one feminine. Atwood apocalyptically foresees the failure of humanism, liberalism, individualism, capitalism, *and* feminism. My aim is first to examine the novel's formal relations to epistolary traditions, particularly in terms of masculine writing versus feminine speech. I shall then analyze the novel as an anatomy of ideology, in order to show that apocalyptic politics are as vital as poetics in the postmodern epistolary mode.

MASCULINE WRITING/FEMININE SPEECH:
ATWOOD'S EPISTOLARY ANTECEDENTS

The Handmaid's Tale has been compared thematically to *The Scarlet Letter* and to "fearsome future" novels like *1984*,[1] but its epistolary origins can be traced to the *Heroides*, for like Ovid's heroines Offred narrates from exile, a ceaseless reiteration of her desire and her despair. She is multiply exiled: in obliterating the world she used to know, the Gileadean regime transforms her into "a refugee from the past."[2] When she flees Gilead, she is literally exiled; she makes her tapes (presumably) while being hidden by the underground resistance movement. Thus, as in *The Golden Notebook* and *The Color Purple*, Offred's psyche and the nation are both in a state of siege among warring factions; in narrating, Offred situates herself in a landscape that is simultaneously physical, psychic, and political. In this respect, these epistolary heroines recall Ovid's Briseis, Dido, Penelope, and Medea.[3] Whereas in earlier epochs the heroine addressed a reader (real or imagined), Offred addresses an imaginary listener. But like previous epistolary heroines, she reveals her pain and compulsively repeats it, as when she confesses:

1. Mary McCarthy, *New York Times Book Review*, 9 February 1986, pp. 1, 35.

2. Margaret Atwood, *The Handmaid's Tale* (Boston: Houghton Mifflin, 1986), 227; hereinafter cited parenthetically.

3. For an analysis of the *Heroides* as a *locus classicus* of epistolarity, see Kauffman, *Discourses of Desire*, chap. 1; see also Janet Altman, *Epistolarity: Approaches to a Form*, pp. 118–20.

It hurts me to tell it over, over again. Once was enough: wasn't once enough for me at the time? But I keep on going with this sad and hungry and sordid, this limping and mutilated story, because after all I want you to hear it. . . . By telling you anything at all I'm at least believing in you, I believe you're there, I believe you into being. Because I'm telling you this story I will your existence. I tell, therefore you are. (267–68)

Atwood thus expands the traditional epistolary *je crois te parler* motif to encompass a vast audience, for what Offred wills is nothing less than a future for the human race, since at the moment when she actually speaks, its destruction seems imminent. In this respect *The Handmaid's Tale* resembles *The Golden Notebook*: the cataclysms Lessing prophesied a quarter of a century ago simply seem all the nearer now. By positing a listener, Offred is trying to affirm her faith in human survival. Far from being a solitary testament of individual feelings, a purely interior discourse of the heart, Offred's obsessions of necessity center on history, politics, and apocalypse. Those obsessions link her not just to Anna Wulf but to the unnamed heroine of Lessing's *Memoirs of a Survivor* (1974). Apocalypse generally connotes catastrophe: terrorism, mass torture, nuclear accidents, deadly new contaminations in the body and earth. But apocalypse also signifies revelation of what was, is, and will be; in this sense, Offred is a "handmaid" metaphorically as well as literally; she is the handmaid of history, prophetically revealing the monstrous shape of things to come for a listener she can only imagine but whom she wills into being by telling. At other moments, however, she subverts the *je crois te parler* motif and reveals both the effort involved in sustaining the illusion and her deepening despair: "I'll pretend you can hear me. But it's no good, because I know you can't" (40).

Since the epistolary gesture often entails the invention of a confidant who is absent at the moment of narrating, it is an act of dissimulation as well as of confidence. Offred's narrative embodies both impulses: she dissimulates by disguising identities and by scrambling the order of her tapes; she confides by repaying tenacious listeners with her remarkable revelations. As Janet Altman points out, "The epistolary confidant is most fundamentally an archivist"; Offred's eventual listener in 2195 turns out literally to be an archivist.[4] Just as the heroine's narrative provides a glimpse into a past that

4. Altman, p. 53. Chap. 2 examines the oppositions of confidence and dissimulation in epistolary fiction. The dissimulation and duplicity of epistolary heroines (Ovid's, Héloïse, Mariane, Clarissa, and the three Marias) are discussed in Kauffman's *Discourses of Desire*.

the archivist barely comprehends, his own historical notes provide a glimpse into a future that neither the heroine nor the reader could have foreseen, for by 2195 the entire map of the world has been transformed in terms of territory, language, culture, religion, and politics. Whether any of us ever understand history at the moment it is in the making, whether we are ever able to view the present in perspective, is one of the many questions the novel raises. Offred readily confesses her ignorance about events leading up to the coup and beyond it; I would argue that the archivist is just as ignorant about his own historical moment. But his narrative smacks of a smugness that Offred's lacks. (In this respect, his closest analogue is Nabokov's John Ray, Jr., in *Lolita*.) He endorses the myth of Enlightenment progress by implying that his own society in 2195 is far advanced over the "primitivism" of Offred's in the 1990s.

The text thus articulates the problems of transmission and reception, an articulation for which epistolarity is justly renowned, and in which the female voice is particularly problematic. Bernard Duyfhuizen's explanation of those problems can be applied to *Zoo, Lolita, The Post Card, The Golden Notebook,* and *The Color Purple* as well as to *The Handmaid's Tale:* "If a novel in letters is to exist, the act of transmission must include its inverse: the act of retaining or collecting. . . . One part of the narrative of transmission . . . is the story of the collection—how the letters became available to an 'Editor.'"[5] That is precisely the story that the historical notes tell. Only after the reader finishes Offred's discourse and turns to those notes do the novel's epistolary origins become apparent: the fiction of found tapes is the next century's equivalent to the traditional fiction of found letters. Professor Pieixoto, Cambridge University's director of twentieth- and twenty-first-century archives, recounts his discovery of Offred's tapes at the Twelfth Symposium on Gileadean Studies in 2195. More than thirty tapes are found in what used to be Bangor, Maine; they were purposely recorded at random intervals on different musical cassettes to camouflage their chronology, coherence, and significance. Pieixoto determines that the tapes are authentic rather than forged and draws deductions about the handmaid's culture. The very sequence of the sentences we read results from Pieixoto's guesswork; he arranges Offred's "blocks of speech" in what seems to him a plausible order. He is aided by voice-print experts and technicians who re-

5. Bernard Duyfhuizen, "Epistolary Narratives of Transmission and Transgression," p. 5.

construct a machine long obsolete: the tape recorder. The narrative we read is thus a reconstruction, an approximation, subject to numerous interventions, all of which undermine the voice(s) of authority, the validity of interpretation, and the notion of a center.

Perhaps the most celebrated predecessor in the tradition of the fiction of found letters is *The Letters of a Portuguese Nun*, published in France in 1669 by Claude Barbin, who added an *avis au lecteur* asserting that the letters were written by a Portuguese nun, Mariane, after her seduction and abandonment by a French chevalier. Barbin recounts his difficulties in "translating" the letters and "verifies" their authenticity, but he may have perpetrated one of the greatest literary hoaxes of all time, for many now believe that Racine's friend Gabriel-Joseph de Lavergne de Guilleragues authored the letters.[6] Both editor and author, well aware of the public's distaste for fiction, accurately predicted the scandalous appeal the "history" of the nun's passion would have for the public. Like Barbin, Atwood's archivist insists on the authenticity of his discovery, and repudiates those forgeries "for which publishers have paid large sums, wishing to trade no doubt on the sensationalism of such stories" (302). Like *Lolita's* John Ray, Professor Pieixoto's lecture is filled with pious (his name in pig Latin means "Oh-so-Pious"), moralistic editorial intrusions: "It appears that certain periods of history quickly become, both for other societies and for those that follow them, the stuff of not especially edifying legend and the occasion for a good deal of hypocritical self-congratulation" (302). But—again like John Ray—the archivist commits the very crimes he condemns, for he has little sensitivity to Offred's predicament or her pain. His tone is jocular; Offred's narrative comes to be entitled "The Handmaid's Tale" as a bawdy joke

---

6. See Frédéric Deloffre and J. Rougeot, "L'énigme des *Lettres portugaises*," in *Lettres portugaises, Valentins, et autres oeuvres de Guilleragues* (Paris: Garnier, 1962), pp. v–xxiii. While in the editors' view the identification of Guilleragues as author is definitive, others argue that, although no Portuguese original has ever been found, the work was at least inspired by authentic letters of a Portuguese woman. The controversy is far from being settled; Peter Dronke maintains in the *Times Literary Supplement* (5 November 1976, p. 1397) that "the entire issue remains . . . wide open"; Yves Florenne, in "Introduction," *Lettres de la religieuse portugaise* (Paris: Librairie générale francaise, 1979), p. 77, argues for a female voice; Jean-Pierre and Thérèse LaSalle offer new evidence and additional letters by the same hand in *Un manuscrit des lettres d'un religieuse portugaise: Leçons, interrogations, hypothèses*, Papers on French Seventeenth-Century Literature 6 (Paris: Biblio 17, 1982). See also Kauffman, *Discourses of Desire*, chap. 3.

among his colleagues: "the word *tail* . . . being, to some extent, the bone, as it were, of contention, in that phase of Gileadean society" (301). In this pun, the issues of genre (tale) and gender (tail) are joined. Since Professor Pieixoto does not know how to describe the document as a genre, he diminishes its impact and veracity by defining it as a "tale." He is equally condescending in terms of gender, ascribing the aleatory construction of the discourse and its lack of style to the poor education of North American females in the 1980s, and apologizing for the inferior quality of Offred's mind. He wishes her record contained more data about the Gileadean regime, and he yearns for some of the Commander's computer printouts. He ignores the fact that it is precisely because she is female that she is denied access to the kind of information he desires, and he devalues the kind of information (intuitive, emotional, sensory) that she provides. Pieixoto and his cohorts are merely the most recent of a long series of male epistolary editors who appropriate the female voice for their own purposes—fame, fortune, power, self-aggrandizement, and self-congratulation. Like Nabokov's satiric portrait of John Ray's pretensions, Atwood satirizes male academicians distanced from women's history.

Pieixoto's obsession with literal facts is particularly ominous since Gilead, like Puritan America, is founded on a literal interpretation of the Bible, specifically Genesis 30:1–3, where Rachel tells Jacob, "Behold my maid Bilhah, go in unto her; and she shall bear upon my knees, that I may also have children by her." These words result in a monthly "flesh triangle": Offred lies on her back between the knees of Serena Joy, the Commander's wife, while the Commander attempts to inseminate Offred. If and when she delivers a healthy baby, its appropriation and the handmaid's dismissal will follow—an ugly perversion of the spirit of the biblical dictum. How does one respond to such perversions if one is stripped of power and struggling to survive? "One detaches oneself. One describes," says Offred (95).

As so often in epistolary narration, Offred gives us the sense not just of narrating in the moment but of urgently narrating under compulsion: "I don't want to be telling this story," she confesses (273). Just as traditional epistolary heroines draw attention to the blots on the paper, the tearstains on the page, and the self-reflexivity of their acts of writing, Offred repeatedly reminds us that

This is a reconstruction. All of it is a reconstruction. It's a reconstruction now,

in my head. . . . When I get out of here, if I'm ever able to set this down, in
any form, *even in the form of one voice to another,* it will be a reconstruction
then too, at yet another remove. It's impossible to say a thing exactly the way
it was, because what you say can never be exact, you always have to leave
something out, there are too many parts, sides, crosscurrents, nuances; too
many gestures, which could mean this or that, too many shapes which can
never be fully described, too many flavors, in the air or on the tongue, half-
colors, too many. (134; emphasis mine)

Even speech is a reconstruction, irrevocably distanced from truth—an insight Derrida also takes pains to demonstrate. Atwood emphasizes syn-
esthesia, the poetic mixing of sensory impressions, because it is the texture
of life that language cannot capture; that texture is too ineffably rich and
temporally fleeting. Like Lessing, moreover, Atwood is suspicious of all attempts to label, to sum up, to encapsulate, to define: Gilead has shown
Offred too well the repression that results from literally enforcing one way,
one truth, one interpretation. The compulsion to describe what cannot be
put into words is one of the hallmarks of epistolarity; as the Portuguese nun
reflects, "It seems to me that I am doing the greatest possible wrong to the
feelings of my heart in trying to make them clear in writing to you."[7] Like
Anna Wulf, Offred is overwhelmed by the incapacity of language to encompass experience or feeling; it is always approximate, as she says in describing
her affair with Nick: "I'm not sure how it happened; not exactly. All I can
hope for is a reconstruction: the way love feels is always only approximate"
(263). Despite his training as a historian, what is lacking in the archivist's
commentary about Offred's discourse is precisely any sensitivity to taste,
texture, touch, sound, sight—to the particularity of material existence in a
specific historical moment.

Since the regime is erasing the past, redefining language, history, and
reality before her eyes, Offred struggles to preserve her hold on an increasingly fragile "reality," reminding herself while observing the bodies hanging on the wall:

Each thing is valid and really there. It is through a field of such valid objects
that I must pick my way, every day and in every way. I put a lot of effort into

7. Frédéric Deloffre and J. Rougeot, eds., *Lettres portugaises, Valentins, et autres oeuvres
de Guilleragues,* p. 43, my translation.

making such distinctions. I need to make them. I need to be very clear, in my own mind. (33)

Such specificity is a trademark of epistolary writing-to-the-moment, but Atwood expands the parameters of the classic epistolary novel by relating private emotions to political atrocities. Like Lessing and Walker, Atwood explodes the private/public dichotomy. Exiled, imprisoned, cloistered, or "shut up," many epistolary heroines transform writing into means of sub-version and revolt. As the three Marias proclaim, "When woman rebels against man, nothing remains unchanged."[8] Sex and politics are indistinguishable as transfer points of power and oppression in a society under siege. Even the Portuguese nun's seduction is metonymic: she is enthralled by (and in thrall to) a Frenchman stationed in Portugal to expand the empire of the Sun King; once the conquest of woman and colony is accomplished, the chevalier sails home. In Gilead, woman's body becomes the territory to master; female sexuality is harnessed to the "higher good" of the body politic; and viable ovaries become a "national resource" (65).

The appropriation of the female body and voice is therefore closely allied with other political acts of appropriation and conquest. One begins the process of mastery by stealing the language, a theft that is a recurrent theme in Atwood's poetry as well as her fiction. In the "Circe/Mud" poems in *You Are Happy* (1974), for example, Circe is initially mistress of the island and namer of all things on it, but Odysseus vanquishes her by possessing her sexually and stealing her words: she spends her days "with my head pressed to the earth, to stones, / to shrubs, collecting the few muted syllables left over." She resists speaking in the "received language," as if aware that mythology always reproduces the same stories—of seduction, betrayal, conquest, power. She tries to subvert the glorious epic of omnipotent patriarchs by referring to Odysseus' "stupid boat, / your killer's hands." Yet she is helplessly doomed to silence, for she recognizes that he is the narrator of his odyssey, and she knows that "it's the story that counts." Despite her magical powers and prophetic capacities, she beseeches him to answer her questions: "When you leave will you give me back the words? Don't evade, don't

---

8. Maria Isabel Barreño, Maria Teresa Horta, and Maria Velho da Costa, *The Three Marias: New Portuguese Letters*, p. 158. The three Marias were prosecuted by the Caetano-Salazar dictatorship from 1972 to 1974. See Kauffman, *Discourses of Desire*, chap. 8.

pretend you won't leave after all: you leave in the story and the story is ruthless."⁹ She knows that since he is master of the myth, his story will depict her as evil; she cannot change its contours or course. Offred expresses the same powerlessness, the same awareness that she has no control over the outcome of what she narrates. Atwood also follows Lessing in purposely blurring the boundaries between fiction and reality: "I would like to believe this is a story I'm telling. . . . If it's a story . . . then I have control over the ending. Then there will be an ending, to the story, and real life will come after it" (39). The catastrophic events she witnesses are so unreal that Offred tries to deny them, but she fails. Her circumstances are too desperate, and the regime is too ruthless.

The archivist fails to appreciate the profound implications of Offred's act, for he does not comprehend the effort of will and the leap of faith it requires for her to imagine a listener. Nor does he fully understand her objectives, for the particularity of her predicament is closely allied to the collective fate of women in her society, and one of her aims is to memorialize their individual voices as well as her own. Traditionally, the epistle brings the absent beloved before the writing heroine; the motif of *je crois te parler* enables her to "hold him in her hands." For Offred that process is made more complex because she must first reconstruct her former self, since the regime has turned her into a "missing person . . . disembodied . . . deserted . . . like a room where things once happened and now nothing does" (103–4). She must first reclaim herself, retrieve her voice; once she does so, she proceeds to reinscribe the voices of other women. Poignantly, in this context, *je crois te parler* amounts to raising the dead, for Offred tries to bring into being a nonexistent archive of women so as to memorialize, for history, the women she will never see again: her daughter, her mother, her friends, her coconspirators. She re-presents the speech of Moira, for example, the gutsy lesbian friend who ends up as a prostitute in the Commander's private club. Offred consciously tries to mime Moira's iconoclastic, witty speech: "I've tried to make it sound as much like her as I can. It's a way of keeping her alive" (243–44). As a result, the entire narrative is a polyphony of distinctive female voices, but the archivist is deaf to these nuances. His

9. Margaret Atwood, "Circe/Mud Poems," in *You Are Happy* (Toronto: Oxford University Press, 1974), reprinted in *Norton Anthology of Literature by Women*, ed. Sandra Gilbert and Susan Gubar (New York: W. W. Norton, 1985), pp. 2296–98.

scholarly, detached approach to the tapes reflects the assumptions of scientific research, technology, and objectivity; it assumes the status of truth. But his "truth" is not the same as these women's. In Gilead, as in all previous periods of history, women's history is repressed; Gilead is merely the most recent regime to suppress their voices by prohibiting them from reading, writing, or speaking. The conditions of existence under which Offred labors do not permit the luxury of the archivist's so-called objectivity. As Pierre Macherey observes,

> The act of knowing is not like listening to a discourse already constituted, a mere fiction which we have simply to translate. It is rather the elaboration of a new discourse, the articulation of a silence. . . . What can be said *of* the work can never be confused with what the work itself is saying, because two distinct kinds of discourse which differ in both form and content are being superimposed.[10]

Atwood juxtaposes the handmaid's discourse with "what can be said" by the archivist, who presumes that knowledge is an act of mere translation, once he assembles the proper technological equipment. The traditional definitions of "feminine" speech versus "masculine" writing are simultaneously reaccentuated and satirized by Atwood: the feminine is subjective, disordered, hysterical, illogical; the masculine is objective, orderly, rational, logical. Such dichotomies have been reiterated by theorists of epistolarity through the ages and have been used to decide whether the letterwriter's gender can be determined solely by internal stylistic evidence; with such texts as *Letters of a Portuguese Nun*, for example, the question continues to be intensely controversial.[11] Since tape recordings enable one better to hear whether the speaker is male or female, the speaker's gender will presumably be less ambiguous in "high-tech" epistolarity, although voice alone is not an infallible key to gender, as Balzac's *Sarrasine*—the story of a male sculptor who falls in love with a castrato disguised as a diva—so eloquently demonstrates.

10. Pierre Macherey, *A Theory of Literary Production*, trans. Geoffrey Wall (London: Routledge & Kegan Paul, 1978), p. 6.

11. See, for example, Peggy Kamuf, "Writing Like a Woman," in *Women and Language in Literature and Society*, ed. Sally McConnell-Ginet, Ruth Borker, and Nelly Furman (New York: Praeger, 1980), pp. 284–99; Nancy K. Miller, "The Text's Heroine: A Feminist Critic and Her Fictions," *Diacritics* 12 (Summer 1982): 48–53; and Kauffman, *Discourses of Desire*, chap. 3.

Ovid's heroines and the Portuguese nun are clearly Offred's ancestors, but in her relationship with her missing husband, Luke, she resembles Héloise. Years after Abelard's castration and her convent incarceration, Héloise still refuses to face the fact that their separation is permanent; instead she sustains her illusions and her passion in her letters. Offred is equally defiant and illogical; she cannot reconcile herself to the fact that she and Luke may never be free, may never make love again, that he may not even be alive. She imagines three alternative fates for him: that he was killed when they were captured, that he is a political prisoner, that he escaped and is working in the resistance movement. She confesses, "The things I believe can't all be true, though one of them must be. But I believe in all of them, all three versions of Luke, at one and the same time. This contradictory way of believing seems to me, right now, the only way I can believe anything" (106). "Three versions of Luke": since Luke wrote only two books of the New Testament (the Gospel and the Acts), a third version suggests the Gileadeans' distorted version. Atwood may also be alluding to the indeterminancy of scriptural exegesis, translated in many hands and languages, which makes the regime's literalization of the Bible all the more ludicrous. The dichotomy between fact and truth, letter and spirit is a structural source of the narrative's tension, dividing Offred from her oppressors and her letters from Pieixoto's notes. Offred searches for spiritual solace amid the aridity of Gilead's repressive theocracy. "In reduced circumstances you have to believe all kinds of things. I believe in thought transference now . . . I never used to" (105). This passage recalls Anna Wulf's reflection that her schizoanalytic interaction with "Saul" was a "record of a hundred different people living now, in various parts of the world, talking and crying out and questioning" (623). It also recalls Celie's tenacious faith in Nettie's survival, even after she receives notification from the State Department of her "death." Thus, irrationality, which in former times could be seen as merely personal—and feminine—is transformed into an explicitly political act, for Offred's survival is at stake in sustaining herself in order to witness to posterity about the fate of other political prisoners. Given the horror of her predicament, her danger, and its apocalyptic proportions, irrational faith is her only defense, for to be able to imagine one listener, she has to imagine the survival of thousands capable of vanquishing Gilead; these are the conditions of her survival and hence her narration. She explicitly relates her discourse to letters when she says:

> A story is like a letter. Dear *You*, I'll say. Just *you*, without a name. Attaching a name attaches *you* to the world of fact, which is riskier, more hazardous; who knows what the chances are out there of survival, yours? . . . *You* can mean more than one. *You* can mean thousands. . . . I'm not in any immediate danger, I'll say to you. I'll pretend you can hear me. (40)

Letters have long functioned to defamiliarize the distance between fiction and reality by drawing attention to the fictiveness of the narrative act, as Offred does here. But here, *je crois te parler* is linked not solely to sexual desire but to the survival of the human race.

The same transformation of the personal to the political through the act of forbidden discourse applies to forbidden reading, which has long been a feminine transgression in fiction, as with the forbidden letters Clarissa receives from Lovelace. But in Gilead, it is not just personal letters that are forbidden; all reading is forbidden to women. That injunction is one of the taboos that links Atwood's novel to slave narratives, for slaves were similarly forbidden to read and write. The Commander indulges Offred's craving by offering her a secret supply of banned books and magazines: Charles Dickens, Raymond Chandler, *Ms. Magazine*, *Mademoiselle*, *Vogue*, *Esquire*, *Reader's Digest*. She reads voraciously, trying to absorb as much material as quickly as possible in stolen moments. These materials help her remember a time before Gilead redefined even the language, inventing such terms as "unwomen," "unbaby," and "gender traitors" (for homosexuals and lesbians) to reshape reality. The banned books and magazines also help her to remember a time when print media still played a crucial role in preserving culture; the shift to electronics has fortified the regime's power and enforced the powerlessness of the populace. Like Celie, Offred wrests the alphabet to resist the dehumanizing definitions that subject her. To the wives, for example, the handmaids are "little whores . . . they aren't even clean . . . the *smell*" (115). That is why her surreptitious Scrabble games with the Commander are significant: it is her method of stealing the language back again, a proleptic hint of the tape recordings she will eventually make. Through language, she tries to steal knowledge and power; she demands to know what is going on.

The epistolary novel is the site of numerous transgressions, the formal codes of which are all familiar: adultery in *Les liaisons dangereuses*, prostitution in *Clarissa*, suicide in *The Sorrows of Young Werther*—forbidden reading in all of these. Atwood transforms these familiar codes while leaving their traces legible: since the previous handmaid killed herself when her trysts with the Commander were discovered, suicide is never far from Offred's mind. She is, moreover, defined by the regime as an adulteress since she married a divorced man. Furthermore, she deceives Serena with the Commander and later deceives the Commander with Nick. Finally, when the Commander takes her to Jezebel's, the private men's club and brothel, she is forced to play the prostitute. But the formal codes are here transformed into political crimes, for reading is not merely "an imaginary or metaphorical transgression,"[12] instead it is a literal crime, punishable by the amputation of a hand. The Gileadean regime punishes those who commit the crime of "unchastity" by amputating an arm and the crimes of fornication and adultery by execution (275). In Gilead, these codes reflect an ideology devoted to the repression of human desire in general and female sexuality in particular.

Atwood shares Lessing's efforts to understand the appeal of fascism. What makes people desire their own subjection? What causes such sudden and severe societal repression? The Commander reveals that men engineered the coup because they were becoming increasingly sterile, impotent, and irrelevant. Just as Paul's repeated refrain about Ella applying ice to her ovaries and pushing all men "off the edge of the earth" signifies a pervasive male anxiety in *The Golden Notebook*, the Commander confesses that before the coup men felt the same anxiety:

12. In "Flaubert's Presuppositions," *Diacritics* 11 (Winter 1981): 2–11, Michael Riffaterre traces a causal connection leading from forbidden reading to adultery, and from adultery to prostitution or suicide:

> The first fatal step leads inevitably to the last fatal leap. These inseparable and complementary poles thus set the limits of the fictional space extending from an imaginary or metaphorical transgression (wicked thoughts nurtured by immoral and forbidden readings) to the most definitive of all actual and literal transgressions—the one that drags the heroine out of existence, and out of the text, simultaneously putting an end to what can be lived or to what can be told in words. The adulteress either commits suicide or sinks into prostitution.

The main problem was with the men. There was nothing for them any-
more. . . . There was nothing for them to do with women. . . . The sex was
too easy. Anyone could just buy it. There was nothing to work for, nothing to
fight for. . . . You know what they were complaining about the most? Inability to feel. Men were turning off on sex, even. (210)

This revealing statement implies that male identity derives from and depends on domination. The film adaptation of the novel, with a screenplay by
Harold Pinter under the direction of Volker Schlöndorff, cleverly evokes the
artificiality of men's war games by depicting the Commander in his office
surrounded by plastic toy soldiers; in other scenes soldiers cuff each other
and roughhouse like overaged fraternity boys. Only by wrapping women in
veils and habits, by persecuting "deviants," by suspending civil liberties, do
such men derive a raison d'être. As the three Marias observe, "The basic
repression, the one which . . . lies at the very core of the history of the human species, creating the model and giving rise to the myths underlying
other repressions, is that of the woman by the man."[13] Just as the regime
inflates the rhetoric of "family values" precisely when biological kinship has
become irrelevant, the men are hypocrites in numerous other ways. Men
strip women of all liberties but retain their own male prerogatives: at
Jezebel's, liquor, cigarettes, pornographic books and movies, and sex with
women they have turned into prostitutes are readily available. The film sar-
donically captures their nostalgia for the "good old days": women prance
about looking like Dallas Cowboy cheerleaders, dominatrixes, Playboy
Bunny playmates, and harem belly dancers. Each woman's costume is a
reflection of male sexual fantasies, clearly implying that sexual arousal
depends on props and female humiliation. Underscoring the traffic in
women, the Commander blandly explains that the club is good for "foreign
trade."

At one point, Offred prophetically envisions not just a listener for her
tape recordings but specifically a male listener. She addresses him directly.
After declaring that it is impossible to describe anything accurately, in all its
complexity, she makes a crucial distinction between masculine and feminine
responses to her discourse:

13. *The Three Marias,* p. 219.

> If you happen to be a man, sometime in the future, and you've made it this far,
> please remember: you will never be subject to the temptation or feeling you
> must forgive, a man, as a woman. It's difficult to resist, believe me. But re-
> member that forgiveness too is a power. To beg for it is a power, and to with-
> hold or bestow it is a power, perhaps the greatest. (134–35)

This puzzling statement becomes clearer in the context of Offred's attitude
toward the Commander. She weighs individual responsibility, emotional involvement, and the power of forgiveness as she tries to find the words to
describe his monthly violation of her:

> He is fucking . . . the lower part of my body. I do not say making love, be-
> cause this is not what he's doing. Copulating too would be inaccurate, because
> it would imply two people and only one is involved. Nor does rape cover it:
> nothing is going on here that I haven't signed up for. (94)

Offred's comment about forgiveness must be placed in the context of questioning whether it is possible to forgive the Commander, who puts her life in
peril by breaking the rules of their intercourse. On the one hand, he becomes
an individual rather than a thing to her, and she to him, which slightly eases
her otherwise unbearable existence. On the other hand, she is completely in
his power, and he can turn on her, or turn her in, at any moment, as happened to the previous handmaid. It may seem as if Offred is advocating
forgiveness—a stereotypically feminine virtue—but she goes on to record
her childhood memory of a television documentary about the mistress of a
Nazi SS officer who was responsible for sending Jews to the ovens. Offred
imagines that the mistress "did not believe he was a monster. He was not a
monster, to her. Probably he had some endearing trait: he whistled. . . . he
called his dog Liebchen. . . . How easy it is to invent a humanity, for anyone
at all. What an available temptation" (145–46). What Offred remembers
most about the Nazi's mistress is her makeup; though as a child she didn't
grasp the significance of that memory trace, in retrospect it symbolizes the
cosmetic, superficial attempts to cover up fascism. "To put a good face" on
fascism is what Offred warns against (and what the archivist endorses, as I
will show presently). The temptation of a woman to forgive a man is precisely what Offred abjures; forgiving would result in forgetting, and that is
exactly what she records her narrative to prevent: her listeners must remember history and must not eradicate the memory of what has been done
to the spirits and bodies of the regime's dissenters and its victims.

DOCILE BODIES: AN ANATOMY OF IDEOLOGY

Offred neither forgives nor forgets; she rebels by keeping the past alive, first in her memory, then on tape. What the regime would eradicate, she re-inscribes. Her first words evoke another memory trace, the "afterimage" of a world long ago and far away: she remembers the basketball games and high school dances held through the decades in the gymnasium where she is imprisoned, which has been turned into a "reeducation" center to indoctrinate handmaids in their new roles. "There was old sex in the room and loneliness, and expectation, of something without a shape or name. I remember that yearning, for something that was always about to happen. . . . We yearned for the future" (3). The intensity with which teenagers yearned for the future is grimly ironic in retrospect, since that future has now arrived, emptied of hope, freedom, possibility. The "something without shape or name" is desire, and Offred remembers her own "insatiability," a craving all the more poignant now, since desire is precisely what is banned in Gilead.

Her individual memories illuminate not just her intimate relationships but political and historical moments, ranging from her mother's feminist activism for abortion rights and against pornography to her own combined roles as librarian, wife, friend, mother, citizen. But Gilead strips women of their individuality, categorizing them hierarchically according to class status and reproductive capacity. They are, in fact, metonymically color coded according to their function and their labor: the commanders' wives wear blue (a remnant perhaps of aristocracy's blue bloods); the handmaids wear red, the color of blood; and "econowives," distributed to lesser functionaries in the regime, wear multicolored dresses, to indicate that they have to perform multiple sexual and housewifely functions. The very term, "econowives," makes explicit the hierarchical commodification of the female. Men without any status are not "issued a woman, not even one" (18). The traffic in women eliminates the individual female personality; she merely becomes an interchangeable unit in the body politic. The film visually highlights female commodification: rather than branding them as slaveowners did blacks, or tattooing them as Germans did Jews, each handmaid's wrist is encircled with a slave bracelet engraved with the kind of codes that are electronically read at the supermarket checkout counter; in order to pass checkpoints in the city, the guards pass the sensor over the woman's wrist. In addition, all the women's clothes are identical except for color; ordered from a Sears catalog, they underscore the scarceness of consumer wares in a society under siege.

The novel gives a new and ominous meaning to the phrase "the body politic" by laying bare the devices by which subjects of the state are ideologically constructed. Atwood implicitly inquires, "What is Woman?" The answer: a person of the female sex. Only in certain relations of power and exchange does she become a servant, a womb, or a sexual partner, as Simone de Beauvoir observes in *The Second Sex*, which may have provided Atwood's donnée, for in trying to distinguish production in the Marxist sense from biological reproduction, de Beauvoir observes:

> It is impossible simply to equate gestation with a service, such as military service . . . no state has ever ventured to establish obligatory copulation . . . all that can be done is to put woman in a situation where maternity is for her the sole outcome—the law or the mores enjoin marriage, birth control and abortion are prohibited, divorce is forbidden.[14]

That is precisely the situation Atwood imagines: mass marriages are arranged; divorce is prohibited; free will and individual choice cease to exist. Like Héloise, Mariane, and the many nuns in *The Three Marias*, Offred takes the veil not from religious conviction but because external pressures coerce her to harness her sexuality. The only difference between her existence and a nun's is that the latter is forced to be chaste, whereas for Offred and all handmaids, copulation is obligatory; birth control and abortion are prohibited; woman is compelled to bring forth or face death.

Apocalypse depicts what has been, what is, and what will be. Atwood depicts what "Woman" has been in the Judeo-Christian tradition, from biblical times through the 1980s to the end of the next century. From Medusa to the Virgin Mary, from the biblical handmaid Bilhah to Hester Prynne, from Mary Webster[15] to Maryann Crescent Moon in 2195, the novel assembles the constructions of "Woman": angel/monster, fairy/witch, castrator/ nurturer, dutiful daughter/revolutionary, saint/heretic, madonna/whore. Revolutions come and go, but women remain subject to the same negative

14. Simone de Beauvoir, *The Second Sex*, trans. and ed. H. M. Parshley (New York: Vintage, 1974), pp. 65–66.

15. Atwood dedicates the book to Perry Miller, her professor of American literature at Harvard, and to Mary Webster, her Puritan ancestor who was hanged as a witch but survived. "She had a tough neck," Atwood wryly observes.

definitions, straitjacketed by the same crippling dichotomies. The three Marias share the same insight in *New Portuguese Letters*, as they similarly shift forward and backward through time, asking in a woman's diary entry from 1800:

> What woman is not a nun, sacrificed, self-sacrificing, without a life of her own, sequestered from the world? What change has there been in the life of women through the centuries? . . . We are living in an age of civilization and enlightenment, men write scientific treatises, and encyclopedias, nations continually change and transform their political structure, the oppressed raise their voices, a king of France has been sent to the guillotine and his courtiers along with him, the United States of America has gained its independence. . . . What has changed in the life of women?[16]

Far from progressive, history, for women, is regressive. Atwood unflinchingly depicts the oppression of women *before* the coup as well as after: before the coup, women were not safe on the streets; portable "Pornomarts" were on every corner; "snuff" films celebrated the murder and dissection of female bodies. The new regime promises an end to rape, pornography, and violence. As Atwood observed in an interview, "A new regime would never say, 'we're socialist; we're fascist.' They would say that they were serving God. . . . You can develop any set of beliefs by using the Bible. . . . Repressive regimes always have to offer up something in return."[17] Women believed the regime's promises and participated in book burnings, inadvertently colluding in their own enslavement; it is precisely the cooperation of feminists with right-wingers that helps bring about the fundamentalist coup: pornography is banned, but so are all civil liberties.[18] Martial law is

16. *The Three Marias*, p. 154. Even after the junior officers' coup overthrew the Caetano-Salazar dictatorship in 1974, the women were still forced to stand trial, an injustice that further demonstrates the validity of their argument that revolutions do little to change women's oppression. See Kauffman, *Discourses of Desire*, chap. 8.

17. Interview with Cathy N. Davidson, *Ms.* (February 1986): 24–26. Regarding the current debate about pornography vs. censorship, Atwood observes, "Women are in the position of being asked to choose between two things, neither of which is good for them. Why can't they have a third thing that is good for them . . . some kind of reasonable social milieu in which pornography would not be much of an issue because it would not be desired by men?"

18. One wonders whether Atwood had in mind the activities of feminists Catharine MacKinnon and Andrea Dworkin, who contributed to then Attorney General Edwin Meese's *Final Report of the Attorney General's Commission on Pornography*, which appeared the

imposed and all undesirables—prostitutes, lesbians, and feminists like the narrator's mother—are forced to clean toxic wastes until they die from contamination. All are labeled "unwomen." Language thus irrevocably defines reality, which is one reason that Offred spends so much time meditating about words, comparing their meanings before the coup and after, and exposing the arbitrariness of construction. Of the word *chair*, for example, she reflects, "It can mean the leader of a meeting. It can also mean a mode of execution. It is the first syllable in charity. It is the French word for flesh. None of these facts has any connection with the others" (110). But, in fact, there is an associative connection, for the leaders of the revolution enforce their power by torturing the flesh of dissenters. Resisters receive no charity, no mercy; instead, they are executed.

The Handmaid's Tale functions as an anatomy of ideology, exposing the process by which one constructs—physically, psychologically, and politically—subjects of the state and then enlists their cooperation in their own subjection. One begins at the level of the flesh. In the reeducation centers, the handmaid is taught to have an entirely different relation to her own body, her "self." As Offred confesses:

> Each month I watch for blood, fearfully, for when it comes it means failure. I have failed once again to fulfill the expectations of others, which have become my own.
>
> I used to think of my body as an instrument of pleasure, or a means of transportation, or an implement for the accomplishment of my will. I could use it to run, push buttons of one sort or another, make things happen. There were limits, but my body was nevertheless lithe, single, solid, one with me.
>
> Now the flesh arranges itself differently. I'm a cloud, congealed, around a central object, the shape of a pear, which is hard and more real than I am and glows red within its translucent wrapping. Inside it is a space . . . huge. . . . I see despair coming towards me like famine. To feel that empty, again, again. (73–74)

---

same year (1986) that Atwood's novel was published. In 1983, MacKinnon succeeded in getting an antipornography ordinance passed in Minneapolis (subsequently repealed). Closer to Atwood's home, censorship in Canada has become increasingly virulent, especially in some radical feminist groups, as Linda Hutcheon reported in "The Still Sad Music of the Humanities" (paper delivered at a symposium on "Redefining the Humanities," Brooklyn College, 8 December 1989).

Offred's relation to her own body has been utterly transformed now that others have reduced her to a womb, a reproductive factory. Her destiny is irrevocably linked to her anatomy, and she lives under a death sentence should she fail to "deliver" on this her last assignment.

The novel dramatizes the paradox that the ideology of the biological family really comes into its own when the complexity of a class society forces the kinship system to recede.[19] Children have always been viewed as paternal property; here biological bonds are systematically destroyed and children are distributed like commodities to strangers. The patriarchs nevertheless justify their reign of terror by trumpeting the ideology of the family to the heavens, basing it on an extremist's interpretation of the Bible. The closest historical analogue to the Gileadean system is slavery in the American South, where families were similarly destroyed and where black women were similarly prized and priced as breeders. In slavery, despite the black woman's labor, the white slaveowners (like the men in Gilead) retain legal property rights over the product of the woman's body; religiously and legally, it is the man who "produces" the child, just as it has always been. The closest contemporary analogue is the 1987 Baby M case, in which Mary Beth Whitehead agreed to surrogate motherhood for a fee and then reneged on her contract with William and Elizabeth Stern. The case brought into sharp focus the injustices of class and gender in the United States. It was framed by the media and the courts as a case of nature versus nurture, private versus public, good parents versus bad parents. What emerges in the final New Jersey Supreme Court ruling is an attack on Whitehead and a defense of the bourgeois individual and the traditional "family" ("family" defined as economically self-sufficient as well as nurturing), personified in William Stern, as Janice Doane and Devon Hodges point out:

> The traditional family creates this [bourgeois] individual, and contract law protects *his* rights. Indeed, the ideology of contract and the ideology of familialism both define and defend him. . . . The discourse of "rights" prompts us to focus on private individuals and their property. As Paul Hirst remarks, "Rights are expressions of the attributes of subjects and are possessive. Secondly, all rights are modelled upon ownership." . . . Rights discourse has al-

19. Juliet Mitchell, *Psychoanalysis and Feminism: Freud, Reich, Laing, and Women,* p. 378.

ways been more firmly attached to the masculine subject, for the obvious reason that women are not often considered subjects: paternal rights have long been more important than maternal rights. . . . Rights discourse does not need to privilege men but it has almost always done so because men are the paradigmatic individuals with property.[20]

Discussion of all the parallels between Atwood's novel and the Baby M case lies beyond my study's scope, but there are several haunting similarities: surrogate mothers may sign contracts, but the choices they make are hardly "free"; instead, they are driven by economic necessity. Offred is placed in a similar double bind: nothing is done to her that she hasn't "signed up for," but that hardly means that she freely chose her fate. Atwood purposely invents a bizarrely surreal insemination ceremony and system of exchange (of handmaids and babies) to highlight the gap between the rhetoric of the patriarchs and the reality; the Baby M case similarly "highlights the artificiality of the ideology of familialism and demonstrates its continuing power to shape our desires for happiness and to restrict our responses to the actualities of production, parenting, and sexuality."[21] Just as the novel stages competing modes of discourse (male versus female, objective versus subjective, rational versus "hysterical"), the Baby M case revolved around the same dichotomies: William Stern took his case to an "objective" third party, a court of law; Mary Beth Whitehead was variously accused of being a "homicidal" or "suicidal" mother, "overidentified" in and with her children, suffering from a "mixed personality disorder."[22] "Objectivity" is as flawed in legal discourse as in "scientific" and historical research like the archivist's.

Few legal cases in recent times have had such a Foucauldian cast; Atwood's novel is a desedimentation of the processes that lead to such subjection. Foucault argues that bodies are turned into machines in the army, the school, and the hospital; in Atwood's novel, the Red Centers combine all three functions. They are run by the "Aunts," menopausal women whose job is to create a sisterhood and a women's culture, a grim parody of one of

20. Janice Doane and Devon Hodges, "Risky Business: Familial Ideology and the Case of Baby M," *Differences* 1, no. 1 (Winter 1989): 67–81.

21. Ibid., p. 67.

22. Ibid., pp. 70–72.

the quaint feminist impulses of the 1970s and early 1980s. It is as if Atwood took Elaine Showalter's ideas to their absurd but logical conclusion, for "gynocriticism" is a joke in the novel: "You wanted a women's culture. Well, now there is one. It isn't what you meant" (127). The Aunts are licensed to torture recruits who resist reeducation. This emphasis on the collusion of women with their oppressors is significant; one of the regime's strokes of genius is the discovery that the least expensive way to enforce its policies is by using women against each other. The Red Centers are also hospitals, for here the handmaids practice Lamaze exercises and undergo drug and shock treatments. Their identities as women, wives, mothers, lovers are all erased through discipline, punishment, and torture. As Foucault asks, "Is it surprising that prisons resemble factories, schools, barracks, hospitals, which all resemble prisons?"[23] Offred is simultaneously a prisoner, a pupil to be reeducated, a patient who is forcibly subjected to monthly gynecological exams to optimize the chances of pregnancy. The novel thus condenses two of Foucault's major subjects: the birth of the prison and the birth of the clinic, the gaze of the panopticon and the gaze of the medical amphitheater. In Gilead, human identity is reduced to the level of the embryo and subject to electronic and microscopic surveillance; genes and reproductive organs alone signify.[24] The slave trade in *The Color Purple* is replaced by the gene trade.

In revealing the inextricable connections between power and sexuality, Atwood demonstrates the validity of Foucault's observation that "[s]exuality is not the most intractable element in power relations, but rather one of those endowed with the greatest instrumentality" (*DP*, 103). Offred's reckless trysts with Nick seem to refute Foucault's thesis, but when she is discovered, she says,

> I'll sacrifice. I'll repent. I'll abdicate. I'll renounce. . . . Everything they taught at the Red Center, everything I've resisted comes flooding in. I don't

23. Michel Foucault, *Discipline and Punish: The Birth of the Prison*, trans. Alan Sheridan (New York: Vintage, 1979), p. 228; hereinafter cited parenthetically as *DP*.

24. See Foucault, *The Birth of the Clinic: An Archaeology of Medical Perception*, trans. A. M. Sheridan Smith (New York: Vintage, 1975). For an analysis of the manipulation of electronic surveillance by anti-abortionists, see Rosalind Petchesky "Fetal Images: The Power of Visual Culture in the Politics of Reproduction," *Feminist Studies* 13, no. 2 (Summer 1987): 263–92.

want pain. . . . I want to keep on living, in any form. I resign my body freely, to the uses of others. They can do what they like with me. I am abject. I feel, for the first time, their true power. (286)

This statement illustrates an important feminist point, for Foucault rejects the repressive hypothesis too readily, although he maintains that he does not deny sexual repression so much as situate it within a larger dynamic. Nevertheless, Gayle Rubin is right to insist:

> Sexuality in Western societies has been structured within an extremely punitive social framework, and has been subjected to very real formal and informal controls. It is necessary to recognize repressive phenomena without resorting to the essentialist assumptions of the language of libido. It is important to hold repressive sexual practices in focus, even while situating them within a different totality and a more refined terminology.[25]

The suicide of Offred's predecessor similarly attests to the powerful mechanisms in force to control sexuality. In Gilead, all citizens are classified in binary categories that control and contain everyone: licit versus illicit, reproductive versus nonreproductive, white versus black, religious believer versus heretic. Homosexuals are executed as "gender traitors"; abortionists are hanged for crimes against the species; Jews must emigrate or convert; blacks are "resettled"; feminists and other deviants—Quakers, Baptists, Catholics, atheists, liberals, leftists—are "disappeared." Around the time that Atwood was completing her novel, while living in Alabama, David Duke distributed a plan for resettling Asians in "East Mongolia" (presently Hawaii), African-Americans in "New Africa" (presently the American South), Mexican-Americans in "Alta California," and Native Americans in "Navahona" (the last two in the Southwest). Cuban-Americans would be segregated in "New Cuba," (Miami, Miami Beach, and Dade County), American Jews in "West Israel" (Manhattan and Long Island), Puerto Ricans and Americans of Italian and Greek descent in "Minoria," encompassing the rest of New York City. Americans of French-Canadian descent would be settled in "Francia," near the Canadian border. The rest of the nation would be "reclaimed" by "Aryan Americans." The proposals were dissemi-

---

25. Gayle Rubin, "Thinking Sex: Notes for a Radical Theory of the Politics of Sexuality," in *Pleasure and Danger: Exploring Female Sexuality*, ed. Carole S. Vance (Boston: Routledge and Kegan Paul, 1984), p. 277.

nated in the December 1984 newsletter of the National Association for the Advancement of White People, a group Duke founded. Duke is a member of the Louisiana House of Representatives; he ran for Senate in the Louisiana primary in the fall of 1990 and was defeated by a far narrower margin than expected.[26] In one sense, Atwood "invents" nothing; she merely defamiliarizes the work of ideology that seems to go on invisibly all around us.

To make visible the invisible work of ideology and subjection, Atwood's archeological investigations uncovered two theocracies as models: Puritan Boston of *The Scarlet Letter* and modern Iran under the Ayatollah Khomeini. Like Hester Prynne, the handmaid is defined by her sexuality, literally marked as a scarlet woman. Like Hester, she lives in a utopia gone awry, where the prison and the cemetery are omnipresent. Hawthorne's "Custom House" seems to have inspired Atwood's preoccupation with the ways in which we subject ourselves to the prison houses of custom: repression is first horrific, but soon comes to seem necessary, then customary, and finally "natural." At one point, Offred offhandedly remarks that at present "only" two bodies hang on the wall in what used to be Harvard Yard. The present reality in all its horror is already coming to seem normal—even to her—and the next generation will have no memory, no means by which to measure the relative normality or abnormality of the regime. Indeed, time is carefully manipulated so that all remnants of the past, pre-Gilead reality are obliterated: there are no dates after the 1980s; all historical documents are destroyed, and the Gileadean regime periodically wipes out even its own computer records after various purges. Atwood thus shares Lessing's and Walker's obsession with history. The Gileadeans are the logical inheritors and cunning assimilators of Stalinist strategies (as in Lessing) and racist strategies (as in Walker) to systematically distort, erase, and rewrite history.

In a society under siege, when the brutal force of a coup prescribes the law of the land, subjects are defined solely by obedience: by a grim tautology, the subject who is constituted as subject is the one who obeys. As Foucault observes:

26. Lucian K. Truscott IV, "Hate Gets a Haircut," *Esquire* (November 1989): 174–84. The title emphasizes the same cosmetic attention to concealing fascism that characterizes the mistress of the Nazi in Atwood's novel.

> The historical moment of the disciplines was the moment when an art of the
> human body was born, which was directed not only at . . . the intensification
> of its subjection, but at the formation of a relation that in the mechanism itself
> makes it more obedient as it becomes more useful, and conversely. What was
> then being formed was a policy of coercions that act upon the body, a calcu-
> lated manipulation of its elements, its gestures, its behaviour. The human
> body was entering a machinery of power that explores it, breaks it down and
> rearranges it. A "political anatomy," which was also a "mechanics of power,"
> was being born. (DP, 138)

Disciplined like soldiers, the handmaids learn to control their bodies, to respond mechanically, to think and act as a collective unit. As with a soldier or
a nun, each handmaid's body and gestures must reflect her status; she is
commanded by signals, not by comprehension. Perhaps the closest model
for the behavior desired of her is *dressage*—the leading of horses through
their paces—which metaphorically signifies blind, unthinking obedience
(DP, 166).

Obedience is also ensured through the careful regulation of time. Offred
notes that "the bell that measures time is ringing. Time here is measured by
bells, as once in nunneries. As in a nunnery too, there are few mirrors" (8).
Offred's bodily movements are minutely monitored: so many minutes in
the bathroom; so many chances (three) to conceive. She mimes the moni-
toring of time through her method of narration: each entry is brief, descriptive, recorded in random moments—similar in this respect to the style of
slave narratives and *The Color Purple*. Seven out of fifteen chapters are entitled, "Night," which signifies metaphorically the darkness of impending
doom, of ignorance, of despair. The repetition suggests the repetition of
other holocausts, as in Elie Wiesel's *Night*.[27] Offred's entire existence as
handmaid consists of waiting: waiting for the monthly sexual "ceremony,"
waiting for the results, and if they are positive, waiting to deliver the baby.
Another way to ensure obedience is to enforce silence; since spies are everywhere, the entire society ceases to speak freely, and the handmaids are only
allowed to speak in prescribed pious clichés. Through parody, Atwood defamiliarizes the misogyny of the Bible, substituting "There is a bomb in

27. Janet L. Larson, "Margaret Atwood and the Future of Prophecy," *Religion and Literature* 21 (Spring 1989): 27–58; hereinafter cited parenthetically.

Gilead" for "balm" (218), and rewriting St. Paul: "From each according to her ability: to each according to his needs" (117; cf. Acts 4:35) (Larson, 48). St. Paul is particularly significant because Atwood parodies his epistles in her own epistolary text. As Janet L. Larson observes,

> The Handmaid's Tale exposes "Pauline" misogyny with sardonic wit, but the novel also "compasses," protects, the best parts of his letters for Offred's use. She can compare the fragments of Scripture preserved in Gilead to parts of a dismembered body . . . bits and pieces of Paul keep turning up, scattered members Atwood gathers into the body of her text.[28]

Despite the grimness of its subject matter, mordant absurdist comedy abounds in the novel. Atwood is as much the master of parody as Lessing is: one recalls The Golden Notebook's parody of the Communist party "line," and the prescribed clichés comrades are required to parrot in conversation, as well as the dreadfully trite fiction of social realism written by the party's aspiring novelists. Parody is one of Atwood's most devastating devices: she ridicules the regime's rhetoric and satirizes its true believers.

Atwood portrays a regime in the process of establishing the mechanisms of repression that will eventually be invisible. At the moment, those mechanisms can still be seen: executions still abound, checkpoints stop citizens from fleeing the city, police vans suddenly materialize on the streets and whisk unsuspecting citizens away. Once Gilead works out the kinks in its repressive mechanisms, however, all citizens will, like the handmaids in their red habits, exist in a state of conscious and permanent "compulsory visibility" that will ensure the automatic functioning of power. The agents are called the Eyes, and eventually, as in Bentham's panopticon, surveillance will become permanent in its effects, even if discontinuous in its action, for the institutional gaze will be invisible but omniscient. Atwood follows the other writers in my study from Shklovsky onward in portraying the enormous power of the image to monitor, control, and restrain its subjects. The film aptly captures this facet of the novel by depicting T.V. monitors on every street corner; the T.V. logo is an eye on a pyramid (reminiscent of the CBS logo); this eye, however, spies on the citizens while they stare at the tube. No one can overestimate the sweeping range of visual surveillance in

---

28. Larson draws extensive parallels between St. Paul's letters and Offred's as well as providing a detailed analysis of other biblical allusions.

contemporary life: video technology controls every aspect of existence, ranging from the transvaginal scopes used to detect defective ovaries to the propaganda and "disinformation" disseminated on televised "prayvaganzas." Atwood, Schlöndorff, and Pinter all adamantly insist that they are depicting the present as much as the future, as Schlöndorff reports:

> Atwood said she didn't invent anything, she just assembled pieces of mankind's puzzle in a different way. . . . It is really very much more oriented to see where we are at and how we got here rather than to look into the future. . . . Pinter . . . scribbled on the screenplay: "This story takes place a few years from now, but the aim is not to show a futuristic world. Apart from special elements—clothes for instance—appearances are in the main familiar. It is the customs which changed."[29]

One of the grim paradoxes in the novel is that the present is as invisible to us as the future, because perception has been dulled by habitualization—the very danger Viktor Shklovsky warned against in 1917. Atwood's novel is thus an exemplary response to the challenge Michèle Barrett addressed to feminist literary critics:

> I can find no sustained argument as to why feminists should be so interested in literature or what theoretical or political ends such analyses of literature serve. . . . related to this is the inadequacy of feminist attempts to explore the ways in which material conditions have historically structured the mental aspects of oppression.[30]

Atwood's aim is to demonstrate precisely how material conditions structure mental oppression, for despite all of Offred's efforts to remember her prior existence, she inevitably begins to internalize the perception the regime wants her to have of herself. When she sees a pregnant woman, for example, she feels the emptiness of her own womb and experiences a sense of failure, futility, and worthlessness. Her breasts become swollen and ache. This is exactly how the material and mental aspects of oppression work in concert, for the Red Center trains her to reflect in her material body the mental impression it strives never to let her forget: that she is nothing but a passive

29. Jami Bernard, "The Filmmaker's Tale," *Starlog* (March 1990): 45–48, 56.

30. Michèle Barrett, "Ideology and the Cultural Production of Gender," in *Criticism and Social Change: Sex, Class and Race in Literature and Culture*, ed. Judith Newton and Deborah Rosenfelt (New York: Methuen, 1985), pp. 65–85.

receptacle. (When Moira is tortured by electroshock for her attempted insurrection, she is told, "For our purposes your feet and your hands are not essential" [91].) Essentialism no longer has anything to do with identity, much less with feminist politics, gynocriticism, or *écriture féminine*: instead what is essential turns out to be what is defined as such by those in power and valued accordingly: a fertile womb. Atwood echoes de Beauvoir when Offred remarks, "My self is a thing I must now compose, as one composes a speech. What I must present is a made thing, not something born" (66). The biopolitics of bodies in the late twentieth century explode all organic and essentialist mythologies, as Donna Haraway explains in examining the role and rhetoric of science and technology: "bodies . . . are not born; they are made. Bodies have been as thoroughly denaturalized as sign, context, and time. . . . one is not born an organism. Organisms are made: they are constructs of a world-changing kind."[31]

Although Offred internalizes the oppression to which she is subjected, she also resists it. She seems to reclaim desire by making love with Nick, an act for which she could be executed; she is compelled toward him, "expecting at any moment to feel the bullets rip through me" (268). By telling him her real name and history, she unburies the body, the voice, the intelligence that the regime sought to annihilate.

The subplot with Nick is a risky one for Atwood, full of paradoxes. On the one hand, it seems to illustrate de Beauvoir's assertion, "It is impossible to bring the sexual instinct under a code of regulations. . . . What is certain is that it does not permit of integration with the social, because there is in eroticism a revolt of the instant against time, of the individual against the universal."[32] On the other hand, Foucault maintains that our liberation does not lie in freedom from sexual repression and that (as Barthes and Derrida also argue) identity does not lie in sexuality. The tensions between these two viewpoints are revealed when Offred and Nick "make love each time as if we know beyond the shadow of a doubt that there will never be any more, for either of us, with anyone, ever" (269). At first, these words merely seem to support de Beauvoir's contention. But closer scrutiny reveals that far from

---

31. Donna Haraway, "The Biopolitics of Postmodern Bodies: Determinations of Self in Immune System Discourse," p. 10.

32. de Beauvoir, p. 65.

viewing lovemaking as liberating, Offred approaches it as if death is imminent. Far from seeing sexuality as the source of her liberation, she recognizes that her act may simply hammer the nails in the coffin of what *at the time* seemed to be her already-sealed doom. One must constantly keep in mind the complex temporal manipulation of the narrative by distinguishing the Offred who is speaking (in the "present") from the Offred (of the past) who is the focus of her narrative. ("Present" belongs in inverted commas because, by the time her narrative is transcribed, 150 years have passed.) As Offred speaks these words, she is presumably already at least temporarily safe in a halfway house outside Gilead. (Whatever her eventual fate, she apparently remained safe long enough to record her tapes.) But the reader is not yet aware that her narrative is retrospective; one has to wait for the archivist's endnote to discover that. Offred, similarly, is trying to portray her own impressions as they unfolded at the moment, and at that moment, each time she slept with Nick, she thought it would be the last time; that she was shortly to feel the bullets ripping through her. Nothing in the passage suggests that she has any illusions that sexuality will liberate her. Some may object that her sexuality does in fact liberate her, since her affair with Nick results in her rescue by the Mayday organization. It is not her sexual activity, however, but her willingness to aid the Underground that paves the way for her presumed rescue. (To the very end, her rescue remains a matter of surmise.)

Atwood's novel is obviously no mere application of Foucauldian theory, for where Foucault rejects the repressive hypothesis, Atwood clearly exercises poetic license by inventing a society that is relentlessly repressive *and* oppressive. Moreover, despite the numerous ways in which Foucault's work illuminates the novel, one could argue that this issue reveals his blindness where feminism is concerned, for—as we saw above—feminist theorists ranging from de Beauvoir to the three Marias to Gayle Rubin insist that men's oppression of women is a fundamental historical reality. When the Commander explains the rationale for the coup, he makes it clear that the coup occurred precisely because repression was lacking: "[T]he sex was too easy. . . . Anyone could just buy it. There was nothing to work for, nothing to fight for." But what passes for freedom from repression from men—the "freedom" to buy sex—entails oppression for women: the economic necessity of prostitution. These paradoxes are represented in the novel without resolution or closure. Offred's section ends indeterminately; it is followed by a gap, a silence of over a century, and then resumes with an archivist's interpretation that raises more questions than it answers. Atwood dramatizes the ambiguities of repression through temporal manipulation, contrasting our obliviousness to it as it begins to take shape latently with its manifest phase, which then once again becomes seemingly invisible—as indeed it may be invisible in the archivist's society. That is why Offred reflects that "[n]othing changes instantaneously: in a gradually heating bathtub you'd be boiled to death before you knew it" (56).

Another risk is that the subplot with Nick could easily have turned the novel into a sentimental romance, but Atwood simultaneously inscribes a counterdiscourse that deconstructs the ideology of love. In this respect, she continues the efforts of both Lessing and Walker. Just as Lessing describes Ella putting her mind to sleep and floating darkly on her love for Paul, Atwood estranges the word "love":

Falling in love. . . . It was the central thing; it was the way you understood yourself. . . . *Falling in love*, we said: *I fell for him*. We were falling women. We believed in it, this downward motion: so lovely, like flying, and yet at the same time so dire, so extreme, so unlikely. . . . The more difficult it was to love the particular man beside us, the more we believed in Love, abstract and total. (225–26)

Ironically, that ideology was disseminated in magazines like *Mademoiselle* and *Vogue*—the very magazines now banned. It is tempting to interpret the novel as a paean to individual freedom, but Atwood's critique is more complex, for advertising invariably ties a concrete product to an abstract concept, like youth, freedom, or love. ("The Pepsi Generation," "the Heartbeat of America," etc.) For many before the coup, Atwood suggests, "freedom" merely signified the right to choose between products like Chanel or Opium perfume. Schlöndorff describes his strategy for defamiliarizing this aspect of contemporary life in the film, noting that the Washington political wife

invariably wears a blue dress, a blue coat and a blue hat, and she doesn't look so good in it. Now, if you have a hundred of those, you are all of a sudden in a Stalinist society. . . . Ditto for cars, objects, lamps, beds. We eliminated what characterizes our society: the apparent wide variety of objects and choices. But in fact, they are not so different even today, they are all more of the same, they're just recycled so that they look a little different, like our TV pro-

grams. . . . by the fact that there are so many of this one type, it gets
strange.[33]

The magazines that disseminate the ideology of love are underwritten by
advertisers committed to sustaining our illusions of individualistic freedom
and choice. In contrast, far from merely endorsing the free enterprise system, Atwood repeatedly stresses that the obsession with the superficial and
cosmetic hides myriad social ills and multiple atrocities. Offred comments at
one point that "context is all," but it would be equally accurate to say that
"appearance is all." That is certainly the function of the televangelists who
carefully censor the news. Serena Joy resembles Tammy Faye Bakker, whose
trademark was her grotesquely overly made-up face: Serena Joy

> was ash blond, petite, with a snub nose and huge blue eyes which she'd turn
> upwards during hymns. She could smile and cry at the same time, one tear or
> two sliding gracefully down her cheek, as if on cue. (16)

Tammy Faye was also famous for smiling, weeping, and singing simultaneously. Her husband, Jim Bakker, founded the PTL prayvaganza industry,
and is now serving an eighteen-year prison sentence for bilking millions of
the faithful. "PTL" was supposed to mean "Praise the Lord," but in retrospect "Pass the Loot" seems more fitting; in the novel, similarly, "In God we
trust—all others pay cash" is one of many jokes. The mercantile motives of
fundamentalism are indissolubly linked to its ideological motives—a link
that has perhaps been indissoluble ever since the Puritans joined up with the
Massachusetts Bay Company. As William Faulkner once observed, the
Puritans didn't come to America to escape a tyranny so much as to establish
one. Although Jimmy Swaggart, Jim Bakker, and Oral Roberts have fallen
on hard times since Atwood's novel was published, the power, threat, and
zeal of fundamentalism remain. Jerry Falwell was on the podium when
President Bush was inaugurated to symbolize Bush's and Quayle's soli-
darity with the so-called Moral Majority—particularly in their opposition
to abortion. Television evangelist Pat Robertson was a candidate for president in the 1988 election, and recently formed a new grass-roots organization called the Christian Coalition, which plans to have organizations in
thirty-two states by the end of 1990, in order to continue its anti-abortion,
pro-Creationist crusade to promote Christianity "in neighborhoods, school

33. Bernard, p. 45–46.

boards, city councils and state legislatures."[34] In April 1990, Reverend Donald Wildmon and the American Family Association targeted photographer David Wojnarowicz's work by taking two homosexual images out of context from a larger collage and mass mailing the enlarged images to every member of Congress, as well as to 178,000 pastors on the American Family Association's mailing list. These actions were part of a massive effort by fundamentalists to dismantle the National Endowment for the Arts and to censor "pornography." A bill introduced in the Olympia, Washington state capital in February 1990, sponsored by Republican State Senator Jim West from Spokane, would make it a crime for people under the age of eighteen to engage in sex, including "heavy petting." The fine: ninety days in jail and a $5000.00 fine, unless they decide to marry.

Atwood also deconstructs the ideology of love by showing how collective oppression undermines the notion of individual salvation through love. After the regime strips women of their jobs, their bank accounts, and their autonomy, Offred's relationship to Luke is irrevocably altered because she is utterly dependent upon him:

> Something had shifted, some balance. I felt shrunken, so that when he put his arms around me . . . I was small as a doll. I felt love going forward without me.
>
> He doesn't mind this, I thought. He doesn't mind it at all. Maybe he even likes it. We are not each other's anymore. Instead, I am his. . . .
>
> We never talked about it. By the time I could have done that, I was afraid to. I couldn't afford to lose you. (182)

Atwood thus reaccentuates the epistolary motif of trial throughout the novel: Offred conducts silent dialogues in her mind, like the one above, in order to sort out the complex web of motives, interactions, desires, and intentions that have entrapped her and led to society's disintegration. She alternately assumes the role of judge, jury, witness, and criminal, shifting backward and forward between past and present, relentlessly putting her relatives, friends, colleagues, husband, and society at large on trial. Like Celie in *The Color Purple*, she puts God on trial, too, asking how *He* (in her view, it must be a he) could permit such distortions of the spirit by the letter to take place in His name; unlike Celie, she is not able to affirm God's exis-

34. *Washington Post*, 14 March 1990, p. A6.

tence by the conclusion of her narrative, however desperately she tries to cling to her own conception of God.

She also puts herself on trial. Paradoxically, one of the ways in which she manages to resist the regime is by taking responsibility for her actions. She recognizes that she is guilty of numerous "sins"—albeit sins different from those defined by the regime. She castigates herself for not paying enough attention to the alarming signs of intolerance—religious, racial, and sexual—in her society before the takeover; and for colluding with the regime in order to survive. Her confession of these sins recalls one of the most remarkable characteristics of women's epistolary literature, for from Héloise to Mariane to Clarissa heroines have used their letters to engage in merciless self-condemnation. Like Clarissa and the three Marias, Offred simultaneously suffers trials and tries herself.[35] She reveals her participation in the rite of "salvaging," for instance, which means that when a woman is hanged, Offred touches the rope in unison with the other handmaids, then places her hand on her heart "to show my unity with the Salvagers and my consent, and my complicity in the death of this woman" (276). She also confesses to sharing the sensations the regime wants her to have when a political prisoner is brought before the handmaids on trumped-up charges of raping and murdering a pregnant handmaid. In a ritual called "particicution," they dismember him; only by an extraordinary effort of will does Offred restrain herself, but even she nevertheless experiences the "bloodlust; I want to tear, gouge, rend" (279). And she memorializes both her complicity and that corpse in her text:

> I wish this story were different. I wish it were more civilized. I wish it showed me in a better light, if not happier, then at least more active, less hesitant, less distracted by trivia. I wish it had more shape. . . . I'm sorry there is so much pain in this story. I'm sorry it's in fragments, like a body caught in crossfire or pulled apart by force. (267)

While apologizing for the pain in her story, Offred emphasizes that the fact that she is unhappy is less relevant than the fact that she should have been more engaged in collective action to save her society from fanatics. In this fashion, Atwood undermines the ideology of bourgeois individualism; her

35. For an analysis of the trial motif in epistolary literature and the heroines' self-condemnation, see Kauffman, *Discourses of Desire*, pp. 44–45, 77–78, 133–36, 187–94.

emphasis in this respect is similar to Anna Wulf's insistence that she is sick of her emotions and subjectivity. In retrospect, Offred is able to compare the present with the ominous signs of growing oppression in the past before the coup:

> We lived as usual. Everyone does, most of the time. Whatever is going on is as usual. Even this is as usual, now. We lived, as usual, by ignoring. Ignoring isn't the same as ignorance, you have to work at it. Nothing changes instantaneously: in a gradually heating bathtub you'd be boiled to death before you knew it. (56)

She was an apathetic, self-absorbed member of the "post-feminist generation."[36] Of interest in the art-imitates-life category, Natasha Richardson, who plays Offred in the film, and who is the daughter of the actress and ardent political activist Vanessa Redgrave, admits that she is guilty of the very malaise and apathy that Bolotin describes and Offred embodied in her earlier life:

> The fact that my mother is a very political person has, unfortunately, put me off politics for the rest of my life. In politics you have to be willing to stand up and say what you think. You have to defend yourself and I'm not like that. I'm not like Margaret Atwood or like my mother. I'm not politically well-educated enough to talk about things.[37]

The unfortunate tendency to leave things to the "experts" is precisely the phenomenon responsible for the ascendancy of men like the Commander as well as of other marketing research wizards, sociobiologists, scientists, and CIA strategists who make up the "Sons of Jacob Think Tanks." The Sons of Jacob embody what Haraway calls "the informatics of domination," which

---

36. See Susan Bolotin's "Voices from the Post-Feminist Generation," *New York Times Magazine*, 17 October 1982, pp. 28–31, 103–7. Performance artist Laurie Anderson eerily echoes Offred's words:

> I feel like a lot of people have kind of napped through the Reagan years, politically. You know how you feel when you wake up from a nap, sort of real disoriented and cranky and stuff? That's how this time is striking me. . . . As I looked around I saw things weren't the way they were being described at all. You remember that old "safety net" thing they used to talk about? You don't hear about that any more. People fell right through. (Interview with Joe Brown, "'Angel' Voice: Anderson's Art," *Washington Post Weekend Magazine*, 16 March 1990, p. 23)

37. "'Handmaid' on the Hill," interview with Jim Naughton, *Washington Post*, 10 March 1990, pp. D1, D5.

are "scary new networks" dedicated to formulating human diversity in terms of frequencies and parameters. "Any objects or persons can be reasonably thought of in terms of disassembly or reassembly."[38] Offred's Commander seems to be a composite of two figures whose joint skills embody the most wretched excesses of contemporary society. Like Donald Trump in the 1980s, Frederick Waterford's expertise lies in marketing, packaging, public relations and ritual; he is credited with resurrecting the ancient rites of particicution and salvaging. B. Frederick Judd's genius lies in military tactics; like Oliver North, he specializes in destabilizing foreign governments and securing huge sums of money nefariously. He is credited with planning the massacre of the nation's leaders and with privatizing the Jewish repatriation. Habitualization prevents us from noticing the various forms of "privatization" that are aided and abetted by new technologies. As Haraway notes,

> the new technologies seem deeply involved in the forms of "privatization" . . . in which militarization, right-wing family ideologies and policies, and intensified definitions of corporate property as private synergistically interact.[39]

Although staged in dramatically different terms from either *The Golden Notebook* or *The Color Purple*, *The Handmaid's Tale* similarly demonstrates how a particular situation contains both the forces of oppression and the seeds of resistance, for while Offred in some respects internalizes the oppression the regime enforces, she simultaneously resists it first by confessing her individual responsibility and later by making the tape recordings. From *Clarissa* to *The Golden Notebook* and *The Color Purple*, the heroine's discourse in epistolary fiction simultaneously reveals her oppression and resistance, her collusion and rebellion. Quakers and Catholics also resist the regime; even Southern Baptists instigate civil war, which to Atwood suggests that in the event of such a takeover there would be considerable resistance, even among groups one would have thought would support the fundamentalists. Her view of the Southern Baptists seems overly

38. Donna Haraway, "A Manifesto for Cyborgs: Science, Technology, and Socialist Feminism in the 1980s," in *Coming to Terms: Feminism, Theory, Politics*, ed. Elizabeth Weed (New York: Routledge, 1989), pp. 173–204; hereinafter cited parenthetically as "Cyborgs."

39. Ibid., p. 192; see also Rosalind Petchesky, "Abortion, Anti-Feminism, and the Rise of the New Right," *Feminist Studies* 7, no. 2 (1981): 206–46.

optimistic in reality, for the 14.6 million member denomination in 1987 elected a leader who endorses a literal interpretation of the Bible, insisting that "the narratives of Scripture are historically and factually accurate." A moderate minister who dissented from the majority vote noted that the election "seems to reflect the agenda of the fundamentalist takeover."[40]

My motive for consistently alluding to "real life" as I write these words in December 1990 is not to resurrect a naive mimeticism, but to demonstrate that art does have a connection to reality, a connection we ignore at our own peril. Barrett is right to insist that "representation *does* bear a relation to something which we can know previously existed."[41] While some have blamed literary theory for disguising or negating those connections, it should by now be clear that semiotics, poststructuralist- and materialist-feminism provide invaluable strategies for deciphering the codes authorizing technology in multiple discursive practices. Few of us completely comprehend the extent to which our lives have been utterly restructured by what Haraway calls "the social relations of science and technology"; nor is it accidental that women and people of color remain scientifically illiterate in these disciplines:

> Communications sciences and biology . . . indicate fundamental transformations in the structure of the world for us. Communications technologies depend on electronics. Modern states, multinational corporations, military power, welfare-state apparatuses, satellite systems, political processes, fabrication of our imaginations, labor-control systems, medical constructions of our bodies, commercial pornography, the international division of labor, and religious evangelism depend intimately upon electronics. ("Cyborgs," 188–89)

Novels like Atwood's thus merit close scrutiny because they are less about the "fearsome future" than about the "fearsome present." She dismantles received ideas and unquestioned assumptions about religion, sex, politics, women's culture—and feminism itself. Atwood audaciously creates a heroine who is in a very real sense responsible for the Gileadean coup: she is apathetic politically, complacent about women's struggles, absorbed

---

40. Atwood's comments appear in the *Ms.* interview; the Southern Baptists' Convention was reported by the *News and Observer*, Raleigh, North Carolina, 17 June 1987, pp. 1, 13A.

41. Barrett, p. 70.

solely in her individual existence. All around her she sees racial hatred, religious intolerance, and sexual repression intensifying daily. If *The Handmaid's Tale* were solely a tragic tale of one woman's victimization, it would merely reinforce the emphasis bourgeois ideology places on the individual, but by focusing equally on the decimation of a culture, a gender, and several races, Atwood follows Lessing and Walker in expanding the parameters of the epistolary mode. The genocidal and suicidal impulses of humanity propel letter writing far beyond the boudoir of the bourgeois gentlewoman.

Perhaps the most chilling statement in the novel is that of Professor Pieixoto, who observes, "There was little that was truly original with or indigenous to Gilead: its genius was synthesis" (307). The oppressions Gilead devises are a synthesis of all previous "civilizations": it borrows from the Spanish inquisitors, the Puritans, Khomeini's Iranian followers, the KGB, the CIA. Gilead borrows Hitler's tactics for encircling urban centers, persecuting the Jews, eliminating undesirables, and using female bodies as laboratories for genetic reproduction. Pieixoto comments, "The sociobiological theory of natural polygamy was used as a scientific justification for some of the odder practices of the regime, just as Darwinism was used by earlier ideologies" (306). As in the slave trade, oppression and exploitation lead to ideological constructions of the persecuted groups as "other."

Since such ghastly practices come to seem normal while Offred is witnessing them, one inevitably wonders what hope there is of sustaining any sense of outrage nearly two centuries later. Because readers in the 1990s are close to the period Offred describes, our horror at what Atwood imagines as our imminent destiny is proportionally greater; Pieixoto and his colleagues, however, look back coolly on a remote past. Whereas Offred sees nothing but pain in her narrative, 150 years later, it is merely a source of quaint curiosity to the historians, archaeologists, and anthropologists who hear it. The immediacy of her danger and her descriptions of the evils she witnesses are so remote in 2195 that her audience cannot even rouse itself to murmur against "the banality of evil"; nothing is condemned by Pieixoto, who warns: "We must be cautious about passing moral judgment upon the Gileadeans. Surely we have learned by now that such judgments are of necessity culture-specific. . . . Our job is not to censure but to understand" (302).

This statement is a direct contrast to Offred's own defiant outrage, for

like survivors of other holocausts, she insists that we pay attention to the
material conditions of the suffering of specific individuals in a particular historical moment:

> Maybe none of this is about control. Maybe it isn't really about who can own
> whom, who can do what to whom and get away with it, even as far as death.
> Maybe it isn't about who can sit and who has to kneel or stand or lie down, legs
> spread open. Maybe it's about who can do what to whom and be forgiven for
> it. Never tell me it amounts to the same thing. (135)

You can only forgive atrocities that you forget, and Offred reminds us never
to forget, never to bury the horrors of history amid vague clichés in which
there are no agents and no evils. Judgment is necessary, she insists, to prevent the past from repeating itself. As in *The Golden Notebook*, Atwood dramatizes how difficult it is to sustain a sense of the copresence of others and to
interrogate world events as they are unfolding. Atwood forces us to ask ourselves how aware we really are of the world around us; how many knew, for
example, that at the very moment when Atwood was writing, the Romanian
regime of Nicolae Ceausescu was forcing Romanian women to bear up to five
children to increase the nation's power? Women were forced to have
gynecological exams every three months to make sure they hadn't had abor-
tions, which were illegal. Thousands of women were nonetheless hospi-
talized or imprisoned for attempting to self-abort; hundreds of thousands of
orphaned children are now warehoused in primitive hospitals, many of them
maimed and brain damaged from botched abortion attempts. The enormity
of these crimes has only come to the world's attention since the Romanian
Revolution in 1989, although Atwood's archivist alludes to them quite
explicitly:

> Rumania . . . had anticipated Gilead in the eighties by banning all forms of
> birth control, imposing compulsory pregnancy tests on the female popula-
> tion, and linking promotion and wage increases to fertility. (305)

How many in 1989 knew that, in the United States, the Department of
Health and Human Services bans doctors and counselors in federally funded
family planning clinics from discussing abortion with clients? Judy Epstein,
the spokeswoman for Planned Parenthood in New York City, comments,
"The effect is blackmail. They will pay us, if we keep our mouths shut." For
the first time, in an effort to control women's sexuality, the Government is
ordering physicians to counsel their patients in prescribed ways and to with-
hold information from them. The word "abortion" has been excised from

birth control pill pamphlets and the words "periodic abstinence" substituted.[42]

Not just clinics but schools are under attack: How many object to the
fact that in the guise of promoting "accuracy" in teaching, a league of right-
wing students report to right-wing politicians about the activities of professors with whom they disagree? These students are particularly active in
Jesse Helms's home state of North Carolina; since Duke University's liberal
and left-wing professors have been one target in these attacks, it seems fitting that the movie version of *The Handmaid's Tale* was filmed at Duke.[43]

Since eyes are everywhere—in the form of spies, electronic monitors,
and surveillance equipment—the symbolism of darkness as blindness is
particularly ironic. The archivist's myopia is ironically underscored by the
last words of the text: "Are there any questions?" The novel leaves us
haunted by myriad questions: What was Offred's eventual fate? What happened during the intervening century and a half to the United States and
North America? The human race has survived, and the planet seems to have
replenished itself—there are fish, oceans, forests—but what kind of society
exists in 2195? Is it less fanatical? Is it more just? Or is it a telling comment
that the archivist refuses to condemn Gileadeans? Perhaps his society has
merely perfected Gilead's "genius for synthesis," making the mechanisms
of power and oppression completely invisible—and thus all-pervasive.
What, if anything, have we learned from history?

42. Lynnell Hancock, "Censoring Abortion," *Village Voice* 35, no. 2, January 1990,
pp. 29–31. Both the Romanian and the U.S. example demonstrate that "bodies and works"
haven't entirely been replaced by texts and surfaces, in contrast to Haraway's statement:

> It is time to write *The Death of the Clinic*. The clinic's methods required bodies and
> works; we have texts and surfaces. Our dominations don't work by medicalization and
> normalization; they work by networking, communications redesign, stress manage-
> ment. ("Cyborgs," p. 177n)

43. Charles Sykes's *ProfScam* (New York: St. Martin's, 1988) is among the most recent in a
long series of ideological attacks to single out Duke University, particularly liberal, left-wing,
and feminist members of the English Department. As *Special Delivery* goes to press, yet another diatribe has appeared: Dinesh D'Souza's *Illiberal Education: The Politics of Race and
Sex on Campus* (New York: Macmillan, 1991). While seeming to plead for tolerance, D'Souza
should really be remembered for editing a nasty magazine called *Prospect*. Financed by right-
wing millionaires and distributed to all alumni at Princeton University, *Prospect* vehemently
denounced women, racial minorities, and gays. It described Princeton's distinguished
women's studies program as "the pockmarked face of feminism." See *The Washington Post*,
20 April 1991, p. A19, and 16 April 1991, pp. B1, B4.

The novel resists closure, leaving us with disturbing questions rather than soothing answers. Atwood records the failure of humanism, liberalism, individualism, and feminism, but she offers no substitutes, no solutions, no comforting fictions of personal or political redemption—including feminist fictions. As Elaine Hansen, referring to *Bodily Harm*, observes, "This kind of fiction and feminism alike insists that we uncover and examine the contradictions, the disequilibrium and insufficiency masked by the sense of an ending."[44] Thus in form and content, Atwood purposely dismantles received ideas about the present, as well as about the past and future, a strategy that evokes Fredric Jameson's reflection on future fiction: "The reader will there find an empty chair reserved for some as yet unrealized, collective, and decentered cultural production of the future, beyond realism and modernism alike."[45] Atwood invents just such a decentered cultural production, for the narrative we read is a collective endeavor, made possible by the resistance movement that presumably rescued Offred, by her courage and defiance in taping her discourse, and by archaeologists and technicians who reassemble her speech. The concentric construction of Atwood's apocalyptic novel encompasses past, present, and future. She makes readers into detectives, trying to reconstruct the political history from which Offred's daily chronicle emerges. Readers discover the struggles and tensions that resulted in the establishment of Gilead's theocracy, and with the appended historical notes they see history portrayed in its vastest sense, projected into the next century. Through this triple framework, Atwood decenters both history and narrative. By dialogically superimposing the archivist's writing over the heroine's speech, she decenters the representational status of writing while reaccentuating the epistolary postmark.[46]

44. Elaine Tuttle Hansen, "Fiction and (Post)Feminism in Atwood's *Bodily Harm*," *Novel* 19 (Fall 1985): 5–21.

45. Fredric Jameson, *The Political Unconscious: Narrative as a Socially Symbolic Act* (Ithaca: Cornell University Press, 1981), p. 11. The novel embodies Jameson's concept of "symbolization," for its structure consists of

> three concentric frameworks [which] function to mark a widening out of the . . . social ground of a text through . . . first, . . . political history, in the narrow sense of . . . a chronicle-like sequence of happenings in time; then of society, in the . . . sense of a constitutive tension and struggle between social classes; and ultimately, of history now conceived in its vastest sense of . . . various social formations, from prehistoric life to whatever far future history has in store for us. (75)

46. Cf. Jameson, pp. 285, 296. On Bakhtinian dialogism and epistolary reaccentuation, see Kauffman, *Discourses of Desire*, pp. 18, 23, 25, 33, 79, 82, 282, 298.

Atwood's contribution to the long tradition of female voices in epistolary literature is to combine epistolary poetics with apocalyptic politics. Despite Gilead's attempts to ban desire, Offred's remains unvanquished. Despite the self-aggrandizement of masculine editors, the interventions of time, and the ideologues who sought to eradicate her, the distinctive female voice of Atwood's heroine remains. Her discourse is a defiant testimony of her innocence and culpability, her defiance and desire, her submission and rebellion to the history being rewritten before her eyes. Like Rennie, Atwood's heroine in *Bodily Harm*, her experiences of a brutal regime so radicalize her that she becomes "a subversive: She was not once but now she is. A reporter. She will pick her time; then she will report."[47] Far from turning inward, as writers confronting politically exhausted cultures often tend to do, Atwood—like Lessing and Walker before her—turns outward, mapping the correspondences between others in a global and temporal panorama.

The novel is finally a testament to the urgency of the analytical project which lies at the interstices of feminism and literary theory, for the future Atwood describes is not distant. Instead, like 1984, it has already arrived. Atwood merely defamiliarizes the world around us: whether one thinks of the trials of surrogate motherhood, or the Vatican's doctrinal edict against anything but married "normal sexuality," or of the AIDS epidemic and its attendant repressions, or of the erosion of civil liberties by the Supreme Court, or of the resurgence of racial and religious intolerance—the seeds of hatred, violence, and repression are already prepared. Whatever "issue" is slouching towards Bethlehem is now more than an embryo, and the seeds of disciplinary power and punishment of the body politic have already been sown. Atwood has written a history of the present.[48]

---

47. Atwood, *Bodily Harm* (New York: Simon and Schuster, 1982), p. 265.

48. Mary McCarthy disagrees. She sees nothing "in our present mores that I ought to watch out for unless I want the United States . . . to become a slave state something like the Republic of Gilead." One wonders whether McCarthy perhaps lived in Paris too long, but many of the reviewers of the film version of Atwood's novel took the same "it-can't-happen-here" stance. George Orwell's 1984 had the same reception, but that was long before Watergate, Irangate, and the invention of doublespeak like "disinformation" and "plausible deniability" perhaps dulled our sense of outrage.

EPILOGUE

*E*pistolarity is a destabilized and destabilizing category in both twentieth-century fiction and critical theory. From *Zoo* forward, the epistolary novel becomes the subject of profound deformation and experimentation. In keeping with the narrative orientation of writing-to-the-moment, each text in my study dramatizes *the present* as a grammatical tense and as a historical tension—albeit in markedly different ways. Shklovsky tries to make sense of the chaotic events leading up to his exile and beyond. While Russia is being pulled apart by cataclysmic upheavals, he remains forcibly caged in Berlin, trying to decipher the competing claims of history, politics, aesthetic theory, and unrequited love. Acutely conscious of the remarkable transformations science and technology have wrought on perceptions of time and space, Shklovsky translates the techniques of Cubism and montage into narrative. He mimes the immediacy of writing by accentuating the text's temporal constructedness and the partiality of perception.

Shklovsky is the first of my writers to grapple with the power of the image, to examine the implications of living in a society that nourishes itself with images rather than beliefs. This explains why he attacks European consumerism so vehemently. Each subsequent writer in my study similarly attempts to historicize desire, showing how it is shaped by literature, art, the media, and commodity culture. With *Lolita*, Nabokov returns some thirty years after Shklovsky to write another anatomy of obsession. John Ray's preface reflects the ideology of behaviorism; Humbert's picaresque journey reflects America's avid postwar consumerism, its love affair with Madison Avenue, movies, advertisements, and commodities. Lolita (nicknamed "Dolly") resembles nothing so much as a department store mannikin upon whom consumer wares are exhibited, mutely turned into an object by Humbert. Humbert's heart, fed on fantasies nourished by his reading and voyeurism, grows brutal from the fare. Lolita never really exists for him, which is why he is so obsessed with "fixing" her in a still life or freeze-frame of film. Since the power of the image has political ramifications as well as personal ones, *The Golden Notebook* complements *Zoo* in many respects, for where Shklovsky in 1923 tries to predict the eventual results of communism, Lessing in 1962 looks back at the long nightmarish aftermath of destruction and disillusionment. Lessing relates the fascination with images to the rise of fascism, one of the topics that ties her novel to Margaret Atwood's. What exactly accounts for the social genesis of psychosis? What forces conspire to make the masses desire their own repression? What are the implications of living in a politically exhausted culture? Before the coup in *The Handmaid's Tale*, the United States is described as a society dying of too much choice; Gilead tells citizens what to believe by disseminating electronic images that command and spy at the same time. As with Lessing and Atwood, Alice Walker systematically deconstructs the processes by which one first devises a strategy of exploitation and then develops an ideology of otherness to authorize it, moving backward and forward through history from slavery's Middle Passage to African colonization to the American South before and during the Second World War.

Given their obsession with the power of the image in photographs, films, television, and advertisements, it is not surprising that so many of the writers in my study confront the inadequacy of language, although that lament is one of the classic characteristics of epistolarity. Where Shklovsky focuses on discarding outworn language and conventions, Nabokov portrays the limitations of criticism: neither John Ray's sociological prose, nor legal rhetoric, nor psychological jargon, nor Humbert's lyrical literariness capture the "truth" of *Lolita*; every critic of the novel must similarly confront the partiality of his or her reading. The same applies to *A Lover's Discourse* and *The Post Card*; every critic confronting each of those texts (much less the two in combination) must acknowledge how much remains to be said. That point is emphasized *in* the texts as well as being a major point *about* them. Derrida declares the death of the epistolary genre as a result of the advent of the new technologies of telecommunications, but *The Post Card's* very composition delays the execution, thus demonstrating that epistolarity is both a paradigm and an exception to the rule, the law. Each text in my study repeats this paradox: while reaccentuating the ancient generic conventions of epistolarity, each text goes beyond the paradigms it delineates.

In different ways, each writer in my study examines the implications of living in "the post-age,"[1] a term variously invoked to signify the effects of

---

1. Gregory L. Ulmer, "The Post-Age," *Diacritics* 11 (Fall 1981): 39–56.

postmodernism, poststructuralism, postfeminism, postrepresentational, or postparadigmatic productions. The word "post" suggests not just something we have gone beyond (or desire to go beyond) but uncertainty about what will come next. The term helps to explain why no totalizing theory applies to these texts individually or collectively. Instead, paradoxes abound: Shklovsky attempts simultaneously to justify Russian Formalism and to push it beyond its limits. By striving for the integration of language and history, form and content in *Zoo*, he approaches the dialogism of Bakhtin. Nabokov proffers a theory of reading as "aesthetic bliss," but those who endorse it wind up as Humbert's dupes. Barthes and Derrida point up the limitations, not just of Marxism and psychoanalysis but even of poststructuralism: when confronted with amorous discourse, it is necessary to write exactly the opposite of all axiomatics. What they each desire is precisely what poststructuralism specifically deconstructs: living speech, presence, proximity. Doris Lessing also goes beyond numerous paradigms: she reconceptualizes the theories of R. D. Laing, enabling us to trace the line of descent that links Laing to Deleuze and Guattari. Lessing reproduces bourgeois realism in *The Golden Notebook*, but she criticizes its paradigms by embedding it in an antirealist novel, purposely constructed to make readers confront the limitations of genre. In *The Handmaid's Tale*, similarly, those who impose their will to power on the text end up making the same kinds of interpretive and moral mistakes as the myopic Prof. Pieixoto. To trace the process by which the relationships among writer, reader, and critic have become relativized in the twentieth century is one thing. It is quite another to conclude, as Pieixoto does, that the relationships between oppressor and oppressed—that evil itself—are relative. The critic's and historian's role is to understand *and*, where evil abounds, to identify its agents and censure them. Far from being a refuge, writing in all these texts is a site of struggle—as Celie's painful path toward literacy and historical consciousness illustrates in *The Color Purple*. Alice Walker draws on African-American theories of literary production, orality, and culture to dramatize those struggles. The epistolary mode enables each writer to illustrate how the text is produced, while simultaneously exposing the mechanics of oppression. Indeed, the Gileadeans are the logical inheritors of the Stalinist strategies anticipated in *Zoo* and exposed in *The Golden Notebook*; like the racists in *The Color Purple*, they systematically distort, erase, and rewrite history.

Each of the seven texts in my study exploits radically different techniques to widen the fictional space of narrative and to reconstruct history. Each epistolary experiment goes "beyond" in multiple senses: beyond the ideology of romantic love, beyond the Oedipal triangle, beyond mimesis, beyond the confines of identity. Lessing, Barthes, and Derrida attempt to wrest desiring-production from the oedipalizing constraints of Western thought; in different ways they each envision a politics of desire. The premises of bourgeois individualism and the patriarchal family are also dismantled by Walker and Atwood, who expose the invisible work of ideology. Neither Anna Wulf, nor Celie, nor Offred are allowed to be innocent victims; they each participate in persecuting others and each suffers for her complicity. Nevertheless, each heroine's situation contains the seeds of resistance as well as of oppression; in different ways their narratives testify to their defiance and rebellion.

Perhaps what is most remarkable about these texts is the meticulous description of the *cheminement*—the myriad ways they represent the working-through process of reading, writing, desiring. They highlight the vicissitudes of psychic life and show how it resists regimentation and repression. They depict the simultaneous movements of deconstruction and reconstruction: they deconstruct the ruses of identity while reconstructing history. My aim in drawing upon deconstruction, psychoanalysis, materialism, and feminism has not been to authorize a master discourse but to interrogate each of them. Just as the texts in my study engage in dialogic contestation with one another and with epistolary predecessors, so, too, these theoretical discourses are contestatory and contested. Thus the effort to deconstruct representation does not eradicate materialist analysis. Instead, the strategies of deconstruction are particularly vital when representation is used to exploit the ideology of bourgeois individualism, as has been the case at least since the eighteenth century. Similarly, one can delineate the decentering of the human subject, from Shklovsky to Atwood, without repudiating the notion of agency. That is why each writer places such emphasis on collusion and complicity.

The texts in *Special Delivery* are wakes, simultaneously commemorating and contributing to the "deaths" of the author, literature, and the unitary subject, while leaving their traces visible nonetheless. They are counterdiscourses, written against the grain of genre and gender. Political exile, linguistic estrangement, sexual and textual silencing and cunning recur in myriad combinations in these seven texts. As symptomatic narratives of a discontinuous history, they are marked more by difference than by similarity, yet each reaccentuates and defamiliarizes epistolarity to dramatize the special delivery of desire in the "post-age."

INDEX

Abbott, H. Porter, *Diary Fiction*, 135, 137n

Abel, Elizabeth, 165n

Abelard, Peter, 19, 232

Abraham, N., and M. Torok, *Le verbier de l'homme aux loups*, 122n

Acker, Kathy, *Great Expectations*, xxi

Alger, Horatio, 207

Althusser, Louis, 139n

Altman, Janet Gurkin, 135, 224; *Epistolarity*, 134, 223

Anderson, Hans Christian, 34; *The Little Mermaid*, 65

Anderson, Laurie, 255n

Andrews, William L., *To Tell a Free Story*, 190

Appel, Alfred, Jr., 61n, 65n, 74

Aragon, Louis, 4, 23n

Aristotle, 11

Armstrong, Louis, 214

Armstrong, Nancy, xiv n

Arnim, Bettina von, 90

Artaud, Antonin, 153, 181

Atwood, Margaret, xii, xiii, xviii, xx, xxiii, 35; *The Handmaid's Tale*, x, xi, xiii, xv, xvii, xviii, xxi, xxii, xxiii, 26, 65, 128, 133, 134, 135, 139, 142, 158, 160, 166, 170, 171, 174, 179, 186, 187, 192n, 195, 198, 199, 217, 220–237, 239, 240, 242–258, 261, 262, 264, 266, 267; *Bodily Harm*, 261, 262; "Circe/Mud Poems," 229; *Survival*, 222

Axmatova, Anna, 15

Babb, Valerie, 194n, 195n

Baby M case, 241, 242; *see also* Doane and Hodges

Bahktin, Mikhail M., xv, xvi, xx, 4, 5; *The Dialogic Imagination*, xx n, 15, 16, 150, 187, 189, 192, 193, 203, 261n, 265; *The Formal Method in Literary Scholarship*, 5n, 13; *Problems of Dostoyevsky's Poetics*, 135

Baker, Houston A., Jr., *Blues, Ideology, and Afro-American Literature*, 194n, 206n, 207

Bakker, Jim, 252

Bakker, Tammy Faye, 252

Balzac, Honoré de, 25, 33; *Sarrasine*, 33n, 107, 173, 180, 231

Bann, Stephen, and John E. Bowlt, *Russian Formalism*, xvi n

Barbin, Claude, 226; *see also* Guilleragues

Barnes, Julian, *A History of the World in 10¹/₂ Chapters*, xxi

Barreño, Maria Isabel, *The Three Marias: New Portuguese Letters*, xiii, 221, 224, 229, 235, 238, 239, 250, 254

Barrett, Michèle, 78n, 248

Barth, John, 6, 15; *Lost in the Funhouse*, 24; *Letters*, xxi, 24; "The Literature of Exhaustion," 6n, 25, 94

Bartheleme, Donald, 182

Barthes, Roland, xi, xii, xv, xvi, xvii, ix, xx, xxiii, 12, 15, 18–19, 23, 27–28, 30–33, 35, 39, 48–49, 51, 57,

269